Chehalis Stories

Chehalis Stories

EDITED BY JOLYNN
AMRINE GOERTZ WITH
THE CONFEDERATED
TRIBES OF THE CHEHALIS
RESERVATION

As Shared by Robert Choke, Marion
Davis, Peter Heck, Blanche Pete Dawson,
and Jonas Secena

Collected and Translated by Franz Boas

UNIVERSITY OF NEBRASKA PRESS, LINCOLN AND LONDON

RECOVERING LANGUAGES LITERACIES OF THE AMERICAS

This book is published as part of the Recovering Languages and Literacies of the Americas initiative. Recovering Languages and Literacies is generously supported by the Andrew W. Mellon Foundation.

♾

Library of Congress Cataloging-in-Publication Data
Names: Amrine Goertz, Jolynn, editor.
Title: Chehalis stories / edited by Jolynn Amrine Goertz with the Confederated Tribes of the Chehalis Reservation; as shared by Robert Choke, Marion Davis, Peter Heck, Blanche Pete Dawson, and Jonas Secena; collected and translated by Franz Boas.
Description: Lincoln NE: University of Nebraska Press, [2018] | Includes bibliographical references and index.
Identifiers: LCCN 2017026646 (print) | LCCN 2017036807 (ebook) | ISBN 9781496204110 (epub) | ISBN 9781496204127 (mobi) | ISBN 9781496204134 (pdf) | ISBN 9781496201010 (cloth: alk. paper) | ISBN 9781496207654 (paper: alk. paper)
Subjects: LCSH: Chehalis Indians—Folklore. | Chehalis Indians— Biography.
Classification: LCC E99.C49 (ebook) | LCC E99.C49 C47 2018 (print) | DDC 979.7/601—dc23
LC record available at https://lccn.loc.gov/2017026646

Set in Huronia by Tseng Information Systems, Inc.

CONTENTS

ILLUSTRATIONS

Following page 124

MAPS

FIGURES

PREFACE

The edited text of *Chehalis Stories* is a reconciliation of fragments. This text is based on the typescript prepared by Ethel Aginsky but is greatly informed by the following sources:

- Franz Boas's fourteen Chehalis field notebooks
- Boas's letters
- Boas's lexical files
- Notes copied from Boas's field notebooks by both Aginsky and Boas
- Boas's interlinear translations of "Bear and Bee" and "Daughters of Fire"
- Boas's "A Chehalis Text"
- M. Dale Kinkade's "'Daughters of Fire': Narrative Verse Analysis of an Upper Chehalis Folktale"
- Kinkade's "'Bear and Bee': Narrative Verse Analysis of an Upper Chehalis Folktale"
- Kinkade's *Upper Chehalis Dictionary.*

Throughout this text, notes indicate the source of each story, particularly corresponding field notebook and typescript page numbers. Absolute transparency would be unnecessarily cumbersome, and many changes that resulted from negotiating the content of the field notebooks with the typescript have been made silently.

I began by making a diplomatic transcription of the typescript, maintaining original line breaks, marginalia, and page numbers. This allowed me to cross-check the text with the field notebooks and to work through passages that contained discrepancies. After this work was completed, the text was made continuous by eliminating the original line breaks, marginalia, and page numbers. Corresponding field notebook and typescript page numbers are included as a note to each story.

After the text was made continuous, punctuation, spelling, and typographic errors were corrected. For instance, pilcrows (¶) have been replaced with paragraph breaks. Comma splices have been corrected by separating complete clauses with a period. Aginsky frequently used semicolons in place of colons or commas; the appropriate punctuation has been used in these cases. Aginsky indented songs, put songs in quotation marks, or both. I have consistently indented songs and omitted quotation marks. Spelling, specifically of characters and place-names, has been modified to reflect Americanist transcription practices and is consistent with Kinkade's *Upper Chehalis Dictionary*. For instance, the spelling of place-names within the text come from Kinkade, but notes indicate the spelling used in the typescript or field notebooks and provide cultural and geographic contexts. Indisputable typographic errors were silently corrected. Words crossed out on the typescript were omitted, words penciled in were added, and duplications of words such as "and" or "the" were deleted.

Grammatical issues are more complicated. It is difficult to make corrections without Anglicizing the text to the point of erasing circumlocutions or idioms that have carried over from Upper Chehalis. Usually the corrections are straightforward, such as a word missing from a sentence. As an example, the typescript of the first story contains the sentence "x̌ʷəné·x̌ʷəne went up the river, where there no more women." The field notebook translation is quite rough for this section, but similar vocabulary and syntax are later translated as "there were no more." I have added the missing "were" in brackets so the sentence reads, "x̌ʷəné·x̌ʷəne went up the river, where there [were] no more women." When an addition or change to a sentence is clearly supported by the field notebook, I have silently made the correction. When the addition or change is made after looking at contextual clues, I have modified the text and indicated modification through the use of brackets. When further explanation is warranted, I include a note explaining discrepancies between the field notebook and the typescript. In regard to editing Adamson, Jay Miller notes, "Idiomatic Indian or Red English expressions indicate that Adamson . . . was recording verbatim statements" (1999a, 2). Boas's translations also contain these idiomatic expressions, and I have attempted to preserve the original.

Proper names are inconsistently capitalized and spelled throughout the typescript. In the same paragraph, characters such as Beaver, Moon, and Mountain Lion are referred to with and without a definite article. "Moon" and "the Moon" are interchangeable. For the sake of consistency, the definite

article has been removed. I have capitalized the names of individual and collective entities. Capitalized names reflect the spirit form of the being, while lowercase names reflect its modern species. I have also capitalized environmental entities when these entities function as animate beings. These include Fire, Rock, Lake, Wind, Creek, and Trail, consistent with Kinkade's editing in "'Daughters of Fire': Narrative Verse Analysis of an Upper Chehalis Folktale" (1983). They are not capitalized in the typescript. An exception to this is in "A Story," in which "daughters of the fire" become "Daughters of Fire." Similarly, collective entities such as Children of the Southwest Wind have been capitalized. Whether or not to capitalize proper names in Upper Chehalis is problematic. In the native-language text, the names are not capitalized. In the typescript, Upper Chehalis native names are sometimes capitalized, sometimes not. Kinkade does not capitalize Upper Chehalis names. I have followed his lead, and x̣ʷəné·x̣ʷəne, k'ácx̣ʷe, and other names are rendered lowercase.

I have assumed that when I have a question about the text, the answer can be found in either Boas's field notes or the typescript, and if it cannot be found in these originals, editorial decisions should cohere with Kinkade's methodology. When neither the original manuscript nor Kinkade can offer an answer, I believe it is better to consult storytellers and descendents of storytellers within the Chehalis community than it is to make editorial decisions based on trending editorial conventions. The editorial voice behind this volume attempts to be collaborative.

Kinkade's "Guide to Pronunciation" from the *Upper Chehalis Dictionary* is reproduced below. This is to help readers with the pronunciation of character names and place-names used throughout this text. Kinkade provides the following alphabetical order for Upper Chehalis: ʔ a b c c' č č' d dᶻ e ə g h i j k k' kʷ k'ʷ l l' ɬ ƛ' m m' n n' o p p' q q' qʷ q'ʷ s š t t' u w w' x xʷ x̣ x̣ʷ y y' (1991, xii).

Kinkade's "Guide to Pronunciation" (1991, xii–xiii)

Since this dictionary is intended for the use of Indians, linguists, and non-linguists alike, this guide to pronunciation is provided to explain the phonological symbols (letters) used in this dictionary for those who are not familiar with Americanist transcription practices. International Phonetic Alphabet symbols are added where they differ significantly from Americanist usage.

b, d, g, h, k, m, n, p, s, t, w, y sound very much like English sounds those letters usually represent (y = IPA [j])

ʔ - represents the catch in your throat that you make when you say "Uh-uh" (meaning 'no') in English, although it is never written in English

a - like the a of f<u>a</u>ther

e - like the a of f<u>a</u>t ([æ])

ə - varies a great deal depending on the consonants around it, but basically is like the u of b<u>u</u>t or the a of <u>a</u>bout

i - like the a of l<u>a</u>te, or the i of mach<u>i</u>ne ([e, ɪ, i])

o - like the au of c<u>au</u>ght ([ɔ])

u - like the oa of c<u>oa</u>t, or the u of r<u>u</u>le ([o, ʊ, u])

long vowels (a·, e·, etc.) are identical to short vowels, but held about twice as long ([:])

c - like the ts of ha<u>ts</u> ([ts])

č - like the ch of <u>ch</u>ur<u>ch</u> ([tʃ])

dᶻ - like the ds of be<u>ds</u> ([dz])

l - like the l at the beginning of <u>l</u>ean (*not* like the l at the end of ca<u>ll</u>)

ł - sort of like an l but is very breathy ([ɬ])

q - like k, except that it is made by touching the back part of the tongue further back in the mouth

š - like the sh of <u>sh</u>ine ([ʃ])

x - the tongue should be in the same position as for k, but not quite touching the roof of the mouth, resulting in a light scraping noise

x̣ - the tongue should be in the same position as for q, but not quite touching the roof of the mouth, resulting in a scraping noise ([χ])

kʷ, qʷ, xʷ, x̣ʷ - like k, q, x, x̣, respectively, but the lips should be slightly rounded; qʷ is like the qu of English <u>qu</u>ick ([kʷ, qʷ, xʷ, χʷ])

c', č', k', k'ʷ, p', q', q'ʷ, t' - these are like the same sounds without the ', but are made with a sharp popping sound; to get this popping sound, make a ʔ, hold it, and say the other sound (c, k, p, etc.) at the same time ([ts', tʃ', k', k'ʷ, p', q', q'ʷ, t'])

ƛ' - this has the same sort of sharp popping sound that the sounds immediately above have; to make it, begin with ʔ and make a t, keeping the tongue closed against the roof of the mouth; then, instead of letting the tip of the tongue come away from in back of the upper teeth, keep it there, but let the air out to one or both sides (just as in making l or ɫ) ([tɬ'])

 l', m', n', w', y' - like l, m, n, w, y interrupted by ʔ; at the end of a word the sound is chopped off abruptly; in the middle of a word there may be a ʔ right in the middle of the sound, but mostly they just sound sort of "squeezed" or raspy ([l', m', n', w', j'])

´ - this marks the part of the word that sounds loudest or most prominent (['])

ACKNOWLEDGMENTS

This volume is a collaborative endeavor that would not have come to be without the contributions of the many people committed to returning these stories to the Chehalis community. Special thanks to Confederated Tribes of the Chehalis Reservation Business Committee for encouraging this project, especially Chairmen David Burnett and Don Secena for continued support of the work. Past and current staff of the Culture and Heritage Department, including Joyleen McCrory, Dianne Devlin, Lynn Hoheisel, and Walter Lewis, and members of the Chehalis Culture and Heritage Committee, including Cindy Andy, Virginia Canales, Sylvia Cayenne, Christina Hicks, and Heather Youckton, have provided much encouragement and corrected the path of this project many times. Past and current Education Department staff—Nathan Floth, Jason Gillie, Racheal Mendez, and Jodie Smith—graciously shared their space with me and provided insight into these stories' contexts. I would also like to thank the Elders who generously spent time with me and taught me about the storytellers and storytelling more generally: Curtis Du Puis, Beverly Johnson, Elaine McCloud, Helen Sanders, Roberta Secena, Jerrie Simmons, and Mel Youckton. A few younger Chehalis tribal members, some of whom are related to the storytellers whose words form this volume, sat down with me to talk about Chehalis storytelling and how these stories might be reintroduced to the Chehalis community: Christina Hicks, MDC, J. William Gleason, Fred Shortman, John Shortman Jr., and William Thoms provided much insight. Thoms's original art, inspired by these stories, graces the cover. His encouragement and participation were always perfectly timed. The Chehalis Tribe will receive the royalties from this volume, further funding community culture and language revitalization efforts.

There are many people who have helped return these stories—and information about how they were shared, translated, and edited—to the Chehalis community. I would like to thank Brian Carpenter, Charles Greifenstein, and Michael Miller at the American Philosophical Society; Marilyn Graf at the Indiana University Archives of Traditional Music; Andy Skinner and Margaret Shields at the Lewis County Historical Museum; Daisy Njoku at the National Anthropological Archives; Henry Davis at the University of British Columbia (M. Dale Kinkade's literary executor); Perry Cartwright at the University of Chicago Press; and Anne Jenner and Clare Tally-Foos at the University of Washington Special Collections for granting permissions and providing research support. This project owes much to Matt Bokovy and all those at the University of Nebraska Press involved in the publication of these stories. Laurel Sercombe and Bill Seaburg, both of the University of Washington, shared their research about Thelma Adamson, Franz Boas, George Herzog, and Melville Jacobs, and the very productive summer of 1927; Gary Lundell at the University of Washington Special Collections guided me through the M. Dale Kinkade Papers, the Melville Jacobs Papers, and the Edmond S. Meany Papers; Ewa Czaykowska-Higgins at the University of Victoria pointed me in the right direction when I had questions about translation; and Madronna Holden shared her insight. Brittn Grey and Janice Hamilton kindly read and copyedited early drafts, and Anna Plovanich helped me decipher Boas's handwriting. Amy Hildreth Chen encouraged me to think about the role of the archive and the importance of access throughout this process. Thank you all so much for your generosity and willingness to contribute.

It has been most fortunate to have Amelia Susman Schultz's assistance in editing drafts of the stories, as she was Boas's last graduate student, working with him in the late 1930s and early 1940s. Special thanks to Jay Miller for coordinating this connection, and for his generosity of time and knowledge at every step in the process, from our first—very welcome—conversation about Boas's field notebooks to our troubleshooting at the Poodle Dog. Every email and phone call gave this project momentum. I could not have done this work without you.

For my own sake, I would like to acknowledge those at the University of Alabama who have encouraged this work from the beginning: first, those who gave me a home in the English Department—Nikhil Bilwakesh, Catherine Davies, Tricia McElroy, Heather White, and Emily Wittman; and second, those who welcomed me into the Anthropology Department—Ian Brown, Marysia Galbraith, Kareen Hawsey, Steve Kosiba, Michael Murphy, Clay Nelson, and Matthew Wolfgram. My family has been incredibly supportive throughout research and writing. I would like to thank Harvey and

Janice Hamilton and Scott and Cheryl Amrine for always listening, and especially Harvey, for taking me up to visit with Chairman Burnett in the first place. Ben, you have thoroughly read this volume, in all its various forms, with tremendous patience. Thank you for enduring hundreds of dinner table read-throughs. And Theodore and Eleanor, you have both joined us since I began working on this project. You are as much a part of this work as anyone, and I am grateful for your companionship.

Finally, I would like to thank those of you who asked to remain unnamed but who have contributed your knowledge and time and who have ensured that this project move forward in a good way. I would also like to acknowledge those who chose not to participate, and those who have yet to make their contribution. There is an assumption that once something is set to type, the work is over. That is not the case; this work has only begun. Please share these stories as appropriate. If you are reading this volume now and believe your voice should have been included, please come forward and share. As an "Oakville girl," I often prioritized discretion over detail and have often erred on the side of respecting privacy. It is never too late to contribute, to correct bad information, or to amend what has been written here to include another perspective. This is only one part of a conversation that has been ongoing for generations, and, hopefully, will continue for many more.

Chehalis Stories

Introduction

Weaving is a vital tradition within the Chehalis community, and Chehalis weavers emphasize the importance of going to the places their ancestors gathered to collect bark, grass, and roots. They spend months preparing this material—stripping, soaking, shredding—until it is ready to be used in the making of something. Each thing they make is connected to the land that Chehalis people have called home for millennia. So, too, the stories in this volume have come to be through many generations of gathering, preparing, and making. Chehalis people have carried and shared these stories, first with their families and communities and then with those of us who want to be part of the preservation of these stories—though at times we are complicit in, even responsible for, their displacement and disappearance. These stories, and the traditions and values held within, are firmly rooted in Chehalis ancestral lands. But many of these stories have been taken to places far away from where they originated, both geographically and ideologically. We are making this volume to bring these stories back—to gather them here so that they may once again be held by the families that first generously shared them.[1]

These stories were collected at a critical moment in Chehalis history. By the 1920s, assimilation efforts had affected almost every aspect of Chehalis life. Many Chehalis families had been removed from their ancestral villages and relocated to the Chehalis Reservation near Oakville, Washington. These families were assigned allotments—secured through homestead—on which they were expected to farm; traditional fishing, gathering, and hunting were regulated by government officials. In the name of formal education, children were sent to government schools. There were boarding and day schools on the Chehalis Reservation, but many children were sent to other boarding schools, some of which were hundreds of miles away. At these schools, speaking one's native language was punished and traditional religious practices were forbidden. Stories, which were the means of transmitting cultural knowledge from one generation to the next, were still told, but as the knowledge contained within them became less relevant to day-to-day survival, many of these stories were put away.

Chehalis people have shared their stories with non-native people since contact. Indian Agent James Swan and ethnologist George Gibbs provided some of the earliest accounts of Chehalis mythology—yet these were not collected until the 1850s. Puget Sound missionary Myron Eells made note of a few legends in the 1880s. Some language material was also collected during this period. This volume includes three Lower Chehalis stories that Charles Cultee, a Clatsop man, shared with Franz Boas, a German man, in 1890–91 and 1894 at Bay Center, Washington (appendix 1). In 1905 Edmond Meany, a University of Washington professor who taught botany and history, visited the Chehalis Reservation and interviewed a number of Chehalis people; his notes contain abstracts of stories shared by Jacob Secena, sisína?xn, the grandfather of Jonas Secena (appendix 2). The following year, Robert Jackson, Sard-Khom, a Chehalis man who attended Carlisle Indian School, published "The Story of Sun: A Legend of the Chehalis Indians" in *Washington Magazine*, a periodical edited by Meany. Anthropologists and linguists visited the Chehalis Reservation in the 1900s and 1910s, motivated by a desire to document Native American cultures and languages before they were lost forever.[2] Interest in Chehalis stories surged in the 1920s, resulting in three major projects: George Sanders shared *Honne, the Spirit of the Chehalis: The Indian Interpretation of the Origin of the People and Animals* with Katherine Van Winkle Palmer;[3] members of the Ben[n], Charley, Davis, Heck, Iley, Johnson, Pete/Peter, Sanders, Secena, Williams, and Youckton families related cultural knowledge to Thelma Adamson in 1926 and 1927, which she used in *Folk-Tales of the Coast Salish*; and Robert Choke, Marion Davis, Peter Heck, Blanche Pete Dawson, and Jonas Secena worked with Boas in 1927. The stories the last group shared with Boas make up this volume.

CHEHALIS HISTORY

Chehalis people have fished, gathered, and hunted along the Chehalis River and its tributaries since time immemorial, occupying a territory extending from the Pacific Ocean to the Cascade Mountains, trading with neighboring tribes along the Northwest Coast, and sustaining themselves—both physically and spiritually—by following seasonal rounds. Intertribal trade brought European goods—and horses—to the Northwest Coast before the explorers and settlers arrived, with the Perez Expedition of 1774 and the Vancouver Expedition of 1792 frequently cited as contact incarnate. Lewis and Clark and Work and Wilkes explored (what would become) Southwest Washington, eliciting the aid of Chehalis people to guide them through the territory and negotiate trade relationships. These interactions furthered the spread of European diseases, which decimated native families and villages. Treaty negotiations came soon after: these included Anson Dart's efforts (which the U.S. Congress never ratified), the Chehalis River Treaty Council in 1855 (which Isaac Stevens left unfinished), and the Treaty of Olympia in 1856 (to which Chehalis people did not consent). In 1864 the Chehalis Indian Reservation was created by order of the secretary of the interior, which President Grover Cleveland reaffirmed in 1886 by executive order.

While this is an expected, and often sufficient, rendering of Chehalis history, this type of account privileges the postcontact period presented through a western lens—and is premised on an assumption that Chehalis people were a static entity prior to European exploration and U.S. expansion. The histories of the Chehalis people cannot be conscribed to a linear chronology. Oral tradition and narrative material provide other ways of looking at Chehalis histories—and these histories are often family-based and cyclical,[4] not lent to radio-carbon dating. Families carry knowledge pertaining to the historical events mentioned above, but they also impart wisdom regarding their relationship to the environment and to each other that is not time-bound.

An example of this is a story that Lucy Heck,[5] a renowned storyteller and weaver, told Adamson in 1926. In "Mʊspʻ and Kəmoʻl" the Transformers travel the coast from the Columbia River to the Strait of Juan de Fuca, returning eventually to their Humptulip home. This story is a cumulation of cultural knowledge, gathered and shared for generations. History is preserved not as a reconstruction of the past events but as a series of transformations rooted in specific places. The stories herein contain the same vital cultural knowledge and might easily be situated in mythic time. However, the dichotomy of mythic and historic time is also a western construct, as though the contents of these stories belong to a time no longer relevant to contemporary audiences.[6] Understanding time as cyclical, rather than chronological, one can see the relevance of the stories today. These stories, like Moon, are not relics of the past but part of a continuous cycle of going away and coming back.

Many of the stories in this volume are situated in specific landscapes,[7] and the storytellers who told them have particular family and village affiliations. Some of these affiliations are difficult to reconstruct, especially those that were fractured when families were relocated from ancestral villages to the Chehalis Reservation. A brief discussion of Chehalis lands and principal communities will provide a spatial—and social—context for readers unfamiliar with these stories' settings.

The contemporary Confederated Tribes of the Chehalis Reservation is made up of two primary groups: Lower Chehalis and Upper Chehalis,[8] with Lower Chehalis including affiliated people who fished, gathered, hunted, and lived "along the Chehalis River and its tributaries" between Grays Harbor and Satsop,[9] and Upper Chehalis people occupying the area from Satsop to the headwaters of the Chehalis River "just north of Pe Ell"[10] (Kinkade 2008, 350). Bands of the Lower Chehalis correspond to principal communities along Shoalwater Bay, Westport, Hoquiam, Wishkah, Wynoochee, and Humptulips (Hajda 1990, 503). Bands of the Upper Chehalis correspond to principal communities near Mud Bay, Tenino, Chehalis, Pe-Ell/Boistfort, and Oakville/Porter (Kinkade 1991, v). Together, all these bands have come to be known as Chehalis. The name derives from c'əxíls, a native word that means "sand" in Upper Chehalis, as well as in Cowlitz (Kinkade 1991, 283; 2004, 190). It was the name of a village site near present-day Westport, the first coastal point of contact for native and European visitors making their way up the Chehalis River for trade or exploration from the Pacific Ocean. Thus the village name was used to refer to native people who occupied the watershed that emptied into Grays Harbor, especially those people who occupied its lower portion. Correspondingly, q'ʷayáiɬ, the name of a village site near Mud Bay and the first point of contact by portage from Puget Sound, refers to Upper Chehalis language and people.

The c'əxíls and q'ʷayáiɬ village sites were the thresholds of two important trade routes: (1) The Salish Funnel connects Puget Sound to Grays Harbor by way of the Chehalis River and its tributary, the Black River (Miller 2012c, 168). This passage makes it possible to travel from the Salish Sea to the Columbia River without navigating the Olympic Peninsula and the perilous Strait of Juan de Fuca. (2) The Cowlitz Portage, a land route by which people traveled from Puget Sound to the Cowlitz River by way of Grand Mound Prairie,[11] made possible travel between Puget Sound and the Columbia River without navigating the Columbia Bar. These two trade routes allowed for travel that avoided the Graveyard of the Pacific, a region stretching from Oregon's Tillamook Bay to Vancouver Island's Cape Scott.

Trade was not only material—songs and stories also traveled along these routes. Chehalis people shared stories with neighboring tribes, and elements of Chehalis narratives are present throughout the Northwest Coast traditions (or these traditions are carried by Chehalis storytellers). Chehalis people's most immediate neighbors included Quinault (Tsamosan) to the northwest, Skokomish (Twana) to the north, Muckleshoot, Nisqually, Puyallup, and Squaxin (Lushootseed) to the north and northeast, Klikitat (Sahaptin) to the east, Cowlitz (Sahaptin and Tsamosan) to the south and southeast, and Chinook (Chinook) to the southwest. Similarities between the stories gathered in this volume and stories shared by people from these tribes are apparent.[12] (Trade extended far beyond these groups, but these were the tribes with whom Chehalis people had the most frequent and direct contact.) As Chehalis storytellers belonged to families affiliated with these neighboring groups, the stories they told often incorporate these neighboring traditions. While the affiliation of the storyteller is important, the stories are Chehalis not only because of who told them but also because of where they are situated (bays, lakes, rivers, prairies, and mountains within Chehalis ancestral lands), which cultural practices are emphasized (building fish traps, catching lamprey, digging camas, gathering berries), and which entities (Bluejay, Moon, and x̌ʷə́n) are most prominent.

FAMILY TRADITIONS AND THE CONCEPT OF OWNERSHIP

As previously mentioned, the goal of this volume is to return the stories that were shared with Boas to the Chehalis people.[13] This returning, however, is not premised on the assumption that these stories—in their current form—are a restoration of the stories told ninety years ago, or that they were not also preserved within the families who carried them. Only the families who carry these stories know what has been lost or put away and what has been carried forward through oral tradition. The stories presented in this volume have undergone tremendous transformations. The language of restoration suggests that what is being returned is — or is at least true to — the original. But sometimes the "original" — the story shared with the person filling a notebook — varies significantly from the story shared within the community.

Discussions pertaining to sharing, taking away, and returning of stories are strongly tied to ownership. There are many perspectives regarding the ownership of stories — and the right to share and publish them. Some people hold that stories belong to a particular family, while others believe that stories belong to the community more generally.[14] Silas Heck, brother of Peter Heck, told Adamson about storytelling in the Heck family. Adamson notes, "When get old, made a practice of telling [story] to young people. Never heard of borrowing stories. My mother got her stories from her grandfather. One night, Peter Heck learned his stories from his uncle. Peter [Heck] went to sleep. After that uncle wouldn't tell him any more for no use to tell them to a person like that" (1926–27, 148). While many storytellers learned stories from older members of their families, the teaching of stories was not restricted to one's own descendents. Regarding family ownership, Peter Heck told Adamson, "Seems to be nothing of the sort. 'Some people have stories all mixed, all different, maybe will see mine, and say they aren't right. The Var. winter stories are different.' Never heard of any 'family' stories" (1926–27, 275). Today some storytellers will not tell a certain story because it does not belong to his or her family. Value is placed on direct oral transmission from one generation of storyteller to the next.

Also from Adamson's notes, Marion Davis explained that Chief Yawnish, an Upper Chehalis chief from Grand Mound, "held a class to teach stories to boys" (Adamson 1926–27, 62; Miller 1999a, 53). Attention to and respect for the storyteller were expected, and in some circles children were required to go to the river and swim after hearing a story (Adamson 1926–27, 54). Jonas Secena remembered that "Mrs. Youc[k]ton told Clarence and Bob Choke, who were practicing stories, that they should go to swim" after a Lower Cowlitz and Taitnapam custom (Adamson 1926–27, 387). In these instances, cohorts seem to be based on the age of the learner, not his or her family affiliation.

Jonas Secena provided more insight into the telling of stories, as well as borrowing stories from other communities. "Not confined to children of own family — any child who like may come.[15] Are some 'professional' story tellers. That's his business to tell stories — his boys who are taking lessons will take good care of the old fellow—will be respected. Would go a long ways to get another story—from a different country. Would tell it with his story and make it good. Sometimes again father and mothers would tell their children their own story" (Adamson 1926–27, 387). Although many people knew one or two stories, only professional storytellers knew many stories. Anyone could learn stories, and Secena noted that slaves might be just as good storytellers as their chiefs, from whom they would learn stories (390). Secena noted that Moon "is the story of the chiefs. All the chiefs always know it, because moon is the chief. Fire is also a great chief, but it is a story of the girls," referring to the Daughters of Fire (345). Secena explained, "All chiefs' stories have the 'law' on the end. Any one who knew the moon story could tell it. No matter who—the Moon has his own commandment, so chief doesn't have to make it" (346). So in some instances chiefs told stories to reinforce Chehalis values.

Chehalis people hold similar views on the ownership of stories today. In Upper Chehalis, ʔacwé·txʷ means "to have" as well as "to own," and the concept is intricately tied to use. J. William Gleason, a Chehalis artist, education specialist, and language teacher,[16] explained that the western concept of ownership[17] does not directly apply to how stories were shared and have been carried. Gleason says, "It's an Anglo way of looking at things, as if the only way you can pass them down is through your direct descendents. In any Indian culture—the aunt, the uncle, the grandma, everybody raises one child—so, so all those stories that he may have had, that may have had family ownership, were spread to everyone else. That being the reason, well, who owns this story—it wasn't an owned story. We didn't own anything. The land wasn't something we could own; how could we own something that somebody says?"[18] Gleason's analogy has far-reaching implications. When Chehalis people shared their lands and resources with early settlers, they often lost control of those lands and resources. Settlers interpreted this sharing as a transfer of title, as is illustrated by Sidney S. Ford's[19] occupancy—and ownership—of tá·ɬn'c̆šn', or "resting place," a prairie on the Chehalis River near Centralia, Washington. According to Tové Hodge, a Ford family descendent, the Chehalis "liked my great-great-grandfather. They saw that he was kind and honest in his dealings, and they invited him to live there also." They told him, "'If you know how to use the land, you can have it'" (1995, 78). Ford built a home and farmed the land and held a donation land claim for the place that has come to be known as Ford's Prairie. But in sharing the land with Ford, the Chehalis people, who had occupied the prairie for millennia, did not relinquish ownership of it, as they conceptualized ownership differently than settlers did. This distinction must be remembered—and respected—when considering the risks and repercussions of sharing a story.

Secena family members also shared their perspective on the ownership of stories. Christina Hicks, chair of the Chehalis Culture and Heritage Committee and great-great-niece of Jonas Secena, expressed a view similar to Gleason's. She indicated that while stories might have been carried by a particular family, there has been a loss of "ownership." Ownership, it seems, is an act. To own a story is to cultivate it, to carry it forward through listening, remembering, and sharing. When people no longer do this work, the ownership is lost because the story has been put away.

John Shortman Jr., Chehalis Education Department supervisor and a great-great-nephew of Jonas, explained that ownership has become less important over time and seems to be more important to older Chehalis people than to younger Chehalis people.[20] His uncle, Fred Shortman, Chehalis communications coordinator and a great-nephew of Jonas, explained that if a story is shared (orally) it is owned by a family, but if it is written down, then it is owned by everyone who reads it. If a story or legend is told, the storyteller or singer should state who they learned it from, to give credit and honor to those who told it. Learning stories required a tremendous amount of dedication from both the person telling the story and the person learning it. Stories were learned not only by listening to a story but by memorizing and repeating it through intentional practice. The story-learner was drilled on performance aspects as well, such as gesture and voice inflection.[21] These aspects bring the stories to life.[22]

TRANSFORMATION

The stories presented here are different from the stories shared in two important ways. First, they are textual representations of stories that were shared orally. Second, they are English translations of stories that were told in Upper Chehalis (or Lower Chehalis, in the case of the three stories shared by Cultee). When a story is transformed in these ways, a part of it is lost. Gleason helps explain this. He holds that hearing a story from a person directly is important because, "Every time the story is told, when these stories were being told as a form of entertainment, people wanted to maintain that they were exactly right. They were telling them in the right way, making sure everything was covered. And as we moved forward, sometimes those things are lost." There is loss, too, in the translation of the stories from Upper Chehalis into English — the translations are not quite "as fantastic or amazing" as the original. Gleason advocates for presenting both Upper Chehalis and English versions of the stories side by side, so that readers have access to the material collected in Upper Chehalis. Indeed, there is still much work to be done.

Though we often favor original — past and "pure" — forms of these stories, the stories shared with Adamson, Boas, and other collectors would not necessarily be the same stories shared today if they had, in fact, been carried forward through oral tradition. John Shortman Jr. maintains that "stories change so much over time," and he uses his family's oral tradition to illustrate this. Murphy Secena, Shortman's great-grandfather, was Jonas's brother and a Chehalis storyteller and Chehalis-language speaker. Shortman holds that the stories shared with him — through Murphy's decedents — may be different from the stories Jonas told because stories change from storyteller to storyteller, even though the stories Shortman remembers hearing as a child were carried forward from a shared ancestor.

These variations might be due, in part, to the belief that when a story is shared and written down, that version of the story belongs to whoever holds that handwritten account. MDC, a member of the Hazel Pete family, explains that once a story is shared, "You never have that particular story in your pocket anymore. You might have a story and have these different versions that you use at different times depending on your audience, or depending on the situation.... Once that one version goes out, you can't pull it back out. It's like throwing a handful rocks in the river, you know. You're not getting those rocks back at all, no matter how many other rocks you're picking up." As a result, storytellers sometimes change a story for public presentation, omitting details or episodes that are reserved for sharing within the family or community. When a particular version of a story is told, "that version can be considered lost by the speaker or teller" (MDC). This is because, more often than not, when Chehalis people have shared their stories or other cultural knowledge with missionaries or scholars, these people have taken away what has been shared, and that knowledge has been used to benefit the church or university, for instance, not Chehalis people. The result is that Chehalis people lose control over what they have shared, it leaves the community, they never get to see it again, and they do not benefit from it (MDC).[23]

Chehalis sculptural artist William Thoms also talks about how stories carried through oral tradition change over time and what that change has looked like in his own family. Thoms is a great-grandson of George Sanders, the storyteller who shared *Honne, the Spirit of the Chehalis* with Palmer, and is a great-great-nephew of Jonas Secena. In our talk about the differences between orality and textuality, Thoms discusses these changes (presented in interview form to preserve context):[24]

WT: Then we get into that question of the problems of oral history versus the problems of written history. Clearly the problems of oral history are . . . extreme individual bias based on an individual's memory, an individual's ability to speak, what sort of command they have over rhetoric. Just as we were talking about my Grandma:[25] she heard the stories, but the limits of her ability to speak the language, which, she said, a lot of the time she could kind of tell what they [elders, storytellers] were saying, but she always said she couldn't make the sounds. So she could never, she never relayed that way, she never related to the old language. So obviously there's some translation occurring there, which also causes issues orally. So you kind of never know what you're going to get, not to mention people's creativity. Which is both a problem and an advantage in passing on stories, right? What you bring to it makes it unique and what makes it yours and makes it part of your family's [oral tradition]. But that also fundamentally alters the story over time. You know, the game. What's that game where you whisper something in someone's ear and you have to pass it around?

JAG: Oh yeah, Telephone.

WT: Game of Telephone. And maybe that's the way history is supposed to be told. Because we keep doing it. We take what we learned and we re-edit it with our own perspective, and then we pass it forward. In that way oral history feels more honest, you know, because it is, it's admitting that it's going to change over time. Whereas writing it down makes it, especially . . .

JAG: It's less dynamic.

WT: It's way less dynamic. And all those sort of things still exists, but it presents itself as being inscrutable. But the reality is, that I am still doing interpretation when I read something written. I'm still bringing my own baggage to it when I read it. But it's that aim at uniformity. It's that aim at making it permanent. But that's also, I think, false too, you know?

We talk about historic distrust of writing things down, and then return to how oral tradition—and stories in particular—changes over time.

WT: Is this an original experience, or is this a reproduction? So that's a really hard question to answer—"How are things being transformed?"—because, one, you don't know the origin, and two, you don't know where they stand today.

JAG: You just have a little snapshot of a moment in time.

WT: We just have little tiny snapshots. With these ethnographic records, we see what Jonas said that day, and we don't know the reasons why, and we don't know whether that's the whole, or just a fragment, what he's willing to share—we don't know how that's attached to other pieces. So it's just this tiny little sliver, and then, as time goes on, just like any other culture, or any other art, we decide what's important and that changes, consistently, and it's always intriguing to see what survives the cut, and I think more intriguing to see what doesn't survive the cut. Why do we think that these stories are so important, but we never talk about other sort of rituals that were happening in the day-to-day life, two hundred, five hundred, a thousand years ago, which may, if interpreted and adapted properly, be more important than these stories. Like functional living may give us a better idea as to what was going on in the culture than these stories, that have been morphed an infinite number of times.

To present stories that have been carried through oral tradition in textual form gives a false sense of permanency and wholeness—these representations are fragments of a larger whole, a whole that is ever-changing. Some of those changes are related to language; stories that were told in Upper Chehalis may have been understood—but not carried forward—by people whose survival and success were dependent on their knowledge of English, not their native language(s). Also, stories may have served as a means for processing new information—as a way of assimilating European beliefs and values into Chehalis traditions.[26] Thoms explains that it is difficult to determine how stories have been and are being transformed because we will never know where the stories started and where they will end up. This volume—like Thoms's artwork—is just one manifestation of these various forms.

Though much is lost in the transformation of these stories from orality to textuality, there is a hope that material collected by Boas might be reintroduced into Chehalis oral tradition. Gleason speaks to this transformation:

> Just because [those stories are] not being spoken doesn't mean that there aren't people who would like to be able to read those stories and read them to their children, and put in character and add voice, and add emotion and body to it. You can't eliminate the group of people who really want to be a part of keeping with that tradition, simply based on the idea that oral tradition is how it was supposed to be done. There are people whose stories have been completely lost, [and] are luckily at least preserved in writing, and to be able to bring them back alive is probably one of the most important things in tribal preservation that there is.

Having a form of these stories preserved through print gives current and future generations the option of reading these forms and incorporating them back into the oral tradition. This is especially important in instances where the relationship between a past storyteller and a future storyteller was interrupted—often through government interventions such as boarding school or foster care. Gleason maintains that this volume might serve as "a means to an end," that the stories might be preserved and once again become part of the oral tradition. The best way to do this, he says, is to tell these stories to Chehalis children, so that the children may carry the tradition forward.[27] He emphasizes the importance of repetition—of making the stories part of the children's day-to-day lives—in reviving cultural traditions.

This sort of sharing would be consistent with the ways stories were taught in the past—similar to Chief Yawnish's story classes. Stories were—and are—

communal. Both MDC and Gleason recall that stories were told at community gatherings, but this does not seem to be the case now. MDC describes how things have changed:

> Storytelling used to be an integral part of the different community gatherings and monthly tribal meetings. Way back when, this would have been when my dad was young then,[28] they did tell stories, they gathered around, there were a lot fewer tribal members, and that became the focus. But I think as the tribe developed economic independence, and we had to, all of our meetings have gradually shifted towards business and business decisions that had to be made, and I don't know if there's always time for telling stories, and that made the stories become more family originated. ... I know the tribe still values the stories but I don't hear them recited or shared at any gatherings, like at any monthly meetings or General Councils or anything like that, but historically they have been, and that was even as late as the fifties and maybe sixties.

This economic independence coincided with the improvement of utilities on the Chehalis Reservation—including electricity and paved roads. And with electricity came television, perhaps one of the greatest distractions from oral tradition. Gleason holds that television and gaming consoles entertain and distract, insomuch that children do not seek out stories from their elders and that elders are not so ready to share. But it is possible that these mediums—film and gaming, especially—might serve as a way forward for these stories' transmission. Young people proficient in these technologies might serve the community by reimagining stories in new forms. As Thoms explains, the oral tradition is carried forward through new perspectives. It might also be carried forward through new mediums.[29]

"THE STORY OF HOW THE STORY WAS MADE"

Scholars

Many explorers, government agents, missionaries, scholars, and settlers documented Chehalis culture, but these early observations were often informed by colonial agendas.[30] In an effort to "record the precious culture before it disappear[ed] forever," salvage ethnographers hurried to the field—the hearths and porches of their informants (Rosaldo 1989, 81). The stories in this volume were shared by Chehalis storytellers with Franz Boas, the father of American anthropology.[31] Boas first recorded Chehalis stories in 1890 and 1891 when he was conducting fieldwork along the Oregon and Washington coasts.[32] In his introduction to *Chinook Texts*, Boas notes that the Chinook people at Bay Center had "adopted the Chehalis language" and that the Chehalis occupied "the whole country," that is, the area north of the Columbia River and on Shoalwater Bay (Boas 1894, 5). Chehalis stories were thus being shared in this community.

Boas worked with Charles Cultee and other storytellers at Bay Center, a Clatsop and Chinook settlement on Willapa Bay. Boas also worked with Cultee to make *Kathlamet Texts*, collected during the same summers as *Chinook Texts*, with additional material gathered in December 1894. A "veritable storehouse of information," Cultee was married to a Chehalis woman, his "mother's mother was a Katlamat, and his mother's father a Quila'pax'; his father's mother was a Clatsop, and his father's father a Tinneh of the interior" living on the "upper Willapa river"[33] (1894, 6; 1901, 5). Boas notes, "At present he speaks Chehalis almost exclusively, this being also the language of his children" (1894, 6). Boas collected three Chehalis stories from Cultee: "Qoné'qoné,"[34] a version of the kidnapping of Moon that commences at Toke Point, near Willapa Bay; "The Women Who Married the Stars"; and "The Sun" (appendix 1).

In 1895 Boas met James Teit, a Scottish clerk, trapper, and hunting guide. Boas notes, "The great value of Teit's contributions to ethnology is due to his painstaking accuracy, his intimate acquaintance with the Indians, and his ability to converse with them in their own language" (1923, 102). Teit helped Boas make connections along the Northwest Coast and collected cultural material—including linguistic data and Salishan and Sahaptin stories—which supplemented Boas's own research (Boas 1923, 102–3; Wickwire 2003, 1). In 1910 Teit wrote at length to Boas about Chehalis, mapped the distribution of tribes in Southwest Washington, and described the linguistic and cultural diversity of the area. He also observed that the people he met were "fast losing knowledge of every thing old" and that in order to glean what he could from the memory of "old people reported to have old time knowledge," he had

to travel considerable distances (July 10, 1910, "Annotated Maps and Notes to Maps of the Pacific Northwest"). Boas encouraged students and graduates to conduct fieldwork in Washington and staff the newly formed Anthropology Department at the University of Washington. Herman Haeberlin began work in Puget Sound in 1916; T. T. Waterman conducted research in the same area and served as an associate professor at the University of Washington from 1918 to 1920; Erna Gunther and Leslie Spier continued this work in the early 1920s, with Spier serving as a founding member of the department and Gunther serving as chair for twenty-five years (Garfield and Amoss 1984, 394). Though Gunther, Haeberlin, Spier, and Waterman worked near the Chehalis Reservation, these anthropologists focused their attentions farther north.

But then Boas sent two of his graduate students, Thelma Adamson and Melville Jacobs, to "undertake field research with Native Americans in Washington State" during the summer of 1926 (Seaburg and Sercombe 2009, x). Adamson worked with Upper Chehalis, Cowlitz, Humptulip, Wynoochee, Satsop, Puyallup, White River, and Skokomish storytellers, and Jacobs worked with Klikitat people. Adamson collected stories in 1926 and ethnographic material in 1927. The summer of 1927, the same year he published *Primitive Art*, Boas joined Adamson and Jacobs in the field. Boas and Adamson worked near Oakville at the Chehalis Reservation, and Jacobs continued his work with Kittitas, Klikitat, Upper Cowlitz, and Yakama people near Morton.[35] The *Oakville Cruiser*, a local newspaper, reported the anthropologists' activities. "Dr. Franz Boas head of the department of anthropology at Columbia University, New York City, was here a few days last week, doing research among the Chehalis Indians. Miss Thelma Adamson, who has been engaged in the same work here for several weeks, is his assistant, doing graduate research work in that department" (July 8, 1927). Boas recorded the Upper Chehalis language in the form of stories and Adamson focused on collecting ethnographic material. Boas and Adamson also recorded Chehalis songs on wax phonograph cylinders, later transcribed by ethnomusicologist George Herzog.[36] Adamson's description of the summer's activities, written in a letter to Herzog dated August 2, 1927, provides a glimpse of her sense of humor as well as her take on Boas: "Well, Dr. Boas has come and gone. He was here for a month and as far as I know we got along quite well. He was very sweet most of the time. I particularly enjoyed him the last few weeks. He worked on the language quite steadily for a month." Boas left Oakville for Berkeley, via Portland, to visit Alfred Kroeber at the end of July. Adamson's letter continues, "Dr. Boas will return here the middle of August and stay a week or so longer working on Chehalis. Then the twenty-seventh of August, he and Mel and I plan a two day run up to Mount Rainier, a very beautiful crater, covered with three glaciers, and one of the highest peaks in America" (Indiana University Archives of Traditional Music). Boas then continued on to the University of Washington, where he was instrumental in establishing and negotiating the hiring of the permanent staff of the Anthropology Department. He then traveled to Victoria, British Columbia, to meet with George Hunt.[37]

Boas's summer in Oakville was productive, in spite of logistical difficulties. Boas recounted his daily comings and goings to his wife, Marie, in a letter dated August 17, 1927. He writes, "These few days here are still very strenuous. I am working mornings from eight to twelve with Blanche [Pete Dawson], who learns quite quickly. At noon a bus picks me up. At this hour it is too hot to walk in the sun. This way I am there at 12:30 and work with Jonas [Secena] until 6 p.m. Then I walk back, which takes me one and one-half hours" (Rohner 1969, 287). Boas organized his day to maximize time spent with Jonas Secena, whose stories spanned mythic and historic time, and with Dawson, whom Boas trained to transcribe and translate. But the glorious hours spent devoted to preserving the adventures of xʷəné·xʷəne and Moon were made mundane by hot bedrooms, late buses, and sore feet. Boas and Adamson were both dependent on sometimes-reliable buses and walking to get from the town of Oakville to the Chehalis Reservation. They easily walked ten miles a day in the summer heat. Boas's letter continues, "It has been awfully hot here these past two days, 104 degrees in the houses and not a bit of breeze. Even at night it hardly gets cooler. Tonight however it is nice and cool, and one feels relieved. I still have to prepare myself for tomorrow, so that I really don't have time to write letters" (Rohner 1969, 288). In a letter written two days later, Boas describes the rush to get as much material as possible before leaving and complains about missed connections. The letter also provides insight into Boas's fieldwork, revealing that he had to spend at least two hours at night going over material collected to prepare for the next day's activities (Rohner 1969, 288). Boas worked with the Chehalis material upon his return to Columbia University and enlisted graduate students in the copying, translating, and editing of the stories. Due to Boas's age—he turned sixty-nine on the trip—this was one of his last seasons of fieldwork on the Northwest Coast, followed only by a visit with Hunt at Fort Rupert in the winter of 1930–31.

Storytellers

These comings and goings of scholars and students frame the story of how the stories were made, but little is known about particular collaborations— field notebooks and personal letters do not provide much insight into the lives of the storytellers. Adamson was able to lay the groundwork for Boas's work prior to his arrival in 1927, and Boas maintained contact with Chehalis people after his fieldwork ended. For instance, Boas wrote to Dawson throughout 1927, exchanging a few letters with her and sending her a book. (Dawson later worked with other anthropologists, as well as Salish linguist M. Dale Kinkade.) Adamson's and Boas's letters indicate that Chehalis people were skeptical of working with scholars who might sell their stories, as some believed Palmer had done when she published *Honne, the Spirit of the Chehalis* the year before Adamson arrived in Oakville. Even after establishing rapport with storytellers, Boas notes that Adamson "pumps and pumps for ethnological information" (July 10, 1927, Indiana University Archives of Traditional Music). In her letter to Herzog, Adamson uses similar language: "In spite of my boredom at the present, I really have had a most satisfactory summer in many ways. And my material is pretty good, considering it was 'pumped' out of a decaying civilization" (August 2, 1927, Indiana University Archives of Traditional Music). These comments, articulations of a salvage paradigm, indicate that Adamson and Boas solicited some, if not much, of the material, and it is difficult to determine the extent to which the investigators shaped the content of the material they gathered.

Boas's intermittent identification of storytellers makes tracing each text's origin somewhat difficult. In his introduction to the *Upper Chehalis Dictionary*, Kinkade notes that Boas "identified his informants, although he did not consistently indicate the source for all his data. Jonas Secena was his principal source, and Blanche Pete Dawson probably the second most important. He also collected texts from the Tenino dialect speakers Marion Davis, Peter Heck, and Robbie Choke" (1991, vii). In this volume, the name of each storyteller is listed after the title of the story attributed to him or her. When a story is not attributed to a storyteller, I have noted the story's context, within both the field notebooks as well as the wider context of recorded Chehalis literature. For instance, Boas does not indicate who told him "Skunk," but the story directly follows Peter Heck's "The Flood" and a short section on hunting in Boas's notebook 9 (1927a). However, in *Folk-Tales of the Coast Salish* Adamson attributes another version of "Skunk" to Davis and "X̱wanä'x̱wane and Skunk" to Jonas. It may not be possible to determine who told "Skunk" to Boas, but I have provided contextual clues in order to support educated guesses. I have assumed that Jonas narrated the unattributed material, particularly those stories that contain the X̱wanä'x̱wane variation of x̣ʷə́n, the Secena family form of this familiar figure's name. Loss of textual provenience muddles distinctions between oral traditions. The following biographical notes emphasize this distinctiveness and serve to remind us that multiple Chehalis traditions are communicated through the voices of storytellers who both carry and construct the stories valued by the Chehalis community. Brief biographies of each storyteller are provided below, along with pertinent information gleaned from field notebooks, letters, and newspaper accounts.

Robert Choke (September 16, 1894–April 26, 1965), frequently referred to as Robbie or Bob, told "x̣ʷə́n and Bluejay," a concise version of the story of Moon, to Boas. His grandparents were William and Sally Choke, and his parents were Jack and Nellie Choke. Choke was a member and minister of the Indian Shaker Church. He was active in traditional fishing and gathering activities, as noted in an issue of the *Oakville Cruiser* published while Adamson and Boas were working on the Chehalis Reservation. According to "Reservation News Notes," "Mr. and Mrs. Robert Choke have been catching salmon from the Chehalis river all last week" and "went to Cowlitz Prairie to pick blue berrys last Monday" (August 12, 1927). He also worked for the N. and M. Lumber Company and as a dairy farmer and fisherman ("Robert Choke" 1965).

Marion Davis (1855–February 20, 1932), teller of "Bluejay" and "Mink," was born near Centralia[38] (Adamson 1926–27, 50). Davis lived on the Chehalis Reservation and was a political and religious leader within the Chehalis community. His father, Jack Davis, was Cowlitz and possibly Puyallup, and his mother, Eliza, was Cowlitz, Nisqually, and Puyallup (Adamson 1926–27, 50, 229; Kinkade 1991, viii). Anthropologist Jay Miller explains that Eliza "moved to the Upper Chehalis from the White River when she was five and she taught [Davis] some Lushootseed Puget Sound tales recorded by Adamson" (2012a, 8). Kinkade also notes that Davis had Southern Lushootseed connections. These family lines might account for Davis's Mink speaking in a Nisqually dialect, and Katherine Barr,[39] Davis's daughter, recalls that "Chehalis, Nisqually, Chinook, and English" were spoken at her home (*Interview of Chehalis Tribal Elders* 2005; MDC). Davis was married to Bertha Petoie[40] at the time of Boas's visit. Bertha was the daughter of Charlie Petoie and Emma Heck, and thus niece to Peter and Silas Heck. Davis told Adamson that Robert Jackson, the storyteller who shared "The Story of Sun: A Legend of the Chehalis Indians," was his younger brother, as was Bruce Jackson. The boys were given different last names when they went to school; the three brothers attended Forest Grove Indian Training School in Oregon in the early 1880s.

At Forest Grove, Davis took an interest in ministry. Eells, who had strong ties with the school, knew Davis through missionary work on the Skokomish Reservation. At Skokomish Davis shared his knowledge of native languages with Eells. Edwin Chalcraft, superintendent of the Chehalis boarding school, noted that Davis helped him with "Indian language," specifically Chinook Jargon[41] (2004, 22). Chalcraft also noted that Davis was a member of the early Indian Shaker Church and recounted that in 1888 Davis was the first Chehalis man to vote. To support his family, Davis worked in a logging camp and was a skilled hunter and fisherman.

Davis worked extensively with Adamson, providing her with a great deal of cultural knowledge, ranging from burial practices and marriage customs to explanations for landforms. For instance, in detailing the origin of Grand Mound, an important cultural place about seven miles southeast of the Chehalis Reservation, Davis told Adamson that there "was no hill there, and suddenly they saw a hill. Something told them, their Ta[manous][42] or something, that a piece of star had broken off and fallen there" (1926–27, 59). Davis's stories are rooted in the landscape of the Chehalis; specific prairies and rivers are central to plots of "Bluejay" and "Mink."

In their introduction to *Folk-Tales of the Coast Salish*, anthropologist

William Seaburg and ethnomusicologist Laurel Sercombe closely examine the first paragraph of Davis's "Bluejay Goes to the Land of the Dead," a version of which is contained in this volume as "Bluejay." Seaburg and Sercombe note that although Adamson's 1926 and 1927 field notebooks have been lost,[43] "a handful of typed transcripts of stories remain." They explain, "Comparison of the typed-up notes with the published texts reveals Adamson's (and perhaps others') editing practices." An analysis of the two versions shows how changes made "silently gloss . . . Davis's rural Indian English" and, in a critique similar to those made of Boas's tendency to erase the voice of the storyteller, "one consultant begins to sound like any other consultant" (Seaburg and Sercombe 2009, vi, vii). Adamson's ethnographic notes include an alternative, or supplementary, version of "Mink," as well as a more thorough version of "Skunk." Adamson records Davis's commentary regarding two central Chehalis figures: x̣ʷə́n and Bluejay. According to Davis, "Xw&n was kind of a smart man, and B. J. was good and smart, too. Something like a fortune teller. I believe in B. J. now because our old people say, 'You must listen to B. J., because if going to die Katc Katc——but when he says Kac Kac——something will happen pretty soon, for good luck. I believe it. I always did'" and "Xw&n don't tell us what happened to him. Mn. Story last nearly one night lying flat. If sit would get crooked back and couldn't straighten up, and keeps saying hamu qi—like 'amen' in prayer" (Adamson 1926–27, 50). Adamson worked with Davis during the last years of his life (Miller 2010). Though he was ill, he was able to sing, and some of his songs were recorded on wax cylinders. Davis passed away five years later from tuberculosis, an illness that claimed so many Chehalis people in the early twentieth century (*Interview of Chehalis Tribal Elders* 2005; Miller 2011). At the time of his death, he was "the oldest Indian on the Reservation" ("Reservation News Notes," February 26, 1932).

Peter Heck (1854–April 23, 1951), teller of "The Flood," was the son of Mary Heck,[44] of Tenino and White River ancestry, and Thomas Heck, whose ancestors came from the southern side of Grays Harbor, the place near Westport known as c'əx̣íl's, or "sand," in Lower Chehalis, and ɬaq'ʷə́lm, near where Cloquallam Creek meets the Chehalis River, "just above Elma" (Adamson 1926–27, 24). Peter was "about sixty years old" when he worked with Adamson and Boas (Adamson 1934, ix). He was an active member of the Chehalis commu-

nity, serving as bishop of the Indian Shaker Church and as a policeman for
the Chehalis Reservation. Peter talked to Adamson about marriage customs,
religious practices, and village sites, among other things. Both his mother,
Mary, and his brother, Silas, worked with Adamson. Kinkade recorded Silas
telling "The Kidnapping of Moon" and made a thorough analysis of this tale,
situating Silas's version in the wider context of Chehalis oral tradition.[45]

Blanche Pete Dawson (January 21, 1909–May 4, 1971) was the daughter of
Maggie Smith Pete, "whose mother was Lower Chehalis and Chinook, and
whose father was half Upper Chehalis and half Puyallup," and Joseph Pete,
"whose mother was Upper Chehalis, and whose father was half Upper Chehalis and half Puyallup" (Kinkade 1991, vii). According to Kinkade, "Joseph
Pete's mother was a sister of sisínaʔx̣n," Jacob Secena (1991, vii–viii). Thus the
stories she shared with Boas might also be considered Secena family stories.
Other family connections include Tenas Pete, her paternal grandfather, and
John Smith, her maternal grandfather. She married John Dawson. In a letter
to Jacobs, Boas notes that he supplemented the material Secena provided
"every now and then by work with an intelligent girl," that is, Dawson (July
10, 1927, Jacobs Papers). Indeed, Dawson worked diligently to learn how to
collect and transcribe stories. Boas writes, "In some cases it has been possible
to interest educated natives in the study of their own tribes and to induce
them to write down in their own language their observations. These, also, are
much superior to English records, in which the natives are generally ham-
pered by the lack of mastery of the foreign language" (1911, 62). Dawson's
handwriting appears many times in Boas's field notebooks, though it appears
that Boas copied her versions into his notebook in his own hand. At times,
Dawson transcribed full stories in Upper Chehalis and provided the interlinear English translation.[46] She also helped Boas translate the ethnographic
material and stories that he collected.

Dawson and Boas exchanged letters after he returned to Columbia. In
August Dawson wrote that she had not yet transcribed a promised story for
Boas due to her mother's illness. Boas then sent a copy of "the tales that
Charley Cultee dictated," either *Chinook Texts* or *Kathlamet Texts* (Septem-
ber 27, 1927, Boas Papers). Dawson's mother, Maggie, wrote back thanking
Boas and informing him that Dawson was sick and had not been able to fin-

ish the story. On October 27, 1927, Boas wrote to Dawson and, trusting that her health had improved, asked if she had found time to finish the story. He added, "I remember with pleasure the hours that we worked together. I hope you enjoyed it as much as I did." Dawson replied and included a story with her letter, presumably "The Five Brothers," which Boas copied from Dawson's letter onto the last few pages of his field notebooks. On November 23, 1927, Boas replied, "I am very glad to have the story. It seems to me that you have written carefully and well. Be sure to pay close attention to the stops . . . over the line." Dawson indicated that it took her four hours to write the story, and Boas sent her payment (two dollars, at fifty cents an hour) for her effort. He concludes his letter with "I do trust that you will be willing to go on with this work and do as well as you can during the winter" (November 23, 1927, Boas Papers). It seems that the correspondence ended shortly after. "Cougar and Wildcat" may also be Dawson's work. A handwritten, partially translated draft is on file at the American Philosophical Society (APS) among Boas's notes on the Chehalis material and is not reproduced in this volume.[47] The exchange between Dawson and Boas shows that Boas maintained contact with members of the Chehalis community and that Dawson's work was integral to the transmission of texts.

Our principal storyteller, **Jonas Secena** (February 16, 1884–February 17, 1929), was "about forty" when he worked with Adamson and Boas. Boas notes that Secena had "an inexhaustible patience" and provided Adamson and Boas with both linguistic and literary material (July 10, 1927, Jacobs Papers). Jonas was blind, though it is not clear if he was blind from birth or if he became blind later in life. His mother, Alice, a respected faith healer, pie maker, and storyteller, was also blind. According to family tradition, Jonas would walk from the Chehalis Reservation to Oakville with twenty dogs, and the dogs would kick up so much dust everyone would know it was Jonas coming down the road. Jonas spoke mostly Chehalis, and the dogs understood Chehalis, too.[48] Though Jonas had no children, his impact on his family and community is still felt today, with many people acknowledging his good work as both a storyteller and a spiritual leader.

Kinkade describes the Secena family structure: "The Secenas are a large and still prominent family; Dan Secena was the father of Boas' main informant Jonas, as well as of Murphy (from whom [Leon] Metcalf recorded a story). Dan Secena's father was sisínaʔxn (a name also held by the latter's father and paternal grandfather; his maternal grandfather was one of the Kitsaps of Southern Puget Sound, and was part Sahaptin)" (1991, vii). Dan Secena indicated that his father was Upper Chehalis, his mother was Lower Chehalis, and the Secena family lived on "Mountain Prairie," probably Mound Prairie near Rochester, before relocating to the reservation (*U.S. v. Halbert* 1929, 598–99).

Jonas Secena told Adamson that his paternal grandfather died in 1907 and "saw it before the whites came," suggesting that he remembers the time before contact, and added that he lived to be about 115 years old, with an estimated birth year around 1790 (1926–27, 379). Secena also related his grandfather's story of Europeans coming to the area:

My grandfather said, when he was a boy, (this was the Spanish or the Hudson Bay) that either the Squaxin or Mud Bay were camping one time. Big crowd of Indians camping on the shore. People came who were white. That is a ghost. When came closer, the Indians said, "They smell strong like ghosts." The Indians were so clean—as went on someone said, that must be people, others said "No—ghosts."

Others decided that the ghosts shouldn't come again. That would cause the people to die.

Indians watched them in white's camp. Had boat, made fire, had something in their mouth to smoke.

Some said, ghosts, are different that they come back from land of dead. One warrior said, "What shall we do with them?" Someone suggested, "Shall be no ghosts here. We'll get rid of them." The chief agreed.

When the whites went to sleep, hit him on the head. One squeeled—hit the other. Burned them up and everything they had. Thought they were really ghosts. Didn't kill them from meanness, but were really afraid. (Adamson 1926–27, 381)

A version of this story continues through Chehalis oral tradition today. The continuity of storytelling in the Secena family reaches back to precontact time, and, remarkably, this family has shared their stories with scholars through many generations, providing a glimpse into how oral tradition changes from one generation to the next and how the family preserves their cultural knowledge.

Jonas's mother, Alice, also carried a rich oral tradition. Alice, wa'x̣əmlut, was a daughter of a Chief Kitsap,[49] and she was affiliated with Kittitas people near Ellensburg. Alice worked with Jacobs when he was visiting Oakville in August 1927 and talked about her family life east of the Cascades and shared a couple of stories. She is referred to as Mrs. Dan Secena throughout. According to Jacobs, Alice was "a well traveled and respected shaman" and, according to Miller, informed by Roberta Secena, "though blind later in life, was famous for her pies (berry, apple, peach), made every day to serve to people from all over who came to her as a healer" (Jacobs 1934, 15; Miller 2011, 8; Roberta Secena, conversation). Jacobs presents the cultural knowledge Alice related to him as "Reminiscences of Kittitas Life" in *Northwest Sahaptin Texts*. This knowledge includes family lineage, who family members married, how and where people lived, how they gathered berries, fished salmon, and caught eels, how social classes were structured, how chiefs ruled, and how spirit powers were acquired and shamans were trained (Jacobs 1934, 269–72). The Secena family has carried, and continues to carry, this cultural knowledge through many generations.

While we do not know much about how, and if, Chehalis people were paid for sharing stories and other cultural knowledge,[50] other forms of compensation may have encouraged participation. For instance, Boas thought it might be possible for Jonas's eyesight to be restored, and Boas wrote to Jacobs, "If you can arrange to get your man then and let us take him to Portland, we can get the x ray pictures. I intend to take Jonas along and perhaps your Secena[51] could take care of him. I think it is possible that a decent ophthalmologist could restore the sight in his right eye and I should like to give him the chance. Let me hear from you if that can be done" (July 10, 1927, Jacobs Papers). In her August 2, 1927, letter Adamson notes, "Sunday [Boas] left for Portland to take a few X-rays of sounds;[52] he took his informant from here with him. Mel took his informant, also, and 'motored' them all to Portland" (Indiana University Archives of Traditional Music). The *Oakville Cruiser* corroborates these reports: "Professor Franz Boas of Columbia University of New York, and Miss Thelma Adams[on] also of that place were studying Indian dialect language of this place, instructed by Jonas Secena, a blind young man of this place. Professor Boa[s] has been here for about four weeks and he can almost speak the language very well. He left for San Francisco last week, taking Jonas Secena, the blind boy, as far as Portland, Oregon, to consult and [*sic*] eye specialist there. Professor Boa[s] will be back in about three weeks to finish his study of the Indian language" ("Reservation News Notes, August 12, 1927). There is no mention of the visit to the ophthalmologist being a success.

It is likely that Jonas provided the majority of the material Boas recorded during his time in Oakville. He was the narrator for the material Boas translated as both "A Story" and "x̣ʷəné·x̣ʷəne: A Story," and Kinkade notes that Jonas probably told "Bear and Bee," here titled "Bear, Yellow-Jacket, and Ant" after Boas's own table of contents (1984, 246). Boas attributes "A Farewell Speech" to Jonas and, as noted above, I suspect that Jonas shared most of the unattributed material within the field notebooks. Jonas provided Adamson with commentary on both the art of storytelling and the stories as well. He notes that storytellers "used to make a business of it. Would go to other places and learn what they didn't know" (Adamson 1926–27, 345). This accounts for the diffusion of cultural traits among Northwest Coast narratives — storytellers would travel to share stories, telling their own, learning from others, and bringing word of distant adventures home.

Jonas also talked to Adamson about storytelling protocol. Storytelling would start after supper and would continue until midnight. The person telling the story would lie down, and everyone would listen, lying flat. Only the man tending the fire would get up during storytelling, but then he would lie back down. When the man tending the fire got up, all others lying down would say "ososos," so that he would not get a hump in his back. According to Jonas, "This was the only thing was allowed to say. When story is getting good, would say this" (Adamson 1926–27, 387). Adamson notes that there is no translation for this word (1934, xiii). Stories were told in the winter, to forget the winter, and telling stories on long winter nights would make the winter shorter. In order to make stories last all winter, storytellers would get "new stories with the old ones" to make "it just right" or complete (Adamson 1926–27, 390). Stories were not told in the spring because people were busy hunting, particularly for mountain beaver. In order to make the summer stretch long, storytellers would stop telling stories in the spring. It is problematic, then, that Adamson and Boas collected stories in the summer—entreating storytellers to break cultural protocol for the sake of preservation.

Boas worked with many storytellers when he visited the Chehalis Reservation but spent most of his time with Jonas, with Dawson aiding him with transcription and translation on a regular basis. Kinkade notes, "It is clear from Boas' transcriptions that Mr. Secena was an accomplished story-teller, and the more I work with his stories, the more I am impressed with his narrative ability" (1983, 267). Kinkade worked closely with this material, both in its narrative form (see appendixes 4 and 5) and at a lexical level (see the *Upper Chehalis Dictionary*, Kinkade 1991). Boas's notebooks are strictly focused on linguistic and narrative material; paratext is rare. But at the end of "A Farewell Speech," Boas includes a transcription of Jonas's name, with the note, "I thank you my people, Jonas B. Sesene̲x̲an, Storyteller of Chehalis" (1927a, 885). Jonas passed away less than two years after telling these stories to Boas, in the winter of 1929.

TRANSLATION

Boas filled fourteen field notebooks while he worked on the Chehalis Reservation. The notebooks, now housed at the American Philosophical Society, contain over nine hundred pages of Upper Chehalis stories with corresponding vocabulary lists and grammatical paradigms. Boas recorded the stories in Upper Chehalis and then made interlinear translations in English. When Boas returned to Columbia University, he organized a large bank of linguistic data (represented by an eight-thousand-slip lexical file at APS) and worked with graduate student Ethel Aginsky[53] to make typescripts of the stories he collected. The typescripts Boas and Aginsky made are the textual bases for the stories presented in this volume, and I have consulted the field notebooks to clarify ambiguous passages. One of the goals of this project is to provide clear and consistent versions of the stories Boas collected for a wide audience and to continue the conversation regarding this material that has gained momentum in the last decade.[54]

A few scholars have worked with Boas's Upper Chehalis field notebooks and linguistic data, often as part of broader, comparative projects. For instance, Aginsky worked with Salish languages, studying Puyallup and Twana and making a comparison of Puyallup and Upper Chehalis in the mid-1930s. Charles F. Voegelin and Zellig S. Harris prepared an index to the Franz Boas Collection of Materials for American Linguistics after the material was donated to APS in the 1940s. There, Morris Swadesh worked with Boas's linguistic data, analyzing and classifying Upper Chehalis material.[55]

Kinkade began his study of the Chehalis material in the late 1950s, a connection facilitated by Voegelin. Voegelin served as Kinkade's advisor at Indiana University and, knowing that Kinkade was born and educated in Washington and interested in Salish, suggested that the young linguist work with the Chehalis material at APS (Kinkade 1991, iv). Boas's field notebooks were integral to Kinkade's work; Kinkade describes these records as "the second primary source of vocabulary" for the *Upper Chehalis Dictionary*, second to data he "gathered directly from native speakers of Upper Chehalis between 1960 and 1974." Kinkade notes, "Boas had under way a dictionary of Upper Chehalis which was never completed" (1991, vi, v). In the introduction to the *Upper Chehalis Dictionary*, Kinkade provides a thorough overview of Chehalis bands, dialects, and speakers and a history of the collection of linguistic material. His study spanned nearly fifty years, and he conducted occasional language classes, at tribal request and grant-funded, on the Chehalis Reservation up until his death in 2004.

According to Seaburg, Kinkade was working on a translation of Secena's "x̣ʷəné·x̣ʷəne: A Story" before he passed away, but unfortunately he did not complete this work. Seaburg is the caretaker of Kinkade's unfinished translation, and there are strong hopes that the work—the most comprehensive Upper Chehalis text in existence—will be completed and shared with the Chehalis community.[56] As with "Bear and Bee" (appendix 4) and "Daughters of Fire" (appendix 5), Kinkade restyled the material Boas collected. He made new interlinear transcriptions of the stories and divided them into acts, scenes, stanzas, and lines following the ethnopoetic form developed by Dell Hymes.[57] "The Kidnapping of Moon: An Upper Chehalis Myth," told by Silas Heck, should also be mentioned here. This story is an abridged—or alternate—version of Secena's "x̣ʷəné·x̣ʷəne: A Story," which Kinkade put into ethnopoetic form. (This version is presented in English only.) Much of the introduction to Silas Heck's version applies to the versions presented in this volume as well, and Kinkade provides commentary specific to Secena's "x̌ʷəné·x̌ʷəne: A Story."

Kinkade spent the better part of his career analyzing, preserving, and teaching Upper Chehalis, and his work provides a model for future analysis and preservation efforts—in part because Kinkade identified—and found practical solutions for—problems associated with translating and working from Upper Chehalis material collected in the hundred years before his own efforts began. He notes, "There are certain difficulties in reanalyzing and retranscribing Boas' material. It is not always clear what his vowel notations mean, and his handwriting is often difficult to decipher"[58] (1991, xi). Kinkade relied on Boas's field notebooks, and not the typescript prepared by Aginsky, because in the recopying "some errors crept into" the linguistic material (1991, vi). As noted above, Aginsky's typescript serves as the textual foundation for these stories, and I have consulted the field notebooks to clarify ambiguous passages.

Still, some circumlocutions are simply carried across the translation of a passage from Upper Chehalis into English. For instance, Kinkade notes, "The use of the name Moon in Upper Chehalis is ambiguous because there is a single word for 'moon' and 'sun' in the language [ɬukʷáɬ]. When a speaker wants to refer specifically to the moon, the circumlocution 'night-sun/moon' must be used" (2008, 352). Circumlocution is present in grammatical structures and even within the plots of the stories: one knows that the protagonist of the kidnapping of Moon stories is, in fact, Moon through roundabout clues, as Jackson explains in "The Story of Sun." (See appendix 2 for a more thorough discussion.)

Although Kinkade preferred the ethnopoetic form—and indeed, this style is better representative of Chehalis oral tradition as it preserves (or seeks to re-create) the performance qualities of the texts—I have left the stories in paragraph form following Aginsky and Boas's precedent. Boas would have found this volume incomplete, as it does not include his Upper Chehalis transcriptions of these stories. Boas prepared handwritten transcriptions of both "Bear and Bee" and "Daughters of the Fire" from his field notes, and these transcriptions contain clues to understanding Boas's translation methodology. Boas valued the publication of interlinear texts, pursued the publication of both English and native-language versions of the material he collected, and encouraged his students to do the same. When it was not possible to publish English and native-language versions of the stories he collected as one volume, he often pursued publication of a second volume that contained the native-language version. Boas notes, "When the question arises, for instance, of investigating the poetry of the Indians, no translation can possibly be considered as an adequate substitute for the original. The formal rhythm, the treatment of the language, the adjustment of text to music, the imagery, the use of metaphors, and all the numerous problems involved in any thorough investigation of the style of poetry, can be interpreted only by the investigator who has equal command of the ethnographical traits of the tribe and of their language" (1911, 62). Unfortunately, I do not possess this equal command, and no one has yet come forward to work with this material who does, making an interlinear presentation impractical at this time.[59] The need and opportunity are obvious. To work with these stories in Upper Chehalis—and to reintroduce the stories to the community in the language in which they were first told—will be possible only with concerted language revitalization efforts. Ideally, this will come from within the community.

One project that will provide tremendous support for this work is the documentary edition of the Franz Boas Papers—a collaborative effort led by Regna Darnell and M. Sam Cronk and bringing together the efforts and resources of the University of Western Ontario, the American Philosophical Society, the University of Nebraska Press, the University of Victoria, and the Musgamagw Dzawada'enuxw Tribal Council. The Franz Boas Papers have been available to scholars who have the means to visit APS or through microfilm or specific digitization requests. With the documentary edition, "Digital materials will be available for use, first by Indigenous communities with an ongoing proprietary stake but also by academic and archival institutions, including museums. The documentary edition, particularly in its digital form, will constitute a research tool for further collaboration and documentation of the relationships between First Nations and researchers." Indeed, "the contents of the papers provide materials for language revitalization" (Smith, Darnell, Hancock, and Moritz 2014, 97). Boas's Upper Chehalis field notebooks are part of the American Council of Learned Societies Committee on Native American Languages collection and so are not included in this first wave of digitization. If and when these materials are digitized, they will be a valuable resource for members of academic and tribal communities—especially for those people engaged in reservation-based language revitalization efforts. The importance of direct access to these materials by the families of the people who shared them cannot be overstated.

PUBLICATION

Many Chehalis stories were shared prior to Adamson and Boas's visit to the Chehalis Reservation, but only a few were published. These include Boas's German translation of Cultee's "Qonē'qonē," Meany's abstracts of stories shared by Jacob Secena, sisína?xn, as part of a *Seattle Post-Intelligencer* series featuring Washington tribes, and Jackson's "The Story of Sun: A Legend of the Chehalis Indians." In the early 1920s Palmer worked with Sanders on *Honne, the Spirit of the Chehalis*. In her introduction Palmer notes, "There has passed down the generations to the last a series of legends which explain the existence of the world in which they live; imaginative and supernatural, naïve and truly reflecting the thought, habits and customs of the Indian himself and the animal and plant life of the valley which the Indian knew so well" (1925, 1–2). Erna Gunther reviewed the book in 1926, calling it a "welcome addition" motivated by a "real interest in these people and a desire to perpetuate their body of unwritten literature." She acknowledges, "That there are fragments to be gleaned by the ethnologist is shown by the present publication." Still, Gunther calls attention to the weaknesses of the volume. She notes that the collection does not "help solve the question of cultural affiliation of the Chehalis." The question of cultural affiliation of the Chehalis is not neatly answered—even now. Gunther points out that it is not clear whether Sanders was telling stories passed down to him by his father (who was Nisqually) or whether he was "telling the tales of the locality in which he lived" (1926). Indeed, the "Sanderses descended from the Nisqually patriot Quiemuth, a brother of Chief Leschi" (Miller 2012a, xi). But the "tales of the locality" cannot be assumed to come from a single origin, as the Chehalis Reservation was—and is—home to people affiliated with many Coast Salish tribes, often serving as a refuge for displaced Native peoples (Gunther 1926, 67).

The publication of *Honne* made it difficult for Adamson to gain the trust of Chehalis storytellers when she first visited the Chehalis Reservation in 1926. Adamson assured those with whom she wished to work that she "wasn't going to sell their stories and make a fortune from them," as some people assumed Palmer had done (August 9, 192[6], Boas Papers). Indeed, the economic climate of the late 1920s and early 1930s made it difficult for Adamson to get the stories she collected into circulation, much less profit from their publication. Adamson was plagued with tuberculosis in 1929 and may have suffered a relapse—or even showed indications of the onset of mental illness—by 1933.[60] For these reasons, Ruth Benedict and Boas oversaw the 1934 publication of Adamson's *Folk-Tales of the Coast Salish*, a volume containing stories from Upper Chehalis, Cowlitz, Wynoochee, Humptulip, Satsop, Puyallup, White River, and Skokomish storytellers, through the American Folklore Society. Adamson had pursued, at Gunther's invitation and Boas's encouragement, the University of Washington as a publisher, but, ironically, the press passed on this material. Boas worked with Jacobs to negotiate the publication of *Northwest Sahaptin Texts* through the University of Washington in 1929 and a more extensive two-part volume of the same title through Columbia University Press in 1934.

Boas published a fragment of "Bear and Bee," a guide to the translation of Upper Chehalis, as "A Chehalis Text" in the *International Journal of American Linguistics* in 1935 (appendix 3). Kinkade finished the translation nearly fifty years later,[61] using the original field notebooks as his source, and published it as "'Bear and Bee': Narrative Verse Analysis of an Upper Chehalis Folktale" (appendix 4). Kinkade explains, "Only one folktale has ever been published in Upper Chehalis, a Salishan language of southwestern Washington. This was the story of Bear and Bee. . . . The story was published solely to provide a basis for extensive grammatical notes on the language (and they are very good notes), and nothing whatever is said about the text itself. In fact, Boas only published about a third of the story" (1984, 246). This lack of textual commentary is consistent throughout the Boasian literary corpus, as Boas focused on collecting, editing, and publishing native texts, not analyzing them. Kinkade presents the completed story "as transcribed in Boas' field notebooks" and rearranged "into the narrative verse format," that is, an ethnopoetic form that Kinkade believed "correctly portrays its structure" (1984, 246). Kinkade also published "Daughters of Fire: Narrative Verse Analysis of an Upper Chehalis Folktale," a subsection of "x̣ʷəné·x̣ʷəne: A Story," in the same style (appendix 5).

MOVING FORWARD

Talk—sometimes oral tradition, sometimes gossip—about the visiting anthropologists persisted in the Chehalis community long after Adamson and Boas finished their work. The linguist and ethnologist John P. Harrington visited the Chehalis Reservation in 1942.[62] John Vosper, an Oakville man, related Adamson and Boas's visit. Harrington notes, "It was some 12 yrs. ago that a man already elderly visited here (clearly Prof. Franz Boas). He was accompanied by a young lady, whose name Vosper forgets. Vosper drove this young lady out to some Indian's house. She was writing down Ind. lore & was from New York. She told Vosper that the old man had been in British Columbia and *talked* Indian dialects (not jargon but native langs.) The professor taught anthropology in N. Y. C." (1942–43, 74). The "man already elderly" description of Boas was carried forward through oral tradition. When I started working on this project, I was told that an old German man had come to the Chehalis Reservation and collected stories and that it would be good for those stories to be returned to the Chehalis people. There is a strong desire within the community that these stories be returned and shared, and this volume is only a small piece of that effort. One thing is almost certain: if these stories do not continue through oral tradition, the talk surrounding them most definitely will. Either way, the stories will persist.

When Boas and his graduate students came to "the field" they sought to preserve languages and literatures that assimilation efforts rendered nearly unrecognizable. In fact, the act of transcribing the oral tradition fundamentally changed the way these stories were carried forward, and in this sense, salvage ethnographers were complicit in destroying what they sought to save. While it is impossible to know exactly why Robert Choke, Marion Davis, Peter Heck, Blanche Pete Dawson, and Jonas Secena shared their stories with Franz Boas, changes brought about by government schooling, regulation of fishing, gathering, and hunting, and the privileging of literacy over orality threatened the survival of precontact Chehalis culture. Fortunately, these forces were not successful. These moments of sharing were, in fact, acts of resistance against the loss of what was, and by reintroducing these stories to the Chehalis people, the truth and wisdom contained therein can once again be part of what will be.

Upper Chehalis Stories

A Story

Jonas Secena

I

x̌ʷəné·x̌ʷəne and k'ʷə́cx̌ʷe

It is always told how the world and the animals[1] were long ago.[2] They were people and were not in the right way,[3] therefore they were changed by the Chief.[4]

"Why then," said x̌ʷəné·x̌ʷəne,[5] "Let me go to the ocean." He gathered little brushes which were hollow inside.[6] He cut them short. He strung the brushes on the string and tied them together. He made a necklace. From there he went to the mountains. He was near the mountains. Then he was very hungry. He stopped then on the trail and sat down. It was almost night. Then he heard someone coming. He saw a woman was coming. She was coming near. That x̌ʷəné·x̌ʷəne gentleman said, "Oh, it is a big woman." She came nearer. Oh, it was a monster. She was k'ʷə́cx̌ʷe,[7] that one who ate people. "What may it be that she is carrying on her back? I'll try to take camas[8] for my necklaces." Then he went after her and x̌ʷəné·x̌ʷəne said, "Oh, my elder sister, I am very hungry. I am starving. I have a necklace of dentalia.[9] Could I buy from you bulbs of camas for my necklace?" Then k'ʷə́cx̌ʷe said, "Oh, although your necklace is not good I'll give a few to you to eat. I'll just help you out so that you may not starve." x̌ʷəné·x̌ʷəne was given camas into his hand. Then x̌ʷəné·x̌ʷəne said when he got it, "Thank you for what you give me to eat. We are five, four younger brothers. We all look alike. You will happen to meet them whenever[10] there is a mountain. If he looks like myself, that one is my youngest brother. Now I am going to leave you. I am going into the woods. From there I'll go home." The monster said, "Goodbye, now I am going." x̌ʷəné·x̌ʷəne went along into the woods. He sat down and ate the camas. After he[11] had finished eating he braced up and felt stronger. After he had been starving he wondered, "How shall I do it? Let me rest a little while here. Oh, that is not good. It would be better if I ran to the next mountain. Maybe I'll take a rest." Then he ran to another mountain. He arrived at a clear place. He lay down there near a trail. Then he lay there for a long time. Then k'ʷə́cx̣ʷe came. He went after her again. Now his necklace was different. x̣ʷəné·x̣ʷəne said, "Oh, you must be traveling a long distance?" k'ʷə́cx̣ʷe answered, "My younger brother, I am just going to my house." x̣ʷəné·x̣ʷəne said, "Did you see my elder brother?" "My younger brother, I saw him. He is bad." Then x̣ʷəné·x̣ʷəne said, "I am very hungry. Might I buy a little from your lot?" k'ʷə́cx̣ʷe answered, "I do not gather camas to sell it. I only gather it for my food. I'll give you a few." x̣ʷəné·x̣ʷəne took the camas. "Oh, my sister, thank you. You feed me with your food. Now she speaks well, brother. Now I am starting off. Goodbye." x̣ʷəné·x̣ʷəne went out of the woods and ate. After he had eaten he sang. When he had finished eating then he started over again. He ran now faster and arrived at another mountain. First he gathered grass. He found some dry grass. It was shiny. He walked now and sat down. He cut the grass into short pieces and threaded it on a string. He tied it together and put it around his neck. Then he waited for k'ʷə́cx̣ʷe. Now k'ʷə́cx̣ʷe was coming. "Oh, my elder sister, are you traveling? It looks as though you had a heavy load. Oh, my elder sister, I am very hungry. May I trade this my necklace for food for a part of your load?" k'ʷə́cx̣ʷe answered, "You are bad. You are always cheating me. Never mind, I will give you something to eat." She took the cover off her basket and gave him a few pieces of camas. "I will just give you something to eat. Your necklace is bad." "Thank you for feeding me. Goodbye, now I am going along," said he and went into the woods and ate. After he had finished eating he ran again and ran with all his might. He arrived at a mountain and sat down next to the trail. There he waited for k'ʷə́cx̣ʷe. He had not waited long when k'ʷə́cx̣ʷe came along. "Oh, my elder sister, I am very hungry. Might I buy a little food from your load?" k'ʷə́cx̣ʷe answered quickly, "My younger brother, I am feeding you from my load. I do not sell my camas. I only prepare it for my food for the winter. I only take pity on you, therefore I always feed you." Now she gave it to him again. x̣ʷəné·x̣ʷəne took it. x̣ʷəné·x̣ʷəne said, "Oh, my elder sister, thank you for feeding me. Now I'll go along." Now x̣ʷəné·x̣ʷəne went into the woods first.

Field notebook II, 87–96; typescript, "A Story," 1–3. Also referred to as "The Adventures of x̣ʷəné·x̣ʷəne."

II

x̣ʷəné·x̣ʷəne Loses His Eyes

k'ʷə́cx̣ʷe looked at her load and she saw that only a few camas were left. k'ʷə́cx̣ʷe said, "What shall I do with him? He is bad." Now she started. She went and she said, "Now this is too much. x̣ʷəné·x̣ʷəne is making me poor. If I give him my camas it will be gone, what belongs to me as my food. Let me not give him anything to eat. Let me cheat him. He is bad. He told me in the first place there were five. I am always walking. Then I always meet him. He is the same x̣ʷəné·x̣ʷəne. Let him die. He is bad." k'ʷə́cx̣ʷe had something like a beehive. She wrapped it up. She told the Bees, "When he unwraps you, at that time sting his eyes. Take out his eyes. Sting him until he is nearly dead. Leave him when he goes into a hollow cedar stump. When he is inside the cedar stump shut up the cedar stump. You will sting him." She had made her plans. Then k'ʷə́cx̣ʷe started again. She came to a mountain and there again was x̣ʷəné·x̣ʷəne. He was waiting for her. "Oh, my elder sister, I am very hungry. Could you feed me with some of your load?" k'ʷə́cx̣ʷe answered again, "Oh, younger brother, I have very little. Oh, never mind, I'll give you all." She pulled out a little basket with something wrapped over it. "Oh, that is what I have for you. Take it. Do not eat it here until you are inside a cedar stump and you will eat." x̣ʷəné·x̣ʷəne took the bundle. "Thank you, you give me something to eat. Later on I will return it to you, some other time." k'ʷə́cx̣ʷe said again, "When you are going to eat this camas, don't open it until you are inside a cedar stump. Then eat it." x̣ʷəné·x̣ʷəne went, "Goodbye, now I'll go. I'll look for a cedar stump." He started. x̣ʷəné·x̣ʷəne shouted five times, "Wä, wä, wä, wä, wä." k'ʷə́cx̣ʷe said in the evening, "He is bad. If I give him my camas it will all be gone." x̣ʷəné·x̣ʷəne went after he shouted. He found a cedar stump and entered the cedar stump. When he got inside it closed. He could not get out. He unwrapped the bundle and opened it. A buzzing sound came from the bundle. It was a buzzing sound. Then they buzzed and he was stung all over in his eyes. He became dizzy. And x̣ʷəné·x̣ʷəne lost his sense. His eyes were taken off by the Bees. They got them. They took them way out. Then x̣ʷəné·x̣ʷəne came to life again. He could not see. There was no way of getting out. He could not do anything and he gave up hope. He said, "Now I may die." He lay down inside the stump and went to sleep. For five days he was there.

Field notebook II, 96–102; typescript, "A Story," 3–5.

III

x̣ʷəné·x̣ʷəne Meets Woodpecker and Takes New Eyes

Then he heard pecking from above. He shouted, "Oh, who are you?" He was answered, "I am Woodpecker." x̣ʷəné·x̣ʷəne replied again, "What are you doing?" Woodpecker said, "I am just looking for winged ants for my food. What are you doing inside the cedar stump?" x̣ʷəné·x̣ʷəne replied, "I was shut up by k'ʷə́cx̣ʷe. Can you help me? Can you make a hole in the tree large enough that I can get through?"[12] Woodpecker said, "I do not do that, but I'll try." Now Woodpecker went down. He made a hole downward. It was not very long when it opened inside. First he went in and found x̣ʷəné·x̣ʷəne. He had no eyes. He asked, "What has become of your eyes?" x̣ʷəné·x̣ʷəne said, "My eyes were taken away by the Bees. Maybe they took them along. Come on." Woodpecker went out first. He called and x̣ʷəné·x̣ʷəne came to the hole. He was pulled out by Woodpecker. Woodpecker said, "It is almost night. I cannot wait for you." Then Woodpecker went home to his house. First x̣ʷəné·x̣ʷəne was thinking he would not know which way he was going. He took hold of a stick. He broke it and made a cane. Now he walked. He just felt with his foot. Thus he walked for a long time. Then he bumped his face. It seems that it was a house where he bumped his face. Then he turned back to a good place. There he found a wilted flower. He made it into a good form, almost round, and he stuck it into its orbit. He also put on another one. It looked as if he had eyes and could see with it [them] nearby, which looked like the sea down below. Then he went after this in the house. He came to those in the house. Again he hit the house of Slug. Then someone said, "What are you doing? What are you looking for?" "I am only trying to find out how long your house is." Then he went around the house of Slug. He just felt with his hands. Then he found the door of the house. He got in. Then he saw a little nearby by means of the flower. He was asked by Slug, "What kind of person are you?" "Oh, I am x̣ʷəné·x̣ʷəne. I only came to visit you." He gave him a seat and he sat down. They talked. x̣ʷəné·x̣ʷəne told him about everything he knew of far away countries. Then x̣ʷəné·x̣ʷəne said, "Could we not trade eyes? My eyes are good. I want to have small eyes so then I can see nearby. I see too far with my eyes." Slug said,[13] "They are too big, therefore I do not want them. No I do not want to trade for your eyes." Then x̣ʷəné·x̣ʷəne said, "Let us go out." They went out, x̣ʷəné·x̣ʷəne leading. They came out of the house. x̣ʷəné·x̣ʷəne said, "Do you know where we can sit down where we can see the waterfront?" The other one said, "Come here. Here is the stick you set down." x̣ʷəné·x̣ʷəne said, "Look at the sea. Do you see the people on the other side of the ocean?" "Oh, there is no land. You could not find land beyond the ocean. All over there is water around." "My, what is the matter with your eyes? Look again. Way yonder the people are running back and forth. Look." Slug looked and could not see anything. x̣ʷəné·x̣ʷəne said again, "Oh, try these my eyes, and take off your eyes. First I'll put on your eyes." Slug took off his eyes. x̣ʷəné·x̣ʷəne put on the eyes of Slug. "I'll try your eyes to see whether I can see with them. Oh, your eyes are good. Here are my eyes. Put them on. Then you will see with them across the ocean." Slug put on the flower eyes. Then x̣ʷəné·x̣ʷəne went away. When he got far away he shouted. Slug put on the eyes of x̣ʷəné·x̣ʷəne. Slug wanted to see with them. But he could hardly see with them. He could not distinguish anything with them. "Ai, ai, ai, ai, ai," shouted x̣ʷəné·x̣ʷəne.

Field notebook II, 103–9; typescript, "A Story," 5–7. "x̣ʷəné·x̣ʷəne [illegible] woodpecker & takes new eyes" in original table of contents.

IV

x̣ʷəné·x̣ʷəne Recovers His Own Eyes

Then he walked slowly. He went somewhere far away. Then he heard from far some tamanous.[14] At first he stood up. Then he listened from which way he heard it. Then he found out from where it came. He went toward it and he came near. "Oh, a wheel game.[15] I'll see who they are." He walked slowly and got there. He saw then there were many people. Behold! The Bees were playing the wheel game. He went up to them and looked at the disc. He was looking at the disc of the people. Then these people were shouting. One of the Bees got from another, one of the rings. The Big Bee sang and the other Children of the Bees were making a noise. Others shouted. One rolled it along. Then it was seen by x̣ʷəné·x̣ʷəne that the discs were his eyes. "Oh, they made discs out of my eyes." He said to the Bees, "Oh, younger brothers, let me look at your discs." He got one. It was one of his eyes. They were both his eyes. He was holding them and took hold of both. Then he jumped up and ran as fast as he could. He got far way. There he stood and first took off the eyes of Slug and put on his own eyes. After he had put them on he threw away the eyes of Slug. He shouted, "Hai, hai, hai, hai, hai," because he had his own eyes again.

Field notebook II, 109–11; typescript, "A Story," 7–8.

V

x̣ʷəné·x̣ʷəne Flies with Geese

From there he went far away. He came to a country of traveling people. He came near. He asked, "What are you doing?" "We are traveling far. First we'll eat." Those people ate. Some of them said, "Why do you not give anything to eat to x̣ʷəné·x̣ʷəne?" One of them said, "Come on so that you will eat with us." x̣ʷəné·x̣ʷəne ate. He finished and started. Then x̣ʷəné·x̣ʷəne said to one of them, "May I come along?" "Oh, come along with us. We will lend you some wings and a tail." They taught x̣ʷəné·x̣ʷəne how to do it, when he should fly. He began to fly and first he did not fly well. Then he learned it. They went along. It was night. Then it became day. When they came to people, x̣ʷəné·x̣ʷəne talked. The Chief of the Geese[16] said, "Don't talk. Don't make fun of the people down on the ground. It is forbidden in our customs." They all flew away. They came near some people. x̣ʷəné·x̣ʷəne talked. The people on the ground said, "Did you hear it? It seems talking comes from those flying. It seems it is different, the one flying with them." They flew. It became night and it became day again. They came to one swimming. "Oh, Lady, you are showing yourself." One of the Chiefs of the Geese said, "x̣ʷəné·x̣ʷəne has broken our rules. Let us leave him on a big mountain." They flew and came to the highest one. They left him. First they took away their wings and their tails.[17] Then they left him. The Geese flew away to the northern part of the world.

Field notebook II, 112–15; typescript, "A Story," 8–9.

VI

x̣ʷəné·x̣ʷəne Kills Owl and Takes His Eyes

x̣ʷəné·x̣ʷəne stayed. It was night. He could not get down. It was too steep. He stayed there for four nights. Then it became day again. Now he was starved. "What can I eat?" He took out one of his eyes and ate it. Again he was hungry. He had no eyes. He stayed there five nights. Then he heard a noise from above. "Hou, hou, hou, hou, hou." It was Owl. x̣ʷəné·x̣ʷəne swore, "You child of a dog. Shut up, you wake me up." The hooting Owl answered, "If you are not quiet, you bad one, I'll grab you by the face, you bad one." "You are too weak. You cannot overcome me." And Owl said again, "Hou." "Ah," said x̣ʷəné·x̣ʷəne, "Confound it, you make too much noise." Owl answered, "If you are not quiet I'll beat you. I'll break all your bones. I am a hooting Owl. I overcome everybody, no matter who it may be. I am always overcoming everybody no matter who it is. I am the hero. The night and the mountains are mine." He stopped talking. x̣ʷəné·x̣ʷəne said again, "Screecher, son of a hooting Owl, what are you doing here? Come on down and let us fight on this level ground." "Hou, hou, hou, hou, hou, you will find out after a while. I'll break all your bones." x̣ʷəné·x̣ʷəne said, "When can you overcome me?" Owl came down but x̣ʷəné·x̣ʷəne had no eyes. x̣ʷəné·x̣ʷəne said, "I always play like that. If you think you are a man, come here. If you think you are a strong person, you first take hold." Owl jumped at him and took hold of x̣ʷəné·x̣ʷəne. x̣ʷəné·x̣ʷəne held on to the throat of Owl. They fought for a long time. Then Owl got tired. Then he was thrown down by x̣ʷəné·x̣ʷəne and was stepped on by x̣ʷəné·x̣ʷəne. He punched out his eyes and he hit his face with one hand and he punched him senseless with the other hand. Owl was knocked senseless. He broke the throat of Owl and then Owl died. He took his eyes and put them into his orbits. After he put them on he could see. Then he took his wings and his tail and put them on. First he tried them and when he tried them he went but not very far. He almost fell always.

x̣ʷəné·x̣ʷəne said, "I am hungry, let me turn back." He turned around and went back to the body of Owl. He made a fire and when the fire got hot he cooked the body of Owl. He put it on a stick[18] and ate it when it was done. After he had eaten he warmed himself by the fire. He became stronger and his mind recovered. When it was day, he said, "Let me start out." He flew away and he almost fell from above. He came to another mountain. First he rested. Then he fixed himself up and flew again. He flew steadily and got there. He almost fell. He got to the bank of the river.

Field notebooks II, III, 115, 144–48; typescript, "A Story," 9–11.

VII

x̣ʷəné·x̣ʷəne Makes Self-Acting Maul

He walked about on the level bank. Indeed he was starving. He thought, "What kind of food can I prepare?" Then he saw Spring Salmon jumping. First he looked at the water. It was too deep where Spring Salmon was. He walked up the river and came to a shallow water. He saw that it would be good there. He could make a fish trap.[19] He made a fish trap. In a short time he finished it, because it was not wide. He watched on the bank. Nothing came up. He walked downriver and when he had gone off, something went in it, went right through and went into his fish trap. He came to his fish trap and found that it was broken. First he repaired it, then he wondered what he could do to capture his Spring Salmon. He was making a canoe. He always was chipping[20] the canoe that he was making. There was a noise of hammering. It was night. Then he said, "I guess I'll make something to hammer slightly on my canoe. I'll go near the bank of the river and I'll just peek out of the bushes to look at my fish traps to see who may be hammering on my canoe so that I can get the better of the fish. This is very far away from the people." Then he said, "Let me make a maul to hammer my canoe." He said to his maul, "Tap on my canoe." Then it hammered the canoe and it sounded just like some person.[21] "Now I'll go down the river." He got down to the river. When he came to the river it stopped hammering. He went back again. The maul was not working well. Then he worked at it again. When he had worked it again he went back to the river. He came to his fish trap. Then he saw the Spring Salmon going up. He broke off the sticks and made it so as to strike his head. The Spring Salmon[22] got through the trap and got into it. x̣ʷəné·x̣ʷəne jumped after it. He hooked one on the head and threw it on the shore. He hooked another one on the head and threw it on the shore. "This is enough, what I kill. Let me go home." He came to the maul. "Qul, qul, qul, qul, qul," x̣ʷəné·x̣ʷəne said. "Now finish your work. I killed two." He went to his house. x̣ʷəné·x̣ʷəne prepared his food. He cut it and he found the intestines. He looked a little at it. "How pretty are all these insides." He found the gills, "Oh, how pretty is the inside of the head of the salmon." He took the gills and put them behind himself. He cooked the body on a spit. He fixed the fire and threw into the fire some of his beechwood. It burned. It was cooking for a little while. Then he ate. He finished eating.

Field notebook III, 161–66; typescript, "A Story," 11–12.

VIII

x̣ʷəné·x̣ʷəne Makes Girls Out of Gills

Then he went to gather the gills and other parts from the inside of the Spring Salmon. He said, "What could be made out of it? Let me make two women out of the gills. They will be my wives." Then he took them to his house. He spilled ashes all over the insides and he piled a large amount of ashes over them. Now he lay down the gills. He did not go far for he came back. There was nothing. The gills had just disappeared. Again he went far away. First he worked at his canoe. He made a noise. Then he stopped. He went slowly. There was nothing. Then he saw what looked like tracks of children. Then he went to work. He adzed his canoe. Then he made a noise although he was working. He was not working well because his mind was changing because he always thought of his wives. x̣ʷəné·x̣ʷəne said, "Well, let me take a rest." He went to his house. When he was still far away he heard the high voice like children. He sneaked to the house and looked inside. No children must have been running about. All must have been running about inside the house. He walked back slowly and went back to work. Now he was broken-hearted. He went back to his canoe and he just tapped his canoe. He did not want to work because he was heartsick. His head always thought of his wife. For a little while he tapped and again went to his house and he came to it. Not far from the house he heard the noise of little children. They were singing. Slowly he went near and looked. He saw them running and saw the dust in his house. Again he went back slowly and went to his canoe. First he sat down for a little while. Then he wondered. He talked to his mind, "Four times I sneaked in to these girls and I could not see them, but my maul could not work even if it was making a noise." "But it would not be like a person," answered his own mind. "Oh, you can make a person just to deceive him if you take your insides out of your body first," x̣ʷəné·x̣ʷəne wondered. He said, "It would not be possible to take out the insides from a person. Even if I should do that I should have to cut my insides. Let me not do it. Other people might do that." First he sat down for a while. "What part of my insides would be easy to make like a person?" said he. "I always eat food and it passes [through] me, then it steams. I think that is what I will make like a person. The passed food." He said to the passed food, "You would hit my canoe. It would not be lighter with my maul, younger brother. Try it." The passed food answered him, "Slowly or fast?" x̣ʷəné·x̣ʷəne said, "Hammer quickly so that it sounds like many people." The younger brother of x̣ʷəné·x̣ʷəne hammered. "Oh," says x̣ʷəné·x̣ʷəne, "That sounds good. Now I leave you." x̣ʷəné·x̣ʷəne went toward the house. He sneaked in really slowly. First he stood there. First he listened to his younger brother. "The adzing of my brother sounds well." He started slowly toward it and now he heard singing, and there was noise of laughing. He heard one say, "There, he is still working." Then x̣ʷəné·x̣ʷəne went inside. The girls did not see him. They were facing the other way. x̣ʷəné·x̣ʷəne sneaked after them. Suddenly x̣ʷəné·x̣ʷəne took them. x̣ʷəné·x̣ʷəne said, "You are my children. You will always remain with me. Do not hide again. When I work anywhere you will stay in the house. Do not run away when I come in." x̣ʷəné·x̣ʷəne stayed there for five years, at the place where he was, far away from people, in the woods near the mountains which were steep everywhere. x̣ʷəné·x̣ʷəne stayed there and after he had worked hard every day and night he went fishing and picked berries. He only gathered fern roots[23] and all things[24] to feed his children for many days and nights, all the time. It was four years, one summer and one winter. Then they were big women. They looked like pretty girls.

Field notebook III, 166–74; typescript, "A Story,": 12–15.

IX

x̣ʷəné·x̣ʷəne Travels with Girls

He remained there five years. Then x̣ʷəné·x̣ʷəne said, "These girls are big enough. Let me take them far way. Let me take them up the river. I'll take them up the river to the mountains. Then we'll pick berries and I'll make them my wives. All the people wish for wives." x̣ʷəné·x̣ʷəne said to the Children of the Gills, "Let us pray go up the river. I'll go on ahead and you stay behind in the canoe. You shall have paddles and I'll pole." x̣ʷəné·x̣ʷəne started punting. They went so[25] far and they came to rapids. They went up the rapids. They almost reached the place where there were no rapids. At the place of the rapids the river had a bend. The canoe only turned to the bank, when they were going up the rapids. x̣ʷəné·x̣ʷəne said to the women, "Push the canoe out from the bank. Try hard. Push your paddles down to the bottom." They went on. They came a second time to rapids. "Push hard, push my children." They came to a place where there were no rapids and the girls said, "There are too many rapids in the river. We are getting tired." They went up and they came a third time to rapids. x̣ʷəné·x̣ʷəne said, "Push hard, children, we are traveling down the river." He pulled strongly again. He said, "Try hard, women." They came to a good water where there were no rapids. Then one of the girls said, whispering, "What did he say to us?" They went on. A fourth time they went up and now they came to the rapids. Then x̣ʷəné·x̣ʷəne said again, "Push hard, women." They went on and they almost came to a place where there were no more rapids. He said again, "Push hard, my ladies." And they came to where there were no more rapids. Then said one of the girls, "What is he saying to us?" "It seems he said to us that we are his wives," the other one said. "Yes, it seems as though he said that." They arrived at another rapid. They whispered, "Let us leave him when we come to the bend of the river, when the canoe lies close to the bank. It is too much. It is not good that he says we are his wives." They started going up again this time. "Oh, look out, we have almost arrived. This is the last rapid. Push hard, my wives. Push hard, Children of the Gills." Then x̣ʷəné·x̣ʷəne said again, "Oh, push hard this time." His heart was breaking and he said again, "Push hard, my wives." Then the youngest one said, "It is bad what he is saying." They went on and came to the bend of the river and their canoe came near the bank. The stern of the canoe touched the shore. Then the youngest one jumped ashore. She said, "What are you doing? Come down quick." She came down and the youngest one took a large rock. She put it aboard.[26] The other one got quite a little rock. She put it aboard and there were two rocks in x̣ʷəné·x̣ʷəne's canoe. First they pushed it off and then they ran inland. They got far away. They were singing. x̣ʷəné·x̣ʷəne went up the river, where there [were] no more women. Then x̣ʷəné·x̣ʷəne said, "The canoe is getting heavy.[27] Push hard my wives." Nobody answered. He went on and he almost came to where there were no more rapids. Then he slipped and almost upset. He tried with all his might to go up when he came to where there were no more rapids. Then x̣ʷəné·x̣ʷəne said to the women, "My wives, we are almost arriving at the place where we are going." Nobody answered. After that he turned around and he saw the two stones which were with him. "Oh, maybe they left me! They ran away. Let me try to shout." He shouted, hallooing five times, "Hou, hou, hou, hou, hou." Nobody answered. He went and came to where there was a level ground. He came ashore. First he tied up his canoe, then he went to the level ground. He was crying. After he had cried he was very sick and his heart was breaking. "Let me die, let me hang myself. First, I walk."[28] He came to a good piece of land and there his heart became good. He walked on and sat down under a little red fir. x̣ʷəné·x̣ʷəne said, "Don't let me hang myself. Let them go, the bad ones. It will be just that way. Sometimes men will leave their wives and if anyone is deserted he will never hang himself among later people."

Field notebook IV, 185–94; typescript, "A Story," 15–17.

X

The Girls Kidnap malé's Grandchild

The girls finished singing. Then they talked while they were walking. Then one said, "Let us stop." They stood still and they went to a level piece of land. Here they sat down. Then the elder female said, "Let us make a plan. If we are walking too much at random we do not know which way we are going." "Which way in the world shall we go?" said the youngest one. "We cannot go anywhere. We only could return to the Country of the Spring Salmon where all the spring salmon live. Let us start and go there," said the elder one. "That is the right way. Now let us start for the land of all the salmon."[29] Now they walked with all their might fast, night and day. On the fifth day in the afternoon they came to a river. They rested a little. Then they drank a little water and sat a little.

At that time there was no moon. It was just always night and day.[30] After they had rested they started again. They walked along for a short time. Then they came to a meadow. They heard singing. The name of the place to which they came was ɬakʷítu.[31] This is the meadow of the Chehalis where the Chehalis assembled in summer. malé[32] was camping under many juniper bushes. There were many juniper bushes all around the edge of the meadow. It was juniper berry season. Her daughter was picking berries. She had a daughter by immaculate conception from the bursting of red hot stones in front of her body. From these her child was born. This baby was Moon.[33] The child was a Chief because malé and her daughter and her grandson were the real Chiefs of the world. He was going to rule the world. These were Chehalis. When the daughter of malé was out gathering berries she left her child with his grandmother.[34] She made a cradle for her child. She went a long ways. Then she went back again. malé was singing a cradle song when she left her. First she arranged the cradle. The string of the cradle of the child was very long. Then she pulled the string of the cradle of her grandchild. Then this mother went picking berries. malé was singing a cradle song to her grandson. She sang every day.

> Sleep my master
> Oh my master sleep
> Sleep oh my master
> Aiya, aiya, aiya, aiya, aiya

malé was blind. She just had supernatural power. She knew how to send her power. Then the daughters of x̣ʷəné·x̣ʷəne came. They were running away, down below to the other side to the other world because they did not want x̣ʷəné·x̣ʷəne. When they passed the child the younger one said, "The old woman Chief in her song says, 'Chief,' and the old woman is blind. She is far away. When we pass the cradle, we might pull it out of the cradle. Let us take it out of the cradle. We will replace it with rotten wood." Then the younger one took the baby. She took it out and the elder one replaced it with rotten wood. The elder one said, "Let us run as fast as we can. When we get far away then we'll plan what we will do with this pretty baby. He is a Chief's child. He will be Chief." They were always running. They stopped at a river. First they drank. Then the elder one said, "What shall we do with this baby?" Then the younger one said, "Let us make this child our baby." Then the elder one said, "No, let us make him our husband. We are going to make him our husband when he grows up." After this they started again. They ran as fast as they could because they knew the mother of the child was coming.

When they got the child malé knew it. When she found out that her grandchild was stolen she knew that they had replaced her grandson with[35] a short piece of decayed wood. Then she changed her song.

> Rotten wood, rotten wood
> Is my little grandchild,
> Rotten wood is my little grandchild
> Rotten wood

Her daughter heard it. "It is bad what my mother is saying. She says her grandchild is rotten wood." After she had stopped she said, "Maybe her grandchild has been stolen." Then she ran to her house. She came to her house. She saw that her child[36] was not there. She said to malé, "Do you know who stole[37] your grandchild?" She said, "I cannot see, but I heard whispering that sounded like girls." She said, "Oh, my mother, your grandchild has been stolen. I shall pursue them." The daughter of malé was pretty. She was a large, tall woman. She could run fast. The daughter of malé said, "I am a fast runner. I can run fast. My breath is long. These bad girls just passed us too far. Maybe the girls are a[38] different kind. I am going to run. Now I leave you."

Field notebook IV, 204–14; typescript, "A Story," 17–20. This section is titled ". . ? . . . Male's child" in the original table of contents.

XI

malé's Pursuit

Now she ran, ran as fast as possible. She went that way. It was now night. Now she could not see anything like people. She was on a steep mountain. She always saw the tracks of both girls. She said, "I cannot catch up with them. I started too far behind them. These girls who stole my child are also strong. First I must run to my mother." She ran and came to her house at night. She came to her mother. She cried and said to her mother, "I could not overtake those who stole your grandchild. I think we ought to send somebody to go get your grandchild." Then malé answered, "Oh, my daughter, we cannot wait, it would take too long. Let us chase them. Let me go along." malé talked to her about her supernatural[39] power. "I have gained power when I was a child. I was a strong woman. I have power and I know how to use charms. When I got my supernatural power I was able to wrinkle up the country. You must take me along." Then they started. malé walked on the ground. When she used her supernatural power while they were running malé sang

> Wrinkle up ground, Wrinkle up ground,
> Wrinkle up so that I may catch up with my grandchild
> Wrinkle up, wrinkle up, wrinkle up ground

They went. It was day. Then indeed the ground wrinkled up. They heard singing. The daughter of malé tried harder. They came near the Girls of xʷəné·xʷəne. They saw them. Then they almost got from them their child. She was always carrying her mother. Then she let go of her mother in order to get her child from the girls. Then she dropped malé. Then the world stretched out again and the girls left her far behind. Again she took up her mother and they ran again.

> Wrinkle up ground, wrinkle up ground,
> Wrinkle up ground,
> Wrinkle up that I may catch up with my grandchild

They ran as fast as possible. Again the ground wrinkled up. They were running all the time. Now they saw the girls nearby. They were quite near them.

She let down quickly her mother in order to get her child. When she put
down malé the land stretched out and she was left behind by the bad girls.
Then she took up her mother again. Again they went in pursuit. They ran as
fast as possible and malé said

> Wrinkle up ground, wrinkle up ground,
> Wrinkle up ground, wrinkle up

They came to a mountain. They saw them nearby and they almost caught
up with them. Then she let down her mother to get the bad ones who had
stolen her child. Almost she got it from them, but again the land stretched
out. She lost for the land again stretched out. Again she took up her mother
and malé said

> Wrinkle up ground, wrinkle up ground,
> Wrinkle up ground, wrinkle up

They ran as fast as possible and they almost overtook them. She let down her
mother and the ground stretched out. She lost them. Again she took up her
mother, then the fifth time malé said, "Do not let me down so that we may
get them." Again malé sang her supernatural song

> Wrinkle up ground, wrinkle up ground,
> Wrinkle up ground, wrinkle up

Then they ran as fast as possible. Now they heard them nearby. They saw that
they were near to them and they got there where the ground was buzzing.
Pou.[40] The sky went up and rejoined the earth. There was a little opening so
that a person could almost go through where it rejoined the earth.[41] She tried
to get the child. Then she was going to get in but she failed to get hold of it.
When she failed to get hold of it the Children of Spring Salmon[42] jumped
and went through where it opens and rejoins this world (the horizon). They
lost out and there was no way to get to the other side because it was a different country. malé said to her daughter, "Now we have lost. If I had been
able to get hold of her we should have her. If my supernatural power and my

power of sending out had been used we would have obtained her right in the beginning. They were too far gone when we started. We started too far be-hind them, else you would have got your daughter.[43] I might have used my power and we should have got her. We are too far behind. Now I give it up." Her daughter said after her mother had talked, "Let us start for our house." Again she carried her mother on her back and they both went home, she and her mother. They were weeping. They were saying while they were traveling what malé said, "Oh, my master, you were stolen from us, my master." They cried while they were walking. They had walked that far and arrived at their house.

Field notebook IV, 214–23; typescript, "A Story," 20–23. This section is titled "Pursuit of Male" in original table of contents.

XII

The Animals Try to Pass through the Opening and Rejoining of the World

First they rested. Then she said to her mother, "Is there any way of getting your grandchild? I will go to other people. I will try to assemble strong young men. We will send for the strongest of all young people." malé said, "No. First call the Chiefs. First we will make a plan, and at that time we will pick out the one who will be the first to go to the other side of our world, the one who will be the strongest. Then he passes through the opening at the rejoin-ing of the world." The daughter of malé replied, "I will leave and now I am going to get the people." She came to all the animals. She told them that her child had been stolen. "I want you to come to the place where I live. There we are picking out the one who will go to the buzzing of the world." As soon as she finished talking, all the people ran from everywhere. They said, "The Child of the Chief has been stolen." Said the Child of Bear and all the other big animals, "Gracious! Maybe x̌ʷəné·x̌ʷəne did this." Mountain Lion said, "x̌ʷəné·x̌ʷəne's hip is wearing out.[44] Let us be quick and go to the house of malé." All the Chiefs and every one of the people were running. Those who were the oldest ones and all the youngest ones, they ran and came to the place of malé. There must have been over a thousand, all the animals. When they arrived the people said, "Let us first make an assembly." One said, "Make haste, send all the strongest young ones all over the world, as large as the world is so that all the people may come." The messengers had been out for a short time, then the people came over the land, and others came across the rivers. Others arrived in any way. Some were flying from above. The people arrived from all over the world, as big as the world is. First the Chiefs gave them to eat. When they had finished, one said, "Let us first have performance of supernatural[45] power."

Then they did so. Then they talked about the supernatural power. Beaver said, "I am a hero. I have power." They started to sing. Then other animals sang together. Then they danced and all the other people, every one old and young, showed their supernatural power, from day until night. They showed their supernatural power, every one. They did so until the morning. After they had finished showing their supernatural power, they picked out the one who was first to go through. One of them said, "The one who has power shall start first. The one who has a supernatural helper shall go first." Beaver said, "I will be the first. I have real supernatural power." Then malé said, "You will go to the other side of the place where it opens and rejoins. I will pay him with a blue blanket." When malé finished talking all the people started quickly. They went off. Then Hou, hou[46] and there [were] many people.[47] Beaver went first. He went and came to the buzzing of the world. They all stopped on level ground, not far from the horizon of the world. When they had all arrived, one of the young men said, "Now do not let us wait, go ahead. Beaver first." Then Beaver went and just came to where the horizon opened and closed. He was blown back. He was almost knocked unconscious. He turned back. "There is no way for anyone to pass through. This is difficult." After he had said so, others said, those who were the greatest heroes, those were Bear and Lynx and Wolf, said, "Oh, our elder brothers, let Mountain Lion go first."[48] He started. Mountain Lion went. He came to the horizon of the world. He just looked. He said, "How can I go through? If I should jump, it would get me before I can pass through. If it should get me the ground would crush me. Let me go back." Then it was said, "You runner, you are a hero, you Wolf." Wolf ran. He said, "I know how to go after it. I will run from a distance and I will stop on the other side." He went and he stopped. "It is hard. I might die. Let me go back." He said, "No," and finished talking.

Chicken Hawk said, "Let me try." Chicken Hawk flew near to the hole. He also blew back and almost lost his senses. He turned back and when he came to the other place he said, "Oh! There is a strong wind." Then Snake jumped up quickly and squeezed through a small hole. "I can go through anything." He started and did not stop. He came to the horizon. It splashed soil and sand and he was knocked out of his senses. He was caught. He was picked up and many took him far away. All those helped Snake, who was wounded. Then Bear said, "Now I will try." Bear started and he just came near and then he gave up. "This is hard." Bear turned back. "This is hard. It is altogether hopeless. Lynx, now you go." Lynx went fast. He just came near the horizon. Then he said, "There is no way to get through it. It is deadly. Let me go back, I do not want to die." They changed about with the young men. They just came near the horizon. Then they went back. Now it was night. Then one said, "Let us first take a rest." Then they ate. After they had eaten they said, "Let us first have tamanous ceremony." First the shamans talked about their powers. Then they started singing again. They performed the tamanous ceremonies until midnight. Then they rested. "Now let us eat." Before eating the people fed them first with some of their food. Then they prepared their tamanous ceremonies again for a short time. They finished singing. Then they ate again. They finished eating. First they went around, counterclockwise. Five times they went around where their food was spread. When they had finished the shamans first talked about their tamanous power. After they had talked about their tamanous power they performed the tamanous ceremony. They danced. Some of the young men of the heroes shouted. It was almost day when they stopped. "Now we will stop." They all wished very much for the blue blanket. They thought, "I might get a blue blanket." They started. A little Chief who had a great heart, Crane, said, "Let me start first." He shouted, "Xwas, xwas, xwas, xwas." He came to the horizon and gave it up. "This is difficult. Let me go back," he said. "This is difficult." After he had talked Bee said, "I might go through." Bee started and went to the horizon. He said, "No, if I should try I should be crushed by the ground. Do not let me go." He went back. He said to all the people, "Oh, my people, this is difficult. There is no way for anyone to go through to the other side." Again one went. He came and it was a strange person from far away people. Another person went. He came to the horizon. They were changing about. It was night. Then the Chief said, "Let us eat." After they had eaten they talked about tamanous power. People from far away finished. They performed their tamanous ceremonies until midnight. Then they ate. After they had eaten they talked about their tamanous power. These were still the people from far away. They performed their tamanous ceremony and when day came they finished. They started. They came to the horizon in the morning. Now a person from really far away went first. He started. They talked a different language. They changed about, going to the horizon. It was night and the Chief said again, "Let us eat." After they had eaten they talked about their tamanous power. They performed their tamanous ceremonies until it was midnight. Then they took a rest. They ate and after they had eaten a very different person from the edge of the world performed his tamanous ceremony until day came. They finished, and then in the morning they went to the horizon. Some of the people said that those under the world started. "Let us quickly go." They started for the horizon. Then he came up and turned back. He said, "No one can go through the horizon." After he had finished talking, Bluejay was wondering, "How can I do it to this horizon when the people go back and forth from the horizon?" He went and got a stick. He thought he would place the stick in the horizon. The people went one by one from all parts of the earth. It was night and they ate again and after they had eaten they performed the tamanous ceremony. It was midnight and they ate again. After they had eaten, when it was almost day, the people said, "We will give up. Who will start?" "I will start first," said Bluejay. For five days the people from all over the world had tried. "Let me try. Bluejay belongs here. He is a Chehalis." Bluejay went. The other people laughed at him. Bluejay went. First he looked at the horizon. "I will place upright my stick before it comes down again." He put up his stick. It was long enough for one to go through. After he had put it up, Bluejay flew from outside as fast as possible. "Káčə, káčə, káčə, káčə, káčə."[49] Bluejay disappeared. He went through. Not very long after he had gone through, the horizon came down again and joined the ground. Then Bluejay took off the stick. Bluejay laid it down. He flew "Káčə, káčə, káčə, káčə, káčə."

Field notebooks IV, V, 224–34, 245–54; typescript, "A Story," 23–28. Titled "Animals try to . . ." in the original table of contents.

XIII

Bluejay Meets Moon

Bluejay went not very far and came to level ground. He found one person. This country had a red sky, and red, black, and white clouds, just like storm clouds in this country. The Country of the Salmon was altogether different. He asked the person, "Do you know the Chief here?" He replied, "The Chief is near, not very far from here. He has two wives and many children. He is always working at his house. He came from a place far away." Bluejay said, "Thanks, that is what I wanted to know." He thanked him, "Káčə, káčə, káčə, káčə, káčə." Again he flew along. Far away he heard a ringing sound, a nice sound. He went and flew above this ringing sound and alighted above a tree. He thanked him. He knew this was the Chief. "Káčə, káčə, káčə, káčə, káčə." He flew from a distance far away. Then he wondered. After he had wondered he said, "Let me go near him." Again he flew. He stood near the little work that he was doing. Bluejay thanked again, "Káčə, káčə, káčə, káčə, káčə." Then Moon said, "What is Bluejay saying? Why did he come here?" He took ashes and threw them. Bluejay was hit in the eyes. Bluejay fell off. It hit his eyes and he could not open his eyes again. Bluejay said, "What are you doing to me, my master?[50] I was sent to get you by her who was your mother and by your grandmother." "What does Bluejay say? He said, 'My mother.'" He went up to Bluejay, washed his face, and after he had washed it, he tapped the back of his head with his hands and the ashes came out of his eyes. Now Bluejay could see again. "What happened to my mother? What did you say?" Bluejay replied, "The people are tired because they were looking for you. Nobody could go through the horizon, but I passed through. Your mother and your grandmother said to me, you should go home." Moon replied, "I have many children. I have two wives. First I will make toys for them." After he had finished making toys he divided his toys that he got ready. When he was ready he said to his children, "Do not cry. After I have traveled far to the other world, I will come back. You will be looked after by your mother." After he had done so Bluejay said, "Now let us go." They started. They went quickly and it was not very long when Bluejay and Moon arrived together at the horizon. Moon said, "Let me put in the stick." He put it up. Moon said to Bluejay, "Now fly to the other side as fast as possible." Bluejay started, "Káčə, káčə,

káčə, káčə, káčə." He passed through to the other side and Moon ran after him. He got through. Then Moon took out the stick and the horizon closed up. First they went to level land and camped. Moon said, "Let us camp here, even if it is not night. We will cook our food." Moon made a fire under a little tree. Now it was night and when they had eaten they went to sleep. Early in the morning they arose. First he made a fire. After he had made a fire they cooked their food. When the food was done, they ate. After they had eaten Moon said, "Now let us start."

Field notebook V, 255–261; typescript, "A Story," 28–30.

XIV

Moon and Man Who Hammers with Head

They went. They traveled slowly. They had not gone far when they heard some noise. They passed it. Moon said, "What was it we passed?" Bluejay said, "What is it? It is a person." Moon replied, "Let us turn back and see what he is doing." They got there. He always put up sharp pointed sticks and hammered them with his head. The person was thus: he was slim but he had a big head. He was asked by Moon, "What are you doing, boy?" He answered him, "I am working and splitting this wood to make a house." "Go ahead split it. How do you hammer?" "I hammer with my head." Then he hammered with his head, tə́p, tə́p, tə́p, tə́p, tə́p. The wood did not split. Then Moon said, "This is quite impossible. This is not the way to split wood. Stop. I will make wedges for you and a maul." Moon made wedges and a hammer. He put these wedges into the wood and hammered them with the maul. Then the wood split. Then Moon and Bluejay sat down. High up on a big fallen log they looked on for a while and the boy split up many planks. The boy said, "This, your tool, is good." Moon replied, "I just made it. The wedges and maul are yours. Only in this way the people will work. You will not again use your head. Now I will leave you."

Field notebook V, 269–71; typescript, "A Story," 30–31.

XV

Raven Uses People as Fish Trap

He and Bluejay went on. They had not gone far when they came to Raven. Many people were standing in the water holding one another from this side out, long, clear across. Then Moon said to those people and to the other men, "What are these people doing?" "This is my fishing trap. I am catching fish." "Do you catch food?" "Sometimes," said the Raven. Moon went to the water. Some of the people were grunting. Others were grinding their teeth. Others were shivering. Moon said to the people. "What are you doing in the creek?" "We are working for Raven. We are fishing." Moon said, "Do you always do that?" "Always, even if it is very cold. We are afraid of Raven. He is mean." Moon replied, "Go ashore." The people went to shore. "That is not the way a fish trap is made. The people shall not do that way. Let me make a fish trap for you." He cut many little sticks. He finished making the fish trap. "The people are to make fish traps like this. They shall never make fish traps of people. They shall never use them badly in later times." Moon started. Raven said, "You are bad. You work for other people. You had better leave today." Moon said, "You will not be a person. You will be a bird. You will fly about in the houses. You shall gather all bad scraps of food of the people," said Moon. "Now fly." Then the Raven flew. Moon said, "You will say, 'Sqwaq, sqwaq, sqwaq, sqwaq.'" Then Raven answered, "Sqwaq, sqwaq, sqwaq, sqwaq, sqwaq." Then he flew away. When he had finished Moon and Bluejay started.

Field notebook V, 271–75; typescript, "A Story," 31–32.

XVI

Moon and Deer

They went, they say, and they heard singing. There was a noise and behold a deer was whittling. "Oh, I will stab him. With this I will stab the Chief. I will stab him after a while when the Chief comes." Bluejay and Moon went. They came to the man who was singing. "What are you saying?" said Moon. "I am saying nothing, I am just singing." "Bad one, don't lie," said Moon, "You said, 'I will stab the Chief with this sharp pointed stick.'" Moon said, "Bring your sticks." That fellow, Deer, took them up and gave them to Moon. Moon said, "Stretch out your arm." He took the arm of Deer and jabbed the stick into the arm and then he jabbed in one more. "Now run." Deer ran. He did not run far away and was told, "Now turn around." Deer turned around. "Now run again." Now Deer jumped. Moon said, "You have been bad. You were too mean. It is a disgrace. You said to me, you would stab me with your sticks. Now you will be good food for the people later on. When the people find you, you will first be frightened. You will run but you will not go far. Then you will turn around. Then you will run. Forever you will be the food of the people." Moon and Bluejay started again.

Field notebook V, 275–77; typescript, "A Story," 32. This is titled "Moon . . ? . . Deer" in the original table of contents.

XVII

Bluejay Goes to malé

It came to be night. Moon said, "Let us camp near this creek." They cooked their food and then it was done. Then they ate and after they had eaten they slept under the branches of a small tree. First he made a fire, a large fire. Now they were asleep. When the next day came, Moon said, "Let us first eat much. Then we will start." They cooked and ate. When the food was done they ate much. They got enough, he and Bluejay. They were sitting down. Moon said, "Let us make a plan. How shall we do? After a long time I will go to my mother because first I want you to set right the country. You had better fly right along. I will follow behind. I will go for many days." Then Bluejay flew to malé. He came to the two malés. There were many people. Bluejay arrived. "I have returned. I came ahead for Moon is going to straighten out the world. He said I should return first." Then Bluejay finished talking. They thanked Bluejay because he brought back the Chief. He was given a blue blanket. Bluejay took the blanket. He put it on. He stepped far away. The people shouted. Everyone sang. Then the people finished singing.

Field notebook V, 277–80; typescript, "A Story," 32–33. Titled "Moon . . ? . . Bluejay goes to Male" in the original table of contents.

XVIII

Sun out of Diaper

When they had run away with Moon, the Mother of Moon rinsed the diaper in water and drank the water. It was not many days when the daughter of malé had a child. It was a boy, Sun. Moon had a younger brother. The people were eating. They finished eating. In the afternoon they performed the tamanous dances. The people finished their tamanous dances, then they were dismissed and they went home to their part of the world. Bluejay went along.

Field notebook V, 280–81; typescript, "A Story," 34.

XIX

Moon and Beaver

He went along. When Bluejay left he heard someone talking, "I hear the Chief coming. I will kill him." It was known by Moon what Beaver was saying. He came to Beaver. "What did you say? Did you say you would kill me?" said Moon. "Go on, say it again the way you said it." "No," answered Beaver, "I did not say anything, I was just talking." "The bad one," said Moon. "Turn around." Beaver turned around. Beaver was taken and his paddle was stuck into him in his hind part. He said, "Go on. Swim. Strike the water a little with your tail." Beaver struck it with his tail making a noise on the water all around, "Tepou, tepou, tepou, tepou, tepou." "Hereafter you shall be in the water. You will fell trees near the bank. You will eat wood and mud. You will be the food of the Indians in later times."

Field notebook V, 281–83; typescript, "A Story," 34.

XX

Moon and Bears

He was left by Moon. He had not gone far when he found a monster. Behold! There were Bears. The Bears were bad ones. Moon said, "You are not right. You often frighten other people. Go that way. Stand up. Dance. Go ahead, run.

You shall be the food of later people. If you hear the noise of people coming you shall first stand up and listen, then you shall run away. You shall be killed and you shall be food." He finished and Moon started.

Field notebook V, 283–84; typescript, "A Story," 34–35. Boas does not provide a subtitle for this story.

XXI

Moon and Man with Headband

He walked on that far, then he heard a noise from far away. First Moon stood still and listened. He went toward it and came to an old man who was working. He was a good-looking person. Behold! He was very old. He had many tools. He was chopping wood. Moon looked on. Moon said, "Grandfather, this work is really good. Your clothing is good. I should like very much to have your headband.[51] What are you making?" Then Moon also said, "Your tool[52] is very curious. It is big. It is long. How does it chew after it chips?" The old man replied, "My Grandson, I am always making canoes, every day since I was young. I am getting old. I have many wives in my house. I feed my tools with the chips so that they become strong." Moon said, "Oh, Grandfather, I wish for your headband and your partner. Let us trade. I give you my headband for yours. Let us trade our tools." "All right my Grandson." They traded. They finished. The old man said again, "Oh, Grandson, you must always feed your tools chips and meat.[53] Then you will get along well. Then it will always search for work. Now I finish teaching you." Moon said, "Grandfather, I leave you. Goodbye. Thank you for your headband."

Moon started. Then Moon went. It was not yet night when he looked for a place to camp. Before night he looked for a girl who should prepare food for him and he found one who was going to help him. He said to her, "Cook a great deal. First I work." He went and he tried his tool. He took an ax and found a tree. Every time a chip dropped down it was eaten by his tool. He chopped the tree until it was night. Then he went home to his camp. He arrived at his camp. The woman had cooked. The girl said to him, "It's been a long time since I finished cooking." Moon said, "Let us eat." And they ate.

After they had finished eating they slept. After they slept it was day. First they ate. After they had finished eating, he said, "I am Moon. I am always traveling. I am setting right the world. I leave you. Sometimes a woman will make love. If he is a good youth, he will steal away with a good girl. Thus it shall be." Moon started. Moon said, "Goodbye, I leave you." Moon forgot to feed his tool. He walked on a warm day and his tool became hungry. Whatever he did it bit everything. It bit himself. The headband was not good to him because he did not do as the old man had told him. He did not feed his tool with chips before he had started. Moon ran as fast as possible. The headband bit him. It almost cut his head. His eyes were rolling. He came to a creek and found a Toad. "Grandmother, I am dying, can you help me?" "Yes, I can do it easily. Take off your headband."[54] She took grease and rubbed it all over his head. His headband came off. She straightened the eyes of Moon for they were almost popping. His eyes were almost popping out. She straightened his eyes and his nose. After she had finished rubbing him with oil, his face and his mouth and his head, she finished rubbing all over his body. She said, after she had rubbed Moon, "Oh, Grandson, go back and trade back. It is bad, the headband and the tools of the old man make you very poor." Moon had been straightened out. Again Moon said, "Oh, Grandmother, I will return them." Then he said, "Goodbye, I am going." Moon walked as fast as he could. Then the tools of the old man became excited and bit his legs. He came to the old man. Then Moon said, "Oh, Grandfather, here you are still working." The old man replied, "I am still here, Grandson." Then Moon spoke again, "Oh, Grandfather, your headband and your partner almost killed me. I have come to trade back." The old man replied, "Oh, Grandson, that is what I thought. I told you [that] you should always feed my tools,[55] then it would be well. You ought to feed them with chips but you did not do so, therefore it punished you. Let us trade back." They finished trading back and Moon said, "Thank you, Grandfather. I have troubled you. Now I leave you again."

Then Moon started off. He went so far. He camped. First he cooked. When the food was done he ate. He talked before he was going to sleep. "I was badly treated by the old man. I have broken my own rules. Let me take this off from the world. A man shall have his tools but they shall not eat chips. Only sometimes when people meet they may trade their hats[56] and caps. They shall never bite the head or make his eyes pop out or shall put the heads out of shape. Chiefs will just trade headbands. They shall never kill him. Thus it shall be among people of the world later on." He slept.

Field notebook V, 284–94; typescript, "A Story," 35–38.

XXII

Moon and Tapeworm

He got up in the morning. First he made a fire. After he made a fire he went for water from a spring dripping down. He cooked. After eating he started out. He walked. It was not long before he came to a big river. Moon stood there. He looked across and saw something like a person moving about far inland. "How can I get across? Let me shout." Then he shouted "Eh, eh, eh, eh, eh"[57] five times. It was not long when a boy came with a big stomach. He was also short, round, and fat. His face was very ugly. Moon said, "Boy, I want to go across." Tapeworm answered. This boy was one of the Tapeworms. Tapeworm answered, "Oh, boy, I want to go across." "Have you a canoe, boy?" Moon said. Tapeworm answered, "I want to get across. Have you a canoe?" And Moon said again, "I want to go across. Have you got a canoe?" Answered Tapeworm, "Oh, I want to get across. Have you got a canoe?" Moon said, "Bad one makes me angry." Tapeworm answered, "The bad one makes me angry." Moon said, "You will find out, bad one," and Tapeworm answered, "You will find out, bad one. I'll kill you." Moon got angry. He made a stone arrowhead. Two sharp stones for his arrowheads. He found out that these Children of Tapeworm were monsters in this world who defeated everyone. "I know how to kill him." He tied a sharp-edged arrowhead under his breech clout.[58] He tied the arrowhead on as firmly as he could. He fixed his knife. Then he swam. He swam a little. He landed. He jumped out as quickly as he could. He said to the boy, "I am Moon. I have killed everything. Oh, this big stomach!" Tapeworm answered, "Oh, this big stomach!" Then Moon said, "Oh, this one who is short all over!" Then Tapeworm answered, "Oh, this one who is short all over!" "Where is your house? Oh, you son of a bitch," said Moon. After he had said so he punched him. He fell down. He kicked him. Tapeworm shouted, "Come out, come out my folks."[59] Moon looked inland but no one came. Then he struck him with his knife on his chest. "Come out my folks." Then something came out from behind the hips. They came out of his mouth. Behold! He was coughing the worms out of the inside. Behold! These were his folks. Long ones like snakes came, a great many. He struck one and it broke in two. Others came and they wrapped themselves around his legs. He struck them as hard as he could. He cut them in two with his sharp-edged arrowheads on his legs with his knife. They fell down. Then he struck another one and still others came to wind themselves around. Then they were cut in two. He fought with them so long until they were all gone — all the little monsters were gone. He stabbed them with his knife. He cut off the neck of the boy and he died. He made a fire and he piled them on the fire and burned them up. Moon said, "On this day I have killed the tapeworms. There shall be no tapeworms in this world who will kill people. Only sometimes it shall happen that the insides of a person have a tapeworm and anyone who has a tapeworm may be cranky, but not every person. They shall not be monsters."

Field notebook VI, 303–10; typescript, "A Story," 38–40.

XXIII

The Daughters of Fire

There was a Fire. Fire had five daughters. They stayed in their house near the mountains. It was always burning, burning in their house, but they were Chiefs. It was just forbidden that they should sing for young unmarried men and for other people. The Children of Fire were pretty women. There was one, the youngest one, of them who was always singing. Once in a while they would all sing. Nobody is now like the Daughters of Fire. They were pretty women. Once in the morning one of the five girls, the youngest one, was singing

> Fire, fire put out your tongues
> Blaze flames, flames

Then a handsome person came along the road. The girl saw him and she continued to sing. The young man reached her and the young man said, "I heard you singing well. I am a Chief. Maybe you heard of Moon? I have been walking a long ways. I am very tired. Go ahead. Sing the same song." This girl said, "No, I cannot sing for you. That is forbidden to sing to anyone. I am a Fire girl. It would be the end of this world if I should sing for you." Moon said, "Although it is thus, I heard your tune from far away. You better sing again." The girl said, "We are five girls. Now we will sing for you." Then she was singing

> Fire, fire put out your tongues
> Blaze flames, flames.

All the five girls came to help her sing, the other Fire girls. They sang and the Chief listened. Then Fire blazed up all over and everything was burning. Moon said, "I think the whole world is on fire," and Moon went away. Fire came near him and he came to Rock. Moon said to Rock, "Elder brother, can you help me? Fire is coming." Rock said, "Oh, my younger brother, no I cannot help you. When Fire comes to me I crack and burst." Then Moon ran harder. He arrived at Lake and he asked, "Can you help me? Fire is coming. Maybe I'll get burned." Then Moon ran again. He was running and reached Wind, "Can you help me? The world is on fire." Wind said, "No, I cannot help you. When I blow Fire burns still stronger." He ran to the Creeks. "Maybe you can help me?" Moon ran again. He came to the Creeks and he said to Creek, "I am dying." Creek said, "Surely you got the Fire girls. Surely you are going to die. There is no way for me to help you. When Fire comes this world will get hot. I'll boil and you would be cooked. Surely you will die. Run, run as fast as you can." He ran along. Moon said, "I am a Chief. I always destroy everything in this world. I have defeated everything. Now today I am going to die. I will be burned and I'll die." He tried to run hard. He went along and Fire came near him. Everywhere Fire surrounded him. Only a small piece of land was not burning. He ran to it and came to a small Trail and said, "Now I am going to die. Maybe I will be burned. You, my Grandfather, could you help me?" Trail looked at Fire. Fire was blazing. Everything was crackling. The trees fell. The creeks and the lakes were boiling. Trail said, "Behold! Indeed Fire has almost caught you, but I am the only one who is never burned by Fire around me. It passes above me. Come on, my Son, lie on my back," the little Trail said. "Although you will get hot do not move. Lie down with your eyes and your mouth close to the ground." Then he just lay down on Trail and Fire reached him. It was blazing everywhere. Moon perspired. He had not been lying for a long time when Fire passed him. He almost died. Then Fire went. Moon stood up. He said, "After all I shall not die for five days. I'll stay here. I'll bathe first then I'll start off." He stayed for five days and Moon bathed. After he had bathed for a while he dressed up. He said, "At this time I might have died just because the Fire girls sang for me. It shall be different for the future people. From this time girls will sing and the water will not burn. Girls will only sing for a Chief, but their bodies will never burn up."

Field notebook I, 57–62, 72–76; typescript, "A Story," 41–43. See Appendix 5 for Kinkade's "'Daughter of Fire': Narrative Verse Analysis of an Upper Chehalis Folktale."

XXIV

Moon and Vagina Dentata

He went along. Then he came to a house. He arrived. A woman came out. She was laughing. "Where are you going young man?" Moon answered, "I am walking a long ways through this world. I am going home." "First stay here and eat with me." Moon answered, "Never mind. Well, I may rest here." This was a big woman. She was also tall. Behold! She was one of the daughters of k'ʷə́cx̣ʷe. Moon went in. k'ʷə́cx̣ʷe cooked. When k'ʷə́cx̣ʷe was cooking she first played with him. They were laughing and Moon became happy. The woman had a pretty face. Her hair was very curly. k'ʷə́cx̣ʷe said, "First I will get water." k'ʷə́cx̣ʷe went away. Moon said . . .

The translation stops here. The second version of this story contains a full translation. See pages 105–6.

Field notebook VI, 311–17, 313–17 not translated; typescript, "A Story," 44.

XXV

Moon Teaches Making Fire and Cooking

He went not far. He could hear her singing. First Moon stood still. He listened. He started to where he heard the noise. Then he arrived. Behold!

There were many Prairie Chickens. He arrived there. The people were singing. There were many people singing on a level land. They were always dancing on their meat until they perspired. Then the meat became hot. When the
meat had been hot for a long time it became soft. They said, "Now it is done."
At that time they ate the meat. Moon looked on the prairie people on the
level land. Moon went up to them. To one of the Prairie Chickens he asked,
"What are you doing?" "Oh, I am cooking our food." Moon said, "Tell your
people to be quiet. I am Moon. I am straightening out the world. This is not
the way to cook food. I will make a fire drill for you." Moon made a fire drill.
He finished it. He gave many to the people. "With this you will make fire."
Moon gathered sticks and made a fire. The sticks caught fire. Then he went
and made a wooden bucket.[60] He heated stones and he poured water into the
bucket and took more red, hot stones and threw them into the bucket. Then
he put the meat in. He took more stones and the meat was being cooked. It
was boiling for a long time and the meat was done. Moon called some of the
people. "This is the way you shall always do and all the people shall use the
fire drill to make fire with." Moon finished talking. Then the Chief of the Prairie Chickens said, "You better eat with us first." Moon went to eat with them.
Before they ate the people sang again. They danced, just as many as were
there. Moon danced with them. After they finished eating the people sang,
"Behold! It will be the custom for the other people always to sing." Moon finished. Then Moon said, "It will be the custom for the people in later times
always to prepare food with fire."

Field notebook VI, 318–21; typescript, "A Story," 44–45.

XXVI

Moon, xʷəné·xʷəne, and Tree Monster

Again he started. He went not far and he camped. He made a fire first. He
went down to the creek and bathed. After he had bathed he went to his fire.
He stirred the fire with a poker. After he had finished preparing food it was
done. He ate and after he had eaten he slept. He went to sleep under a tree.
The next day in the morning first he fixed the fire. He went again to the place
where he had bathed the day before. He bathed and dived five times. Then

he came out of the water. He put on his clothing and went to the fire again. Again he cooked. His food was done and he ate. Then he started again and went far. He came to a boy who had a house. This boy was rather poor (he had no family). It looked as though he were crying before he came. "Oh," said Moon, "What happened to you, boy? It looks as though you had been deserted." "Oh, my uncle, I will answer your words. I have been alone for many days. My seven brothers went hunting and the first one disappeared. The others went to search for him and they were all gone. I believe my elder brothers were killed." Moon said, "Do you know if there are people here nearby?" The boy replied, "There are people, maybe not very far away." Moon said, "I'll go to them." He reached the people. He asked the people, "Do you know the brothers of the boy? I came to the boy who is all alone." He said to them, "His elder brothers had disappeared." One of the people said, "I think they were killed by the monster. There is a monster. He is called Skylark. Nobody can see that Skylark because he is fierce." One said, "Oh, younger brother, many people have disappeared in this land. They have just disappeared, therefore I search for them that I may kill him, but I can never find him." "Oh, my elder brother, I will search for that monster. That Lark did something very bad to the poor boy. I destroy everything in this world." The man replied, "I am the same. I always kill k'ʷə́cxʷe. I am xʷəné·xʷəne." Then Moon left the man. First Moon wondered. He thought, "That is the one who is called xʷəné·xʷəne." Moon came to the boy. He started a fire and after he had made a fire he cooked much. He said to the boy, "All this food is yours. Anything left over by us I leave here." They stayed until night. Then they went to sleep. On the next day in the morning Moon first made a fire. The boy said, "When I slept last night I dreamed that I found my dead people lying in a gulch and found my elder brothers when I dreamed about them. I found a nice trail. Near the trail is a big red fir tree with many limbs above and thick needles. That is where the monster is. The people say it is Lark who always kills the people but it is not that. It is a real monster. It is not a person. This is my dream I had about it last night." Moon said, "Let us go out." They went out. Moon said, "Which way on this world would you look, in what direction in this world do you think is that trail?" The boy said, "I started from there when I was dreaming." "Now this is all," said Moon, "Your dream is true. It was not Lark who killed your elder brothers. It must have been a monster."

They went in and ate quickly. After they had eaten Moon said, "Oh, you boy, your brothers have been killed." This boy was one of the young pheasants. Moon said, "I'll first go find x̌ʷəné·x̌ʷəne. Now I leave you." Moon said, "After a while we will go after that monster with x̌ʷəné·x̌ʷəne." He went. He came to x̌ʷəné·x̌ʷəne and said to x̌ʷəné·x̌ʷəne, "I am coming after you. Let us go after the monster on the mountains." x̌ʷəné·x̌ʷəne said, "Well, let us go." They quickly got ready. Moon said, "Let us first go past the boy." They went. They came to the boy. Moon said to Pheasant, "Now we will leave you. You will always be happy. Don't cry again. Now I leave you." Then they started out. They cut a long pole and Moon and x̌ʷəné·x̌ʷəne walked. They went that far. It was raining in the mountains. It was raining very hard. They went to the trail and found the big tree with thick needles. It looked pretty. Above it were many branches. x̌ʷəné·x̌ʷəne said, "Evidently people camp here. Let us camp. We are getting very wet." "Oh no, I think this is the house of the monster," said Moon. "Go over that way. Go fast on the trail. Make much noise with your feet in the evening. When it is almost dark, come. I shall be on the watch here for the monster. You shall gather much pitch." It was not yet night when at a distance a person appeared coming. Oh, a big man! This was the monster. Indeed, a real monster! "What will he do?" After a while he came to a trail. He looked. There were the tracks of x̌ʷəné·x̌ʷəne. It was night. Then the monster got ready. The monster climbed up the tree. He eats only Indians. He eats the hearts of persons. He does not eat the body of persons, only the heads. He was a real monster. He stayed. Moon walked on the trail looking for x̌ʷəné·x̌ʷəne. He found x̌ʷəné·x̌ʷəne on the trail. x̌ʷəné·x̌ʷəne[61] said, "You shall go make a fire at the foot of the tree. After you have made a fire, sit down at the foot of the red fir tree." He went. After x̌ʷəné·x̌ʷəne had made a fire, he sat down at the foot of the tree. x̌ʷəné·x̌ʷəne said, "What is up there on the tree?" Late in the night x̌ʷəné·x̌ʷəne became quiet. There was a noise from above, "Lo, are you asleep? Lo, are you awake?" x̌ʷəné·x̌ʷəne replied and said, "What are you saying? Come down, bad one, and I will kill you." He did not answer. Moon went to the foot of the tree. He said to x̌ʷəné·x̌ʷəne, "Now we shall fight him and kill the monster. When we fight make a fire, a big fire." Moon went to the foot of the tree and when he came to the foot of the tree he said, "Come down, bad one, you will die this night, bad one." The monster did not reply. Moon said, "He is strong. He is big." He said to x̌ʷəné·x̌ʷəne,

"Let us change about, guarding the monster until day. You will always sing."
x̣ʷəné·x̣ʷəne was singing all the time. It was almost day. Then it creaked
above. Moon ran to the foot of the tree and came to x̣ʷəné·x̣ʷəne who was
half asleep. He shook him and he woke up quickly and Moon said, "Go up the
trail. Now the sound of the monster is coming near." x̣ʷəné·x̣ʷəne ran. Moon
said, "What kind of person are you?" The monster replied from above, "You
just be quiet, I will eat you up." Moon said, "Come down, bad one, I will kill
you tonight." The monster replied, "I will eat you tonight." Moon said, "Come
down, we will fight." Then Moon made a fire all around the red fir. The fire
was burning. The monster yelled, "Bad one, I am coming down and I'll eat
you." Now the monster came down as quick as he could. He jumped into the
fire. He howled, he howled. Moon replied, "I will kill you. You will die today."
Then Moon stabbed him with his long stick. He stabbed him only a few
times. Then he fell into the fire. Then Moon called x̣ʷəné·x̣ʷəne. He said to
x̣ʷəné·x̣ʷəne, "Gather sticks and pile them on the fire." The fir tree was
burned, the flames shot up on the fir tree, and light shot out from the tall fir
tree. It was shining far away on the mountains. Then at last the monster burst
and that was when he died. When he burst the earth shook all over. Then the
tree fell down. Moon and x̣ʷəné·x̣ʷəne stirred the fire and it blazed up and
the white ashes of the dead monster flew up. They were flying about and
looked like birds, not like ashes. He became bats, when the monster was
burned. Now it was day. Moon said when he finished, "There will be no monsters in this world who will eat people. The monster was dead. Its ashes were
transformed into bats. The bats shall not be monsters. They shall only fly back
and forth in the evening, around the houses of the people in future times. The
people shall have houses. They will go hunting and they shall camp under the
trees. Nobody shall eat them. They shall return to their houses. Forever there
shall be no more monsters in the world who will eat people." They were finished. Then Moon started. He said to x̣ʷəné·x̣ʷəne, "You shall go home."
Moon went into a creek and made a fire in the morning.

Field notebook VI, 328–46; typescript, "A Story," 45–50.

XXVII

Moon's Children

When he left his children they cried, every one of his children. Every day she went picking berries, the deserted wife. One day at daybreak all the Children of Moon were crying. One of the deserted wives said, "Let us get ready to go up the river." They went up and every one of them got ready. They were always crying. "Now let us travel through the ocean. We shall go toward land across the ocean. Then we shall land on a river inland." Trout was always crying. He was the prettiest among their children. His mouth became big because he ripped open his mouth crying for his father. The mouth of Sucker became round. The mouth of White Horsefish was round. It was bleeding and his mouth became red. Blood dripped on the side of his chest on account of his crying on account of his father. They always cried. The smallest one was Trout Fry.[62] His mouth became big and they remained that way forever. They started with their mother. Their mother said, "Gather all your toys which your father made for you." The Children of x̣ʷəné·x̣ʷəne went up the river again. On this side of the horizon. When they came to the side the two women said, "Our children are too many. Let us go ashore." The Children of x̣ʷəné·x̣ʷəne said when they were camping near the water of the ocean, "Indeed, we do not know which way Moon went. We have no way of finding him. Let us desert him forever. Only rarely good women shall be deserted, but never shall die on account of crying. They shall take another husband. That will be the way of people of later times."

Field notebook VI, 353–56; typescript, "A Story," 51. The original table of contents refers to this story as "Moon's child . . ? . . ." This section seems to be out of sequence, and it could come after section XIII, "Bluejay Meets Moon," as it does in the version of "Moon" Peter Heck told to Adamson (1934, 162).

XXVIII

Moon Meets His Brother

Moon walked along. In the afternoon he saw something appear near the river. He went for it and he found someone fishing with a hook attached to a pole. The boy had a big stomach. His legs were slender and his arms were slim. He had a good round face. He was very cross-eyed. His nose was crooked and his mouth was crooked. Moon said, "What are you doing?" The boy said, "I am getting food. I am fishing. Did you see what I killed?" Behold! Many kinds of bad bugs were lying nearby. Those the boy had killed. They were lizards, worms, frogs, and all kinds of bad bugs. Moon said, "Do you eat what you killed?" The boy replied, "Yes, that is my food. I always catch this for the small amount of my food." "No," said Moon, "That is not the way to fish. Let me make a fish tackle for you." Moon made a fish hook. He twisted hair and made it somewhat loose. He tied the string to a long pole of hazel wood. He threw a hook on the water and as soon as he had done so he had a bite. It went down and he pulled it. Behold! They had killed a trout. He said to the boy, "With this thing you shall catch fish. This is the kind of real food that is made in different shapes. You should discard what you killed before. It is not a good kind of food. They are only bad, common bugs in the water." He finished. Moon said, "Who are you, boy?" The boy replied, "I am the Sun. It is said they ran away with my elder brother before I became a child. The two malés are my grandmother and my mother." Moon said, "You are my younger brother. Now let us go home." They went from the river inland. They came to a meadow and they came to a house. The boy said, "This is our house." They went in and inside were malé and his mother. Moon said, "I am Moon." malé answered, "Oh, my Chief, you have come back." Moon said, "Yes, I have come back." When he arrived he talked with his mother and grandmother. His mother told about the boy. "He is your younger brother. He is poor. He always stays near the bank of the creek." After the Mother of Moon finished talking Moon said, "Let me set my little younger brother right." He said to his younger brother, "Come." Sun came. He took him by the chest and put his hand into his mouth. All the bad things came out from the inside. He finished and washed his face. He straightened his eyes and his nose and his mouth. He wiped all over his eyes and his head. He finished. Then he wiped all over his body. When he had finished he said to his younger brother, "Run to the river, bathe. First rub your hands with mud from the bank of the river. When you have done so, dive." After Moon had set his brother right he said, "I'll stay for five days. Then I'll go again. I have to set the world right. I have found many monsters in the world. I killed them while I was coming." The two malés replied, "We will first have a feast in our place." Moon said, "It is true what you say." He finished. He prepared all kinds of food for the people. The boy went as messenger to the people. It was not long before they assembled, so many people. They were happy. The people played. In every way that is what they were doing. Many girls came and helped cook. The food was done. Other people prepared the place where they were going to eat. They finished. Then the people ate. They came from all over as big as the world was. Everyone came who had been looking for him. With them were Bluejay, Beaver, Fox, and Coyote. Bluejay talked violently. He talked like a Chief monster. Among them was x̣ʷəné·x̣ʷəne,[63] among the monster people. There were as many as there were animals. The people ate. The people were eating as many as there were. They stretched out a long distance when they were eating so far. They ate and they finished eating. When they had finished Moon talked to the people, "After you have eaten I will thank you, friends. You are displeased,[64] [for] you have just come to eat. Thank you. It shall be made thus for the Indians. They shall feed the Chief when he comes home from far away. It shall be just thus. The Chiefs shall first talk and the children will play. They will be happy during the day. Thus it shall be later on. That will be all. I thank you. First we will make the tamanous tonight."[65] It was night. The people performed the tamanous ceremonial. They made a fire. So far shone the many fires. Then the tamanous talked about their tamanous. They performed the tamanous ceremonial. They began to sing and others answered. They danced. It was midnight. Then they ate. They finished eating and again they performed the tamanous ceremonial. Again it was day. They ate. They always ate three times a day and they performed for five nights. After they had finished only the shamans made a potlatch. After they had performed their tamanous ceremonial in the morning Moon said, "First you eat in the morning." They finished eating. Moon said, "When we dismiss you, when all of you have gone, I will travel again through this world. I am setting the world right. That is all. Thanks for what you have eaten. This is all." The people made a noise. Some got ready and some were going.

It was morning when the assembly was finished. Moon said, "First I'll walk to the mountains, to go hunting." He went. He arrived at the mountain and killed many deer. He dressed them and drew them along to the house of his mother and grandmother—a great many packs. Then he dried the meat for malé, much meat. Every day Moon went hunting. He walked much, and the food of his grandmother and mother became much. He was always walking on account of his younger brother. Often he got tired. Sometimes Moon said to his mother, "I will be absent for many days. I will go far away in the world."

Field notebook VI, VII, 357–61, 373–81; typescript, "A Story," 52–55.

XXIX

Moon Marries Frog

Then Moon started. He walked very far away. He always saw two old people. They had five daughters. The girls were pretty. Moon always ate first. Another man was living in a camp on the bank of the river, far down the river. It was raining hard. Moon got wet although he went inside the house of the old people. It was leaking through the roof of the house. Moon looked at the girls. Moon thought, "I like one of these girls!" Among them was the granddaughter of Toad. The granddaughter of Toad was Frog. Moon finished thinking about this. Then he went out. He went hunting and killed an elk. He carried it to the house and he came to a creek. He waded across and he dropped his pack. Moon wondered. He decided what he would do to his friends and old people. "Let me get married here. These girls are very nice." He fixed up his elk. He finished fixing it. He said to the pack he had been carrying, "If you are carried by a woman who has already known a man do not move. If you are lifted by a girl who has never known a man and who is still good then you move and become light. She who is a strong woman, that one will be my wife." He went ashore in back of the house. He said to the girls, as many as there were and one of them, Frog, the granddaughter of Toad, Moon said, "I left what I killed down by the river. You go and get it." The girls whispered among themselves. One said, "Do not tell Frog about it." Toad said to her granddaughter, "Go ahead and get the meat." The women went and behind them went Frog. They came to the elk. First the eldest one took it. She could not move it on account of its weight. Then the next one took it, she could not move it. Now the youngest one of the five girls arrived. She took the elk. She tried as hard as she could but it would not move. Then they gave it up. It was too heavy. These girls had known men. They laughed. Then they scolded

Frog. They said, "What are you doing, bad one, why do you come along?" The women said, "Go and carry this food, bad one." When the women had finished talking Frog went. She took the meat. She put it on her back and the food moved. She stood up. The other girls laughed. Frog went along and she came to the house and she dropped it. Moon came along. Now the mind of Moon became different. "This is bad what I made for myself. I don't want the granddaughter of the old woman. I want the others badly but they had known men. Never mind, so I will take the granddaughter of this old woman. I shall make her my wife." When Moon finished thinking he said, "First I will break up the meat. I will divide it." He finished. Moon took it to the house of Toad and he put it in. He then had a wife. He went in and it was raining. When the Chief was in the house of Frog it was raining hard. The rain was spattering on the roof on account of the hard rain. A gale was blowing but the roof on the house of the old woman did not leak. She had made the house of her grandchild. She had made it of big leaves of skunk cabbage. They had made the roof of leaves and made it double. They had made the roof round on top. They wrapped the sides with mats. They had made a good door. Then no water could leak through. Inside poles were standing. It was strong. Nobody could shake it, even when there was a gale. The wind could not go through inside. Moon stayed there. The bad weather stopped. When it was bad weather they just lay in bed. Even when it was raining and the wind was blowing it did not go through. When the bad weather had stopped, Moon arose. Moon said to his wife, "Your house is good. It did not leak. Your house is pretty." Then he stopped talking. He went out and went to get firewood. He carried many leaves and bark and he gathered much pitch. After he had gathered wood he sat down outside. He was happy because he lived in a nice house. It was blue. It was shining. The house was very good. Moon said, "Chiefs shall even marry ugly women if the woman belongs to the Chief's family and if she has not known men, if she is still a good woman. That is the way it shall be with all Chiefs and their children as I got married to the grandchild of Toad. For even I shall stay with them, even if the woman has only a grandmother and they belong to the Chief's family. That way it shall be for the future. Even a handsome Chief shall marry an ugly woman if she belongs to a good family. That will be the ways of the Indians in later times." He finished making this rule of future people. He went in again. First he ate. In the evening after they had eaten they went to sleep. While they were sleeping during the night rain poured down. It was a gale. Thunderbird shot forth lightening. It was bad weather. When day came the Wife of Moon arose. She cooked much food. She made much soup, she and her grandmother. They had cooked much food. Then her husband woke up. They ate. After they had eaten Moon went and sat down by the fire. He said, "Even if it is bad weather your house does not leak." The wife replied, "Indeed, my house is good. Nobody has a house like this house I made with the help of my grandmother."

Moon said, "I will go hunting." He went to the mountains. He killed many deer. He carried them down many times. When he had finished he cut up the meat in small pieces. When he had cut it up they dried it in the smoke. He went fishing and caught many salmon in the river. When he had killed plenty, he called his wife. They carried their food in the house. Frog and her grand-mother finished dressing the meat. They finished dressing them and put them on sticks, which they raised high up on poles. They made a fire under it. Moon said, "Thus will people do with their fish in the future. The people will do so all over the world." He finished talking. Moon said, "Now I'll go home. I will go to get my mother and my younger brother. You better accompany me." Frog said, "Let us first get ready." When they were ready they started. They went all the time. And it was almost night when they came to the house of malé. When Moon arrived he said to his mother, "This woman is my wife. And her grandmother belongs to a Chief's family in another country." After he had finished talking Moon went to look for his younger brother. He found his younger brother by the river. His younger brother was a tall youth. Moon said to his younger brother, "I am looking for you. Let us go home to your house and let us eat good food. I have brought much good food. I have a wife. Now we shall eat good food." They went to the house and entered. After their mother and Moon's wife had finished cooking the Mother of Moon said, "Let us eat." They ate. It was so long then they finished. Then they sat by the fire. Then every one of them was very happy. They finished then they went to sleep. Then Moon said, "Tomorrow we will first look for much food, I and my younger brother, for you and my mother and my grandmother." He finished talking and he went to sleep. It became day and Moon made a fire. After he made a fire he heated much water. Then he went out. First he fished with a hook in the river. While he was fishing Frog and her mother-in-law[66] were cooking. Then much food was done. The food was done and they laid it down where they were going to eat. After they had put it down they waited a while and Moon came in with many trout and other fish. He put them down. He came and ate. After they had finished eating Moon said, "I and my younger brother will gather food." He stopped talking and went off. They went to fish in the river. They killed many fish of every kind. They finished and they carried all of them home. It was almost night. They went to their house and the Mother of Moon had much food. Moon said, "This food is enough. It is sufficient to last for many years. Tomorrow we will start, I and my younger brother." They went into the house and the Wife of Moon had cooked the food. The Mother of Moon said, "Now eat." They went and everyone ate. They finished eating. Then Moon said, "This night you ought to sing." They sang. They sang so long. They all sang and among them Moon. They finished and went to sleep again. Day came and Moon started the fire. Moon said, "I am not going to work this morning. I am very tired. I am always very tired in my body. My work is very hard." After his wife had finished cooking the Mother of Moon said, "Now come and eat." They went and ate. They finished eating. When they had finished eating Moon said, "After this we are going to leave you, Mother and Grandmother. You will always be happy. You will always feel good because we shall come back to the earth. Now we leave you, I and my younger brother."

Field notebook VII, 381–88, 404–17; typescript, "A Story," 55–60.

XXX

Moon and Sun

They started and went. Moon said to his wife, "First you shall go home with your grandmother. I shall come to get you if I find a good place for you to stay. At that time I will come for you and I will take you and your whole house and I shall take it." Now Frog went to her house and Moon and his younger brother started. A short time they went to the river. They arrived at the river, and they sat down on the bank of a nice creek. Moon said, "I am getting tired. My work on this earth is too hard and also your work is too hard for you." His younger brother said, "Good is what you say. That is right."

The younger brother finished talking. Moon said, "I made this world good. I have killed all the monsters on this earth. I have transformed many monsters on this earth. I transformed all the bad ones and they will become animals. Only the good ones will be Chiefs in this world. We are going to leave this world for a long time. When other monsters shall come and make the people poor, then we shall come back. Then all the people who had been transformed animals, then they will become people. They will have good ways. All the people whom we are leaving shall be happy. Among them we shall leave my mother and my grandmother. They will be happy together with the other Chiefs. And the other people with my mother they shall be Chiefs in this world. They shall be happy and their hearts shall always be good. We are going far from this world. We have finished setting the world right." Moon finished speaking. They arose, he and his younger brother, and they went home. They came to their mother. "We are leaving you now, I and my younger brother. We shall make something in the sky that shall give light to this world. One shall shine in the daytime and one shall shine at night," said Moon. When he finished talking he said, "Goodbye Mother, may you always feel good." His mother said, "Goodbye my son, look well after yourself that you may not be hurt." Moon and his younger brother started. Moon said, "We will start from the east end of the world. I will start in the day and you will come at night." They went to the east end of the world. Moon started in the morning. He went above in the sky. He went well. He rushed toward the west and the world was almost burned by his heat. Some things in this world were burned. The younger brother came in the night. They were almost afraid of the night. The world was very disagreeable during the night. They came down and they went up above. Moon said, "You shall go in the daytime." Then the younger brother went in the daytime. He went in the nighttime. The world was not really hot. Nothing was burned. Moon came in the nighttime. It was well for the world below. The cold of the night was right. He went when it became day. They went up above. They tried again. They went and it became day and it became night and again it was night and again it was night. For four days they did so. Then Moon said, "Now we are looking well. Maybe we will do this now forever." Moon said, "Let us go home. I will go after my wife." They came down again. Moon came to his wife and said to his wife, "I have come for you. Get all of your things ready." Frog and her grandmother got all ready. The house of Frog was broken up by Moon and his brother. They made a bundle of it and tied up the roof with a rope. All the way around they wrapped it up. Moon said, when he finished, "We shall repeat it as it was before when we reach the place toward which we go." Frog said, "Let us eat first." They ate. Then they finished eating. Moon said, "Now let us start out." They went. They carried all their things together with their food. They went up above over this world. They got there. Moon said, "You, my younger brother, you will travel in the daytime every day for so long then we shall come back. I shall travel forever in the night. We each shall shine on behalf of the people and of our mother. When it will be day then it shall become warm during the summer. The people shall always have light." Then the younger brother went. Moon went at night and the world was made good. The elder brother came in the night. He traveled the whole night and it became day. The world was not disagreeable. Moon said, "Now we are right. Forever when we travel in this way through the world I shall always go with my wife during the night. During the night, that shall be my world. Your world shall be the day forever." Now they traveled. Moon said, "Now we have finished in this world. Your world shall change when anything bad comes near the people. Then we shall straighten the world again." Thus he finished.

Field notebook VII, 418–28; typescript, "A Story," 60–63.

x̣ʷəné·x̣ʷəne: A Story

Jonas Secena

It is told how the world was all the time and the animals long ago. They were the people, only they were not right. Therefore, they were changed by the Chief.

"Why," said x̣ʷəné·x̣ʷəne, "Let me go to the ocean." First he gathered little brushes[1] that were hollow inside. He cut them short. He threaded the brushes and strung them and tied them together. He made a necklace. He went from there to the mountains. When he was near the mountains he became very hungry. He went out off the trail. It was always night. Then he heard the noise of someone coming. He saw how indeed it was a woman who was coming. x̣ʷəné·x̣ʷəne said, "Oh, it seems to be a big woman." The monster came near. It was k'ʷɔ́cx̣ʷe, that one who ate people. "I wonder what she may be carrying on her back. I'll try to trade food, my necklace for camas." Then he went after her. x̣ʷəné·x̣ʷəne said, "Oh, elder sister, I am hungry. I have a necklace of dentalia. Could I trade from you some camas for my necklace?" k'ʷɔ́cx̣ʷe said, "Although your necklace is no good, bring it. I'll give a little to you to eat. I'll just help you out so that you may not starve." x̣ʷəné·x̣ʷəne was given camas into his hand. x̣ʷəné·x̣ʷəne said when he got it, "Thank you for the food you gave me. We are five of us. I have four younger brothers. We all look alike. If you happen to find one on a mountain and if he looks like me, that is one of my younger brothers. Now I am going to leave you. I go to the woods. I'll go home from here." The monster said, "Goodbye. Now I am going." x̣ʷəné·x̣ʷəne went into the woods. He sat down and ate camas. He finished eating. Then he got better. He became stronger after he had been starving. He wondered, "How can I do it? Let me rest here a little while." He said, "Oh, not that. I'll run to the next mountain. There I'll rest a little." Now he ran to another mountain. He arrived at a clear place and lay down there near a trail. He waited for a long time, then k'ʷɔ́cx̣ʷe came again. That time he went to get her again. Now his necklace was different. x̣ʷəné·x̣ʷəne said, "Oh, you must be traveling a long ways." k'ʷɔ́cx̣ʷe answered, "Oh, my younger brother, I am just going home to my house." x̣ʷəné·x̣ʷəne said, "Oh, did you see my elder brother?" "I saw him. He is bad." Then x̣ʷəné·x̣ʷəne said, "I am very hungry. May I trade from you a little of what you are carrying?" k'ʷə́cx̣ʷe answered, "I do not gather camas to sell it. I only gather it for food. I will give you a little." That camas was being taken by x̣ʷəné·x̣ʷəne. "Oh, elder sister, thank you. You gave him to eat when you found my elder brother. Now I am starting off, goodbye." x̣ʷəné·x̣ʷəne went out off the trail to eat. When he finished eating he first sang and when he finished singing he started up again. Now he ran like this[2] faster. He arrived at another mountain. First he gathered grass. He found some other dry grass. It was shiny. He pulled it out. Now he walked. First he sat down and he cut the grass short. He threaded it on a string and tied it together and put it on his neck. Now he waited for k'ʷə́cx̣ʷe. Then k'ʷə́cx̣ʷe was coming, "Oh, my elder sister, you must be traveling. It looks as though you have too heavy a load. Oh, my eldest sister, I am very hungry. May I trade this my necklace for a little food?" k'ʷə́cx̣ʷe answered, "Oh bad one, you are always cheating me. Never mind, I'll give you to eat." She took off the cover of her basket and gave him a little. "I just give you to eat. Your necklace is bad." x̣ʷəné·x̣ʷəne said, "Thank you, you gave me to eat. Goodbye. Now I am going along." He went into the woods and ate. When he finished eating he ran again with all his might. He arrived at a mountain. He sat down beside the trail. He was waiting for k'ʷə́cx̣ʷe there. He had not been waiting long when k'ʷə́cx̣ʷe came again. He went to her, "Oh, my elder sister, I am very hungry. May I buy some food, a little of your load?" k'ʷə́cx̣ʷe answered at once, "Oh, my elder brother, I am feeding you from my load. I do not sell my camas. I only prepare it for my food for the winter. I only take pity on you, therefore I always give you to eat." Now she gave him to eat. x̣ʷəné·x̣ʷəne took it. x̣ʷəné·x̣ʷəne said, "Oh, my elder sister, thank you. Now you have given me to eat. Goodbye. Now I am starting." Now x̣ʷəné·x̣ʷəne went into the woods.

First k'ʷə́cx̣ʷe looked at her load. She looked at her load and she saw that only a few camas were left. k'ʷə́cx̣ʷe said, "What shall I do to him? He is bad." Then she started. Now she was going along. She said, "x̣ʷəné·x̣ʷəne makes me too poor. If I give him my camas it will be gone, what was to be my own future food. Let me not give him to eat. Let me cheat him. He is bad. He told me in the beginning that they were five. I always go, then I always meet him, the same x̣ʷəné·x̣ʷəne. Let him die. He is bad." k'ʷə́cx̣ʷe took something, *x̣ʷəné·x̣ʷəne: A Story* 81

a beehive. She wrapped it up. She told the Bees, "When he unwraps you, at that time sting his eyes. Take his eyes. Sting him until he is nearly dead. Then leave him. When he goes into a hollow burned cedar stump, when he goes into it, the stump shall shut up. The cedar stump will shut up at that time. Sting him." She finished her plans. Then k'ʷə́cx̣ʷe started again. She came to a mountain. x̣ʷəné·x̣ʷəne was there again waiting for her. "Oh, my elder sister, I am very hungry. Could you give me something to eat from your load?" Again answered k'ʷə́cx̣ʷe, "Oh, younger brother, I have only very little camas. Never mind, I'll give you all." She uncovered her little basket with it. There was something wrapped up. "Oh, this is what I have for you. Take it. Do not eat it here. Wait until you are in a cedar stump. There you will eat it." x̣ʷəné·x̣ʷəne took what was wrapped up. "Thank you for giving me to eat. Later on, some other time I shall return the favors." k'ʷə́cx̣ʷe said again, "When you eat this camas, don't open it until you are in the stump. Then eat it." x̣ʷəné·x̣ʷəne went. "Goodbye. I'll go now. I'll look for a cedar stump." He started. He went far away. Then x̣ʷəné·x̣ʷəne shouted five times, "Wä, wä, wä, wä, wä." k'ʷə́cx̣ʷe said, "It's even, the bad one. If I had given him my camas, it would be all gone."

x̣ʷəné·x̣ʷəne went now after he had finished shouting. He found a cedar stump and he went into the hole of the stump. When he got inside, it closed and he had no way of getting out. He unwrapped it and opened it. There was a humming noise coming from the bundle. They were humming. Now they buzzed and he was stung all over his eyes. Now he was fainting there. When x̣ʷəné·x̣ʷəne was senseless his eyes were taken off by the Bees. They took them and carried them way off. x̣ʷəné·x̣ʷəne came back to life. He could not see anything. He had no way of getting out. He could not do anything. He gave up all hope. He said, "Oh, that I may die here." He lay down inside the stump and he slept there for five days. Then he heard pecking from above. x̣ʷəné·x̣ʷəne thought it might be a person pecking from above. He shouted, "Oh, who are you?" He was answered, "I am Woodpecker." Again x̣ʷəné·x̣ʷəne replied, "What are you doing?" Woodpecker said, "I am just looking for winged ants for my food. What are you doing inside the cedar stump?" x̣ʷəné·x̣ʷəne replied, "I was sent up here by k'ʷə́cx̣ʷe. Could you help me out? Could you make a hole in this tree good enough for me to get through?" Woodpecker went down. He made a hole downward. It was not

very long when it opened inside. First he went in and found x̣ʷəné·x̣ʷəne. He
had no eyes. He asked, "What's become of your eyes?" x̣ʷəné·x̣ʷəne said, "My
eyes were taken away by the Bees. Maybe they took them along. Oh, come
on." Woodpecker went out. First he called x̣ʷəné·x̣ʷəne. x̣ʷəné·x̣ʷəne came
to the hole. He was pulled out by Woodpecker. Woodpecker said, "It is almost
night. I cannot wait for you." Then Woodpecker went home.

Now x̣ʷəné·x̣ʷəne was thinking what to do. He did not know which way
he was going. He took hold of a tree. It broke. He made a cane. Now he
walked. He was just feeling with his foot. He was walking this way for a long
time. Then he bumped his face. It was as though it was a house, where he
bumped his face. Then he turned back to an open ground and there he found
wilted flowers. He fixed them and made them almost round and stuck them
into his orbits. He also put on the other one. It looked as though he had eyes.
He could see with it nearby. It looked like the sea down below. Then he went
to those in the house. He came to those in the house. Again he hit the house
of Slug. Then he was told, "What are you doing? What are you looking for?"
"I am only trying to find out how long your house is." He went around the
house of Slug. He was only feeling with his hands. Then he found the door
of the house. He went in. He saw a little nearby by means of flowers. He was
asked by Slug, "What kind of a person are you?" "I am only visiting you."
A seat was placed for him. Then he sat down and they talked. x̣ʷəné·x̣ʷəne
was telling about everything that he knew, far away. Then x̣ʷəné·x̣ʷəne said,
"Shall we trade eyes? My eyes are good. They are too big, therefore I do
not want them. I want to have small eyes so that I can see nearby. I always
see too far with my eyes." "No, I do not want to trade my eyes for yours."
x̣ʷəné·x̣ʷəne said, "Let us go out." x̣ʷəné·x̣ʷəne went out first. They went
outside. x̣ʷəné·x̣ʷəne said, "Do you know where we can sit down so that
we can see the waterfront? Come here. Here is a log." They sat down. Then
x̣ʷəné·x̣ʷəne said, "Look at the sea. Can you see the people on the other side
of the ocean?" "Oh, there is no land. You could not find land in the ocean.
It is water all over." x̣ʷəné·x̣ʷəne said again, "Why, what is the matter with
your eyes? Look again, way over there the people are running back and forth.
Look." But Slug looked again and he could not see anything. x̣ʷəné·x̣ʷəne
said again, "Oh, try these my eyes, and take off your eyes. I'll first put on your
eyes." Then Slug took off his eyes. x̣ʷəné·x̣ʷəne put on the eyes of Slug. "First,

I'll try your eyes to see if I can see with them. Your eyes are good. Here are my eyes. Put them on. Then you will be able to see across the ocean." Slug took the flower eyes. He ran away. When he got far off he shouted. Slug put on the eyes of xʷəné·xʷəne. He wanted to see with them. But he could hardly see with them. He could not distinguish anything. "Ai, ai, ai, ai, ai," shouted xʷəné·xʷəne.

Now he walked slowly. He went some distance. Then he heard from far some singing. He stood up. Then he listened to hear from which direction it came. Then he found out where it came from. He went toward it and he came near. "Oh, they are playing the disc game. I'll see who they are." He walked slowly and he came to them. He saw, oh, many people. Behold, the Bees were playing a disc game. He was looking at the disc of the people. The people were talking. Then one of the Bees took one of the discs. Bee sang his gambling song and other Children of the Bees helped him. The Bees were talking. Others were shouting. One of them rolled it. Then he saw that the discs were his eyes. "They are the discs out of my eyes," he said to the Bees. "Oh, younger brother, let me look at your discs." He took one of the discs. He took one. Here was one of his eyes. They were both his eyes. He held them. Then he grabbed the two and jumped outside. He ran as fast as he could and got far away. Then he stood there. He took off the eyes of Slug and put on his own eyes. After he had put them on he threw away the eyes of Slug. Then he shouted, "Hai, hai, hai, hai, hai," because he had his own eyes.

He went far away from there. He came to a country and he found some people. He went near them. "What are you doing?" "We are traveling far away. First we are eating." The people were eating. Some of them said, "Why don't you give anything to eat to xʷəné·xʷəne?" One of them said, "Come on, say that you may eat with us." xʷəné·xʷəne ate. He finished and they started. xʷəné·xʷəne said to one of them, "May I not go along with you?" "Later on we'll lend you some wings and something for a tail." They taught xʷəné·xʷəne how to do it when he would fly. He started to fly. First he did not fly well. Then he learned it. They went along. It was night. Then it became day when they came to the people. Now xʷəné·xʷəne talked. The Chief of the Geese said, "Don't talk. Don't make fun of the people down on the ground. It is forbidden in our customs." They flew, all of them. When they came near to the people xʷəné·xʷəne talked. The people from below on the ground said, "Did you hear it? It seems there is talking coming from those who are flying. It seems that it is different." He was flying together with them. Then the Geese passed the people. They flew. It became night and it became day. Then they came to one who was bathing. "Oh woman, you are showing yourself." Then one of the Chiefs of the Geese said, "x̣ʷəné·x̣ʷəne broke our customs. Let us leave him on a big mountain." They flew and came to one. Then they left. First they took away the wings and the tail. Then they left him. The Geese went down, northward in this world.

x̣ʷəné·x̣ʷəne stayed there. It was night. There was no way to get down. It was too steep. He stayed there for four nights and when it became day again he was starving. "What can I eat?" He took out one of his eyes and ate it. Again he was hungry. He had no eyes. He stayed the fifth night. Then he heard something making a noise from above, "Hou, hou, hou, hou, hou." It was Hooting Owl. x̣ʷəné·x̣ʷəne said, "You child of a dog, shut up. You woke me up." Hooting Owl answered, "If you are not quiet, bad one, I'll take hold of your face." "Oh, you bad one, you are too weak. You cannot hurt me." Then Hooting Owl sang again, "Hou, hou, hou, hou, hou." x̣ʷəné·x̣ʷəne said, "Damn it, you are too loud." Hooting Owl answered, "If you are not quiet, I'll lick you. I'll break all your bones. I am Hooting Owl.[3] I overcome everyone, no matter who it is. I am always victorious. I am the warrior. The night and the mountains are mine." He stopped talking. x̣ʷəné·x̣ʷəne said again, "You scratcher,[4] son of an owl. What are you doing here? Come on down, so there can be a fight on this level ground." "Hou, hou, hou, hou, hou," said Hooting Owl. "You'll find out after a while. I'll kill you. I'll break all your bones." x̣ʷəné·x̣ʷəne said, "When can you beat me?" They all came down. But x̣ʷəné·x̣ʷəne had no eyes. Hooting Owl said, "Now do you want to fight, x̣ʷəné·x̣ʷəne? I am always like that. I play. If you think you are a man, come here. If you think you are a strong person, then you first take hold." He was attacked by Hooting Owl. x̣ʷəné·x̣ʷəne was taken by the head. x̣ʷəné·x̣ʷəne took hold of the throat of Hooting Owl. They were fighting. For a long time they were fighting. Then Hooting Owl got tired. Then he was thrown down by x̣ʷəné·x̣ʷəne. He was stepped on by x̣ʷəné·x̣ʷəne. He punched his eyes with one hand. He hit his face and with the other hand he knocked him senseless. Hooting Owl was knocked senseless. He broke the throat of Hooting Owl and Hooting Owl died. He took out his eyes and put them in his

orbits. After he had put them in he was able to see. He got them and he took
his wings and his tail and he put them on. First he tried them, and when he
tried it, he went, but not very far. He almost fell down. x̣ʷəné·x̣ʷəne said, "I
am too heavy. Let me turn back." He turned around and got to the body of
Hooting Owl. He made a fire and when the fire got hot he cooked the body
of Hooting Owl. He put it on a stick and ate it when it was done. He ate and
finished eating. After he finished eating he warmed himself by the fire. He
became stronger and his heart became good. When day came, he said, "Let
me start off." He flew and he almost fell down from above. He got to another
mountain. First he rested. Thus he fixed himself up and flew again. Now he
was flying steadily. He got there. He almost fell when he got to the bank of
the river.

He walked about on the bank of the river. Now he was really starving. He
thought what he would use to prepare food. He saw a Spring Salmon jumping. First he looked at the water. It was too deep where the Spring Salmon
was. He walked up the river and came to a place where the water was shallow.
He saw a place where it would be good to make a fish trap. After a short time
he finished it because it was not wide. He watched by the bank. Nothing was
coming up. He walked down the river. When he had gone off something went
into it. It went in and went right through the trap when it went into his fish
trap. He came to his fish trap and found that his fish trap was broken. Then
he fixed it. He wondered what he could do to capture the Spring Salmon. He
was making a canoe. He was always chopping the canoe that he was making.
There was always a noise of chopping at night. Then he said, "Let me find out.
Something seems to be hammering at my canoe, so I will go near the river-
bank so that I may just peep out for it from the bushes, looking at my fish
trap. Who may be hammering at my canoe? This is very far away from the
people." And he said, "Let me make a maul to hammer my canoe." He said
to his maul, "Hammer my canoe." Then it was still hammering at the canoe.
It sounded just as though a person were hammering. "Now I'll go down to
the river." When he got down to the river he stopped hammering. Again he
went back. His maul was not working well. He fixed it and when he had it
fixed again he went again to the river. He came near his fish trap. Then he
saw the Spring Salmon going up the river. He broke off a stick to strike it on
the head. The Spring Salmon came to the trap and got into it. x̣ʷəné·x̣ʷəne

jumped after it. He hooked it and he struck one on the head. Then he threw
it ashore. He hooked another one and again he struck it on the head. Then he
said, "It's enough what I killed. Let me go home." He went home and he got to
his maul. It was hammering, qul, qul, qul, qul, qul. x̣ʷəné·x̣ʷəne said, "Oh, yes,
finish your work. I have killed two." Now he went to his house. x̣ʷəné·x̣ʷəne
prepared his food. He split it. He found the inside. He looked at it a little. "Oh,
how pretty are all those insides!" Now he found the gills. "Oh, how pretty is
the inside of the head." He took off the gills and put them away behind. He
broiled the body on a spit and arranged his fire. Now he threw some pitchwood into the fire. The fire burned hard. For a little while it was roasting and
he ate. Now he finished eating.

Then he went after the gills and the rest from the inside of the Spring
Salmon. He said, "What could be made of it? Let me take two women out
of the two gills. They will be my wives." Then he took them into the house.
He sprinkled ashes all over the insides. He piled many ashes on it. Then he
put down the gills. He went away not far, then he came back. There were no
gills. They just disappeared. Again he went far away and worked at his canoe.
It made a noise. Then he stopped. He went in slowly. Nothing was there.
Then he saw what looked like tracks of children. Again he went. Again he
went to his work. Then he was adzing his canoe. He made a noise as he was
working. But now he did not work because his mind was changing because
he always thought of his future wives. x̣ʷəné·x̣ʷəne said, "Oh, let me take a
rest." He went to his house. When he was still far away he heard the cries
of a child, like children. He sneaked near and looked inside. It was nothing.
Children must have been running around all over the inside of the house.
He went back and slowly went back to his work. Now his heart was breaking. He went and came to his canoe work. He just tapped his canoe. He did
not want to work because he was sick at heart. He was always thinking of
his wife. For a short time he hammered. Then he again went to his house.
He came to it and not far from his house he heard the noise of children who
were singing a little. He came to it and slowly he looked. He heard them running and he saw little in the house. Again he backed out slowly and went
again to his work. He came to his canoe. First he sat down for a little while.
Now he wondered. Then he spoke to his heart. "Four times I sneaked to
these girls. I could not see them. Let my maul work so that it makes a noise."

"But it would not be like a person," answered his own mind. "You can make a person just to fool them, if you take it from the inside of your body." First x̣ʷəné·x̣ʷəne wondered. x̣ʷəné·x̣ʷəne said, "It would not be possible for a person to take out his insides. Even if I should do that, I might cut my insides. Let me not do that." First he sat down a little while. "What would be easy to do to my insides. Could I make them like a person?" he said. "I always eat food and after it passes down through me it is steaming. I think I'll make my passed food like a person." He said to the passed food, "Younger brother, hit my canoe slightly with my maul. Go on, try it." The former replied, "Slowly or fast?" x̣ʷəné·x̣ʷəne said, "Hammer quickly so that it seems like many people." x̣ʷəné·x̣ʷəne's younger brother hammered. "Oh," said x̣ʷəné·x̣ʷəne, "That sounds good. Now I'll leave you." x̣ʷəné·x̣ʷəne went to the house. He sneaked up again slowly. He stood there. He listened to his younger brother. "The adzing of my younger brother sounds well." Then he started toward it, slowly. Now he heard singing and always the noise of laughing. He heard one saying, "Here he is still working." x̣ʷəné·x̣ʷəne went in. Then the girls did not see him. They looked the other way. x̣ʷəné·x̣ʷəne sneaked after them. Suddenly x̣ʷəné·x̣ʷəne took them. x̣ʷəné·x̣ʷəne said, "You are my children. Now you will stay with me. Do not hide again. When I work anywhere you shall stay in the house. Don't run away when I come in." x̣ʷəné·x̣ʷəne stayed for five years at the place where he was, far away from the people, in the woods near the mountains. They were steep everywhere. x̣ʷəné·x̣ʷəne stayed there now. He was always working hard, every day and night. He went fishing and he picked berries. He always gathered many fern roots and everything. Then he gave to eat to his children, many days and nights, all the time, just four years, during summer and winter. Now they were big women. No one is like them. They were pretty girls.

They remained for five years. "These girls are big enough. Let me take them far away. Let me take them up the river. I'll go and take them up the river to the mountains. There we will pick berries. There I will make them my wives." x̣ʷəné·x̣ʷəne said to the Children of the Gills, "Let us go up river. I shall be in the bow and you shall be behind. You shall have paddles. I shall pole the canoe." Then x̣ʷəné·x̣ʷəne started punting. They went so far and came to rapids. They went up to the rapids. They almost came to the place where there were no rapids. At the rapids the river had a bend. The canoe almost turned to the bank when they were going up the rapids. x̌ʷəné·x̌ʷəne said to the women, "Push out to the water. Try hard and push your paddles against the ground." They went on the second time and came to the rapids. "Push on, push hard, my children." They came to a place where there were no rapids. The girls said, "The river has too many rapids. We are getting tired." They went up the third time to the rapids. Then x̌ʷəné·x̌ʷəne said, "Push hard, children, we are driven down the river." Then x̌ʷəné·x̌ʷəne poled strongly. Again he said, "Try hard, women." They came to a good water where there were no rapids. One of the girls said, whispering, "What did you say to us?" They went in the fourth time. They went up the rapids. Then x̌ʷəné·x̌ʷəne said again, "Push hard, women." They went on and they almost came to a place where there were no more rapids. Again he said, "Push strongly, my ladies." They came to a place where there were no more rapids. Then one of the women said to the other one, "What is he saying to us?" "It seems he said we are his wives," said one. "Yes, he spoke like that." They came near to other rapids. Then they whispered, "Let us leave him when we come to the bend, because the canoe lies near the bank. It is not good that he tells us we are his wives." They started again going up the fifth time. "Look out, we are almost arrived. This is the last rapid. Push[5] hard my wives, push hard, Children of the Gills." Then x̌ʷəné·x̌ʷəne said again, "Push hard, this time." The heart of x̌ʷəné·x̌ʷəne was now breaking. Now he said, "Oh, push hard my wives." Then the younger one said, "Oh, that bad one, what is he saying?" They went on. They came to the bend. Now their canoe was near. The end of the canoe struck the land. Then the younger one jumped. He said, "What are you doing? Come down quick." She came down. Now the younger one took a large rock. She put it on board. The other one took quite a little rock and put it aboard. There were two rocks that x̌ʷəné·x̌ʷəne saw and they pushed up and they ran inland. When they got far away they sang. x̌ʷəné·x̌ʷəne was going up the river, but there were no more women. Then again x̌ʷəné·x̌ʷəne said, "The canoe is getting heavy. Try hard my wives." Nobody answered. He went on and almost got to where there were no rapids. x̌ʷəné·x̌ʷəne slipped and almost upset. He tried hard to go up and he came to a place where there were no rapids. x̌ʷəné·x̌ʷəne said to the women, "Oh, my wives, you are almost arrived to where we are to go." Nobody answered. Then he turned around and he saw two rocks with him. There were no women. "Maybe they left me. They ran away. Let me try to shout." He shouted. He hallooed and hallooed, "Hou, hou, hou, hou, hou." Nobody answered. He came to level ground. Nobody answered. First he tied his canoe. He went to the level land and cried. When he finished crying he said, "I am getting very sick. My heart is breaking. Let me die. Let me hang myself." First he walked. He came to a good place and there his heart became good. He went and sat down under a little fir tree. x̣ʷəné·x̣ʷəne said, "Don't let me hang myself. Let them go, the bad ones. It will just be that men will be left sometimes by their wives, and when he is deserted nobody among the later people shall hang themselves."

When the girls finished singing, they talked while they were walking. One said, "Let us stop." They stood there and they went to a level country there and sat down. The elder one said, "Let us make a plan. If we are walking about too much, we do not know where we may be going." "Which way shall we go in this world?" said the younger one. "We cannot go anywhere, but we'll return home to the Country of the Spring Salmon where all the fish live. Let us start going there," said the elder one. "That is right, let us start out to the Country of all the Salmon." Now they started. They walked as fast as they could, night and day. And again it was night, and again it was day. On the fifth afternoon they came to a river. They rested a while. "Let us eat and drink a little." At that time there was no moon. It was always night and day. When they finished resting they started again and came to a meadow. Then they heard singing. This meadow to which they came, the name of this prairie is Kilakwito. malé was camping under the bushes, under many juniper bushes. There are many juniper bushes on the edge of the meadow. It was juniper season. Her daughter was picking berries. She had a child by immaculate conception, a daughter[6] born by the bursting of red hot stones from the fire. Thus this child was born from her. This baby was the moon of the night. This baby was a Chief because malé and her daughter are Chiefs. Her daughter and her grandson are the real Chiefs of this world. He was going to rule the world. Those were Chehalis. When the daughter of malé was out gathering berries she left her child in the cradle with her grandmother. A long ways the cradle went. Then it went backward. malé was singing cradlesongs. When she left she always first arranged the cradle of this baby. It had a long string. She pulled this string for her grandson. Then the mother of the child went picking berries. malé was always singing songs for her grandson. Every day she said,

Sleep my master, oh my master,
Sleep, sleep, my master,
Aiyaie, aiyaie, aiyaie, aiyaie, aiyaie.

malé was blind. She just had power and she knew how to sing out her power.

The daughters of xʷəné·xʷəne came. They were running away down below on the other side of the other world because they did not want xʷəné·xʷəne. When they passed the baby the younger sister said, "That old woman is saying 'Chief' in her tune. It is said, that baby is a Chief. The old woman is blind and far away passes the cradle. When it passes, let me take it out of the cradle. We will first replace it with some decayed wood." Now the younger one took the baby. She took it out and the elder one replaced it with rotten wood. The elder one said, "Let us run as fast as we can. Let us be quick. When we get far away we will plan what to do with this pretty baby. He is a Chief's child. He will be a Chief." They were always running. They stopped at a water. First they drank. Then one said, "What shall we do with the baby?" The younger one said, "No, let us make him for our husband. We will make him our husband when he gets big." When they were done they started again. They ran as quickly as possible because they knew that the mother of the baby was coming. When malé knew that they got the child, when she found out that her grandchild was stolen, and she knew that her grandson was replaced by a short piece of dried wood, she changed her song,

Now rotten wood, rotten wood, rotten wood,
Now rotten wood is my little grandchild.
Now my little grandchild is rotten wood.

Then she was heard by her daughter. "She is bad. What's my mother saying? She said rotten wood is her grandchild." First she stopped. Then she said, "Maybe her grandchild has been stolen." Now she ran from there to her house. She got to her house. She saw that her child was not there. She said to malé, "Do you know who stole your grandson?" "I cannot see, but I heard whispering. It sounded like girls." "Oh, my mother, your grandchild is stolen from us. I shall chase them." This daughter of malé was pretty. She was a big, tall lady. She could run fast. The daughter of malé said, "I am a fast runner. I can run far. I am long winded, only the bad girls passed too far. Maybe they are different girls. I am running. Now I am leaving you."

Now she ran. She ran as fast as possible that far. It was night. It was unknown to what seemed like people. It was on a steep mountain. She always saw tracks of the two girls. She said, "I think I cannot catch up to them. Too far behind I started. These girls who stole my child are also strong. I must just run to my mother." Now she ran. She came to her house at night. She came to her mother. She cried. She said to her mother, "I could not overtake those who stole your grandchild. I think we'll send somebody who can get your grandchild." Then malé answered, "My daughter, we cannot wait. It would take too long. Let us chase them again. Now let me go along." Then malé talked about her power.[7] "I have gained power when as a child. I am a strong woman. I have tamanous and I know how to use my power.[8] When I use my power I can wrinkle up the land. You must take me along." Then they started. malé walked on this world. Then she sang. These were running. And this is the tune of malé,

> Wrinkle up world, wrinkle up world,
> Wrinkle up so that I may catch up with my
> grandchild.
> Wrinkle up, wrinkle up, wrinkle up world.

They went. It was day. Then indeed the world wrinkled up. They heard the song and the daughter of malé tried harder. They came near to the Girls of x̣ʷəné·x̣ʷəne. Now they saw them. They got quite near to get from them their child. She was always carrying her mother on her back. Then she let go of her mother to get her child from the girls. When she dropped malé the world stretched out and the girls left her. She took her mother up again and ran.

> Wrinkle up world, wrinkle up world,
> Wrinkle up so that I may catch up with my
> grandchild.
> Wrinkle up, wrinkle up, wrinkle up world.

They ran as fast as they could. Then again the world wrinkled up. They were running all the time and now they saw the girls all the time. Now they were near them. Then she quickly let down her mother to get her child. When she put down malé the world stretched out and the girls left her. Then she took her mother. Again she pursued them and ran as fast as she could. malé said,

> Wrinkle up world, wrinkle up world,
> Wrinkle up so that I may catch up with my
> grandchild.
> Wrinkle up, wrinkle up, wrinkle up world.

They were near the mountains. Then they saw them nearby and almost they overtook them. Then she let down her mother to get those bad ones who had stolen her child. She almost got it from them. Then the world stretched out again. Again she took her mother and malé said again,

> Wrinkle up world, wrinkle up world,
> Wrinkle up so that I may catch up with my
> grandchild.
> Wrinkle up, wrinkle up, wrinkle up world.

They were near the mountains and the world was wrinkled up. They ran as fast as they could. They almost overtook them. She let down her mother and the world stretched out again and she lost them. Again she took up her mother, the fifth time. malé said, "Don't let me down so that we'll get it." Again malé sang,

> Wrinkle up world, wrinkle up world,
> Wrinkle up so that I may catch up with my
> grandchild.
> Wrinkle up, wrinkle up, wrinkle up world.

They ran near the mountains as fast as they could. They heard them from nearby. They saw that they were near to them, and they got near to the place where the earth is buzzing. Always goes up the sky and rejoins the earth.

It is a little open so that a person might almost go through where it rejoins the earth.[9] They tried to take hold of the child. There she was going to get it. But she missed taking hold one of the women.[10] Then the Children of Spring Salmon[11] jumped when they failed to take hold. They jumped and went through where the world opens and closes. Now they had lost. They had no way to get to the other side because it is a different country. "Oh," said malé to her daughter, "Now we have lost them. If I had taken hold of them we should have gotten them. If I had been able to use my tamanous power and my power of sending, you would have taken them in the beginning. They were gone too far when we started and we were too far behind when we started, else you might have gotten them, you my daughter. I might have used my power and we should have gotten them. We were too far behind. Now I give it up, my daughter." Then her mother had finished talking. "Let us start for our house." Again she carried her mother on her back. Then they went home, the two together, she and her mother. They were weeping. They were speaking while they were walking. malé said, "Oh, my master, you were stolen from us, my master." They cried while they were walking. They had gone so far when they arrived at their house.

First they rested. Then her mother said to her, "There is no way how we could have taken your child. I'll go to some other people. I'll try to assemble strong young men. We'll send for the strongest and all the young people." malé said, "No, first get the Chiefs and then first we are going to plan. At that time we'll pick out who will lead going to the other side of our world, the one who will be the strongest. Then he will pass through the closing and opening of the world." The daughter of malé replied, "I'll leave. Now I'll get the people." She came to all the animals. She told them that her child was stolen. "I want you to come to the place where I live. Then we'll select who is to go to the opening and closing of the world." As soon as she finished talking all the people, everyone, ran. They said, "It is said, 'The child of the Chief has been stolen.'" Said the Children of Bear and all the other big animals, "Gracious, maybe x̌ʷəné·x̌ʷəne did this." Cougar said, "Damn x̌ʷəné·x̌ʷəne. Let us go at once to the house of malé." Then all the Chiefs and every one of the people were running. Those who were almost the oldest ones and all the youngest ones were running. They came to the place where malé lived. There must have been over one thousand. There were many, all the animals.

When the people arrived they said, "Let us first have a great assembly." One said, "Be quick. Send for all the strongest young ones, all over the world. All over the wide world so that if possible all the people come." The messengers had gone a short time when they began to come over land and across rivers. From every way some came. Some were flying from above. All the people arrived coming from all parts of the world as wide as the world is. First the Chief gave them food. When they had finished, one said, "Let us first have a tamanous ceremony." Then they had a tamanous ceremony. First Beaver told about his power. "I am terrible.[12] I have tamanous power." Then they began to sing. Now the other animals sang. Then they danced and all the people, everyone, the old and the young performed their tamanous ceremonies, from daybreak until night. They had strong tamanous ceremonies, everyone, and they performed until daybreak.

After they had finished their tamanous ceremonies, they selected the one who was to pass through first. One of them said, "Let the one who has tamanous power start first. The one who has tamanous power shall go first." Beaver said, "I'll be the first. I have real tamanous power." First malé said, "Who will go through to the other side of the horizon? We'll pay him a blue blanket." When malé finished talking all the people started dancing. Then, "Oh, there were many people." Beaver walked ahead. They walked and came to the closing and opening of the world. They stopped on level ground, not far from the opening and closing of the world. When all those who had been behind had come, one of the young men said, "Be quick, don't let us wait. Now go ahead, Beaver first." Beaver went and he just came to where the world was going back and forth. He was blown away. He was almost knocked unconscious. Then he turned back. "There is no way for anyone to pass through. This is too difficult." After he had said so, others who were the greatest warriors said, that is, the Bears and the Cougar and the Wolves, "Oh, our elder brothers, let Mountain Lion go first." They went. Mountain Lion went and he came to the opening and closing of the world. He just looked at it and he said, "How can I get through? If I should jump it would get me before I could pass through. If it should get me the world would crush me. No, let me go back." One was told, "You runner, you are a warrior. Now you Wolf, try." Wolf ran. He said, "I know how I'll go after it. I should run from far and on the other side I should stop." He went and he stopped. "It is difficult. I might die. Let me go back." He said, "No." He finished talking and Chicken Hawk said, "Let me try." Chicken Hawk flew near the hole. He was blown back. He was almost knocked unconscious. He turned back. When he came to the other people, he said, "Oh, there is a strong wind." Now Snake jumped. He quickly squeezed through a small opening. "I can go through anything." He went. He did not stop. When he came to the closing and opening of the world it splashed dirt and sand over him. He was knocked unconscious. He was picked up and they took him far away, all those who helped Snake who was wounded. Then Bear said, "Now let me try." Bear went. He just came near it and he gave it up. "This is hard," he said. Bear turned back. "This is hard. It is quite hopeless." Then Cougar was told, "Now you go." Cougar ran fast. He just came near the place of the opening and closing of the world. Then he said, "There is no way for us to go through. It would be deadly. Let me go back. I do not want to die." They were changing about. The young men went and they just came near the opening and closing of the world, when they went back. Now it was night. Then one said, "Let us first take a rest." Then they ate. When they finished eating they said, "Let us first have a tamanous ceremony." First the shamans talked about their powers. Then they began to sing again. They performed their ceremonies until midnight. First they rested. "Let us eat first." Before eating the people fed the fire with food. Again they performed their ceremonies for a short time. They finished singing. Then they ate again. They ate. They finished eating. First they made a circuit to the left. Five times they went around, where the utensils for eating were spread out. After they had finished the shamans talked again about their powers. After they had talked about their powers they performed their ceremonies. They performed their ceremonies and they danced. Some of the young men among the warriors shouted. When it was almost day they stopped. Now they stopped. All wished very much to have the blue blanket. They thought, "I might get the blue blanket." They started. Then there was a little Chief who had a big heart. Crane said, "Let me start." First he shouted, "Xwas, xwas, xwas, xwas, xwas." He came to the place of the closing and opening of the world and he gave it up. "This is too difficult. Let me go back." He went back and said, "This is too hard." After he had finished talking Bee said, "I might go through." Bee went and came near the place of closing and opening of the world. He said, "No, if I should try, I should be crushed by the world. Do not let me go." He went back. He said to all the people, "Oh, my people, this is difficult. There is no way for anyone to go through to the other side." Again one went. Then the strangers were leading. All the people from far away, different kinds of persons went. He came to the closing and opening of the world and they changed about. Night came. The Chief said again, "Let us eat first." After they had finished eating they talked about their powers. People from far away, they finished performing their ceremonies and it was midnight. Then they ate. After they had eaten they talked about their powers, the people who came from very far way. They performed their ceremony. When they came they finished. They went. They arrived at the closing and opening of the world in the morning. Then the person from very far away started. He went. He came near and he went back. They talked another language. They changed about going to the place of the opening and closing of the world. Night came and again the Chief said, "Let us eat." They ate. When they finished eating the shamans talked about their powers. They performed until midnight. Then they rested. First they ate. Then they finished eating. When they finished eating quite a different person talked about his powers. He came from the edge of the world. They performed their ceremonies until daylight. Then they finished. Again in the morning they went to the place of the closing and opening up of the world. Some of the people said, "Let those who live below this world begin. Let us go quickly." One came near the opening and closing of our world. Then he gave it up and turned back. He said, "Nobody can go through the opening and closing of the world." When he finished talking then Bluejay was wondering, "How can I go through the opening and closing of the world?" When the people were going back and forth at the closing and opening of the world he went and cut a stick. He thought, "I'll place it in the opening and closing." The people were going and going, one by one from all over the earth until night. Night came. They ate again. When they had finished eating they performed their ceremonies. Midnight came and they ate again. They finished eating and daylight came. Then the people said, "We give it up. Who will begin again?" "I'll try first," said Bluejay. For five days the people all over the world had tried. "Let me try. Bluejay belongs here. He is Chehalis." Bluejay went. The other people were laughing at him. Bluejay went. First he looked at the place of opening and closing. "Enough, I'll put up my stick before you come down again." He got ready. He put in the stick, which was long enough to go through. After he had finished putting it up Bluejay flew through from the outside as fast as he could. "Káčə, káčə, káčə, káčə, káčə." Bluejay disappeared. He went through. Not very long after he had gone through, Bluejay came back through the closing and opening and it clapped together when Bluejay took off. Then Bluejay put his stick down and he flew. "Káčə, káčə, káčə, káčə, káčə."

Bluejay went not very far. He came to a level ground and he met one person. This country had a red sky and red and black and white clouds, just like strong clouds in this country. The Country of the Salmon was altogether different. He asked this person, "Do you know the Chief here?" He replied, "The Chief here is nearby, not very far from here. Two wives and many children always work at his house. He is very far away from the place he came from." Bluejay said, "Thank you, I wish to know about this." First he thanked him. "Káčə, káčə, káčə, káčə, káčə." He flew again. Far away he heard a ringing sound, which sounded nicely. He went and flew above the noise. He alighted on a tree. He was grateful for he knew that this was the Chief. Bluejay said, "Káčə, káčə, káčə, káčə, káčə," and he flew far away. He saw surprises. After he had been surprised he said, "Let me go near him." Again he flew and he stopped near the work of the little one. Bluejay was grateful and said, "Káčə, káčə, káčə, káčə, káčə." Moon said, "What does Bluejay say? Why did he come here?" He took ashes and threw them on him. He hit Bluejay's eyes. Bluejay fell down. It struck his eyes and he could not open his eyes again. "Oh," said Bluejay, "Why do you do that to me, my master? I was sent to get you by the one who was your mother and your grandmother." "What does Bluejay say? What happened to my mother?" He went to get Bluejay and washed his face. After he had washed him he tapped his head from behind with his hands and the ashes came out of his eyes. Then Bluejay could see again. "What happened to my mother? What did you say?" Bluejay replied, "The people are tired because they were looking for you. Nobody could pass the closing and opening of the world. But I went through. Your mother and your grandmother said to me you should go home." Moon replied, "I have many children. I have two wives. First I'll make toys for them." After he had made many toys he divided the toys. He got ready. When he was ready he said to his children, "Don't cry. I am going far to the other world but I am going to come back. You will be looked after by your mothers." When he had finished Bluejay said, "Now let us go." They started and went quickly. It was not very long before Moon arrived in company at the place of the closing and opening of the world. Moon said, "Let me put the stick in." Moon put it up. He said to Bluejay, "Now fly to the other side as quick as possible." Bluejay said, "Káčə, káčə, káčə, káčə, káčə." He got through to the other side. He ran and Moon was running after him. They got through. Then Moon took out the stick and the closing and opening of the world clapped together. They went to a level piece of land and they camped. Moon said, "Let us camp here although it is not night. We will cook our food." Moon started a fire under a little tree. It was night. When they had eaten they went to sleep. Early in the morning they got up. First Moon made a fire and after he had made a fire they cooked their food. Their food was done and they ate. After they had eaten, Moon said to Bluejay, "Now let us start."

They went. They were traveling slowly. They had not gone far when they heard a noise. They passed. Then Moon said, "What was it that we passed?" Bluejay said, "What is it? It is a person." Moon replied, "Let us go back and see him. Let us see what he is doing." They arrived there. He always put up sharp pointed sticks and this person hammered them with his head. His head was slender but large. He was asked by Moon, "What are you doing, boy?" He answered, "I am working. I am splitting wood to make a house." "Go ahead, split it. How do you hammer?" "Oh, I always hammer with my head." Then he hammered with his head, tə́p, tə́p, tə́p, tə́p, tə́p. He did not split. Then Moon said, "This is quite improper. Wood is not split that way. Stop. I'll make wedges for you and a maul." Moon made wedges and a maul and he put on three wedges. He hammered all three with the maul and the wood split. "Now you try it." The person put up the wedges and struck them with the maul. The wood split. Then the man and Bluejay sat down on top of the large fallen tree. He looked on for a while and the boy split all over much lumber. The boy said, "These, your tools, are good." Moon replied, "I just made them. The wedges and the maul are yours. The people will only work in this way. You will not again use your head. Now I am leaving you."

They went, he and Bluejay. They had not gone far when they came to Raven. "Why are many people standing in the water holding one another a long ways from this side?" They stood. They were clear across the river. Moon said to one person, "What are these people doing?" "Oh, this is my fish trap. I am catching fish. Do you catch any fish?" "Sometimes," said the Raven. Moon went to the water. Some of the people were groaning and grinding their teeth. These and others were shivering. Moon said to the people, "What are you doing in this creek?" "We are working for Raven. We are fishing." He said, "Are you always doing that?" "Always, even if it is very cold. Raven is terror. He is mean." Moon replied, "Go ashore." The people went ashore. "A fish trap is not made in that way. The people should not act thus. Let me make a fish trap for you." He cut many saplings. He finished making the fish trap, like the fish traps the people are making. "No fish trap shall be made of people. Never in later days you shall be abused." Moon went. Raven said, "You are bad. You work for your people. Better get out today." "You will not be a person. You will be a bird. You will fly about near the houses. You shall gather everything bad, scraps left by the people." Moon said, "Now fly." The Raven flew away. Moon said, "Now say this, 'Squak, squak, squak, squak, squak.'" And the Raven answered, "Squak, squak squak squak squak." Then he flew away.

After this was done Moon and Bluejay started. They went so far. Then they heard singing. It made a noise. Behold, Deer was whittling wood. "I'll stab him, with this. I shall stab the Chief. Oh, with this I shall stab the Chief. I am going to stab him when the Chief comes." Bluejay and Moon were going. They came to the person. He was singing. "What are you saying?" said Moon. "I'm not saying anything. I'm just singing." "Bad one, don't lie," said Moon. "You said, 'I'll stab the Chief with this sharp stick.'" Moon said, "Go on, bring your stick." That fellow, Deer, took up the stick and gave it to Moon. Moon said, "Give me your arm!" He took the arm of Deer and he stuck the stick into his arm. It was stuck into it once more. He was told, "Run." Deer ran away. He did not run far and was told not to turn around. Then Deer turned around. He was told, "Now run again." Then Deer jumped. Moon said, "Oh, you are bad. You are too mean. It will be disgraceful. You said you would strike me with your stick. You will be good food for the people of later times. When the people find you, you will first be frightened. You will not run far. Then you will turn around and you will run. Forever you will be the food of the people."

Moon and Bluejay were walking. It came to be night. Moon said, "Let us camp near a creek." They cooked food. It was done. Then they ate. When they had eaten they went to sleep under the branches of a small tree. First they made a big fire. Now they went to sleep. When day came the next morning

Moon said, "We'll first eat much, then we'll start." They cooked and they ate. When the food was done they ate much. He and Bluejay had eaten enough. First they sat down. Then Moon said, "Let us first make a plan how to act. After a long time I'll go to my mother because I first make right the world. You better fly right along. I'll follow behind. I shall be going for many days." Bluejay flew to the two malés. He came to the two malés. Then there were many people. Bluejay arrived. "I have returned now. I came ahead for Moon is setting the world right. He said I should return first." Bluejay finished talking. First they thanked Bluejay. "Thank you, Chief, you brought him back." He was given the blue blanket. Bluejay took the blanket. He put it on. Then he stepped far. The people shouted. Everyone was singing. Then the people finished singing.

When they ran away with Moon, the Mother of Moon rinsed the diaper in water and she drank it. It was not many days when the daughter of malé had a child. The boy was Sun. He was the younger brother of Moon. The people ate. After they had eaten in the afternoon they had a tamanous ceremony. The people finished their tamanous ceremony. Then they were dismissed. They went home to where they came from the world and Bluejay went along.

But Moon went along when Bluejay had left. He heard someone talking. "It is said the Chief is coming. I'll kill him." Again it was known by Moon what Beaver was saying. He reached Beaver. "What did you say? Did you say you would kill me?" said Moon. "Go on, say it again, what you said." "No," said Beaver, "I didn't say anything, I was just talking." "The bad one," said Moon. "Turn around." Beaver turned around. He was taken by Moon and he stuck his paddle into him in his hind part. "Go on, swim. Strike the water again with your tail." Beaver struck it with his tail and the water made a noise so loud, "Chpoo, chpoo, chpoo, chpoo, chpoo." "Forever you shall be in the water. You will fell trees near the bank of the rivers. You will eat wood and mud. You will be food of the Indians of later times."

Beaver was left. He had not gone far when he found a monster. Behold, it was Bear. They were bad Bears. Moon said, "You are not right. You often frighten other people. Now do this way. Stand up. Dance. Now run. You shall be the food of later people. When you hear the noise of people coming you will stand up and you will listen. Then you will run. You will be killed. You will be made food." He finished and Moon started.

He walked that far. He heard a noise from afar. First Moon stood. He listened. Then he went after it. He came to a very old man who was working. He was a good-looking person. Behold, he was very old. He had many tools and he was chopping wood. First Moon was looking on. Moon said, "Grandfather, your work is really good. Your clothing is really good. I wish very much to have your headband which you are making." Moon said again, "Your tool is very curious. It is very large. It is long. How are the chips chewed by it?" The old man answered, "Oh, my Grandson, I am always making canoes, every day since I was young. I am getting old. I have many wives in my house. Therefore I feed my tools with many chips so that they become strong." Moon said, "Oh, Grandfather, I wish for your headband. Let us trade. I'll give you my headband for yours. Let us trade your tool for mine." "All right, my Grandson." They traded. After they had done so the old man said, "My Grandson, you must always feed your tool chips and meat so that they may get along well. If you get it you will always look for nice work. Now I have finished teaching you." Then Moon said, "Oh, Grandfather, I leave you. Goodbye. Thanks for your headband."

Then Moon started. Now Moon went along. It was not yet night when they looked for a place to camp before night. He looked for a girl who was to prepare food for him. He found one that would help him. He said to the woman, "Cook many things. First I'll work." He went and tried the tool that they had traded. He got his ax and found a tree. He chopped the tree. Every time a chip dropped it was eaten by his tool. He chopped the trees. When it was night he went home to his camp. He arrived at his camp. The woman had been cooking. The girl said to him, "It is a long time since I finished cooking." Moon said, "Let us eat." They ate. And after they had eaten they went to sleep. They slept. Then it was day. First they ate again and after they had eaten Moon said, "I am Moon. I am always traveling. I am setting the world right. Now I'll leave you. It shall only be this way. Sometimes women will make love. If there is a handsome youth he will elope with the nice girls. It will be that way." Now Moon stopped. Moon said, "Goodbye. Now I feed you." Moon forgot to feed his tool. He walked along and on a warm day his tool became hungry. It was biting everything. It bit his calf very hard. It was not good to him because he did not do as the old man had told him. He had not fed his tool with chips before he started. Moon ran as hard as possible.

His headband was biting him. It almost cut his head. His eyes were rolling. Then he came to a creek and found Toad. "Oh, Grandmother, I am dying. Could you help me?" "Indeed, I can do it easily. I can take off your headband." Toad took grease and rubbed it all over his head and his headband came off. First she set right the eyes of Moon because his eyes were almost puffing out. She straightened his mouth and his nose. When she finished she rubbed his face and his mouth and his head with bear oil. She finished and rubbed all over his body. Toad said after rubbing Moon, "You, my Grandson, go back and trade it back. He is bad. Take the old man's headband and his tool. You will become very poor if you keep it." Again Moon was straightened out. Moon said, "Oh, Grandmother, first I'll go back." Then he started. First he said, "Goodbye. Now I am going." Moon walked as fast as he could. Then the tool of the old man became excited and always bit his body. He came to the old man. Moon said, "Oh, Grandfather, here you are, still working." The old man replied, "I am still here, my Grandson." Moon spoke again, "Oh, my Grandfather, your headband and your tool almost killed me. I come to trade it back." The old man replied, "Oh, my Grandson, that's what I thought. I told you, you should always feed it well with chips but you did not do so. Therefore it bit you." They finished trading back. First Moon said, "Thank you my Grandfather. I've troubled you. Now I leave you again."

Then Moon started off. He went so far. He camped and first he cooked. When his food was done he ate. First he talked before he was going to sleep. "I was treated badly by the old man. I shall break my own law. Let me take this off from this world. The tools shall only belong to man. They shall not eat chips. When people meet they may sometimes trade their hats or headbands. They shall never bite their heads or make them cross-eyed or deform their heads. Chiefs will just trade their headbands. They shall never kill them in the way people will be later on in this world." Then he slept.

He arose in the morning. First he started a fire. After he had made a fire he went for water, from a spring on the mountain. Then he cooked. After eating he started off. He walked along and it was not long before he came to a large river. First Moon stood there. He looked across and he saw something like a person motioning far inland. "How can I get across? Let me shout." Then he shouted, "Eh, eh, eh, eh, eh." It was not a long time when a boy came with what looked like a stout stomach. He was also short. He was round and fat. His face was very ugly. Moon said, "Boy, I want to go across." Tapeworm answered. This boy was one of the tapeworms. Tapeworm replied, "Oh boy, I want to go across." "Have you got a canoe, boy?" said Moon. Then Tapeworm answered again, "I want to get across. Have you got a canoe?" Said again Moon, "I want to go across. Have you got a canoe?" "Eh?" answered Tapeworm. "That bad one makes me mad," said again Moon. "You will find out, bad one. I am going to kill you." Moon became angry. He took an arrow stone, two stones. Both were sharp arrow stones. Now he found that these were some of the Children of Tapeworm. They were monsters in this world. He defeated all of them. "I know how to kill him." He tied a sharp-edged arrow stone under his breechcloth.[13] He tied the arrow stone as firm as he could. First he repaired his knife. Then he swam. He swam a little. He landed and he jumped out as quickly as he could. He said to the boy, "I am Moon. I am killing everything." "Eh?" replied Tapeworm. "I am Moon. I am killing everything." "Eh?" replied that Tapeworm with the big stomach. Oh, this one with the big stomach who was short all over. Tapeworm replied again, "Eh?" Oh, this one who was quite short. "Where is your house?" "Eh?" replied Tapeworm. "Where is your house, you son of a dog?" said Moon.[14] When he finished speaking he punched him. He fell down. Then Tapeworm shouted aloud. "Come out, come out my folks." Moon looked inland and nobody came. Then he struck him with his knife on the chest. "Come out, come out my folks." Then something came out from his body. They came out of his mouth and like it came out behind when he was calling the worms from his inside. Behold, these were his folks. They were long like snakes. Many, very many, came. He struck one and it broke in two. Another one came and it wound itself around his legs. It wound itself around him as fast as it could. He cut it in two with the sharp arrow stone on his legs and with his knife. It fell down. Then he struck another one and others came to trip him up. They were cut in two. He fought with them until they were all gone. Now the worms were all gone. The boy struck them with his knife. They died. Then he cut their necks. There they died. He made a fire and piled them on the fire until they were burned up. Moon said, "Today, I've killed Tapeworm. There shall be no tapeworm in the world who will kill people. Only sometimes a person shall have a tapeworm who has bad intestines. Sometimes anyone who has a tapeworm may be ill tempered. But not every person shall have them. Only the worst people shall have tapeworms. They shall not be monsters."

There was a Fire. That Fire had five daughters. They stayed in the house near the mountains. It was always burning in the house, but they were Chiefs. But it was forbidden for them to sing before young men and for any other people. The Children of Fire were pretty women. There was the one, the youngest one among them, who was always singing. Once in a while they were all singing. There is nobody now like the Daughters of Fire. They were pretty women. Once in the morning, one of the girls, the youngest one, was singing a little,

> Fire, fire, it is blazing
> Blazing are the flames of the fire.
> Häa, häa, häa.

A handsome man came along the trail. The girl saw him and stopped singing. The young man reached her. That young man said, "I heard your nice song. I am a Chief. Maybe you have heard of Moon. I have been walking a long ways. I am very tired. Go ahead and sing your same little song." The girl said this, "No, I cannot sing for you. It is forbidden for me to sing for anyone. I am the Daughter of Fire. It would be fatal for this world if I sing for you." Moon said, "Nevertheless, I heard your tune from far away. You had better sing again." The girls said, "We are the Daughters of Fire. Now let us sing for you. Oh."

> Fire, fire, it is blazing,
> Blazing are the flames of the fire.
> Häa, häa, häa.

She was singing a little. Then all the Girls of Fire came. The other Daughters of Fire helped her singing. They sang a little. The Chief was listening. Then Fire blazed up all over. Now everything was burning. Moon said, "Truly, evidently the whole world is on fire." Now Moon was running. Fire came near him. He came to Rock. The Chief said to Rock, "Oh, elder brother, could you help me. The Fire is coming." Rock said, "Oh, younger brother, I have no way of helping you. When Fire comes to me we should crack and burst." Now Moon ran from there harder. He came to Lake. He asked him, "Could you help me? Fire is coming. Maybe I'll get burned." And Moon ran again. He was running. He reached the Wind. "Could you help me? The world is on fire." Wind said, "I cannot help you. When I blow it will burn rather stronger. Run to the Creeks, maybe they can help you." Then Moon was running again. He came to the Creeks. He said to the Creeks, "Oh, I am dying." The Creeks said, "Surely you reached the Daughters of Fire. Surely you are going to die. I have no way to help you. When Fire comes the world will get hot and I am going to boil. All the same you would be cooked. Surely you are going to die. Go on, and run just the same, as hard as you can." Now he was running. Moon said, "I am a Chief. I have destroyed everything in the world. I have defeated everything. But today, now I think I shall die. I think I will burn and die." Now he was running hard. He was walking. Fire came near. Fire surrounded him from all sides. There was just a little land that was not burning. He ran there. He came to a little Trail. Moon said, "Now I am dying. Maybe I will be burned. You, Grandfather, could you help me?" Trail looked at Fire. Fire was blazing. Everything was crackling. The trees were falling. The creeks and lakes were boiling. The little Trail said, "Indeed, Fire almost caught up with you. However, I never burn. Fire only burns around me and passes above me. Come on, Grandson, lie down on my back," Trail said. "Nevertheless, you will get hot, but do not move. Put down your eyes and your mouth firmly on the ground." He just got down on the little Trail. Then Fire caught up with him. It was blazing everywhere. Moon was perspiring. He had not been lying down long when Fire passed him. Although Fire passed him he almost died. Then Fire went. Moon stood up. He said, "After all I am not going to die. I'll stay here for five days. I'll bathe first. Then I'll start off." He stayed for five days. Moon bathed. When he finished bathing he dressed up for a while. He said, "At this place I almost died, just because the Daughters of Fire sent for me. Future people shall be different after a while. Girls will just sing and it will not burn the world. Chiefs will only be sung for by girls. But your body shall never be burned up."

He went along and then he came to a house. He arrived. A woman came out. She was laughing. "Where are you going, youth?" Moon replied, "I am walking a long ways in this world. I am going home." "First stay here and eat with me." Moon replied, "Oh well, maybe I'll rest." This woman was a large woman. She was tall. Evidently she was one of the daughters of k'ʷə́cx̣ʷe. Moon went in. k'ʷə́cx̣ʷe cooked. When k'ʷə́cx̣ʷe was cooking she first always played with him. They laughed. Moon came to be happy. The woman had a pretty face. She had very curly hair. k'ʷə́cx̣ʷe said, "First I am going to get water." k'ʷə́cx̣ʷe went out. Moon said, "Oh, that woman always kills men. She must be k'ʷə́cx̣ʷe." He took a long stone and heated it in the fire when k'ʷə́cx̣ʷe had gone outside. She came to the water. She sharpened two sharp-edged knives. She put them on. She used these to bite with, so as to cut the man in two. After she had dipped her water she went to the house. She came in. "Maybe you are hungry." Moon replied, "I am never hungry. Sometimes I get tired, my younger sister. Your house is good." "Indeed, I have a good house." "Your camp here is good," said Moon. "That is true. Let me camp here." k'ʷə́cx̣ʷe spread her blanket. She put down the food. k'ʷə́cx̣ʷe said, "Now come, let us eat." Moon thought while he was wondering, "Behold the ways of this woman. We are going to eat good food." They ate. They laughed. k'ʷə́cx̣ʷe was told everything that happened far away. They laughed much. They finished eating. Then k'ʷə́cx̣ʷe stood up. She went to the end of Moon. She arranged her blanket. Behold, there was her bed. k'ʷə́cx̣ʷe said, "Come." Moon went there. "Here you will lie down tonight. Better stay here." Moon went to her. "Come, let us lie down." Moon went. They went to sleep. Moon said, "Let us first shut our eyes tight." When she[15] shut her eyes he took the red hot stone and struck her with it. She cried out. He cut off her head. Then he went out and broke the house of k'ʷə́cx̣ʷe. k'ʷə́cx̣ʷe was the seven Children of k'ʷə́cx̣ʷe. They always ate people. There was much pitch in their house. That is the only thing she likes, men. She ate them. Then the house of k'ʷə́cx̣ʷe was burned. It was burnt up and the body of k'ʷə́cx̣ʷe burst. Then Moon stood up. "There will be no k'ʷə́cx̣ʷe in the world. Women shall only love young men. They will not kill them when a youth comes to them. They will eat and the man will not be killed. They shall be happy. There will be no woman like k'ʷə́cx̣ʷe who eats people in the future. It shall be different with the Indians after this." He finished. Then Moon stopped.

He went along. He had not gone far when he heard singing. First Moon stood still. He listened. He went along and he arrived where he heard it. Behold, there were many Prairie Chickens on the meadow. He arrived there. The people were singing. There were many people on the level piece of land. They were always dancing on the meat until they perspired. Then the meat became hot. For a long time the meat was hot and then it became soft. Then they said, "Now we have cooked it." At that time they ate the meat. Moon looked at the prairie people on the level land. Moon went up to one of the Prairie Chickens. He asked, "What are you doing?" "Oh, we are cooking our food." Moon said, "Tell your people to stop. I am Moon. I set right the world. This is not the way to cook food. I'll make a fire drill for you." Now Moon made a fire drill. He finished many and gave them to the people. "With this you shall make fire." Moon gathered small sticks. He started a fire. Now the sticks were burning. He went and made a bucket. He heated stones and he poured on water, filling the bucket. Then he took more red hot stones and threw them into the bucket. Then he put the meat in. Again he put in more stones and the meat began to boil. It boiled so long. Then the meat was done. He called some of the people. "We shall always go this way and all the people shall use the fire drill to make fire with." Then Moon finished talking. The Chief of the Prairie Chickens of the level land said, "Do first eat with us." Moon went to eat with them. Before they ate the people first sang again. They danced, just as many as they were and with them danced Moon. They finished and they ate. When they had finished eating the people sang again. They danced. Then they finished dancing. Behold, it became customary for the people to sing. They were always singing. Moon finished. First Moon said, "It will only be right for people of later times to prepare food with fire."

He did not go far and then he camped and he made a fire. First he went to a creek and bathed and after bathing he went to his fire. First he stirred the fire with a poker. Then he finished preparing his food. His food was done. He ate and after he had eaten he sat under the tree. He went to sleep. In the morning on the following day he first started his fire and then he went to the place where he had been bathing the day before. He bathed and dived five times. Then he went to the shore and put on his clothing. He went to his fire and cooked again. His food was done. First he ate. Then he started again. He walked far and came to a boy in a house. This boy had no relatives. It was as though he had been crying before he arrived. Moon said, "What has happened to you, boy? It seems you are deserted." "Oh, my uncle, I reply to your speech. I have been alone for many days. Seven days ago or more my brothers went hunting. The first one disappeared and the others went searching. They are all gone. I think my elder brothers were killed." Moon said, "Do you know if there are people nearby here?" The boy replied, "There are people, many, not very far." Moon said, "I'll go to these people." He asked the people, "Do you know about the brothers of the boy? I came to a boy who was all alone. He said that his elder brothers have disappeared." One of the people said, "I think they were killed by the monster. There is a monster called Skylark. Nobody can see that Skylark, because he is a monster." Then one man replied, "Oh, younger brother, many people have disappeared in this country. They only disappear and I search for them. I want to kill him but I cannot find him." "Oh, my elder brother, I'll search for that monster. Skylark, he did bad work to the lonely boy. I remove all the monsters from this world." The man replied, "I am the same. I always kill k'ʷə́cxʷe. I am xʷəné·xʷəne." Moon came to the boy. He made a fire and said to the boy, "All this food is yours. Everything left over by us I leave here." They stayed until night. They went to sleep. In the morning the next day Moon first made a fire. The boy said, "When I was asleep last night I dreamed that I found my dead relatives lying down in a gulch in the country. I found they were my elder brothers. When I dreamed about them I found a nice trail. It is at the far end of the trail. There is a large red fir, and many limbs are above with thick needles. That is where the monster is. The people say it is Skylark. They say he always kills the people. But it is not a real monster. It is not at all a person.[16] This is what I dreamed about it last night." Moon said, "Let's go out." They went out. Moon said, "In what direction in the world do you think is that trail?" The boy said, "I started from there when I was just dreaming." "Now this is bad," said Moon. "Your dream is true. It was not Skylark who killed your elder brothers. It must be the monster." They went in and ate quickly. After they had eaten Moon said, "You, boy, your brothers have been killed." This boy was the youngest of the Pheasants. Moon said, "First I'll go to xʷəné·xʷəne. Now I am leaving you." Moon said after a while, "We will go to get that monster, I and xʷəné·xʷəne." He went and reached xʷəné·xʷəne. He said to xʷəné·xʷəne, "I came to get you. Let us go after the monster in the mountains." xʷəné·xʷəne said, "Let us go quickly." They made themselves ready. Moon said, "We will go first past the boy." They reached the boy. Moon said to the Pheasant, "Now we leave you. Your heart may always be good. Don't cry again. Now I am leaving you." Then they started. They cut a long pole. Moon and x̣ʷəné·x̣ʷəne were walking. They went that far. It was raining in the mountains. It was raining as hard as it could. They walked along on the trail. They found a large tree with thick leaves.[17] It looked pretty and above were many limbs. x̣ʷəné·x̣ʷəne said, "Evidently the people are camping here. Let us camp. We are getting to be very wet." "Oh no, I think this is the house of the monster," said Moon. "Go over that way. Walk fast on this trail. Make much noise with your feet. When it is evening and almost dark, then come. I shall be watching here for the monster. You shall gather much pitch." It was not yet night. A person appeared at the distance coming. Oh, a big man. This was the monster. Indeed, it was a real monster. What was he going to do? After a while he came to the trail. He saw first the tracks of x̣ʷəné·x̣ʷəne. Now it was night and now the monster got ready. The monster climbed up. He eats only Indians. He eats only hearts of persons. He does not eat the bodies of persons, only their hearts. He is a real monster. He stayed there. Now Moon was walking on the trail looking for x̣ʷəné·x̣ʷəne. He found x̣ʷəné·x̣ʷəne on the trail. x̣ʷəné·x̣ʷəne said, "You shall go. You will make a fire at the foot of the tree. After you have made the fire sit down at the foot of the red fir." He went. After he had made a fire x̣ʷəné·x̣ʷəne sat down at the end of the tree. x̣ʷəné·x̣ʷəne said, "What's up there in the tree?" Late at night x̣ʷəné·x̣ʷəne became quiet. Then it said from above, "Oh, are you asleep? Are you awake?" x̣ʷəné·x̣ʷəne woke up. x̣ʷəné·x̣ʷəne replied, "Oh," said x̣ʷəné·x̣ʷəne, "What are you saying? Come down, bad one, so that I may kill you." He did not answer. Then Moon went to the foot of the tree. He said to x̣ʷəné·x̣ʷəne, "Now we'll fight him to kill the monster. When we are going to fight, make a big fire." Moon went to the foot of the tree. When he came to the foot of the tree he said, "Come down, bad one. You'll die tonight, bad one." The monster did not answer. Moon said, "This monster is strong, is big." He went after x̣ʷəné·x̣ʷəne. He said to x̣ʷəné·x̣ʷəne, "We shall take turns in guarding the monster until daytime. You must always sing." x̣ʷəné·x̣ʷəne always sang. It was almost day. Then it cracked above. Moon ran to the foot of the tree. He came to x̣ʷəné·x̣ʷəne. He was a little asleep. He shook him and he awoke quickly. Moon said, "Go on to the trail. Now the sound of the monster is coming near." Then x̣ʷəné·x̣ʷəne ran. Moon said, "What kind of person are you?" The monster replied from above, "You just keep quiet. I'll eat you up." Moon said, "Come down, bad one.

You'll die tonight." The monster replied, "I am going to eat you, bad one."
Moon said, "Come, let us fight." Before he came down the fire was made by
Moon all around the red fir. The fire was burning. It blazed up. The monster
was yelling loud from above. "You bad one. I'm coming down, and I'll eat
you." The monster came down now as quickly as he could. He jumped down
into the fire. He cried and said, "I'll eat you up, bad one." Moon replied, "I'll
kill you. You'll die today." Moon stabbed him with the long stick. Only a few
times he stabbed him. Then the monster fell into the fire. Now Moon called
x̣ʷəné·x̣ʷəne. He said to x̣ʷəné·x̣ʷəne, "Gather wood." They gathered wood
and piled it on the fire. The red fir was burning. The flames shot up on the fir
tree. The tall fir tree blazed up. It was blazing far away on the mountains.
Then at last the monster burst and that was when he died. When he burst the
whole extent of the world was shaking. Then the tree fell down. Moon and
x̣ʷəné·x̣ʷəne stirred the fire. It was blazing and when it was blazing the white
ashes of the monster were flying about. The ashes were different. They looked
like birds. They became bats when the monster was burnt. Now it was day.
Moon said when he had finished, "There will be no monster on earth who
will eat people. The Monster is dead. The fine ashes have been formed into
bats. The bats shall not be monsters. They shall only fly back and forth in the
evening from the houses of the people in later times. The people shall have
homes. They will go hunting. They will camp under the trees and nobody
shall eat them. They shall return to their houses forever. No other monster in
the world shall kill people." Now it was done. Moon started. He said to
x̣ʷəné·x̣ʷəne, "You shall return home." Moon went to a creek and he made a
fire in the morning.

When he left his children, all his children were crying. His deserted wife
was always picking berries. One day when it was almost daybreak all the Children of Moon were crying. One of the deserted wives said, "Let us get ready
to go up the river." They all got ready. "You are always crying. Let us now
travel through the ocean. Then we shall go toward the landside of this ocean.
Then we shall go ashore in the river and go inland." Trout, their prettiest
child, was always crying. Then his mouth became large. Thus his mouth was
torn open on account of his crying for his father. Round became the mouth
of Sucker and also round became the mouth of White Horsefish. Bleeding red
was his mouth and blood dripped on the side of his chest because they cried

much for their father. The smallest one, the Fry of Trout, was always crying and his mouth became large. They were thus forever. They started with their mother. Their mother said, "Gather all your toys made for you by your father." Again the Children of xʷəné·xʷəne went up river, on this side of the opening and closing of our world. When they came to this side the two women said, "Our children are too many. Let us first go ashore to the land." The Children of xʷəné·xʷəne said, when they were camping near the water of the ocean, "Verily, we do not know which way Moon went. We have no way to find him. Let us desert him forever." Good women shall be deserted sometimes only. But they shall never die of crying. They shall get another husband. That shall be the way of the other people of later times.

Moon was walking along. In the afternoon he saw something appearing near the river. He went toward it. He found someone fishing with hook and pole, a boy. The boy had a big stomach. He had almost slender legs and slender arms. He had a good round face. He was very cross-eyed. He had a crooked nose and a crooked mouth. Moon said, "What are you doing?" The boy said, "I am getting food. I am fishing. Did you see what I have killed?" Behold, many, all kinds of bad bugs were lying near him which the boy had killed, salamanders, worms, frogs, and all kinds of bad bugs. Moon said, "Do you eat what you have killed?" The boy replied, "Yes. That is my food. I always catch this for a little food." "No," said Moon, "Do not always fish this way. Let me make fishing tackle for you." Moon made a fish hook. He twisted hair and he made it somewhat loose. He tied the string to a long hazel pole. He threw the hook on the water and as fast as it dropped he had a bite. He pulled it. Behold, they had killed a trout. He said to the boy, "You will fish this kind. This is all real food. Only they are made different shapes. You should discard what you killed before. It is no good food. They are only bad common water bugs." He finished. Moon said, "Who are you, boy?" The boy replied, "I am Sun. They say that my brother has been carried away before I became a child. My mother and my grandmother are named malé." Moon said, "You are my younger brother. Now go on. Let us go home." They went ashore and inland. They came to the prairie and came to the house. The boy said, "This is our house." They went in. malé was inside there with her mother. Moon said, "I am Moon." malé replied, "Oh, my Chief, now you have come back." Moon said, "Here I have come back." When he arrived he first talked with his mother and his grandmother. His mother told about the boy. "It is your brother. He is poor. He always plays near the bank of a creek." After the Mother of Moon had talked, Moon said, "Let me set right my little younger brother." He said to his younger brother, "Come." Sun came. He took him by the chest. He took him by the throat and all the bad things came out from inside. After he had done so he washed his face. He straightened his eyes and his nose and his throat. He wiped his eyes for him and his head. He wiped his body all over. He said to his younger brother, after he had finished, "Run to the river and bathe. First rub your hands with mud from the bank of the river." He finished doing so. "Then dive." After he had set right his brother Moon said, "I'll stay here for five days. Then I'll go again to set right the world. I found many monsters in the world. I killed them while I was coming." The malés replied, "First we shall have a feast gathering in our place." Moon said, "This, what you say, is true." He finished setting right the food for the people. The boy messenger went to the people. It was not long before they gathered, ever so many people. They were happy. They were playing in every way. That is what they are doing. Many girls came and helped the cooking. The food was done. Again there were more people. They arranged the place where they were going to eat. When they had done so the people ate. They came from everywhere as big as the world is, everyone who had been looking for him. He was with Bluejay, Beaver, Fox, and Coyote. Bluejay talked strong. He talked like a Chief monster. With them was x̣ʷəné·x̣ʷəne among the many monster people like many animals.[18] The people ate. All the people that were there were eating. They were stretched out ever so far. They ate. And after they had finished Moon talked to the people. "After we finish eating, I will thank you, friends. How you hurt my feelings if you come just to eat. Thank you. It shall be made this way for the Indians. The Chief shall feed them when he comes home from afar. Just that way shall be the Chiefs. First they shall talk and the children will play. They will be happy all day long. Thus it shall be later on. That is bad. I thank you." Again he said, "First we shall sing our tamanous songs tonight." It was night and the people sang tamanous songs. They made a fire and that far many fires were blazing. First the shamans talked about their tamanous powers. Then they sang tamanous songs. They began to sing and the others answered singing. They danced. At midnight they ate. After they had eaten then again they sang tamanous songs. When

day came they ate again. They always ate three times a day and they sang tamanous songs for five days. When they had finished only the shamans made
a potlatch after they had finished singing the tamanous songs in the morning.
Moon said, "First you will eat in the morning." They ate. After they had eaten
Moon said, "When we dismiss the assembly and when you go, then I will
again travel through the world. I am setting the world right. This is all. Thanks.
Now you have eaten. This is all." Then the people made a noise. Some got
ready and some were going. It was morning when their meeting ended. Then
Wren said, "I will first go to the mountain to hunt." He went. He arrived at
the mountain. He killed many deer. He dressed them and took them to the
house of his mother and grandmother. He often carried a great deal. The
malés dried the meat, much meat. Every day he went hunting. He always
killed much when he came home to his house. The food of his mother and
grandmother became much. He always walked about on behalf of his younger
brother. They worked very hard. Sometimes Moon got tired. He said to his
brother, "I'll be away for many days. I am going far away in the world." Then
Moon started. He walked very far. He always saw two old people. They had
five daughters. These girls were pretty. There Moon first ate. Another one was
living there. He had a camp on the bank of the river, far down the river. It
began to rain hard and Moon was wet although he was in the house of the
old ones. The roof of the house was leaking. The girls were looked at by
Moon. Moon thought, "I like one of these girls among the granddaughters of
Toad." The granddaughter of Toad was Frog, after Moon had thought of it. He
went hunting. He killed one elk. He carried home what he had killed. He
came to a creek. He waded and came to the bank. Then he dropped his pack.
Moon was wonderful. He decided what he would do to his friend the old
man. "Let me get married here. These girls are treating me nice." He tied up
his elk. He finished tying it up. He said to the pack, "If you are tied up by a
woman who has been going with some other man, or who is already known
by a man, then do not move, if a girl who knows a man tries to lift you. If there
is one who is still good you shall move and become light for she will be a
strong woman who will carry the elk. That one will be my wife." He went out
of the water. He went and arrived at the house. He said to the girls, as many
as there were, and with them Frog. She was the granddaughter of Toad. Moon
said, "I left on the river bank what I have killed. You shall get it." They got

ready and the girls whispered to one another. The one said, "Do not tell Frog about it." Toad said to her daughters, "Go and get the meat." The women went. Behind them went Frog. They came to the elk. First the eldest of the girls took it. She could not move it on account of its weight. Next another one took it. She could not move it. They came to the youngest one of the five girls. She took the elk. She tried very hard, but it could not move. And they gave it up. It was too heavy. These girls knew men. They laughed. Then they scolded Frog and one of the girls said, "What are you doing, bad one? What are you that you come along?" Again another one said, "Go on, take it and carry this food, bad one." After the women finished talking, Frog went. She took the meat and put it on her back. But the food moved. She arose. The other girls laughed. Then Frog walked and came near the house. Then she dropped it. There was Moon. Then the mind of Moon became different. "This is bad, what I made for myself. I do not want the granddaughter of the old woman. I really wanted the other girls but they were known by men. Never mind, I'll take the granddaughter of this old woman and make her my wife." When Moon finished wondering, he said, "Now break up the meat. We'll divide it." After this Moon took it to the house of Toad and put it into it. Then he had a wife. He went in and it rained. When the Chief was in the house of Frog it was raining hard. There was a rattling sound on the roof on account of the hard rain and also a gale was blowing. But the roof of the house of the old woman did not leak. She had made the house with her granddaughter. They had made it of big leaves of skunk cabbage. They made a roof of leaves. They had made it double. They had made the roof of the house very round on top and they covered the sides with mats. They had made a good door. Then no water could leak through. Inside, sticks were standing. They were strong and nothing could shake it even when a gale was blowing. The wind could not go through the inside. Moon stayed there and the bad weather stopped. When it was bad weather he only lay on the bed even when it was raining and a gale was blowing. It did not go through the inside. Now the bad weather stopped. Moon rose. Moon said to his wife, "Oh, your house is good. It does not leak. Your house is also pretty." He stopped talking. Then he went out. He went to get wood. He carried many limbs of bark and he gathered much pitch. After he had gathered wood he sat down outside. Now he was happy because he lived in a nice house. It was blue. It was shining and the house was good. Then

Moon said, "Chiefs shall marry women even if they are ugly. She must be a woman of a Chief's family, if she is not known by man, if she is still a good woman. All Chiefs shall be that way, and their children. When I get married with the granddaughter I shall stay with them forever, even if the woman has only a grandmother, but they are of a Chief's family. It shall be this way in the future. A handsome young Chief shall marry an ugly woman, if she belongs to a Chief's family. This shall be the way of the Indians in later times." He finished making this rule to be the rule of the future people.

He went in again and first they ate in the evening. After they had eaten they went to sleep. While they were asleep in the night the rain poured down. A gale was blowing and there was lightning. It was bad weather. Now it was day and the Wife of Moon arose. She cooked much food. She made much soup, she and her grandmother. Much food was cooked by them. Now her husband woke up. They ate. And after they had eaten Moon went and sat down by the fire. He said, "Your house does not leak even if it is bad weather." His wife replied, "Indeed my house is good. Nobody has a house like it. I made this house and my grandmother helped me." Moon said, "First, I hunt." He went to the mountains. He killed many deer and he carried them many times. When he had done so they broke up the meat in small pieces. They cut it in small pieces and they dried it in smoke. When he went fishing in the river he killed many salmon in the river. Then, when what he had killed was plenty, he called his wife. They carried the food inland to the house. Frog and her grandmother finished dressing it. After they had dressed it, they put it on sticks and raised it up high on long poles. They made a fire under it. Moon said, "That's the way the people will do in the future with fish. Thus the people will do all over the world." After he had talked Moon said, "Now I'll go home. I'll go to my grandmother and my younger brother and my mother. You shall accompany me." Frog said, "Let me first get ready." When she was ready they started. They went all the time. When it was almost night they came to malé's house. When Moon came to his mother, he said, "This woman is my wife. She and her grandmother belong to the Chiefs' family in another country." After he finished talking Moon went to look for his younger brother. He found his younger brother at the river. His younger brother was a big youth. Moon said to his younger brother, "I am looking for you. Let us go to your house so that we may eat good food. I have brought much good food. I have a wife now. You shall eat well." After a while they went. Now they entered the house. Their mother and the Wife of Moon finished cooking. Then the Mother of Moon said, "Let us eat." They ate. After some time they finished. Then they sat down by the fire. They were very happy, every one of them. They finished. Then they went to sleep. Moon said, "Tomorrow we look for much food, I and my younger brother, for you and my mother and my grandmother." After they had talked they went to sleep. When it got day, Moon made a fire. After starting the fire he heated much water. He went out. He fished in the river and while he was fishing Frog and her mother-in-law were cooking. Much food was done. Their food was done. They laid it down to be eaten. After they put it down they waited a while. Then Moon came in with many trout and also other fish. He laid it down. He came and they ate. After they had eaten Moon said, "I'll gather food with my younger brother." After they had talked they started off. They went to fish in the river. They killed much of everything. After they had done so they carried it home, every-thing. It was almost night, when they went to their house. The Mother of Moon had much food. Moon said, "This food is enough. Its amount will last for many years. Tomorrow, I and my younger brother will go." They went in and the Wife of Moon had cooked the food. The Mother of Moon said, "Now eat." They went and everyone ate. After they had eaten Moon said, "You shall sing this night." They sang so long, all of them. Moon was singing among them. Afterwards they went to sleep. When day came again Moon started a fire. Moon said, "This morning I am not going to work. I am very tired. I feel very tired. My work is very hard." His wife finished cooking. Then the Mother of Moon said, "Now come and eat." They went and ate. After eating Moon said, "After we leave you, my mother and my grandmother will always be happy and your hearts will be good, because we shall come back to this earth. I and my younger brother are going to leave you." They started. They went. Moon said to his wife, "You shall go with your grandmother. I shall follow you. If I find a good place where we may stay. At that time I'll come for you. I'll take you. I'll take your entire house." Now Frog went to her house. Moon and the younger brother went for a short time to the river. They came to the creek. Then they sat down on the bank of the nice creek. Moon said, "I am tired. My life on this earth is too hard and also your work is too hard for you." His younger brother said, "What you say is good. It's right." The younger brother stopped talking. Then Moon said, "I made this world good. I have killed all the monsters on earth. There were still many transformed monsters on this earth. I transformed all the bad ones. They have become animals. Only the good ones will be Chiefs in this world. You shall leave this world for a long time when other monsters will appear who make these people unhappy. Then we shall come back. Then also all the transformed animals will become people. Then again they will become people and their ways will be good. We are leaving all the people. They shall always be happy. Among them we leave my mother and my grandmother. They will be happy together with other Chiefs, the other people and my mother. They shall be the masters of this world. They shall be happy. They shall have good hearts always. We are going away from this world. We have finished setting right the world." After Moon had spoken they arose, he and his younger brother. They went to the house. They came to their mother. "We are leaving you now, I and my younger brother. We shall make something in the sky. It shall give light to this world. One shall shine in the daytime and one shall shine at night." Moon said after he had finished talking, "Goodbye, Mother, may you always feel good." The mother said, "Goodbye my son, take good care of yourself that you may not be hurt." Then Moon and his younger brother started. Moon said, "Let us start from the east (up river). First I'll start in the day. You, my brother, shall go in the night." Then they went east in this world. Moon started in the morning. He went about in the sky. He went well. He reached a point far away in the evening. He had almost burnt the world with his heat. Everything in this world burned. Then the younger brother came in the night. The younger brother came. Nobody could see well in the night and they were almost afraid in the night. The world was very disagreeable in the night. They came down. They walked up above. Then Moon said, "You shall go in the day." Then his younger brother went in the daytime. He himself went during the night. Then the world was not really hot. Nothing burnt. Then Moon came in the night. He came in the night. Then it was well for the world below. The cold in the night was right. He went and it became day. They went up above. Again they tried. They walked. It became day and it became night. Again it was day. Again it was night. They did so for four days. Moon said, "Now we are work-ing well. Now maybe we'll do this forever." Moon said, "First we will go home. I'll go to get my wife." They came down again. Moon came to his wife. Moon said to his wife, "I come to get you. Get ready all your things, she and her grandmother." The house of Toad was broken up by Moon and his brother. They made a bundle of it and tied the roof with a strong rope. It was very round. They wrapped it up. Moon said after that, "We shall rebuild it in the way it was before, when we reach there where we are going." First Frog said, "We eat first." They ate. After they had eaten Moon said, "Now let us start." They went. They carried all their things and their food. They went up above this world. They got there. Moon said, "You, my younger brother, you will travel away. You will travel in the daytime, every day, for ever so long. Then we shall come back. I shall travel forever in the night time. We shall shine for the people, I and our mother. It will be day and then it shall become warm during the summer. The people shall always have light." Then the younger brother went. And Moon went during the night. The world was made good. The elder brother came in the night. He traveled the whole night. Then it became daytime. The world was not disagreeable. Moon said, "Now we are right forever. It will be thus when we travel through the world. I shall always travel with my wife. Where the night stays, that shall be my world. Where the day stays it shall be your world forever." Now they traveled. Moon said, "Now we finished this world. This world shall change when we'll straighten the world again. Thus we have finished." Ososos.[19]

Bear, Yellow Jacket, and Ant

Jonas Secena

A long time ago the people lived like animals. Once upon a time one day Bear said, "This day is too short. I want more. I am always hungry in winter. It would be well if we make the night a year. One night should be one winter and a day should be one year. One summer would be one day. Then we should eat blackberries and anything else during the summer. When the winter is here when all the berries are gone, then it would be night all through the winter and all the people will sleep. It will be one winter. That is the way the world would be best for the people."

Then Yellow Jacket said, "No, it would not be well if the world were this way: it should always become day and again night. The day and the night should be short." Then Bear said, "Night and day are too short. That is tiresome. I never sleep and then it is day."

Then Yellow Jacket said, "Hold on, wait. I'll go to get Ant." Then Yellow Jacket went to the house of Ant. He came to Ant. "Oh, my younger brother, I am asking you, how should this world be? Bear said it should be night for a year." Then Ant said, "That would be impossible for the people. It would be impossible for the people. It would be impossible if they have the world thus." "Very well then the world shall not be thus. If the world were thus we should die of starvation."

Then Yellow Jacket said to Ant, "Listen, my younger brother, I came to call you. Get ready now, let us go." Then Ant said, "This is difficult, maybe I will die. I have discovered supernatural power. Now I shall use my supernatural power. Oh you, my elder brother, Yellow Jacket, let us make a good belt." Then they made a belt. After the belt was done Yellow Jacket said, "Wait a while. Let us dance before we go after Bear." Then they danced before they went to Bear. "Let us now go to Bear." Then they finished dancing. They started off and walked. Then they arrived at the house of Bear. They reached Bear during the day. When Bear saw them he laughed. "Oh, you, my younger brothers, now you have arrived here where we are arranging the world." Bear said, "Now let us sleep for one year. Then in the spring the day will come. At that time all the people will awake. One summer will be a day, thus the world shall be made." Ant said, "No, the world should not be made that way. It would be impossible for the people if the world were that way. Day and night should just be short." Bear said, "No." Then Ant said, "Let us bet. Let us sing and see who will sleep first. The one who will sleep first will lose, and those who will not sleep will win. If we beat you, then days and nights will always be short. If you beat us we shall sleep one year." Then Bear said, "This is good." Said Bear, "Let us dance."[1] Now it was night. Then they spread out the batons. First Bear started,

> One year will be a day
> One year will be a day
> One year will be a day
> One year will be a day
> One year will be a day

Then Yellow Jacket and Ant started, "Wait, make the belt tight, then start your song." Ant helped singing and Yellow Jacket sang this,

> Day, Day, Day, Day, Day

Then Ant helped,

> Day, Day, Day, Day, Day

Then they finished and Bear said,

> One winter one night
> One winter one night
> One winter one night
> One winter one night
> One winter one night

Then Bear danced and Yellow Jacket and Ant danced. Then they tied their belts tightly.

Day, Day, Day, Day, Day

And Bear's tune was,

> One winter one night
> One winter one night
> One winter one night
> One winter one night
> One winter one night

Then Yellow Jacket said,

> Day, Day, Day, Day, Day

They danced until the morning. They danced until daylight came. They did not eat. They danced until night came. Then Bear said when they started off on the second night,

> One year will be a night
> One year will be a night
> One year will be a night
> One year will be a night
> One year will be a night

Then he finished and Ant sang the third time,

> Short shall be the days
> Short shall be the days
> Short shall be the days
> Short shall be the days
> Short shall be the days

They did not eat until morning. Then Ant said, "Let us tighten our belts." They danced that night and Bear started the fourth night,

One year will be a night
One year will be a night
One year will be a night
One year will be a night
One year will be a night

One summer will be one night
One summer will be one night
One summer will be one night
One summer will be one night
One summer will be one night

Then Yellow Jacket started singing the fourth night,

Day, Day, Day, Day, Day

They danced until the morning and they did not eat. Then Ant said to Yellow Jacket, "Let us tighten our belts." They danced that night.

On the fifth night Bear sang,

One winter one night, one summer one night
One winter one night, one summer one night
One winter one night, one summer one night
One winter one night, one summer one night
One winter one night, one summer one night

Then Ant started singing,

Day, Day, Day, Day, Day

He danced. He danced almost the whole day and then for five nights before day came. Then Bear became heedless. They danced until it was almost morning. Now Bear went to sleep. Then Yellow Jacket sang,

Short will be the night, short will be the
day, Bear is asleep

Short will be the night, short will be the
day, Bear is asleep
Short will be the night, short will be the
day, Bear is asleep
Short will be the night, short will be the
day, Bear is asleep
Short will be the night, short will be the
day, Bear is asleep

They stopped after the fifth night and Yellow Jacket and Ant won at that.
Yellow Jacket and Ant said, "That will be the way for the people in later
times. The night and the day will be short after this. The people will be different, only Bear shall sleep one winter." Bear fell asleep when it was getting
cold. That is the end. From that time Yellow Jacket and Ant were always enemies of Bear. Therefore when Bear finds an anthill or a beehive he destroys
them. He destroys their house and he eats up Ant and Yellow Jackets. That
is the end.

Addition

When first they bet their bodies were straight.[2] For five nights and five days
they were singing. They were always tightening their belts. When they finished they were almost cut in two. When they finished their bellies were
always thin. They were that way when they tightened their belts without
having eaten, although now they used water. Therefore, Bee and Ant were
almost cut in two.

A Visit to the Skokomish

The Chehalis went to the Skokomish. When the Chehalis arrived they were given to eat. Food was placed before them. They were given to drink. It was some soup that they were given to drink. They sat down in this way, many Chehalis. Then one of the Chehalis said, "I am dying of thirst." He said, "Could you please give me water to drink?" One of the Skokomish came and gave him water. When he finished drinking one of the Skokomish said, "One of the Chehalis is drinking water. Maybe they do not like this food." And in the same way they exchanged all of it. It is different. They drink before they eat. Thus they broke the rule of the Skokomish. It is as though he had said, "I do not like the food."

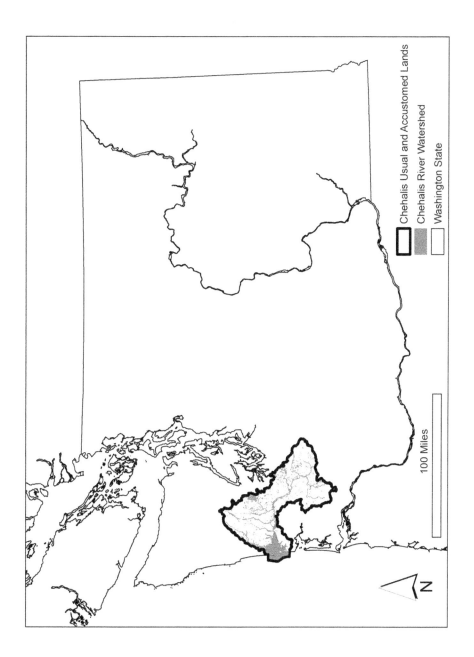

Map 1. Chehalis Usual and Accustomed Lands. GIS data courtesy Washington State Department of Natural Resources. Created by Jolynn Amrine Goertz.

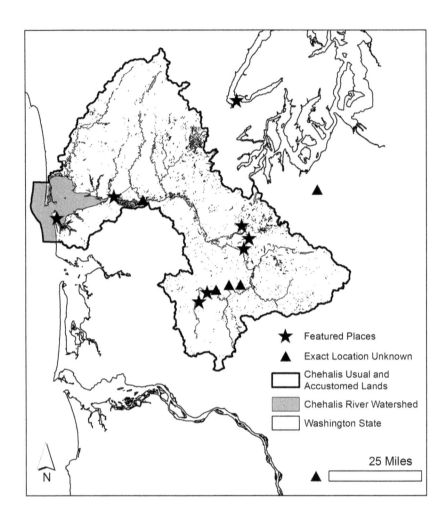

Map 2. Locations mentioned by George Sanders in *Honne, the Spirit of the Chehalis*, edited by Katherine V. W. Palmer. GIS data courtesy Washington State Department of Natural Resources. Narrative data from Katherine Van Winkle Palmer and George Sanders, *Honne, the Spirit of the Chehalis*. Created by Jolynn Amrine Goertz.

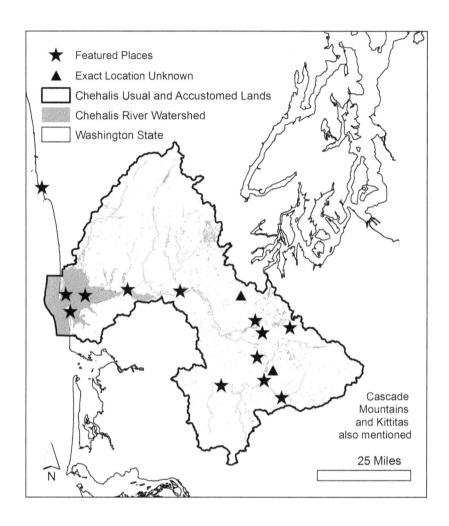

Map 3. Locations mentioned by Upper Chehalis storytellers in *Folk-Tales of the Coast Salish*, by Thelma Adamson. GIS data courtesy Washington State Department of Natural Resources. Narrative data from Thelma Adamson, *Folk-Tales of the Coast Salish*. Created by Jolynn Amrine Goertz.

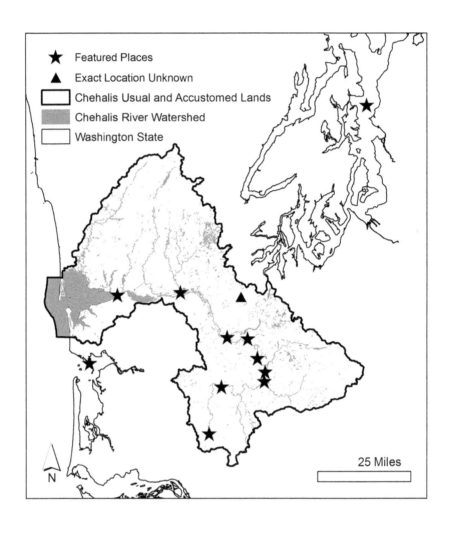

Map 4. Locations mentioned by both Lower and Upper Chehalis storytellers in *Chehalis Stories*, by Franz Boas. GIS data courtesy Washington State Department of Natural Resources. Narrative data from Franz Boas, *Chehalis Stories*. Created by Jolynn Amrine Goertz.

Fig. 1. Franz Boas, the father of American anthropology, in 1920.
Courtesy of the American Philosophical Society.

Fig. 2. Robert Choke, teller of "x̣ʷə́n and Bluejay," with his grandmother Sally.
Courtesy of Lewis County Historical Museum, Chehalis, Washington.

Fig. 3. Peter Heck, teller of "The Flood," in front of a cabin. Photograph taken by Edmond Meany during his visit to the Chehalis Reservation in 1905. Courtesy of University of Washington Libraries, Special Collections, NA1156.

Fig. 4. (*left*) Blanche Pete Dawson (right) provided Boas with much linguistic and literary material, including stories such as "Chipmunk," "The Deluge," and "The Five Brothers." Courtesy of Elaine McCloud.

Fig. 5. (*below*) Jacob Secena, sisína?xn, Chehalis storyteller and grandfather of Jonas Secena, was reputed to have been born in the late eighteenth century and to have remembered the time before European contact with Chehalis people. Photograph taken by Edmond Meany during his visit to the Chehalis Reservation in 1905. Courtesy of University of Washington Libraries, Special Collections, NA1159.

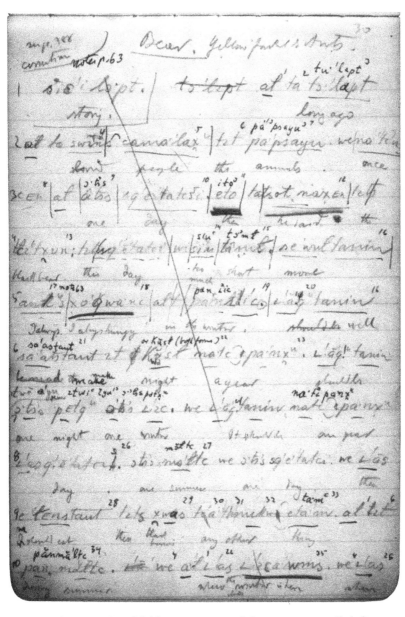

Fig. 6. Boas's "Bear and Bee" field notes. Boas recorded stories in Upper Chehalis and then made interlinear English translations of these texts. Courtesy of the American Philosophical Society.

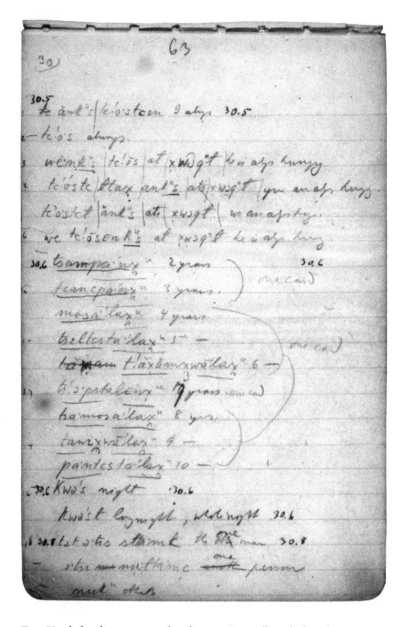

Fig. 7. Vocabulary lists correspond to the texts Boas collected. These lists were usually supplied by Jonas Secena or Blanche Pete Dawson. Courtesy of the American Philosophical Society.

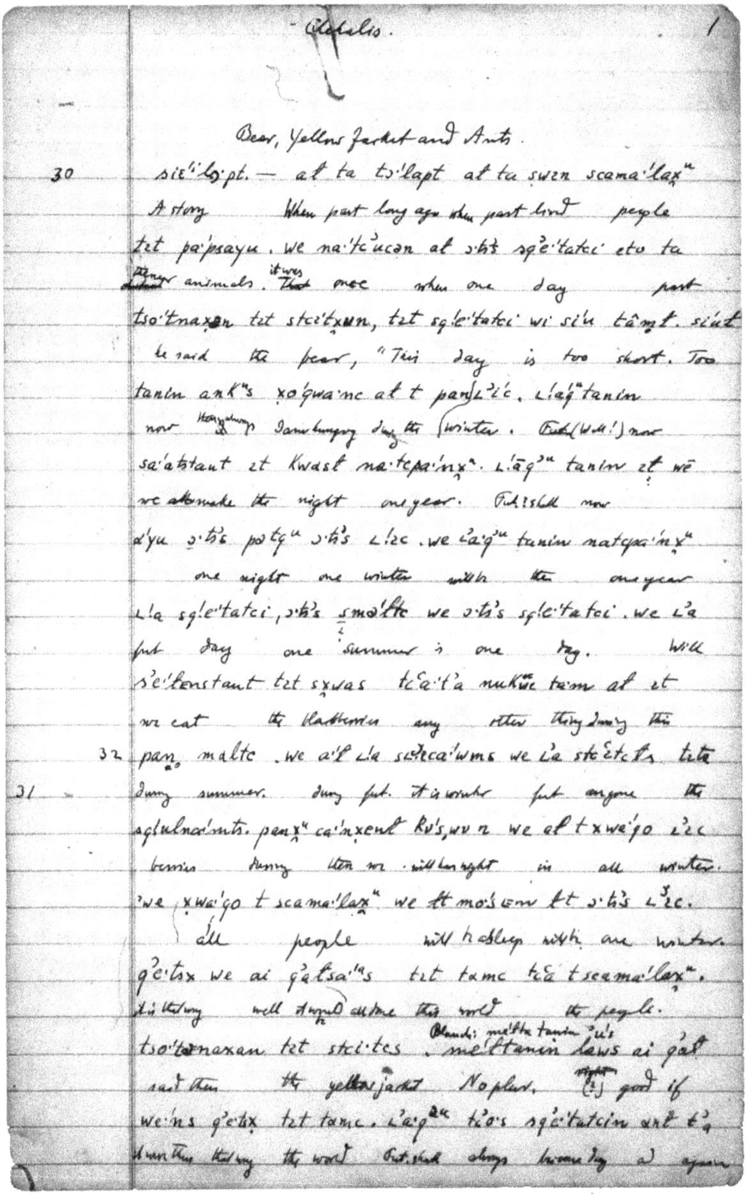
Chehalis.

Bear, Yellow Jacket and Ants.

Fig. 8. A handwritten manuscript shows how Boas revised his field notes into more polished prose. Courtesy of the American Philosophical Society.

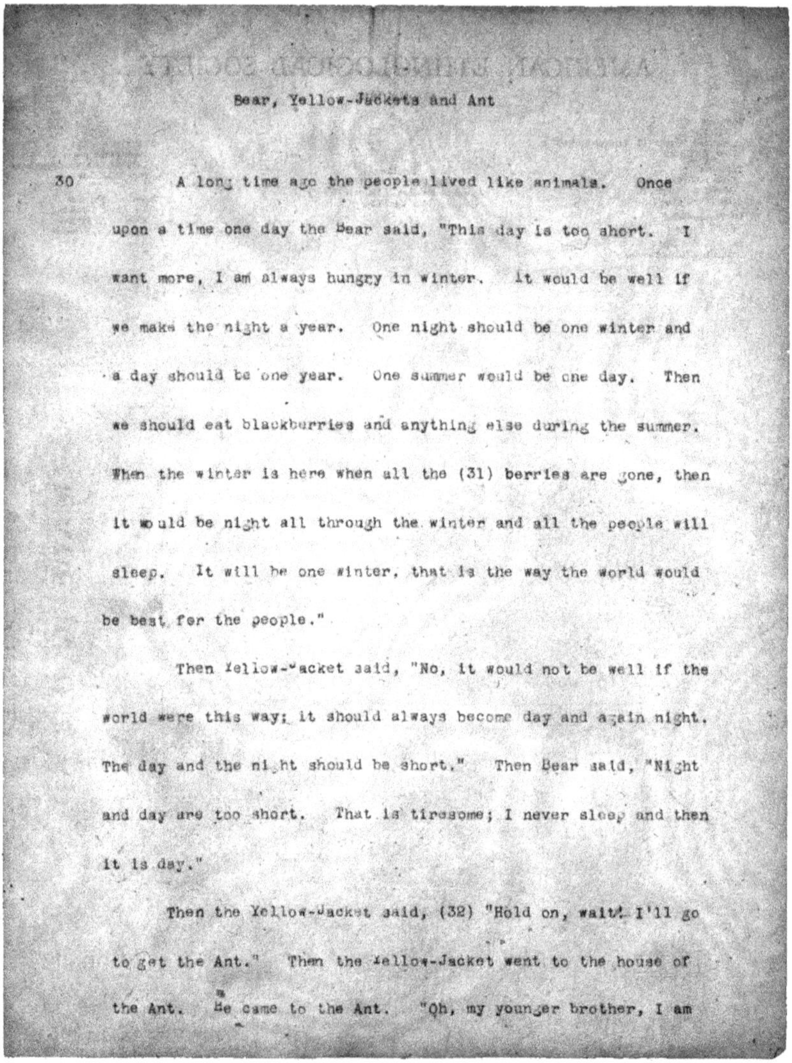

Bear, Yellow-Jackets and Ant

30 A long time ago the people lived like animals. Once upon a time one day the Bear said, "This day is too short. I want more, I am always hungry in winter. It would be well if we make the night a year. One night should be one winter and a day should be one year. One summer would be one day. Then we should eat blackberries and anything else during the summer. When the winter is here when all the (31) berries are gone, then it would be night all through the winter and all the people will sleep. It will be one winter, that is the way the world would be best for the people."

Then Yellow-Jacket said, "No, it would not be well if the world were this way; it should always become day and again night. The day and the night should be short." Then Bear said, "Night and day are too short. That is tiresome; I never sleep and then it is day."

Then the Yellow-Jacket said, (32) "Hold on, wait! I'll go to get the Ant." Then the Yellow-Jacket went to the house of the Ant. He came to the Ant. "Oh, my younger brother, I am

Fig. 9. The typescript shows the text prepared for publication. Courtesy of the American Philosophical Society.

Gossip

One kind of gossip was taken. It was bad. He did not want this gossip to be known by anyone. That person said, "It always causes trouble." He said, "Let me make it so that there is no talking." He took the bad gossip. He hollowed out a round rock. It was a large rock. He put the bad gossip into it. He put it into the rock and shut it up. After he finished closing it, he stuck pitch on it. He put mud over the place, where he shut it in. Then it was shut in firmly. He finished and went home to his house. This hollow stone, hollow inside, is far in the woods. That person stayed many days. He said, "Now I have put away the bad talk. Now there will never be bad gossip." Then one of his own people came and said, "The people are talking. They say you have done something in past days and you are to blame, they say, about trouble with some women." That person said nothing. The one who brought the news went away. That person said, "I have put away a bad thing so that it will disappear in the hollow stone. I thought I had put away the bad gossip. Let me go to the rock. I'll examine it." He came to the rock. He looked at it and rolled it over. Then he saw another hole underneath the stone. "The bad gossip must have made a hole through the stone. The talk would have disappeared, but the evil gossip that had been put away made a hole through the hard stone. Being strong, it made the hole."

Snowbird

In the beginning there were the new people in the world. All the animals were people. In the beginning of the world the people were transformed. All the people were animals. Sometimes they had trouble. They killed one another. After they had finished killing one another they became good and they remained good.

The Children of the Northeast Wind always came and killed the children here. The Children of the Northeast Wind came from above, from the sky. There were seven. There were that many. They were Chiefs of the People of the Sky. At that time there was a star of the darkness. The star, he always hunted the lives of the children in this world. And when he killed the lives of the children they died. It was bad for the children of this earth. He is a star of the night and his name is Elk. The Children of this Northeast Wind always came and attacked this world. When the Children of the Northeast Wind came, the world froze and the people died. They killed people in every possible way. Every year the people assembled to fight the Children of the Northeast Wind. But they could not kill them. Then all the animal children said, "Let the people now assemble everywhere in the world. Let us make a plan. Let us have a war. It has now come to the point that we shall fight, everyone here in this world. The Children of the Northeast Wind always make us very poor. We'll have a war with the Children of the Northeast Wind. We'll go after them up to the sky." The people finished planning. They sent a messenger to the Southwest Wind. The Southwest Wind was an old woman. The old woman was a Chieftainess. She had many children, young men and some girls. The messenger came to the old woman, the Mother of the Children of the Southwest Wind. The messenger said, "I am calling you to the assembly, all the children, you and all your children. Now the people of the world are going to make war upon the Children of the Northeast Wind. They say you are the Chief of these here. All shall be Chiefs in this war. You, Southwest Wind, shall first plan before there will be a great war. We are making a great war in the other world beyond, because we have come to be too poor. He makes us poor. The Children of the Northeast Wind make us slaves." The old woman said, "I am going to be there. I am going to make many baskets and I will make some baskets with little holes, here in this ocean. If you should be beaten I shall fly up. I shall carry the basket with small holes. Hot water will be inside. When the Children of the Northeast come, when you are defeated, my children shall take the large basket with holes. Nevertheless, my children shall go from the sea to the shore the way you are planning. I and my daughters, we shall be making arms by night. We are not going to rest." The old woman finished talking. Now some of her children went with the messenger. They went and arrived at the meeting of the animals. All the children were filling up the world with their number, all, everywhere in this world. Now some people said, "Let us sing. We'll make a trail on which we can go to the sky." Everybody tried and all gave it up. Then Bluejay said, "Oh, my people, all of you, I want to tell you I know a youth. He is a great shaman. He has hidden his power. He said to me that he has power. He can bring it down in small pieces. He can bring down the sky." The people said, "Is he here?" That was Snowbird.[1] They looked for him. He was not found in the assembly. Bluejay was sent to go and get Snowbird. Bluejay went. He came to Snowbird, "Oh you, my younger brother, Snowbird, I came to take you to the assembly. Now the people of this world have a hard war with the Children of the Northeast Wind." Snowbird arrived. Snowbird said, "Damn the Children of the Northeast Wind. I thought so long ago." They went to the assembly. When Snowbird reached the gathering he first shouted five times. Then he called his supernatural power. Snowbird said, "Let me first send word to the Children of the Northeast Wind that we are going to have war with them." They finished singing words through the supernatural power upward. Then they sang. It was day and it was night. It was day again and it was night. On the fifth night, then the blue sky came down. The edge came down and lay on the earth early in the morning. It was not yet really daytime. The edge of the sky was a good place, was a good place for the children to travel on. The people stopped singing and Snowbird was paid with a nice black cap. He was told, "This will be your hat when we have war." Then they finished singing. They finished playing Snowbird. The Children of the Southwest Wind were running ahead because they were the leaders, because they were made Chiefs in this war. Now Snowbird went along with the Children of the Southwest Wind. The other warriors went along, that monster warrior Snake. From here on Snake always makes war. He is always the warrior. War is always in his mind. He was cross-eyed. He was going to fight hardest. He was going to kill many children in the other world. Now went following them the common warriors. They went. They had not been going long when they were met by the Children of the Northeast Wind. One of the Children of Northeast Wind was killed by the Southwest Wind. One was running to a place near a hill in the bluish country. He was pursued by Snake. He was shot. A little while he lasted. Then the child of the Northeast Wind died. These were killed by Snake in the beginning. Now two Children of the Northeast Wind were dead. In the beginning they pursued another one. They went far. They could not find him. First they camped on a nice creek in the other country. Everything was really different there. It was very cold. It was blue all over. They camped. It was not very dark at night. They came. First they ate their lunch. They pursued them and went round a large hill. They had not gone far before they came to a level place in that blue land. You could not see the edge of that world. They saw level land. There were many people like little black spots with the many enemies. They went toward them. They came near and began to shoot. They fought the others with fists. They were fighting until night. Again it was evening. Many people were dead. For four days they fought. When day came, on the fifth day, they defeated them. The Children of the Northeast Wind were dead. Now the short one of the Children of the North-east Wind died, the Chief of the blue country. The stars belong there to the blue country. They were always fighting. When they got there the Children of the Southwest Wind attacked them. The Children of the Northeast Wind got away from them. They fought for five days. They did not rest. They did not eat. The Children of the Northeast Wind went far away. The Children of the Southwest Wind went after them for many days. They could not find them. They reached the creek. Cougar said to the Children of the Wolf, "They, the band of the wolves were many." Cougar said, "Let us rest at this creek." The Children of the Southwest Wind said, "Never mind, let us first eat." They stopped. First they drank at the creek. They ate. Then one of the Children of the Southwest Wind said, "Let us stay here for many days until we have plenty of wetness. Then let us fight again." For many days they stayed at the creek. Those who delivered arms and bows always came and went back down. The others stayed there a long time. Now early in the morning they attacked the enemies. Then the Children of the Northeast Wind were still fighting. They were fighting very hard. Now a child of the Southwest Wind was hurt. They were wounded and also the Chief of the Wolves. Many young men, the Children of the Wolf, died. They killed one more of the Children of the Northeast Wind. Now four Children of the Northeast Wind were dead. They hurt the star of the night whose name is Elk. They wounded him badly, but he did not die. Then the Children of the Wolf and Snake became furious. They said, "Now let us fight. When we are done then we'll rest." Then they fought harder. The people of the upper world did not run away although many of them died. They were many. Many corpses were piled up. Blood was running over the blue land. The blood flowed through a gulch. It flowed like a creek. For many days they fought. They defeated the Children of the Northeast Wind. They ran away after they had been fighting hard. They scattered everywhere. They ran all over the large country when the Children of the Northeast Wind and stars and all the people retired in the blue land. They were badly wounded. Then one of the stars said, "Let us take a rest first with the war. After a short time we shall fight again within a few days." One of the Children of the Southwest Wind said, "We shall not stop the war, not until we kill all the Children of the Northeast Wind and the night star. Then we'll stop." The Chief of the Stars said, "We, the stars, belong to this country. You have badly wounded the one whose name is Elk. He is the night star who shall never fight again for he has been hurt badly." The Chief of the Stars stopped talking. Then all the people engaged by the Children of the Northeast Wind went. They were going now. One of the Children of the Southwest Wind said, "Now we have wounded all over the body of that bad star. He used to take the lives of the people below." The Chief of the Stars said, "It is said, the star warrior stopped fighting. He was one of the bad ones against us. We have taken away his weapons. Let's now go back." Now they went back. Everyone who was alive came and returned below, all the various people and the Children of the Southwest Wind. They counted all the dead in the blue country. They missed one warrior belonging here. One of them said, "One of us did not come. Maybe Snake killed him for us." Snake had for her youngest sister Frog. Frog was always crying in their house. She always said, "Oh, my elder brother, the cross-eyed one, must have died." He lay down. He was cross-eyed. Frog was crying all the time. She was saying this. Then Snake came back. He heard Frog crying. Snake said, "Oh, bad one, what are you saying?" He hit Frog hard and Frog almost died. Snake said, "I shall never have you again as my sister, bad one. You displeased me very much." They went to the assembly. It was not long before they were attacked by the Children of the Northeast Wind. When the Children of the Northeast Wind came they fought. The Children of the Northeast Wind had with them much snow and hail and much ice. These were their new helpers. They always go with them when they fight. Seven was the number of the Children of the Ice. They came with many others from the sky. They fought with all the people of this world. They were making war from morning until night. It was the third day and they were always defeated although they fought as hard as they could. Then came the Children of the Southwest Wind with the baskets with many holes. And they spilled hot water from above. Then the Children of the Snow died. It could not be used against ice. On the fifth day a messenger was sent to the Mother of the Children of the Southwest Wind. He came to the old Southwest Wind. He said, "Let us take the basket with the small holes. Now all my girls will go because we are being defeated and every one of us, the Southwest Winds, we shall go that we may kill the bad ones, that the Children of the Northeast Wind and the Children of the Ice may be attacking us." When they finished getting ready the old Southwest Wind said, "Now my children, all of you must go. I'll go behind you with my next daughter. Then I'll use that big basket." Then her relatives, the clouds, were sent by the old one. The Children of the Southwest Wind had all gone. Then the old one said to her daughter, "Now let us go." She said, "Our weapons are strong." Then they started very late in the evening of the fifth day. They had been fighting for five days. Now the Children of the Southwest Wind got to where they were fighting. When the water was emptied they went back to their country, to the sea, and they came again. The old man and her daughter always came this way. They spilled it from above from the basket with small holes on the Children of the Ice. Now one died who was the real leader of the Children of the Northeast Wind. Then the two little ones gave up[2] for there were now only two Children of the Northeast Wind, leaving[3] five that were dead. They said, "When our people are fighting, let us now run away up[4] so that only we may be alive of our whole family." Then two Children of the Northeast Wind ran away. The Children of the Ice said they were not worth anything. "We will fight until we are dead, every one of us." They fought. That night they sprinkled a fine rain from the small holed basket. It made the world warm. There was steaming fog in the world. Nothing could be seen. It was sprinkled all the time over the Children of the Ice. Then all the Children of the Ice died. And those who had been engaged by the Children of the Northeast Wind and who were alive ran away when it was almost day. One Chief of the Blue World said, "Now we'll finish this fighting. Nobody shall make an attack from the Blue World." Now they all went. Then they went to get Snowbird. Snowbird was told, "Let us now take off the ties from the sky." They went to get him. The bands were untied by Snowbird with his supernatural power. Then the blue sky went fast. That was the end of the war with the Children of the Northeast Wind. The Children of the Southwest Wind said, "This shall be the end of the killing of the Children of the Northeast Wind and of the Ice. We have killed all the Ice. It shall only freeze on this earth and it shall be snowing, but after this the Ice and the Northeast Wind shall not kill anyone. It shall be different now for the future people. Nothing shall come from above to kill the people. This is finished forever for the people of later times."

Rabbit and Mountain Lion

Rabbit was a gambler. He always gambled with all the monsters. He always won over his enemies because he had a spiritual helper, a strong helper. He always referred to his songs. He always referred to the sky. Therefore he was strong. Even if a monster wanted to kill him he would overcome him because he had strength of heart. He had strength from the sky. Although he was a little person he always won over all kinds of monsters. Rabbit was camping on the bank of the river. He was there for many days after he had killed Grizzly Bear. He killed Grizzly Bear for cheating him. After he had killed him he went down the river. It was not long before he arrived where he was staying. He always had it in his mind to play slahal.[1] He was in his house on the bank of the river. This was only his camp. It was not his house. His house was far away. He, Rabbit, always used his helper in all he did. He always sang. Everywhere in this world he went he gambled. Once in the morning he was singing a little. Then Mountain Lion came. Mountain Lion came and sat down on the other side of Rabbit's fire. Mountain Lion said, "Oh, brother, I am a great gambler. I have heard that you always beat the other gamblers. Let us gamble. I'll bet you my blanket for your blanket. Let us try each other, younger brother. If you beat me then we will know who is the real gambler. I am Mountain Lion. Mountain Lion is my name. I am a monster gambler. I beat everybody." Mountain Lion stopped talking. Then Rabbit talked. Rabbit said, "I am Rabbit. I always gamble with my supernatural helper. Nobody ever beats me. We shall not gamble just for fun. Let us really gamble for a heavy bet. I'll bet you your blanket with other things." Mountain Lion replied, "I am not afraid of you. I'll beat you." "I'll bet you all your property," said Rabbit. "Take off your clothing. I'll take off mine. We shall pile them up near the fire near the tally sticks." Mountain Lion said, "Let us put them here in the middle." Rabbit said, "All right." They put them down that way. After they had been betting Rabbit said, "Let us first arrange our seats." After they had arranged their seats Rabbit made a fire, a big fire. After he had made the fire he thought, "This Mountain Lion is a monster. He always eats people. Maybe he wants to cheat me. I shall make a pile of my dung. I'll get it ready after a while. They shall be little round balls. I shall keep them hot. I shall throw it on the ice and thus I shall fix the monster. Mountain Lion is a monster. He is known by everyone. He certainly is a monster." After Rabbit had thought so he went to the fire. He sat down. When he was seated he put up the tally sticks. After he put up the tally sticks he took the baton. He took his bones and threw them to Mountain Lion. Rabbit said, "Now we start." They drew for the deal twice. He got the first deal. After Rabbit sang,

I scrape the bluest sky.

Rabbit shouted five times. He talked about his supernatural power. He said, "Only I have supernatural gambling sticks therefore I always play slahal." Mountain Lion laughed from the other side of the fire. Mountain Lion said, "You braggart. I am going to win by and by." After he had talked about his supernatural fire Rabbit began again. He began to sing a little,

I scrape the bluest sky.

Three times the guess was missed. Then he had five tally sticks. Five times Mountain Lion had missed. When they started Mountain Lion said,

Hoy, I'll swallow the whole body,
I'll swallow him whole.

Rabbit missed five times. Then he hit it. Rabbit said,

I scrape the bluest sky.

He missed five times. Mountain Lion, he said,

Hoya, hoya.
I'll swallow the whole body,
I'll swallow the whole.

It was again missed once. Rabbit hit. Then Rabbit said,

I'll scrape the bluest sky.

It was missed five times. Mountain Lion hit it. Mountain Lion said,

Hoya, hoya,
I'll swallow the whole body
I'll swallow the whole.

Then he did not hit it. Rabbit said,

I'll scrape the bluest sky.

Mountain Lion missed three. First Mountain Lion pointed. He reached across the fire, then stretched out his hands and his body. He stretched the whole length of his body and almost he struck out with his claws. Mountain Lion said, "Oh, my younger brother, I almost struck you." But Mountain Lion wanted to eat Rabbit while he was trying to get hold of him. He wanted to grab the face of Rabbit. Rabbit won five sticks. Mountain Lion had just one stick left when he hit it. He said,

Hoya, hoya,
I'll swallow the whole body
I'll swallow the whole.

It was missed four times. Then Rabbit hit it. Then it was day. Rabbit said, "Let us take a rest first." Mountain Lion said, "Oh, younger brother, let us do so." They took a rest. It was freezing outside. The water froze all over. Then Rabbit heated his dung. He went across and filled his dung over his tracks so that his ice thawed. He spilled it in the middle of the river, much of it, so that when Mountain Lion got there he would slip and the ice would break under him. After he had spilled it across the ice he went across. Then he made more dung. After that he made a fire and put his dung near the fire. Then he went to the place where they were gambling. He came to the place where Mountain Lion was lying down for a little while. Mountain Lion said, "Oh, younger brother, I was asleep. I just woke up. Now let us start gambling again." Rabbit replied,

"I didn't sleep yet for I have been looking at the ice on the river. Let us start our gambling." Then Rabbit said,

> I scrape the bluest sky.

Mountain Lion tried. He stretched his claws across the fire and he almost got Rabbit. He ducked quickly and he missed him. Then Mountain Lion said, "Oh, younger brother, your house is too narrow. I almost struck you." Mountain Lion missed four times. Then one time he hit. Mountain Lion said,

> Hoya, hoya
> I'll swallow the whole body,
> I'll swallow the whole.

It was missed five times. Then Rabbit hit it. Rabbit said,

> I scrape the bluest sky.

Mountain Lion hit it. Rabbit did not get any tally sticks. Mountain Lion said,

> Hoya, hoya
> I'll swallow the whole body,
> I'll swallow the whole.

Rabbit hit it. Rabbit said,

> I scrape the bluest sky.

Again Mountain Lion hit it. Mountain Lion said,

> Hoya, hoya.
> I'll swallow the whole body,
> I'll swallow the whole.

Rabbit hit it. Rabbit said,

I scrape the bluest sky.

It was hit. They were hitting each other. It was evening. Then they were eating. Rabbit was always grabbed in the face. But he always ducked quickly. Therefore he did not catch him. Mountain Lion would always say, "Oh, younger brother, I almost struck you." They were gambling all night. They beat each other in gambling. Day came. When it was day Rabbit said, "Let us rest awhile." And Mountain Lion said, "Let's rest." First Rabbit went out. He made some more dung. And after that he made a fire under it. His dung was near the fire. He took some of the dung to the river. He went across over the ice. And he spilled the dung over his tracks. Then he went ashore and piled up some of it upon the bank of the river. He picked out the dry ones which were very round. Some were round like discs. He piled them up. Then he went across to where they were gambling, he and Mountain Lion. He went in. Mountain Lion was lying down for a little while. When he came, Mountain Lion sat up. "Let us start," said Rabbit. "Never mind elder brother. We will gamble and if we beat each other we will stop." Rabbit started singing,

I scrape the bluest sky.

They gambled. It was evening and when it was night Rabbit almost lost, all but one. Now he gained them back. They gambled and day came. Rabbit said, "Let us rest for a while." Mountain Lion said, "Oh, younger brother, let us take a rest." Rabbit went out. He went to the fire. First he poked the fire, a good fire. It was a big fire. Then he put some more dung near the fire. After that he gathered some of his dung and took it to the river and he spilled it clear across. After he had done so he went back across and came to the bank of the river. He went to where he was always gambling with Mountain Lion. He came to Mountain Lion. Mountain Lion said, "I am waiting for you here. Sit down now." Rabbit sat down. Rabbit started first. They gambled until the evening and Mountain Lion was always beaten. Mountain Lion always cried, "Oh, younger brother, I almost hit you." They bet for what was tied in bundles. It was lying between them and it was almost day. Rabbit had one tally stick left. Then Rabbit thought. He said, "If I miss the last tally stick I shall finish. If he misses I'll run outside." Then Rabbit sang as loud as he could. Mountain Lion pointed and he missed. Rabbit opened his hands and shouted. He jumped. Mountain Lion said, "Bad one, you have beaten me. You will die this morning. I'll curse you and eat you." Mountain Lion jumped. He growled and made loud noises. He ran outside but missed Rabbit. They left their stakes. Mountain Lion came to the bank of the river. He became afraid that the ice would crack under him and he would slide under it. Rabbit said, "Oh, elder brother, why don't you come across?" Mountain Lion answered, "No, younger brother, this ice might crack." Rabbit said, "No, the ice cannot crack. See, I'll throw these round stones." He threw it on the ice and the round balls said, "Tl tl tl tl." Mountain Lion said, "I shall not go across. You had better come to this side. Then we will gamble again." Rabbit replied, "I am not going across. I beat you. I am not going to gamble any more with you. Come to this side and let us fight on this side." Mountain Lion said, "I cannot cross. The ice might break under me." Then Rabbit went to the pile of dried dung. He took it and threw it about over the ice. "Tl tl tl tl." Many times Rabbit threw it. He said, "Look, it made a loud noise." "Oh, probably indeed," said Mountain Lion. "Now I am going across." Rabbit said, "Look out for my tracks. Cross over there." Now Mountain Lion went as quick as he could. Rabbit jumped. He took a long nice pole. He took it. Mountain Lion said, "Oh, bad one, now I am going to eat you." He came to the middle of the ice and his foot slipped on the dung of Rabbit. He got up and as soon as he got up his foot slipped again. The ice broke under him and he fell under the water. He kicked as strongly as he could. Then Rabbit pressed him under the water and it was not long before he was sunk. He lost his breath and Rabbit pushed him under the ice. Then he was dead. Then Rabbit ran for their stakes. He put on his clothing. He beat Mountain Lion. "These mountain lions are many. There are people living far away in another country. They always eat those with whom they play. I have beaten him in gambling. I killed the bad one. After this nobody will eat the one with whom he gambles. The people will only play slahal in later times. Nobody on earth will eat a gambler. The Chief shall only gamble. They shall be happy. The other people shall be glad. That will be the way of the people later on."

Bluejay

Marion Davis

Bluejay was sick and for many days he lay down. Then he said to Náw because she was his sister, she should step over his face. Náw said, "No, I cannot step over your face." Bluejay said again, "Step over my face, Náw." Náw said no. Bluejay said, "I am going to die if you don't step over me." Bluejay was grunting. He said, "My breath is almost gone." Bluejay said again, "Náw, my breath is gone." Then Náw stepped over his face. Bluejay said, "You are stepping too fast over my face." Bluejay said again, "Step over my face slowly." Five times Náw stepped over the face of Bluejay. Then Bluejay said, "That will do. It is alright." Bluejay got well because Náw had done as Bluejay had said because Bluejay had been told by a supernatural power that now he would get well like everyone else. They lived in one house. Now she was in love and Bluejay arranged a wedding to the ghosts. He assembled the people because Bluejay was going to give a wedding. Bluejay placed his people on his side. He placed to whom he was going to give the marriage feast on the other side of the fire. Then Bluejay began to sing, how he had examined Náw. Now Bluejay sang. He said, "What was it you showed me, Náw?" five times. Now Náw was taken to the ghosts. Bluejay stayed alone in the house. Bluejay thought, "I will follow Náw to the ghosts and see how she lives with her husband." Then Bluejay started to visit Náw among the ghosts. He started and he came to the side of the river of the ghosts for the living place of the ghosts was on the other side of the river. First Bluejay rested. He came to the river and shouted for a canoe in the same way as we people shout here, "Hou." No one came for him. He shouted again. Nobody came to get him. He shouted again. He was not taken across. Now the sun was out. Then he shouted again and he was not taken across. He shouted for a canoe and he was not taken across. Now the sun set and Bluejay got tired of shouting. Bluejay was sleepy. Bluejay yawned. He yawned and now the ghosts came to get him. One canoe came but there was no person in the canoe. Still the canoe came quickly. Only bones were lying in the bow of the canoe. He stepped down into the canoe and went aboard. He came to the bones lying in the canoe. He kicked the bones aside. The canoe had holes. Bluejay went across. He could hardly get across. Then he landed and looked for Náw. He found Náw in her house. Then Bluejay told about the canoe that had taken him across had holes and bones were lying in the bow of the canoe. "I kicked them." Then Náw said to him, "What made you kick your brother-in-law who brought you across?" Bluejay said, "How is it that I should have a brother-in-law who was only bones? I did not know that he was my brother-in-law." Now Bluejay lived among the ghosts. When it was night for Bluejay then bones always arose just like people, as we are. Whenever it was day for Bluejay bones were lying about. Bluejay was always walking about. Whenever he got to the bones he kept on kicking about those bones. He came to one bone. It was small, evidently a little child. Bluejay kicked it again. It was night again for Bluejay and these bones woke up. The bones woke up. They cried on account of the little child who had been kicked by Bluejay. Behold! He was a Chief. All the ghosts were crying. Náw said, "If you go about on the ground don't trouble the bones whenever you come to them. Don't kick them for they are people. They are just sleeping." Where Bluejay was he thought the ghosts were shouting, "A whale is coming ashore." Their whale was floating down but it was a big fir tree. They said it was a whale. The fir tree was the whale of the ghosts. It was not a whale for Bluejay. It was just wood for Bluejay. Bluejay always went to get wood from this tree because Bluejay was getting wood here in this country. When he made a fire the pitch of the wood of the tree always melted. The children came to the fire of Bluejay because the pitch of the wood was always melting when it burned. Bluejay was surprised. He said to the children, "Stop children, you will stick to it. Stop, get away from the fire for the pitch is melting. You will stick to it. Get away children." Then she forbade Bluejay, "Don't say get away, get away, children. This pitch is their food. It is their grease for them." Just now Bluejay learned that the fir tree was their food and therefore he had always forbidden the children. Bluejay was thinking of going home. He said to Náw, "I'll go home tomorrow." Night came and the next day Bluejay was told by Náw and his brother-in-law, "I will let you take your water bucket. You will have five buckets for five prairies when you go. Five prairies will be on fire, therefore you must take five buckets. You will spill it little by little over the five prairies. When you come to a prairie and you come to the first prairie take one of your buckets, sing and say, 'Lɛts, lɛts,

lɛts, lɛts.' Then extinguish it and you will go across." Bluejay came out and came to one prairie. He came to a second prairie. Then Bluejay took again some water. He said, "Lɛts, lɛts, lɛts, lɛts." His water was gone. He took another one and poured out many bucketfuls. He took another one and poured out many bucketfuls. "Lɛts, lɛts, lɛts, lɛts." Then the water was gone. He took another one, "Lɛts, lɛts, lɛts, lɛts." Then Bluejay got burned. He had used up his water. After two prairies all the water of Bluejay was gone. It was enough for five prairies and through two prairies Bluejay had used up his water. Bluejay was burned. Bluejay was dead just on the second prairie. It was all gone. It was prepared for the prairies. Then Bluejay went back again for now he was dead. He went and came to the river where he got tired of shouting when he was alive. Now he was dead like the ghosts. Now he shouted in the same way as the ghosts shouted. He yawned, "Hau, hau, hau, hau, hau." They came for him with a new canoe. He was taken across and went to Náw's house. He told Náw, "A good canoe took me across. Wherefrom did they take this good canoe? They are really people here in this country." Náw said, "Oh you are dead like these people here, these people are dead and you are dead because you were burned, therefore you come back to this place. You are just like these persons, therefore everything seems good to you. When you were alive and you came everything in this country was not right for you because you were alive but you got burned. You will probably go across where whoever is burned goes across the river for there live those who are burned. He is there now. He lives there forever." But the bluejay we see now is a spark of the burned body of Bluejay. If he had come back from the ghosts we should be able to visit the ghosts.

Mink

Marion Davis

A Chief lived near the shore of the sea. That Chief had a child. She was a girl. They always wanted to buy this girl to have for a wife. That girl said, "I do not want to marry." From everywhere great Chiefs came wanting to buy her to be his wife. The girl always said, "I do not want to marry." Mink came to find out that this girl was there and where she lived. Mink traveled there. When he walked along the girl smelled him and the girl said, "It smells as though Mink was walking along near the house." The girl would smell him. She said, "It smells like Mink nearby here." When Mink walked about she smelled him.

One night Mink saw a person coming. Oh, what a person! He rolled himself up from the water and rolled himself this way. Again it was night. Mink watched as he was always rolling himself from the water, the one who rolled himself stayed with the girl. The girl dug a way at the side of the house, way down into the ground. Then the one who rolled himself lay with the girl. Mink thought, "That girl is committing adultery." He made five sharp sticks which he hardened in the ashes so that they should stick in the person who always rolled himself. Mink was ashamed that she always complained whenever he walked about near the girl. The girl used to say, "Hm, hm, hm. It smells like Mink walking about. Hm, hm, hm. It smells like Mink." He made sharp the five sticks in the ashes so that they would be tough and not easily break. Then Mink put them into the ashes and after he had finished the five sharp-pointed sticks he set them up where the one who always rolled himself came up to stay with the girl. Mink was watching when the one came who rolled himself. It was night again and for five nights Mink was watching the sticks which he had finished. Then he saw the one come again who was rolling himself. He came to the first sharp stick. Mink heard that the stick stabbed the person. There was a dull noise of striking the ground when the stick stabbed the person. He came rolling along. Then another one stabbed him and cut him. Again one cut him. He was cut by the five sticks Mink had set up. Then the one who came along rolling went back. He came to the water and died in the morning. At that time one person saw him in the water. He saw that evidently it was a whale. Evidently a whale has drifted to shore. He came to the Chief, the one who had the girl. He said, "A whale had drifted ashore on your beach." The people of the village told one another and all assembled from all over the country because of the whale that had drifted ashore in front of the house of the Chief who had the girl. The whale was cut up. It was divided among all the people. The Chief who had the girl cooked it. When the whale was all done he went and asked the girl whether she was hungry for food, for a little piece of the whale. The girl said, "I am hungry for whale." So they took the meat to the girl. The girl ate. There was grease on the mouth of the girl. It was grease of the whale on the mouth of the girl. Mink walked along. He peeped in and saw the greasy mouth of the girl. The grease was near her nose. Mink said (in Nisqually),[1] "You should eat slowly your secret lover," five times. The girl looked around. The girl thought, "This is my lover whom I love." Again Mink said, "You should eat slowly your secret lover." Then the girl really understood what Mink said. She threw away what she was eating. She did not eat it because she really understood what Mink said to her. It was night at that time. She took her sharp bone pin to commit suicide. She stabbed her heart with the pin. The girl wrapped her blanket around her head. When day came in the morning the girl did not arise. They went to look after her. The girl did not get up. They looked for the girl. She was still asleep. Five times the woman whose child she was looked for her. Then she was called when they thought she was just sleeping. Behold! She was dead because the pin had struck at the middle of her heart. She died because she loved her secret lover. When she was dead the people were crying. Mink thought, "What shall I make out of myself? Let me be a boy, or a youth, or an old man. Let me be an old man." Mink went and from there he came and he cried, "I will walk along." When he was nearby he fell down. When he was quite near he fell again. He came to a stick and scratched his knees so that his knees were bleeding. He came crying like this (in Puyallup), "Grandchild, grandchild." Mink was seen. His knee was bleeding. He was falling again and again. Then the old people said, "Take the old one and put him near his granddaughter." The Mink was crying. He almost fainted and fell down near the ground. Then the people said, "Where shall we bury the Chief's daughter?" The people did not know. The people said, "Let the old man say where he wants to bury his granddaughter." Mink said, "Let it be far from the house. Prepare my granddaughter's body." They did as Mink had told them. They put the girl in a canoe and hung her up high on a tree. After they had made the grave the people went away. One day Mink waited near the grave. He pulled the canoe together with the body that was in the canoe because Mink thought, "Oh, my friends, I have five friends. I will take this woman so that they will cure her, that they make her alive." He took her up the river where the friend of Mink lived. He took her first to his friend and they treated her and she did not come to life. He was told by the one who tried to cure her, "Take her to your other friend further above." Mink took the woman along. She did not come to life. He was told by the one who tried to cure her, "Take her to our friends above." Mink took the woman and carried her to his other friend. He said to her, "Your sister-in-law nearly died." They treated the woman and the woman began to move. She just began to move but she could not open her eyes. Mink was told, "Take her to the great new shaman, your brother." He took that woman to the great shaman. He started taking her along. Mink lay down with the woman for she was to be his wife when the woman was going to wake up. "Take her to the great shaman, your friend." Mink took the woman up the river. Now Mink was happy. He always lived with the woman. Mink took her to his friend, the great shaman. He brought her there. Mink said, "Here now your sister-in-law is nearly dead." The shaman uncovered the upper end of his house. He said to Mink, "Lay down your wife in the middle of my house." Mink did so. Then the shaman opened the upper end of the house and sprinkled water on the woman. She moved a little because she came to life when the water was sprinkled over her body. Mink just had the woman for his wife because she had come back to life.

Mink said, "Let your sister-in-law go home." Then he pushed the canoe up river to go home. He came to the house of the woman. She came to her father and mother. Her parents were happy on account of what Mink had done. He said to his wife, "Let us go and get fry." The hired workers of the woman, her relatives,[2] arrived. They became proud. They gave him the hired men of the father of the woman. The hired girls were his, so Mink just stayed in the canoe. He and his wife did not paddle. They were always sitting down in the middle of the canoe. They came to the place where the fry was. The hired women were told, "Now dive and look for what we are trying to get." The hired ones dove and they got some. Their mistress always made bundles out of it. The woman ate it. Mink was told, "Do you want some?" Mink spoke aloud. He said, "No, no." The woman ate. Mink was told again, "Do you want to eat some?" "No," he spit it out. Five times Mink tried the food of his wife. He rolled it about in his mouth and spit it out. "It is bad. It is not at all good. It is bad, bad, bad." They said to Mink, "Eat it, it is good food." Mink was given some. He rolled it about in his mouth and Mink threw it out. He called and said, "It must be better. Bring it here. Let me roll it about in my mouth again." It was given again to Mink by his wife. Mink rolled again the fry about in his mouth. Then Mink said, "Oh, this is good food." Then Mink ate. He ate and ate. Then he said to his wife, "Let me undress. I myself will dive. I'll look for food." His wife said, "No, we have our hired help.[3] Let them dive. They are bringing it." Mink said, "Oh, let me dive." Then his wife said, "It is your wish. Dive if you want to dive." Mink dove. It was not long before he emerged and he had one. He dove for a long time before he emerged again. He had many. He dove still longer. Then he emerged and he did not stay long before he dove again. He stayed a long time. Then it was said, "What has become of Mink?" He did not come up and they looked under the water but Mink did not come up again. Then the hired help looked into the water. Mink was seen and his backside was swollen. Then the hired help said to their mistress, "Look into the water at your husband." The woman looked in the water. Behold! There was Mink, her husband. The woman said, "Take the paddles. Paddle quickly. We must leave him because it is Mink, the one I married." Mink was left there under the water. His wife and her hired help went far away. When Mink came up there was no canoe. Way over there a canoe was going. He was deserted because she recognized that Mink was her husband. She took her child and Mink the boy swam. When Mink came up he said, "My child shall stay with your grandchildren."[4]

The Flood

Peter Heck

There was a bird[1] who married a wife. When it got day in the morning he would never wash his face. He just ate. He was told, "Why don't you wash your face?" It was night again. Day came in the morning and again he did not wash his face. He was told, "Why don't you wash your face?" Again it was evening. Day came in the morning and again he did not wash his face and again he was told, "Why don't you wash your face?" Day came in the morning and again he did not wash his face. He was asked, "Why don't you ever wash your face?" "It would be dangerous for you if I should wash my face." Night came and day came in the morning. He said, "Now I wash my face." He went down to the river. He said, "Now keep inland, my relatives. Now I am going to wash my face all the time." Now he washed his face. His face was streaked with dirt. He scratched down with his fingers making streaks along his dirty face. Then it was raining all the time. It was raining always. The water began to rise and the water became larger and larger. The flood came up to his house. Then they moved inland from the houses. It was not long before the water reached them. Again they moved inland and it was not long before the water reached them. Again they moved inland and it was not long before the water reached them. Again they moved inland and the flood came. They went aboard their canoes and they stayed in their canoes. They put up a post in the water to tie the canoe to. It would not take long until the post to which they had tied their canoes was under water. Again they moved the post to which they had tied their canoes and it was not long before it was under water. Again they moved the post to which they had tied their canoe and it was not long before the flood came. Again they moved the post to which they had tied their canoe and it was not long before it was flooded. Again they moved the one to which they had tied their canoes but they never touched the ground. The water was deep. The world was flooded all over. They could not see any land anywhere. There was water all over. They drifted this way. The canoes were side by side and they were drifting. Everything in this world was dying. Then the Muskrat dove and emerged holding some mud. He put it down. He dove again and emerged. Again he had a handful of dirt. He put it down. He dove again and emerged, again with a handful of dirt. He put it down. He dove again and emerged again with a handful of dirt. He put it down. Then the earth showed above, large enough for houses of the people. They landed on that land. And they stayed. Now the water was flooded the land all over. The people drifted about. Several drifted away. Muskrat made land, therefore these people did not die because they landed and had a home. Therefore they drifted and would not move away with the rest of the people. It got day on the earth and the people lived on the dry land. (masíɬčʼi, Black Hill, a mountain between Chehalis and Olympia, which Muskrat made).[2]

Skunk

There were x^{w}ə́n[1] and Skunk. Where they stayed they were hungry. They had nothing to eat. "Oh, younger brother, tie your belt, younger brother. What shall we do when we are hungry? When we are hungry we will call the Spring Salmon." Then the Skunk tied his belt. Now his stomach blew up. He was getting sick. He went out. Now x^{w}ə́n shouted to Spring Salmon, "My cousins, my younger brother is dying. Come, cousins, my younger brother wants to see you." "There is noise of an old man who shouted saying that his younger brother is dying. Let us go and see." They went there. They got there and from far away they heard him groaning. They entered. Indeed, he was sick. The stomach of the sick one was bloated. They got there. The sick one said, "Goodbye, cousins. Goodbye, you outside." "Now help me so that we may take him out." "All right, now cousin you hold the lower end. I'll hold his head. I will take it and we lift him." They took him out. "Now younger brother, break it." They took him out. When they were outside he broke wind. He broke his belt. The wind went out of his bloated belly. It smelled badly and Spring Salmon were smothered there. They dropped headlong. "Get up now you dog. Hit him over the head." He got up. He took a stick. He knocked him over the head and killed him. Now they had food. x^{w}ə́n put it on a spit. It was done and now he ate it. It was not long before he had eaten all. He did not give anything to Skunk.

"Oh, younger brother, our food is all gone. Tie your belt. Well, what are we going to do?" Skunk tied his belt. "Now I am going. I will call my cousins, Steelhead Salmon. My younger brother is dying." And the other spoke, "An old man is speaking, saying that his younger brother is dying. Let us go." They went to see. They went and arrived. From far away they heard him groaning. They went in. Indeed, his stomach was bloated. They sat down, "Oh, my younger brother is very sick." "Goodbye, you outside. Goodbye, you outside." "Well cousins, help him." "All right. You take him at the lower end I'll take him by the head." They took him out. Then he broke wind, his younger brother. He broke his belt and he broke wind. "Now get up, bad dog. Hit him over the head." He took a stick and knocked him over the head. He killed them all.

Then they had much food. x̣ʷə́n roasted them on a stick. They were done. Then they ate. It did not last long. Then they had eaten all. He did not give anything to Skunk. They were hungry and had nothing to eat. "Oh, younger brother, tie your belt. What shall we do when we are hungry?" Then Skunk tied his belt. "I will go and call my cousin." "Oh, the old man says his brother is sick. Let us go and see." They went. They got there. They entered. Indeed, he was sick. They sat down. "My younger brother is very sick. Oh, goodbye, you outside. Goodbye, you outside. Cousins, you hold him at the lower end, I will lift his head." They took him outside. When he was outside he broke wind. He broke his belt. His wind went out. He fell down headlong. "Get up, old dog. Hit him over the head." He got up. He took a stick and knocked him over the head. They killed all of them. Now they had much food. They put it on the fire and cooked it. When it was all done he ate it all. He did not give anything to Skunk. They lived there and were hungry. "Oh, younger brother, tie your belt. What shall we do? We are hungry." Skunk did not want to tie his belt. Finally he tied his belt. "I will go to call my cousin, Porpoise. My younger brother is dying." "Oh, the old man is talking. He says that his younger brother is dying. Let us go and see." They went there and arrived. They entered the house. They got there. Indeed, he was sick. "Oh, cousins, my younger brother is dying. Goodbye, you outside cousins. Goodbye, you outside old men. Oh, cousin, you take him at the lower end, I'll take him by the head. All right." They took him and lifted him and took him out. Then he broke wind. "Let your wind go out." They dropped down headlong. "Get up. Hit him over the head." He took a stick and hit them over the head. He killed them all. He carried them into the house. Singed it,[2] cooked it and when it was done, he ate. Skunk was going to eat the food. They ate it all. Then they had no food. "Oh, younger brother, tie your belt. What shall we do? We are hungry." Skunk did not want to tie his belt because he had never given him any food. He was forced to tie his belt. When he was willing to tie his belt, "Oh, younger brother, I will go and call our cousins. Oh, cousin Sea Lion." "An old man is calling. He says his younger brother is dying. Let us go and see." They went and arrived. Indeed, he was groaning. They entered. They sat down. "Oh, cousin, my younger brother is dying. Goodbye, you outside." "Oh, cousin, help, so that he may see the outside before he dies." "All right, old man." "At the lower end, cousins, take him. I shall take him by the head."

"Very well." They lifted him. Then they took him out. "Break wind, younger brother." He broke wind. The wind went out and they dropped him. He fell down on the ground. "Oh, old dog, he always does like this." A stick was taken and xʷə́n was hit. He jumped and they hit him again. He ran and escaped. He was taken. He was killed. He was burned up and his ashes were blown. He was told, "You will just be Skunk for later generations. Nobody will die when a skunk blows on him. You will just be Skunk."

x̣ʷə́n and Raccoon

There were x̣ʷə́n[1] and his younger brother. They were hungry for something to eat. "Oh, younger brother, let us work, younger brother." They went
hunting. They found bark and sap. They found it and they went home. They
reached there and x̣ʷə́n put it down under his pillow. This he wished. Raccoon did the same with his. Now they went to bed and they went to sleep.
Then Raccoon got up. He went to the house and climbed up the roof. He
went in and took dried salmon. Then he came down. He went home and he
arrived. He took what he had wished for and threw it away and he put the
dried salmon under his pillow. Then he went to bed. When day came in the
morning he lifted his pillow to look at his wish, but there was nothing. It
was just the same sap. "Oh, younger brother, get up. Let us look at what we
wished for." Indeed Raccoon got up. He had not done anything. Then Raccoon opened his, and what had been his wish had become dried salmon. "Oh,
younger brother, give me some, younger brother. Mine did not become anything. That is good, younger brother. Let us wish again." They went hunting
again for sap and bark. Then they went home and put it under the pillow.
Raccoon went and took his. He climbed up to the roof and went in. He took
dried salmon. Then he came down. He went home. He arrived there and put
it under his pillow. He threw away what he had wished for. Then he went
to bed and went to sleep. In the morning when day came x̣ʷə́n got up and
looked at his wish. Raccoon got up. x̣ʷə́n looked at his wish. There was nothing. Raccoon went to see his and opened it. What should it be but salmon?
"Oh, younger brother, only you get your wish. Give me some, younger brother.
Give me some to eat. Oh, younger brother. Good is what you wished for. Let
us go again hunting for bark." They went to bed. Raccoon went to the house
and climbed up to the roof. He went in and took dried salmon. Then he came
down. He went again and went home. Then he put it under his pillow. He
went to bed and went to sleep. In the morning when day came x̣ʷə́n said, "Oh,
younger brother get up." Raccoon got up. x̣ʷə́n looked at his wish. There was
nothing. Raccoon looked under his pillow. "Oh, younger brother, only you get
your wish. I do not get it. You always succeed. You get something. Let us go

by and by." Then they started. They went there to a house. He got there and Raccoon climbed up. Then he went in. Then Raccoon took it and he went out. He came down and Raccoon went in. He had taken a basket full, full of dried salmon. He lifted it and took it out. Then he fell. He fell into the house. Those in the house woke up. They made a light, and what should it be, the basket was lying down there. Then the stick was taken and x̣ʷə́n was beaten. x̣ʷə́n jumped. x̣ʷə́n was chased out of the house. He got up and ran out of the house. Raccoon was there. "What have you been doing now?" "I was going to take out a basket full of salmon and I fell and I was almost killed." "You went to steal too many and then you fell. I do not get too many and therefore I never fall. You took too many."

x̣ʷə́n Kills k'ʷə́cx̣ʷe

A long time ago there were monsters in the world: k'ʷə́cx̣ʷe. She, whose name was k'ʷə́cx̣ʷe, was a big woman. She was a good-looking woman. She always killed people. She had a home near the mountains, near a creek. She was a strong woman and tall. She always went fishing. During the summer she went to dig roots, camas, and fern roots. When the berries were ripe in summer she also went to pick berries. The young men were always disappearing. Then two youths said, "In summer let us go to the berry patch on a warm day." The other one said, "All right," and they went to the berry patch. One of them was still a boy. The other one was full grown. They said, "Now let us go." They started off and they went and came to the berry patch. They ate the blackberries from the vines. Then they heard something like singing from a thimbleberry patch. She was eating thimbleberries from the bushes. They went quite far away. k'ʷə́cx̣ʷe did not see them. One of the young men said, "It is a girl. It is a woman." "Nobody is here," said the youth to the boy. "Let us go after her, younger brother." "It is too far, she might kill us. She might be a different sort of person. She is too large and too big. Let us go home." The youth said, "Why should this one be a different kind of woman? I will go after her and I will make her my wife." He said, "Let us go and get her." Then they went to get her. They came to the thimbleberry bushes and they arrived there. Then the elder youth said, "Elder sister are you picking berries?" k'ʷə́cx̣ʷe answered, "Yes, I am picking berries. I am eating thimbleberries from the bushes. Which way are you going?" The young man replied, "I am looking for you." Then k'ʷə́cx̣ʷe laughed. The other one, the younger one of the youths, snuck away. He hid in the thick bushes. Then he looked on. Then he heard k'ʷə́cx̣ʷe talking with his companion. The big woman talked well to the man. She did not act like a monster. Then the woman said to the youth, "Oh, you are looking for me, I will take you to my house." The youth said, "Very well, let us go to your house." k'ʷə́cx̣ʷe laughed. "I will take you to my house. You shall always stay in my house. You shall never go home. Whenever the others have come to me they wanted to desert me, therefore I do away with them. If you stay in my house nothing will happen to you. I will look after you well." The

youth said, "Very well, I will go with you for good." k'ʷə́cx̌ʷe said, "Now let
us start off. My house is not far away from here. Near the creek is a trail. My
house is not far." At that time k'ʷə́cx̌ʷe was laughing. She was very happy
now. Then they went. They had not been going long before they arrived at
the creek. They came to the house of k'ʷə́cx̌ʷe. They entered at once. The
other youth was always sneaking behind them, when the woman who was
his companion went into the house of k'ʷə́cx̌ʷe. It was almost night. The day
was almost at an end. Then he said, "Let me go home." He went home to his
house. He was at home to talk about him. He went home. Now k'ʷə́cx̌ʷe was
alone with the other youth. k'ʷə́cx̌ʷe was very happy because she had a good
youth. That youth had k'ʷə́cx̌ʷe for his wife. k'ʷə́cx̌ʷe cooked food. When the
food was done she put it down at the eating place. She put down their food.
k'ʷə́cx̌ʷe said, "Now let us eat." k'ʷə́cx̌ʷe had all kinds of food. The youth sat
down. He said, "You have a great deal of food. You are cooking well." k'ʷə́cx̌ʷe
laughed. "You shall always eat in this way, only you shall never go away, you
shall stay near my house. I make you my husband and you shall stay in my
house all the time. When I have kept others they always deserted me. They
wanted to leave me, therefore, I always kill them. I always cook the bodies of
these men." The youth said, "I like you very much. I shall always stay in your
house." k'ʷə́cx̌ʷe laughed. "Oh, younger brother, you will be my little, younger
brother. I will keep you in my house. I shall take good care of you." They ate.
They finished eating. Now it was very dark. Then k'ʷə́cx̌ʷe said, "Let us go to
sleep." She took her husband to her bed. Her husband slept. k'ʷə́cx̌ʷe went to
the fire. She put it out with water. The fire was extinguished and it was dark.
She went to sleep. She slept with her husband. When day came they got up.
The youth said, "Nothing is better than what I had last night. Now I have
found what is good." They started.

k'ʷə́cx̌ʷe was cooking. She finished cooking and they ate. After they had
eaten, k'ʷə́cx̌ʷe went for a little while outside. She came to look for her husband. He was still inside. k'ʷə́cx̌ʷe said, "Oh, you, my husband, you are good
to me because you do not want to leave." "I shall not go away. I shall always
stay in my house." The youth laughed. They stayed many days and they
always ate. When they finished eating they went to sleep in the evening and
in the day they always stayed in the house. They stayed in all summer. The
youth got tired. He got sick and died. k'ʷə́cx̌ʷe cried. She took her husband

and made a place for him. She made a grave for the youth. She went out and k'ʷə́cx̣ʷe was always crying. She always said, "Oh, my husband is dead, the one I loved."

x̣ʷə́n walked along the trail. x̣ʷə́n passed along the trail. x̣ʷə́n was walking. He was seen by k'ʷə́cx̣ʷe. k'ʷə́cx̣ʷe said, "Oh, turn aside. Let us eat first." x̣ʷə́n replied, "Oh, I heard that my younger brother died." k'ʷə́cx̣ʷe replied, "Indeed he did. I just made a grave for your younger brother." x̣ʷə́n replied, "My sister-in-law, you are my sister-in-law, I used to love my younger brother. You are like my younger sister and now you will take care of me. First I will travel. After a little while I will come back when it is very dark so that nobody may know about us." x̣ʷə́n went. He came to the relatives of the youth who had died. x̣ʷə́n reported, "I have found the house of k'ʷə́cx̣ʷe. I have been looking for a long time for the child of k'ʷə́cx̣ʷe because the oldest sister of k'ʷə́cx̣ʷe has cheated me. The young men always disappeared. Today I have found her. I shall go away with her tonight. Your boy has died. k'ʷə́cx̣ʷe said that he was sick and then he died. I shall heat stones." He heated stones to burn k'ʷə́cx̣ʷe. He finished heating the stones. He put out the fire and wrapped up the stones inside of his clothing. Then he started and went along the trail. He went so long until he came to k'ʷə́cx̣ʷe when it was very dark. When he arrived he first stood outside. k'ʷə́cx̣ʷe heard him. k'ʷə́cx̣ʷe went out. "Oh, you have come. I have been waiting for you for a long time." x̣ʷə́n answered, "Oh, sister-in-law, I waited until it was dark. Now I have come to you and I will stay here forever." He finished, then k'ʷə́cx̣ʷe laughed. "Come in quickly." x̣ʷə́n said, "Well, go ahead." They went in. k'ʷə́cx̣ʷe went to her bed. She lay down. "What are you waiting for?" He lay down. He said, "It is not well when your eyes are open. You better shut your eyes." k'ʷə́cx̣ʷe shut her eyes. She shut her eyes tightly. Then x̣ʷə́n took the hot stones and struck them into the heart of k'ʷə́cx̣ʷe. She cried only once and then k'ʷə́cx̣ʷe was dead. He cut her neck. It was very dark and x̣ʷə́n had no way to travel. He thought, "Let me camp here then I will start." He stayed in the house of k'ʷecx̣ʷe. When it was day he piled up dry wood and pitch wood and he burned up everything in the house. He went out. He burnt everything all around. He burned the house. It blazed up and blazed all over. Then the body of k'ʷə́cx̣ʷe was burned. It burst and everything was consumed and then x̣ʷə́n sat down. x̣ʷə́n said, "I killed k'ʷə́cx̣ʷe because she was cheating my young men. She always ate the people. There was nobody who could go to her house. Young men shall take wives when he finds a strange girl and he shall not die. Married couples shall love each other. I killed k'ʷə́cx̣ʷe. Nobody will any more be afraid of her in this world. Thus the people will do later on."

x̌ʷə́n and Bluejay

Robert Choke

Once x̌ʷə́n went along and came to a river. He wanted to kill fish. He set his trap to kill salmon. He said, "When you kill one, call me." Indeed it killed one. He went and there were just leaves. One time he caught a stick. "Oh, it lied to me." One time it killed moss. Four times then indeed it caught salmon. x̌ʷə́n made a fire and roasted it on a stick. Then he went to sleep. Before he slept he laid down the milt. He said, "My wife or my children." Then he slept. When he got up, behold there were women. They ate what he had killed. It was all gone when he woke up. He looked around for what he roasted, "Oh, those women have eaten it." He touched his mouth and he felt much fat. He thought that he himself must have eaten. "I was going along. The women went up the river in a canoe. I go up the river. I am going far. I say, 'straighten the canoe, my wives or my children.' I always tell them and they get mad and jump off and they run away." x̌ʷə́n went. His canoe was turned around in the river and one of the women went inland. He went and they went going across a prairie. They saw a woman digging camas. They saw an old woman. She was rocking a little grandchild. She pushed it and it came back. The woman was blind. One said, "Let us steal this child." She looked for rotten wood and found it. She took it, and took off the baby. She put it in and pushed it back. Then the old woman found the rotten wood. She said, "My little grandchild became rotten wood. My little grandchild became rotten wood." Then her daughter heard and came and found indeed her child was gone. She said, "I will find the one who stole it." The old mother said, "Do not leave me. I will go along. We will go. I will just speak to the ground. Wrinkle up ground, wrinkle up." Indeed it wrinkled up. They were about to catch him. "I will let down my mother." Then she took her up again. "Oh, mother, speak to the ground." "Wrinkle up ground." "One time I am about to catch this woman. I will let her down." A mountain arose. Then she carried her again. "I will catch that woman. I will let her down." There was a big lake.[1] They did not catch them. She came to the horizon of this world that goes up and down. She jumped to the other side and the mother could not go through. She came back. "I will

156

get one person. I will pay many things to go after my child." He got in past the horizon therefore he could not follow. He came back. He came back and he never found the child. She sent another one. He started and he arrived there. He could not pass the horizon and gave up. He came back. The woman said, "Nobody can pass the horizon." All her property was gone. She got one child. She took the diaper and wrung it out. She drank the water and then she got a child. She sent everybody. Then Bluejay came. "I will get your son."[2] The woman said, "I will pay you whatever you want." Bluejay said, "I will go and get him." Bluejay started. He came to the horizon. He waited. It opened and again it closed. As soon as it opened he jumped and came to the other side. He looked and saw one with many children. He was making a spear for his child. He was whittling the spear. Bluejay started. He jumped back. He jumped. He saw it. Indeed it was the one he had gone for. He jumped. The one who was whittling a spear said, "What do you come for?" He took the dust off what he was whittling and threw it on his face. It struck the eyes of Bluejay. Bluejay said, "I have come for you. Your mother has lost you, therefore I came after you." The other one said, "All right, I will go." He took his children and threw them into the river. He said, "You will be little fish." Bluejay came. He came to the woman. He said, "He has come. He was paid clothing which he has on." He set everything right. He came to one who was sharpening a knife. "I am going to cut up núkʷimaɬ[3] when he comes." He said, "What are you saying?" "Oh, I was just saying I will play with núkʷimaɬ." He said, "Bring it here." He brought his knife and gave it to him. "Now turn around." *He stabbed his behind with it. He said, "Your name will be Beaver. You will eat everything. You will bite around fir trees until they fall."*

Then this one, Moon, started . . .[4]

S'yawyu'wun

Storytelling has only to tell about the way of the world, the way it was long ago before the Moon was traveling. He was a good person. He was the talker of all the people at that time. His name was S'yawyu'wun.[1] He had black clothing on his chest. On his clothing were braids all over. He was shining red, shining like the stars during a frost. On his clothing it was sticking like shining metal, always a reddish color. He was a handsome person, not a very tall man. He was a Chief. He always traveled everywhere. Once he was heard of by the people. It is said now they were shouting "S'yawyu'wun." Sometimes he will be seen traveling on the earth. He will meet people. Some he will find in their houses. Sometimes he will travel above. It was heard that he was coming from below the ocean.[2] They heard that he was coming to other people, all the people everywhere. In one country they were expecting that S'yawyu'wun would pass. They heard a faint noise of ringing. They heard shouting from above. Flounder and other people said, "What would the Chief say?" Others said he said nothing. Flounder said, "No, the Chief is teaching us what we shall do. He, S'yawyu'wun, is just passing." He said nothing and all the people told one another what they should do. But S'yawyu'wun said nothing. Flounder was very much afraid to break the laws of the Chief. Flounder said, "Oh, my brothers, sisters, and mother, and all my people, all you flounders," said the Chief. "Let us change our eyes." He took off his eyes and put it in another place from where his eyes had been. Again he said, "I am moving my eyes because the Chief said, 'Move your eyes.' The ways of the flounders will be the other way forever." Some people said, "Let us get married." The youths and girls ran about and got married. Some said, "Thus said the Chief. He spoke from above." There was a faint ringing noise, then he shouted. Some youths said the Chief said he should make a platform for catching lamprey,[3] on Chehalis River to catch lampreys. They got ready, ever so many people, young men and old ones. They made many platforms for catching lamprey near the bank of the rapids of the river. It was not long before they finished many plat-

158

forms before S'yawyu'wun came passing. They had no platform for catching lamprey. The people only looked for lamprey. They had no platforms. After S'yawyu'wun had passed they had platforms. This happened after the one Chief had traveled.[4]

x̣ʷə́n

When x̣ʷə́n went away from where he had been with Skunk for a long time, he left him. x̣ʷə́n went far up above. At that time the rocks were people. They had life like persons. x̣ʷə́n was traveling along then he came to many rocks near the mountains. These mountains were far from the real people. It was a wild, lonesome country. Then x̣ʷə́n found one stone like a person. He looked at it. He found a little hole through the middle. He found that the Rock was hollow inside like the form of a person.[1] He said, "This is a rock but it is a person."[2] x̣ʷə́n said, "Nobody can be here. This is far away from other people." "Although it is day," said x̣ʷə́n, "let me get married with the Children of the Rock. Let me just marry them. But she will not be my wife. She will be my mistress." The stone was long. It was too heavy. He could not carry it to the woods. These Children of the Rock did not walk. Wherever they stood they always remained. x̣ʷə́n said to the Rock, "I will be staying here for five days. You, Daughter of the Rock, you will be my mistress." Now the Rock became the mistress of x̣ʷə́n. Now x̣ʷə́n stayed with the Daughter of the Rock. She was a sweet woman.[3]

One-Legged Monster

It is told how the world was long ago when the world started. Those who first tell stories, when they die then another one grows up and tells it again, like the one who died. That is the way these stories came to us from the days long ago.

There were monsters in the world. There were some countries that had taboos. One lake was tabooed because it was the house of a monster, on the shore of this lake in the thick woods. The name of the monster was One-Legged.[1] All the people forbade the girls to play near the lake. All the children were told so by all the men. "Do not go near that lake for that monster always kills people. He is a real monster. He always stays there in the lake every year. He is One-Legged and nobody can kill him for he is a monster. His body is different. He is shot by arrows but he does not feel it when he is shot, he just always says it is itching him. If he is shot from the back and all the arrows that the warriors have are gone, he does not feel them, that One-Legged. He just stirs his fire. He cooks his meat, which is roasted on a spit. When he is roasting on the spit he just kneels down near what he roasts. The heroes come from everywhere. One shoots after another from the back, however many warriors there are. Although they shoot at him and all the arms are gone the monster just says, 'What is itching my back?'" One-Legged is a big tall person. His body is like that of a man but he is different. When he had been attacked with bows and arrows and the heroes go home, they always stay. They do not know when the monster comes. It is not known whose child he is. When the heroes from every country come they cannot kill him.

They could not kill him. The monster must have grown long ago. I guess it always belonged to the lake. It is bad to all the people. Whenever he saw a person he killed him. Sometimes he roasted the flesh of the person on a spit when he was very mad. He does not want anyone to come to his house. Everywhere in every country they heard of him. There he was. The monster had his home near the shore of a lake. Those brushes were very thick for nothing could be seen even when it was very near. For many years the warriors of the people wanted to kill him. First they delayed. Their children were forbidden to go to the shore of the lake near these woods for the monster was there. All the girls were told, "Don't go to the woods near the lake."

There was an old man who had six children. The old people had only one daughter. When they came together they told each other that it was forbidden to go near the lake. This girl of the old people did not know that there was a monster at the lake. Only the other girls knew it and they always said that it was forbidden to go to the woods of the lake. She said, "Let me go and see what is forbidden in the woods by the lake." The nice girl went and came to the shore of the lake. She walked about on the open ground. She saw the thick woods. She said, "This is what must be forbidden. Let me go and see." She went. She came to the underbrush. She examined everything in the woods. She was taken from behind. She looked back and saw that it was a man who had taken her. Then she yelled. One-Legged said, "Don't be afraid, I will just make you my wife. If you don't agree, I'll kill you." The girl said, "Let me rather not die. Let me go along with the monster." The monster took her into his house. They stayed in their house. The monster always made love to her. After three days she was pregnant and it was not many days before she gave birth. The monster child was born quickly. She could not get away because the monster One-Legged made it difficult for the woman.

One of her brothers came. He arrived at the house of the monster. When he came he was told by his younger sister, "Go home quickly." Then he ran to the house. When the monster arrived, he smelled the tracks in the house. He smelled the tracks of his brother-in-law. He said, "Evidently there must have been a man here, a secret lover of my wife." He ran to pursue him. He had a dry hide. He made it round. It was hooped on a hazel pole.[2] There was something inside. Round balls of bone. These bones he had taken from the old graves, from the oldest graves. He gathered them so that it would be a strong drum when he pursued his brother-in-law. He shook his drum and the drum rattled with the bones inside. Even though his brothers-in-law were fast runners he always overtook them because when he shook his drum it rattled and the drum had real power. The drum made people weak. When they got tired, they could not run and One-Legged overtook them. And he killed them. When he carried them through the woods and broke up the bodies of the people and roasted them on a spit. He killed four brothers of the Tribe and other youths. There was one of the five young men, the child of the old man. First he kept still. He always was getting ready, the younger one of the five youths. The home of this monster was on the side of a long lake and one was always ready to fight with the monster. One day he went to a place above the river place of the monster. He came to the lake and saw the camp. Mountain Lion and his brother Wildcat[3] came. He went around the lake along the shore. He came to a new camp near the shore of the lake. He came and asked, "What are you doing on this lake? There is a monster on this side of the lake. The monster has killed my brothers. Let us wait and when it is summer I'll fight the monster with many young people at that time. We will send to every distant country for the warriors. When they come that many heroes will surround the lake. Even if the monster should fight we will kill him at that time. Then the young men from distant countries will come because we are tired of the monster. We are planning with all the Chiefs," said he. "No matter how many of us are killed we shall now get the monster and kill him at that time. We and other Chiefs of the country. Thus we are planning. You, Mountain Lion, I heard about you. They say you are a strong person. At that time when we shall make war on the monster we shall call you. My father is one of the Chiefs of this country. One-Legged is always killing people even from far away countries and his enemies will come here from far away. Now I leave you. When next year we go after the monster I shall be glad to see you, Mountain Lion." Mountain Lion said, "I shall be here when you make war on the monsters. I will be here with my younger brother. First we will dry meat here. We cannot stay long because I am always the enemy of the monster. He has chased me for many years. We always move about, I and my younger brother, away from the trails on which people are traveling for many monsters are my enemies in this world. I have killed many, therefore I am always watchful because my enemies might overtake me. It is the same like the monster in this land. This is the end." "First I want to tell you," the youth whose brothers had been killed said, "Good-bye, Mountain Lion and little Wild Cat. Now I am going home." He went along the shore to the lake and came to his house. When he arrived there were already many people from far away. It was very cold because it was winter. The youth said, "We always talk about these new campers on the other side. It is Mountain Lion." He came up to him and his younger brother, Wild Cat. "He is a good looking youth who is called Mountain Lion and he is not a big man. He is almost grown up. He is not very tall but the body of the handsome youth is well made. They are staying there. They have their camp under a cedar stump. It may be seen from this side for it is a big round stump. It looks like a mountain. They say it appears from this side because it was big and round." They stayed with the people. The youth was always happy. The people from afar were always getting ready to fight. In summer Mountain Lion stayed with his younger brother for a long time. He was gone for a long time, beginning in the morning. Then he said to his younger brother, "Always guard my fire." He left in the morning. He said to his younger brother, "Do not go to the smoke in the woods on the other side because it is a monster." Then he went hunting. The fire of Wild Cat went out. Then Wild Cat said, "I'll get into trouble with my elder brother. Let me go for some fire from that what is smoking there." Wild Cat went. He swam across the lake. He got across and came to the house of the monster. First he peeped in and he saw that the monster was asleep. Wild Cat entered. He struck the end of his tail into the fire. Then he crossed and made a new fire.[4] The monster awoke and said, "Mmm, what is that? It smells like Wild Cat." The monster got ready to go across. Mountain Lion came and saw his fire, "Oh, your fire smells differently. Get ready because I will fight the monster whenever he comes. I'll climb up the tree. After a while when we fight, we shall fight[5] in the cedar stump. You make a fire below the tree." Now the monster came ashore. They climbed up and fought. One-Legged was killed. When the body of the monster fell from above on the stump Wild Cat poked his fire and his body was burned.

Mountain Lion gathered his body above in the fire and the monster was dead. Mountain Lion came to life. The cedar stump burned and the light shone that far it was seen by the assembled people. The people said, "Maybe One-Legged is fighting with Mountain Lion because they growled very loud at that fire." Then they ran for the water to the house of the monster. They came to the woman who had married the monster. One of them said, "Where is your husband?" She replied, "He must be fighting on the other side where the fire is." Then the woman stopped talking. She was taken with her child. They ran away with her home. They came to the house and they stayed at her house, she and the child of that monster. When the child came near to people it would dig into the eyes of the people. At last one of the Chiefs said, "Let us destroy the child of the monster, it is impossible to take care of it."

The mother of the child said, "Never mind, it is impossible for me to take care of the child of the monster." A box was made for it. It was put into the box. It was covered tightly. It was put into the river and the Child of One-Legged floated down. The people near the sea said, "What is this floating?" Said one of them, "It is a nice box. Let us take it." They went and one of them took it. He opened it and he saw a baby in the little box. He peeped in to take it and the child dug into one of his eyes. Thus he became one-eyed. The eye was taken off by that child. The child ate only this. The person took the box. He fastened the cover and sent it up. It continued floating down the river to the ocean and always was taking out the eyes of the people. Then there were many one-eyed people. It was only caused by the bad girl who had a child by the monster. She was stubborn. She broke the laws of the people. She went although it was forbidden to go there. After this there will be no more One-Legged in any lake. A girl shall go to a lake and they will not be married by monsters. Girls will only be forbidden anything that is bad because the people were made poor and to see only with one eye by one stupid girl and her older brothers died with other youths just because she was stupid. Girls will marry nowadays. They shall have children but eyes will not be eaten by the child. People will always be happy when they see a newborn baby. Nobody will be one-legged. He shall only be a joke later on. Thus a stupid girl made people die for nothing. This shall not happen again to people.

Chipmunk

Written by Blanche Pete Dawson
August 15, 1927

Chipmunk was foolish. He did not mind his grandmother. Chipmunk was told, "Don't go to that mountain. There is a monster." One time Chipmunk was playing. He thought, "Oh, I will go to that mountain." He came picking blackberries from bushes. Then there was the monster. Chipmunk ran away. He was pursued by the monster. He was bruised by the monster. Therefore Chipmunk now has stripes on his back. Chipmunk came to his grandmother, "I am being pursued by a monster." "Hide under the bed," said the grandmother. The monster arrived. The monster said, "Oh, my elder sister, your tattooing is nice. Could you tattoo me?" The Grandmother of Chipmunk said, "I can tattoo you well." She made a fire, a big fire. "Now come and stand by the fire." The monster came and stood near the fire. The monster was afraid to go near the fire. Just now the Chipmunk was watching. The Chipmunk was holding the fire tongs. He was watching the monster as he was going to the fire. The monster was always afraid to go near the fire but he could not control his wish for being tattooed by the Grandmother of Chipmunk. He thought, "Oh, anyway I'll go near the fire." And he went to stand near the fire. As soon as he got there, Chipmunk sneaked up to him and pushed the monster into the fire. The monster shouted, "Oh, my elder sister, take pity on me. I am dying. Help me." Twice he tried to get up. Chipmunk held him down with the tongs. Then the monster caught fire. He shriveled up. The ashes flew about. These ashes of the monster were mosquitoes. Therefore there are mosquitoes in this world.

Why the Dog Has Marks on His Paws

A little dog was sent to take a message. He was told, "Go quickly. Don't stay away long. If they want to give you to eat, don't pay attention to it. If they want to feed you, don't pay attention to it." The little dog got there. He gave his message. He was told, "First eat." He said, "No, I cannot eat. I was told to be quick, and now I go home." He was told, "Here is camas ready for you to eat." He really desired the camas. "Oh, it will not be known by my parents that I have taken camas." The little dog was told to be quick. Because he stayed his hands were daubed by camas. He stayed to warm his hands by the fire of the people. He wanted to stay by the fire while it was cold outside. When he had warmed his hands suddenly the camas had marked the hands of the little dog. The little dog arrived at home and his hands were seen. Then it was known that he had eaten camas. Therefore the hands of the dog are marked like camas to this day.

The Flood (The Deluge)

Written by Blanche Pete Dawson

Thrush had a wife, a really pretty woman. He was ugly. He never washed his face or his hands. He was always untidy. He was in the habit of walking. He was always scolded by his wife and parents-in-law. They always told him to wash his face. Only he said all the time, "It's forbidden for me to wash my face. Something might happen if I should wash my face. Do not let me wash my face." They always scolded him. Then he said, "Well, let me wash my face. You will always remember that I said so." The little Thrush just lay down for a little while. Then Thrush went down to the river to wash his face. He began. He said, "Let everyone go far inland for now it will rain hard." Before he was going to wash his face he sang and said, "Come my brothers and sisters." As soon as he began to sing it began to rain. It just poured down. The people ran away. The earth was flooded. Therefore when a thrush is seen bathing it is always going to rain. But this world will never be flooded now.[1]

The Crows

The Crows got ready to pick haws.[1] They went to the river to their canoes. Now they paddled. They were working hard. Now they were in a hurry to get there. They perspired on account of their hard work. Then someone shouted to them from inland, "Where are you going, wóli?" They said to one another, "Maybe he wants to go along. Let us not pay any attention to him." They were just working hard again. They always heard someone who kept saying, "Where are you going, wóli?" They did not pay any attention. Suddenly the canoe gave a jump and one said, "Now what is the matter with us?" They came. They wondered that they were staying in the same place. They did not move. Then one of them turned his paddle sideways and so they moved. Then the Crows sang.

Untitled Story

In the beginning, people, birds, and all other beasts were there. Some were really people but their ways were different. These people had really different ways. In the whole world there was one woman in one country who got married to another person. They stayed one year and they had children, boys. These children were quite different in their ways. These children were double. They were stuck together in the middle of their back. They were firmly stuck together. They lived in this one country and their children were growing up. He who had the children belonged to the north people. Other children belonged to the lower part of the world. They always played and they always ate. They did everything as is done by other people. They were good-natured children.[1] Everybody loved them in this world. And they were known in every country. Many children who came from afar wished to see these different kinds of children. The people did so for many years. Sometimes the people gathered from far away, some real people, and some different people. They came and when all arrived the strangers always played together with the double children. Thus were long ago the ways of the people when they assembled. The boys always had bows and arrows and all their children would shoot at targets with arrows. Thus did the early people. Both the double ones were boys. They had a bow and together they would shoot with many children. When one had shot, after he was done shooting, he would run after his arrow. The one who had shot, he ran fast, sometimes faster than the other boy when he was running. He only dragged the other one who walked backward quickly from behind, holding his arrows. When the one who shot first with his arrow, then the other one shot backwards. When the one had finished shooting then he ran backward to get the arrow with which he had shot, while the one who had shot first ran backward. Then the other boys were running together. Thus they always did and the boys were playing. Thus when they were playing sometimes they would have lunch when they were hungry. They took their lunches and both would eat. When they ate they chewed both ways. The other boys loved them and all the boys always played. All the people liked the boys. One summer they made a potlatch and fixed the graves. The people came from all over, all the animals from all over the world. They were people at that time and they talked as is done in the language of the people now. They gathered at the place where the grave was to be re-arranged. All the animals came and other people and they were hungry. Blue-jay came. He did not know the different kinds of children. He never had seen them. He never had heard about them. He came to the place where they were rearranging the grave. When Bluejay came all the other Chiefs went together. Bluejay loves to tell lies. He just joins his lies with the other liars in the assembly. Everyone was there with them. And with them were x̌ʷə́n,² Crane, Beaver, Otter, Mink, Raccoon, Mountain Lion, Wild Cat, Wren, and Rabbit. They belonged to the animals and with them was x̌ʷə́n. He always belongs there and all kinds of animals from far away. The people assembled for many days. The other children were playing on the prairie. Bluejay did not know about it, for Bluejay was contesting in lies with x̌ʷə́n and other liars. All the children were playing. One day all the children and other grownup boys were playing with the different kind of children. They were yelling with all the children. Then Bluejay said, "What is going on on the prairie? These people are yelling. Let me go and see what the children are playing." He came to where the children were shooting arrows. He arrived there and Bluejay looked on. He saw the two children grown together. Bluejay said, "What is wrong with these children? Indeed, it is as though they were stuck together. This is very different." Some of the other animals from far away said, "That is just the way of these children. They became children which are fastened together." Bluejay said, "This is very peculiar." One of the children ran along and got what he went for and the other one went backward and took what he wanted. Then he went backward and Bluejay said, "That is bad, the way these children are. It is a disgrace. Many children might become that way. That would be a great misfortune. Let me fix these children. I'll take them apart so that they will be two children apart when they walk about. Let it be. If this day children are born grown together it would not be good." Bluejay went and sharpened a stick. He went to take the children. He sneaked near them and struck them in the middle. He broke the two children apart. They were bleeding where they were stuck together and both died. Bluejay said, "These double children are dead. It is good that they are disappeared from this world because it is not good if people are in this way, and many children might grow up that way. After this day no child shall appear in this way on the earth. When the world is transformed people will be different later on. Never shall children be born grown together behind. It would be bad if people were grown together. Whenever they are taken off from this world they shall be the way of later generations. The people in this world will be different." Then he finished making plans and laws. Then he ran away because he got into trouble when he killed these children of a different kind.

Beaver and the Woman

Long ago the people had different ways. When a Chief had a daughter and a man came to buy a wife for his son they bought the girl.[1] Thus were their rules in this country. This rule was laid down in this country in the beginning of the world. This rule was always used by the Chief of the country and by all the Tribes. It came down to later times. If a Chief had a nice daughter whom he held dear, she was paid for when she got married. The ancient people did not marry for the parents of the first of the girl that got married to them. If they were industrious, if they were good workers, this they called a good woman. She was strong and industrious. She was the daughter of a Chief. Thus it was in the beginning of the world. In the beginning of the world all the people and animals leavened.[2] They had homes just like houses of the recent people. Many among the animals had houses near a small creek and there were also real people. There was one Chief who had a house, the last one at the end of the houses of many people. The Chief had different ways. His ways were quite foolish. He had daughters. All his other daughters had long been married. They were taken by those who had married them. He had one daughter whom he valued highly. He said if a Chief should come to buy his daughter, if he is valuable, then she will be married. When day came, the girl would go down to the water of the creek. She made baskets near the creek where there was the noise of water. There she worked every day. Where she was working she had a shelter behind her. It was made of cedar bark. Every day she worked there. When she finished her work she left it in the shelter with all her material from which she made baskets. She kept much cedar sap and maple sap and grass for decoration. All these she used to paint when she was working at it. She always held the material and when she finished working she went home to her parents. All the young men wished for her. The youths came looking for women and came to the girl. She would not pay any attention to them. Then the young men went home because the old one[3] was different. He was foolish. He overvalued his daughter. He said that he was one of the Chiefs and he thought a great deal of himself.

One day Bluejay and many other animals came to the one who had a daughter. They came too, the old people who had the daughter. Bluejay said, "I came to buy a wife with all the young men. They are my people. I want to marry your daughter." The foolish old man got angry, "I do not want anyone like you, Bluejay, to make you my son-in-law. You are a common person. My daughter is valuable." Bluejay got mad. Bluejay said, "You have discouraged me. You just make out you are a Chief because you think that you are high although you are a common person." He finished and Bluejay went home. While they went home there was singing along the trail. Everyone shouted. Their shouting made a loud noise. The old man stayed for many years. Always many young men wished to marry her but they could not get the girl on account of that foolish old man, even when a Chief wanted to marry this girl.

One day Beaver was fishing. Beaver was a young man of bad looks but he had a nice blanket. He was broad and his legs were short. He had a stout stomach. His teeth were sticking out and he had a wrinkled nose. He was always working in the water. He was felling trees in the river. He would eat sticks and mud. He was tired of it. One day Beaver said, "Now I am tired of my food. I have eaten too much bark of trees. I'll go up the river and fish for fry." He started and came to a small rapid creek, a small creek. The water was clear. There were many small stones and sand in the bottom. The gravel was bright and smooth. He went upriver to fish. There were many young fish. He went and came to the small creek. He went up to the head of the creek. There was just a little dribble of water there. He met a woman who was making baskets. He stood up and looked at her. Beaver said, "Evidently you are making baskets?" The girl did not reply. She just looked at him. He looked back. She wrinkled up her nose because she disliked him. Beaver said, "Let me leave you. I'll just go fishing in the creek. I am not looking for you, you are too proud." Beaver went. He wondered whether, "Is this really the Chief's daughter whom I passed? Indeed, she is a pretty woman." Now he wanted the woman. He went up the creek and Beaver said to himself, "Let me make medicine. I will make it of castoreum. I will dope that woman." He gathered many things and mixed them. Then he squeezed out his own castoreum. He just made it good, dry and round. He put the medicine into a dry mud. It became moist because he soaked the medicine in the dry mud. He finished. Then he went down to the rippling creek. He did not want to fish with his line because he had changed his mind. He thought much of the girl, although he saw plenty of fish in the rippling creek. He just passed them and came to where the girl was working. She was not there. Beaver said, "That bad proud girl is going to find out. I make her love me by means of her work, so that she may be pregnant and I'll take the princess." He took the medicine in the dry mud and chewed it. He chewed it for a long time and spat it on the place where the girl was sitting. He spat over her baskets, all over her cedar sap, the maple sap, the grass, and everything on the weaving on which the girl was working what was left. Some of his medicine was left. He found a bucket from which she dipped water to soak her material. He dissolved the medicine in the water and sprinkled it over the place in which she worked. He spilt a little in the creek. There was still a little left in the bucket. He dipped some from the rapids of the creek. He put down the bucket where the girl used to work. Beaver said to the bucket before he went home, "First let your mistress drink when she comes to her work." After he had talked to the bucket he returned to his house. He arrived at his house. It was late in the evening. He stayed and it got day again. Then the girl awoke. Before she ate in the morning she ran to the creek where she was doing her work. She said, "First I'll work before I eat in the morning." She came to her work and went to her bucket to dip water. She found the water and filled her bucket. She said, "Now I have much water. I forgot." She took her dipper and first she drank from her bucket. In it was the Beaver's medicine. After drinking she took her basket. She took her bark and bit it. While she was biting her work in the morning she said, "I feel funny. My saliva is getting much." She always swallowed her saliva. She worked and finished one big basket. Then she went home. She came to the house and ate. Then she went to her work and she worked in the morning. Five days she had been working after the Beaver had spat on it. One the fifth morning she got sick. She gagged.[4] She vomited. The shamans came to treat her. One shaman said, "You have no sickness. You are just evidently, well, you were loved by a youth. You are just pregnant." The shaman finished treating her and went home. This girl was pregnant. Then the foolish person who had her for his daughter became angry. He said, "Something bad has been done to my daughter. She broke the laws of the Chiefs." The girl denied that any youth came to her. She said it is just because I took something that was not good. Therefore it happened to me. She stayed one winter. In spring she gave birth. All the Chiefs said, "If anyone has this child for his child that one will be the husband of this girl who gave birth without having a husband." They made an arrangement for guessing whoever was the father of the child, to him the child would jump. "We will see that the boy will laugh at his father and he will cry. If he is another one, not his father, he will just keep still. Let all young men come so that the child will choose." First the shamans came to consecrate the guessing. They were going to work on the child and the mother. The great shamans came and treated the child for a long time. They were treating him. After they had done so all those who had treated him went home. All the youths heard of it, and all the youths felt badly. They went to see the baby. One Chief said, "Let many men assemble to claim the child. Let him choose who wants the woman who has the child. Let us set one baby claiming day." Then all the animals came. There was a seat for the woman who had the child. She was made to sit. Then when all the animals had assembled — Raccoon, Mink, Bear, Mountain Lion, Snake, Grizzly Bear, Lion, Otter, Wolf, Coyote, Bee, Crane, Crow, and x^{w}ə́n. Bluejay and all the animals had come. They came and marched around one by one. Every one of the men marched and everyone stopped. First they talked a few words to the woman. Then they all went and passed the boy. The boy did not do anything. He just kept quiet. All the men came and all passed. Beaver came far behind. They did so from morning until late in the evening. And all had done so. Finally Beaver came. He came to the woman and the boy laughed and Beaver spoke to the woman, talking to her. The boy wanted to go to the Beaver. The boy was jumping about. First he laughed, then the child cried for the Beaver. Then one Chief said, "You, Beaver, take the boy." The boy was taken by Beaver and the child laughed at him. The child was happy. Then all the Chiefs of the guessing party said, "Beaver is the father of this boy. On this day the girl shall become the Wife of Beaver." Then the girl cried, and her father and her relatives, because everybody disliked Beaver. He was an ugly youth. He was a common man. When he had finished one of the Chiefs of the guessing party said, "This will be the way of future times. Sometimes a girl will have a child without having a husband. Nothing shall happen to her parents and her relatives, just those who made love to her shall marry her. They will finish and all the people will be happy. The world is going to change and the people will be different. In the future a girl will grow up and she shall get married. She shall become a wife. She shall not just become an old maid. She shall get married and all her relatives will be happy. Thus will be the ways of the people in the future. This will be the way of the world."

x̣ʷə́n and Crane

x̣ʷə́n[1] was living in the mountains alone. For many days he was waiting for Crane. For five days he waited. Then Crane came to where he was living. Crane came to x̣ʷə́n. Crane said, "Are you still here?" x̣ʷə́n said, "I am always here. I am waiting for you. Let us go to get food where there are plenty of fish, to a place where I know we can take them easily because it is shallow near the bank and there are even many rapids there." Crane said, "That is why I came to get you. Let us go to where you know there are fish. I know how to kill them. If you want to go there let us go right now." x̣ʷə́n said, "Let us go. I have only been waiting for you, therefore I am here. At this mountain is a river where the fish are. It is far. We cannot go there in one day. Let us start." Crane said, "All right." Crane said just the way he always says when he starts, "qʼʷás, qʼʷás, qʼʷás, qʼʷás, qʼʷás." Then they started. They went away from the mountain. They were traveling. It was night and they came to a place where it was not steep. There was a small creek. Crane said, "Let us camp now." They camped. Crane said, "I have much lunch. It is heavy. Let us eat it before we get there where there is food." x̣ʷə́n said, "All right, let us camp. I am too sleepy." They camped. They gathered many sticks and started a fire near the bank of the creek. Crane began to cook. After they had cooked they went to sleep. They slept. Then day came in the morning. Crane awoke. Then he cooked. He awakened x̣ʷə́n. He went to the creek. First he bathed and after he had bathed he came to the shore. He dressed and put on his clothes. He ran that far.[2] He came to Crane. Crane said, "I finished cooking. Let us eat at once so that we may go far today." Then they ate in the morning. After they had eaten x̣ʷə́n said, "Will you go fast after a while so that we may get to a level country in the afternoon? Not far from the level ground we will come to a trail. There is another thing. First we will eat there. When we finish eating we will go through the night because the trail is good." After they finished eating they started off. First Crane said, "qʼʷás, qʼʷás, qʼʷás, qʼʷás, qʼʷás." They went through thick woods in the mountains. They went and although they tried hard they could not travel fast because the bushes were thick. They went far away in the afternoon. They came to level ground. x̣ʷə́n could hardly walk for

hunger. x̣ʷə́n said, "It is not far until we come to the creek. There is the trail."
x̣ʷə́n said, "Oh, younger brother, I die of hunger. I am getting thirsty." Crane
said, "When we reach the creek we will rest for a long time after we have
eaten." They went and reached the creek. First they made a fire. It became
hot that day because it was summer. First Crane cooked. Again he cooked
the food. Then they ate. They ate much. x̣ʷə́n said, "I am going to eat much.
After I have eaten I will drink much for we are going to camp. You will carry
dry pitchwood. I shall hold on to the pitchwood in the night. It is too dark in
the night, therefore, we need light and we'll go with torches." x̣ʷə́n finished
talking. Crane said, "Your plan is good." Crane said, "Well, let us eat." They
ate. They were eating for a long time. x̣ʷə́n ate much. He was laughing. He
finished eating. They started and went to the creek. First they drank much.
After drinking they crossed on a footbridge. Then they came to a trail. They
came to dry pitchwood. First they gathered pitchwood. They split it well.
They finished making bundles of it. When they had done so they started.
x̣ʷə́n went always first. Now x̣ʷə́n became happy because they had reached
level ground. Then x̣ʷə́n was getting strong again. After he had been hungry
he was sleepy. x̣ʷə́n said, "Oh, younger brother, I am getting stronger. I am
awake." Now they walked along and pretty soon it became evening. At that
time it was very dark. It was a black darkness in the night because at that
time there was no moon in the world. It was dark at night. Nothing could be
seen at night. x̣ʷə́n said, "Well, let us light the ends of our pitchwood." They
lit it and they lifted it. There was that much light. Then they started and they
went far throughout the night. Day came but they did not rest. They went
along and evening came. They went through the night. It was day again. They
went and it was night. Day came on the fifth day. They went and they came
to the river. It had fish. It was late in the day, almost night. x̣ʷə́n said, "This is
the river. We get fish." Crane said, "I have not much lunch. Let us go fishing at
once." They went to the bank and saw many young fish. Crane took thin bark
near the bank of the river. He dipped up the fry with the thin bark net and
threw it out on shore on the sand bar.[3] He worked together with x̣ʷə́n. They
had not done so for a long time when they stopped. Crane went to what they
had killed and put it into a small basket in which he kept his lunch. Crane
said, "Tomorrow morning we'll make many baskets to gather fish. We'll stay
here a long time. I'll stay here so that I may make a fish trap and we'll dry

many fish." x̣ʷə́n said, "There is always much food in this river. Let us make it our home this summer." After they finished Crane said, "When it is evening let us go to another place and make fire." And they went and came to a level place. There was a big fir tree. Crane said, "This is a good place to stay over night. We will sleep under the fir tree. This will be our home this summer." They made a fire quite far inland from the sand bar. On the bank of the river there was much sand. On the sand bar much sand was piled up. They finished making a fire and Crane began to cook. They cooked the fish they had caught. When it was done they ate. They finished eating. First they kept awake. x̣ʷə́n was singing with Crane. After they had finished singing they went to sleep. Then day came. Crane made a fire. Then he prepared food. Then they ate. When the food was done they ate. Then they finished eating. Crane said, "Let us first go to a cedar patch and let us gather cedar bark and also various kinds of sticks to make baskets." They went. Then they reached a cedar patch. They stripped the young cedar trees. They took the nice cedar bark. Then they went and found a small cedar patch of trees with good limbs. x̣ʷə́n said, "The limbs of this short cedar tree are always split. Many always make good baskets like those I always see." Crane said, "Let us gather them." They broke off the nice limbs of the cedar. They gathered much. They finished. Then they carried them to the camp. They arrived at their fire and there they laid down their load. Crane said, "I start at once to make a basket to gather the fry." x̣ʷə́n said, "Go ahead. Make a basket. I will go to get many plants and salal leaves for our bedding so that we may have a good bed. I'll make the place good where we stay."

x̣ʷə́n went to get the plants and salal leaves. Then he came and made their beds. He gathered many sticks and many leaves. He placed them upright around the place where they stayed and he walked. Late in the afternoon he finished. Crane said, "First let us fish." They went to the river and they dipped their big baskets into the water. Only five times they dipped them and they got many young fish and other kinds of fish. They took large trout. It was very heavy so that they took one basket with its heavy weight to the bank. x̣ʷə́n said, "One basket contains much food that we caught. These five baskets contain much food. We will work on it many days and we will dry it." They took out the fish and took them to their camp. The two of them worked at it and carried one basket. They carried it inland. After they had done so, Crane said,

"First we'll prepare food." Both of them prepared food. For a long time they prepared much. xʷə́n said, "We'll cook much food so that we'll just eat in the morning. We will have lunch then we fish again." Then they ate and after they finished eating they sang. Then they went to sleep. Day came. Crane made a fire. They heated their food. After that they ate. When they finished eating they went to the river. They dipped their baskets for small fish. Five times they dipped their baskets. Then they finished and they carried it to their camp to preserve it. Crane said, "Let us work at our food. First we will dry it. We shall dry that amount of food." They worked on all the fish they had killed. When they had finished they made a roof[4] for them. They made a fire for it. Crane said, "First let us prepare our food." They prepared much food. After Crane finished preparing the food they ate. They were there a long time until the evening eating. They ate much because they were very hungry. After they had eaten they sang. And after they had finished singing they went to sleep. They slept until day came. Crane awoke and started the fire. xʷə́n awoke. "Let us first go to the river." He dived deep into the water five times. He jumped from above into the deep water. It was very high and he jumped from a fir tree. When he dropped into the river he always splashed loudly. After that he came out. He ran to Crane. xʷə́n said, "Oh, younger brother, I have found a deep water for bathing.[5] There is a fine sand bar." The sand was shining on the bank of the river. Crane replied, "I am getting tired working every day. We will prepare food. After a while we will dry it and tomorrow we will only go to the deep water and bathe the whole day." Crane finished planning and they ate. They ate and after they had eaten they went down to the river. They dipped their basket five times and they caught many young fish and they carried them to their camp. They dried them. After they had dried them they finished quickly. First they ate at noon. They were happy because they had eaten twice in one day. They were going to eat three times. He, xʷə́n, was a great eater. Always when he had eaten he was happy. They ate and they finished eating. xʷə́n said, "Oh, younger brother, let us go to where I used to stay when I was here. It is not far from here. Inland there is a large berry patch." They went there and ate blackberries from the bushes. Then they went back to their camp. First they ate. Then they slept after they had eaten. They slept until day came. Crane got up in the morning and he awakened xʷə́n. Crane said, "Let us cook much food today because we are going to bathe in the deep water today." Then they cooked food. When it was done they ate. They ate and they laughed much. After they had eaten, Crane said, "Let us first dance. Then we will sing a little like my supernatural helper." Then Crane began to sing. x̣ʷə́n beat time. They sang a long time because this day was a good day. "This day is bringing us great gladness to our hearts because we are staying here. We have much good. We have always enough to eat while we are here in this good country." Crane finished dancing. x̣ʷə́n said, "Let us dance the whole day and I will tell you what I found. I'll tell you how I played with women." x̣ʷə́n stopped dancing. Crane said, "I am the same. I know many girls. After a while we will talk together on the sand bar." They started and arrived at the deep water. They dived. They swam about in every way. They always dived. x̣ʷə́n said, "You always dive and then you always come up at the same place. I shall walk along the bottom of the water." Crane laughed. He said, "How can you walk under water?" x̣ʷə́n said, "I am always doing that. Look at me, I walk across the bottom." He took two large stones and walked along the bottom. He came ashore on the other side. When he landed he threw away the stones and swam. He came to Crane. Crane said to him, "Really, you are almost a monster." They went to the sand bar and lay down on the sand bar. He was told by x̣ʷə́n everything that he had done. For a long time they talked together. Then they went to sleep and the young men snored while they were sleeping. He, x̣ʷə́n, always says that he is a good fellow, that he is a girl's man. When they were asleep they were discovered by k'ʷə́cx̣ʷe. Now the girls' men were asleep. k'ʷə́cx̣ʷe was carrying a big basket. They came to x̣ʷə́n and k'ʷə́cx̣ʷe said, "What is that bad one doing here?" While he was asleep she took pitch and stuck it on the eyelids of x̣ʷə́n strongly so that he could not open his eyes. After she had done so she put x̣ʷə́n into the big basket. She was holding him just as though she was handling a tiny mouse. Because she was k'ʷə́cx̣ʷe she was a big person. After she had put x̣ʷə́n in she took Crane and she closed his eyes with pitch. After she had done so she put him in the basket. Then she tied it firmly and they were taken by k'ʷə́cx̣ʷe in her basket. She put it on her back and started. She carried the two youths although they were big men and were heavy. k'ʷə́cx̣ʷe is a tall woman. She is also big. She was one of the Children of k'ʷə́cx̣ʷe. She ate only people. k'ʷə́cx̣ʷe started for the mountains into the thick woods where it was dark. While k'ʷə́cx̣ʷe was walking in the woods, Crane awoke.

He said to x̣ʷə́n, "Oh, elder brother, what is the matter with us?" Crane said, "I cannot open my eyes." x̣ʷə́n said, whispering in the language of the coast, "You, Crane, be quiet. qwɛ́q̓ᵘsnate⁶ took us. Just don't move!" Crane stopped. k̓ʷə́cx̣ʷe started. She stepped slowly with long steps because she was tall. She went far quickly. She started for the mountains and arrived at her home. She brought them both, x̣ʷə́n and Crane, to her home. She put them inside and shut her house tightly. She unfastened her basket and oiled the eyes of x̣ʷə́n and Crane with oil. The pitch melted. When the pitch melted she washed their faces. Then x̣ʷə́n and Crane opened their eyes. They could see now. k̓ʷə́cx̣ʷe said, "Oh, elder brother. I take care of you in my place for now you have come to my place. First you will eat. Then you will sleep." Now they ate. While they were eating they ate with k̓ʷə́cx̣ʷe. She, k̓ʷə́cx̣ʷe, talked kindly to them. She was feeding them in every way as would be done by a good person. k̓ʷə́cx̣ʷe went out. She shut the door tight. When k̓ʷə́cx̣ʷe went out, x̣ʷə́n said, "Let us change off sleeping. You shall sleep a little while. Then I'll awaken you. Then I will sleep a little while. Then you awake me. We will do that all the time." After x̣ʷə́n had talked Crane said, "Not so. Let us stay awake. Then it will be day. We will be talking and it will be day. We will not sleep at all." x̣ʷə́n said, "Oh, you younger brother, you don't know we are going to die. This pretty, big woman is eating young men. She always eats people. There are seven children of k̓ʷə́cx̣ʷe and that one, she is always hungry for people. She just treats us well but she will not be kind to us for a long time although she gives us everything we like. When she gets tired of us, the bad one, we will die. I give it up. I do not know of any way to help myself." Crane said, "Oh, I am Crane, I have power of the ghosts. I use it on those of such kind. I always transform everything with my power. I will try to use it because you say this woman is a monster." They stayed there so long. k̓ʷə́cx̣ʷe came back. k̓ʷə́cx̣ʷe said, "Oh, elder brothers, you are still awake." x̣ʷə́n said, "We are just waiting for you, younger sister. Then we will go to sleep." k̓ʷə́cx̣ʷe said, "Then let us sleep." Now they went to sleep. They slept until late in the night. They awoke in the morning and they ate. And after they had eaten k̓ʷə́cx̣ʷe said to the girls' men, "How did you sleep last night? Was it good for you?" x̣ʷə́n answered, "Oh, my younger sister, there is nothing like it for us. We like it. Only for this we looked, I and my younger brother, this night and this day. You, my younger sister, are taking care of us well, of me and my younger brother." k'ʷə́cx̣ʷe laughed. k'ʷə́cx̣ʷe became happy. After that she went out. She closed the door tight. She left Crane and x̣ʷə́n inside. k'ʷə́cx̣ʷe started for the berry patch to pick berries. She picked many black-berries and ate thimbleberries from the bushes. The Child of k'ʷə́cx̣ʷe always ate thimbleberries from the bushes. After she had eaten thimbleberries from the bushes she went home and brought some home for x̣ʷə́n and Crane, also many blackberries, which they ate. Late at night they went to sleep. The sec-ond morning day came. k'ʷə́cx̣ʷe said, "For five days you shall stay here in-side. Then I send you out." k'ʷə́cx̣ʷe said, "I shall only stay with you." She stayed. Day came and night came. They ate blackberries until all the food of k'ʷə́cx̣ʷe was gone. They went to sleep late and they lay in bed. They never slept. Then day came and night came the third night. Then Crane became hungry. They were only playing with k'ʷə́cx̣ʷe on the third day. Then k'ʷə́cx̣ʷe said, "Oh, we are starving. We are playing too much." k'ʷə́cx̣ʷe said, "You better go out, Crane, and let us go to get good ironwood." Crane went for it and broke off much good ironwood. Then he talked about his supernatural power. "I have supernatural power near the grass. I have the ghost supernatu-ral power. This day I came to great hardship. We are dying, I and x̣ʷə́n. Oh, my power, let me use you today. After a while you shall change the ironwood I have bended. I will change it forever." Then he finished talking to his super-natural power. He took it inside and put it down. k'ʷə́cx̣ʷe said, "You, x̣ʷə́n, whittle the ends of this ironwood." Then x̣ʷə́n whittled the ends of all the ironwood. After he had done so, k'ʷə́cx̣ʷe said, "You x̣ʷə́n, you shall stay first. We will eat Crane today." Then Crane was taken by k'ʷə́cx̣ʷe. "Come here and let me roast you." Crane went near the fire. She took the ironwood and he twisted it with his neck. He twisted all the ironwood that way. It became changed and it was all crooked. Crane was taken by k'ʷə́cx̣ʷe. He was struck against the hip with the ironwood spit but it did not go through because now it was crooked. k'ʷə́cx̣ʷe tried all the ironwood but none of it could go through. Then she let it go and k'ʷə́cx̣ʷe got angry. She said, "Oh, now I'll try you." x̣ʷə́n was taken and the ironwood spits were struck against his hip and all the ironwood could not go through. Then she let them go. k'ʷə́cx̣ʷe said, "Oh, you are bad. I am going to eat you later on sometime." x̣ʷə́n laughed. After x̣ʷə́n had laughed he said, "Oh, younger sister, let us rather sing a little." k'ʷə́cx̣ʷe answered and said, "Well, let us sing." x̣ʷə́n said, "First we will go out and we will take our fine drums.[7] Then we will sing nicely." k'ʷə́cx̣ʷe said, "Well go, but come back quick before evening." k'ʷə́cx̣ʷe went and opened the door and x̣ʷə́n and Crane went out. They went to the good place. x̣ʷə́n said, "Oh, I have a relative, Snake. He keeps his own power." They started and went to look for him. Then they met him. x̣ʷə́n said, "Oh, you my younger brother, I am looking for you. Help us. We want to kill k'ʷə́cx̣ʷe so that she may disappear because she always eats people." Snake said, "Well, we can kill her quickly." "Oh, you my younger brother, I'll make you my head band. You shall wrap yourself around my head and you shall shake as my head band, when you fold yourself around the top of my head. You will shake your head and you will open your mouth wide. Your tongue will loll when I am dancing." Now the Snake was put on by x̣ʷə́n. Then they went. They entered the house of k'ʷə́cx̣ʷe. x̣ʷə́n said, "Now we have come." Crane had a dress tied all over with all kinds of weeds and many flowers. All kinds of leaves were attached to his head. He had a necklace. k'ʷə́cx̣ʷe said, "Oh, elder brothers, really your dresses are nice." Now it was night. x̣ʷə́n said, "Now help us." Then x̣ʷə́n began to sing and Crane helped singing,

> Always is putting out his tongue
> Always is putting out his tongue my plaything.
> Always is putting out his tongue
> Always is putting out his tongue my plaything.

Then they sang. It got day. They danced much. Then it got day. They sang now the whole day. Then it was evening. They sang and until the fifth night, just when it was midnight, k'ʷə́cx̣ʷe got tired. She said, "Oh, my elder brothers, I am tired and I am hungry. Now I will just watch you." x̣ʷə́n said, "Oh, let us only sing." They sang. It was not yet day. Then k'ʷə́cx̣ʷe went to sleep. They sang much. First x̣ʷə́n stopped. He went to k'ʷə́cx̣ʷe. He shook her much. He dragged her about but he could not awaken her. x̣ʷə́n said, "Let us sing until day comes." x̣ʷə́n said to Crane, "Make her sleep." After that they sang again. Then day came. k'ʷə́cx̣ʷe snored. They tried to awaken her but they could not wake her up. After that x̣ʷə́n said to Crane and Snake, "Now go out and gather much dry pitchwood." Then Crane and Snake went. x̣ʷə́n stayed alone. First he played with k'ʷə́cx̣ʷe. Then he piled up much pitchwood. Then he went out. He came to Crane and they piled up dry pitchwood all around. After they had piled up, x̣ʷə́n entered. Then he lighted all the pitchwood in the house. Then he went out. He locked the house. They piled up much pitchwood in front of the door and they set fire to it. Then all the pitchwood caught fire and it burned strongly all around the house. Then they went for a long, good pole to poke k'ʷə́cx̣ʷe. k'ʷə́cx̣ʷe awoke. She yelled, "I am burning. Oh, these bad ones. I will eat you up." Then they poked her. "Oh, the bad ones." The fire collapsed and the flames went up. k'ʷə́cx̣ʷe burst so that the earth shook violently when she burst. The world always shakes then because they have their own power in the world. These just always ate people. Their ways were different. It was poked by x̣ʷə́n and Crane and Snake and the whole house of k'ʷə́cx̣ʷe was burned. Then they threw away their sticks and the dress of Crane. They started to a good country and sat down. x̣ʷə́n said, "We killed k'ʷə́cx̣ʷe today. Now I have taken all this kind of monster from the world. In later days women will not be monsters who eat people in this world. The women will be transformed. When the Chief comes down the people will be different. Young men shall bathe and they shall tell about their lovers. They shall play on sand bars. There shall be no more monster women to carry them away. When they are found by women nothing shall do harm to them. Young men shall not be eaten. They shall bathe in the river and the young people shall just be happy. These shall be the ways of young people. In all the rivers they shall bathe. Thus the world shall be later on. The people shall be different."

Raccoon and His Grandmother

Raccoon and his grandmother had a house near a large river. His grandmother always gathered juniper berries, camas, and acorns. And Raccoon always stole from his grandmother. The grandmother did not know who stole her provisions. Raccoon had disappeared and his grandmother went to where they were accustomed to hide the food. She came to where they kept the camas. Raccoon made a noise. He was eating camas. She sneaked up to him from behind and whipped him only two times. Then he got away from her. Raccoon was very full inside. He was very satiated. His grandmother came from behind with a stick. The old woman said, "I will whip you after a while with a switch." Raccoon got afraid and he climbed a slender crabapple tree. He cried aloud. His eyes were watering and mud was mixed with his tears and made black circles around both his eyes. Therefore he is black around the eyes for all time. His grandmother wanted to whip him. His grandmother looked up. Raccoon yelled above, being afraid, his inside melting. He had diarrhea. His excrement splashed on the eyes and mouth of the grandmother. The old woman said, "Don't do that, bad one." The old woman went home. Raccoon came down. He went to the river. He went into the water in the great river and washed his clothing. First he dived. After he had dived he came to where he dressed and put on his clothes.[1] He went to where it was quite shallow. He looked on the bank of the river and he saw his shadow. He saw his face and he said, "Oh, my eyes have been changed by crying. Where shall I go? I must run away from my grandmother." He played near the bank of the river. He always had a little knife made of obsidian. He always carried it. Then a big person came down the river. Raccoon said, "This is a monster." Behold! Mountain Lion came to the opposite bank. Mountain Lion said to him, "You child, will you bring me a canoe? Have you got a canoe? I wish to cross." Raccoon was laughing. He said to the Mountain Lion, "Why have you got a big head and a big mouth?" Raccoon stopped talking and Mountain Lion growled, "That, bad child, by and by you will know. I will eat you whole, eat your whole body, bad one." Raccoon said, "You only have a big mouth. How can you fight with your big head?" And Mountain Lion got very angry. He swam across and came to the bank of the river. Raccoon could in no way run away. He got his sharp-edged obsidian. He held it firmly in his hands and he fought the monster with it. He ran around in a circle and he ran fast. Although he was stabbing Mountain Lion, his knife was too small. Then Mountain Lion was breathing hard, his mouth wide open. Raccoon said, "Let me jump into his mouth." Mountain Lion nearly bit him and Raccoon jumped into the throat of Mountain Lion. He shut his mouth. The monster swallowed his saliva. Then Raccoon drifted down inside and he stabbed him in his stomach, everywhere inside. Then Mountain Lion became very sick. He defecated and Raccoon drifted out through the intestines of the Mountain Lion. He fell down behind the tail end of the Mountain Lion. He shouted. Just a few times he stepped. Then he fell down. First he growled then he died. Raccoon came and cut his head off with his little knife. After he had done so he went home to his grandmother. When he came to his grandmother he said, "Oh, my grandmother, I killed a mountain lion. Let us go and get its meat." His grandmother said, "Indeed, let us go." Now Raccoon took his ax and big knives and they went to the bank of the river. They reached where he had killed Mountain Lion. Then his grandmother said, "Indeed, you killed a monster." Then they butchered the meat. They cut it up in one day. The meat of Mountain Lion was taken by Raccoon to another house and he put it in there, all that he had killed. He was going to dry it. After he had dressed the mountain lion meat, Raccoon said, "What is the matter with you, grandmother? You do not bring in the meat." His grandmother said, "No, grandson, I never eat meat of a mountain lion. I only eat these two round ones." Then she took the testicles of Mountain Lion and went home. She said to her grandson, "Your place is always in the other house and you can work on the meat." She took the two testicles and made a man. She made him her husband. The testicles became transformed into a man. He talked loud. He laughed loud. Raccoon came for a long time staying in the other house. Then he heard his grandmother always talking. He wished to know, "With whom is my grandmother talking?" He came to his grandmother who was laughing. One person was laughing loud. He sounded like a monster, "He he he." He looked through a hole. Then he saw a man with his grandmother. Then he left quickly because he saw that this man was really a monster. He became scared because he was transformed from the testicles of Mountain Lion he had killed. Whenever he sees anyone he destroys him. He went on a trail and he met Panther and Wild Cat. Raccoon said, "I am running away. There is a monster in my grandmother's house." Panther said, "Come with me. Let us go and kill the monster." Panther went there and he entered the house where the monster was. He entered and went in. He fought with the monster. They fought hard inside. They broke up the house of the old woman. Then they hit the old woman accidentally and she died. Panther did not really fight long with this artificial monster man. Then he died. Panther went out. He set fire to the house and it burned. Then it was destroyed by fire. Panther said, "Let this old one die with the monster. It shall not be thus in later days. Meat shall only be gathered but the bad parts will not be taken. A husband shall not be made in this way. An old woman will make a home with her grandchild. They will stay nicely in one house. That will be the way of later people because in later times it will be different. The way of this woman shall be removed from the world forever. It is not good. Later on people will be different, when the world will be changed, when the Chief will come."

The Five Brothers

Blanche Pete Dawson

A long time ago[1] five young men were living together with one mother. Then they heard that there was a desirable place and that whoever went there was never seen again.[2] He always stayed away. The youngest of the men said, "I have no fear of that monster. I will go and camp there." He went and arrived there. Now it was night. He made a fire under a red fir. A little while later then he lay down. He heard someone saying, "Are you still awake, the one who camps there?" After a little while he heard again, "Is the one who camps there still awake?" "Yes, I am still awake." Then he fell asleep. There he was taken by the monster. Then he was missed by his younger brothers. The one who was the youngest went. He searched for him. He also stayed away. It was always thus until there was only one now, a very young man who was still alive. He was going to search for his younger brothers. He arrived and made a fire. Then he heard someone saying, "Are you still awake, the one who camps there?" He kept still and stayed awake. He thought, "Maybe he thinks I am asleep. Let him think so." Indeed, then the monster jumped right on him. He took him to take him along. He was taken uphill. Now the youth saw that the monster always ate the hearts of people. There lay the bodies of his younger brothers. He took the bodies of his younger brothers and he made them to be just animals. They are the wolves of this day.

The Chief and His House

When long ago in this Tribe the three q'ʷay'iɫq'[1] lived at Lǃaua'iql,[2] the Chiefs of this Tribe lived there. Thus it was told by the old people, the first Chiefs with whom my grandfather grew up. He called the Chief his own ancestors, who was included among the Chiefs together with the other Chiefs of the q'ʷay'iɫq'. Before the white people came they were many. They had houses everywhere along the banks of the nsúlapš[3] from the mouth of the sácapš[4] on this side along this line of the country. They had houses along the banks from there and to the head of the nsúlapš. This nsúlapš was their own river. In the summer they moved away from the prairie to the mountains to the blackberry patches. They went from their homes in Lǃaua'iql because the Chiefs were always with them to gather berries. And they went hunting together. They prepared food and gathered much food, preparing it for the winter at that time. The sqʷalé?amš[5] and the s?ahíwamš[6] and the sácapš[7] sometimes came and others, the spuyálap'amš[8] and with them came the txʷ? á k'ʷamš ?á k'ʷ,[9] and they gathered at náč'aɫ[10] because this prairie had much camas at that time. When they finished digging roots with the other Tribes, relatives of the q'ʷay'iɫq', then they enjoyed themselves every day at náč'aɫ. After they finished picking blackberries, juniper, and salal berries, when they finished camping on the berry grounds in midsummer the Chiefs of the q'ʷay'iɫq' and his relatives from the other countries, sometimes together with Chiefs of other languages, planned to gather in one house of the Chiefs, planning when they gathered in this house and talked about the teachings of all countries at that time. The Chief of this country belonged to them, all the country on both sides of nsúlapš and sácəl'ɫ.[11] These they held and many mountains in their part of the country. After they finished picking berries they planned to burn dry grass everywhere on all the prairies. Everywhere at that time the grass used to be long and there were many flowers. They always burned the whole prairie and also the mountains. They burned the hill to make berry patches just like making gardens for blackberries. They always burned the prairies to plant camas and strawberries. The Chiefs said, "When the earth burns it burns all the badness of the earth and after it has burned it begins to be good." Before they burned the land all the q'ʷay'iɬq' assembled. Everyone prepared to watch all the houses. After this the Chiefs planned to go home to the large houses. All the old people stayed in every house. One watched the large house. The young men and the children and the girls went and scattered all along the nsúlapš down river and up to the head of the nsúlapš. Then they burned all the prairies and some mountains. After they finished burning the land they assembled and had a great feast, which lasted many days. They and the sqʷalé?amš were happy. All the girls and the boys were singing. Everywhere they did this after they finished picking berries. When the grass was dry over all the prairies then they first burned the land of the q'ʷay'iɬq'. After they got back from the mountains they took home all the meat they had dried and the dry blackberries. At that time the sqʷalé?amš and all the other people went home. After they obtained all the food late in the fall the Chiefs went home to L!aua'iql. When winter came they assembled in the large houses and they stayed there during the winter. That was the way of the q'ʷay'iɬq'.

The Way of the q'ʷay'iɫq'

This evening is taboo.[1] It brings evil from the west of the land. It brings the shortening of the life of the people. The evening is taboo. When the darkness is brought down the badness of the world is awakened every evening. When it is just evening then the badness of the world begins to walk about. The badness of the world is just like the soul of a person. The evening is taboo. When the evening begins it is taboo for children and old people to go to sleep because the badness of the evening will come and will take them and will shorten their lives. The sickness is like that. It is hard to be cured by the shamans. Therefore it is a rule for the evening so that the growth of the children will be good. The beginning of the evening is taboo.

A Farewell Speech

Jonas Secena

Honorable ones, first I will talk a few words, when we have finished our work today, when we are looking for good plans today. First I thank you before we dismiss the people. I wish something good would come to this world, to give us light when you go home. While I am talking to you, my people, I am talking from the bottom of my heart. From these I give you my best wishes, my people. I wish that nothing disastrous may come to you when we walk home on this earth. We are looking for the best rule of a Chief in the beginning of the world. They were the Chiefs of this country here. Maybe then[1] we are going to find from the rules of the first Chiefs' good ideas. In the beginning the people and the Chiefs of all countries always respected other people. When a visitor came to the Chiefs we always gave them kind thoughts and the best ideas from the bottom of our heart. Thus it was always with visitors to the Chiefs of the first q'ʷay'iɫq'.

Today we finish following the first ways of the Chiefs in the country. The ways of the Chiefs of L!aua'iql.[2]

SOURCE ACKNOWLEDGMENTS

Franz Boas's "A Chehalis Text" was originally published in the *International Journal of American Linguistics* 8(2) (1935): 103–10 and is reprinted here by permission of the University of Chicago Press.

Dale Kinkade's "'Daughters of Fire': Narrative Verse Analysis of an Upper Chehalis Folktale" originally appeared in *North American Indians: Humanistic Perspectives*, edited by James Thayer, University of Oklahoma Papers in Anthropology 24(2) (1983): 267–78, and is reprinted here by permission of Henry Davis.

Dale Kinkade's "'Bear and Bee': Narrative Verse Analysis of an Upper Chehalis Folktale" originally appeared in *1983 Mid-America Linguistic Conference Papers*, edited by David S. Rood (Boulder: University of Colorado Department of Linguistics, 1984), 246–61, and is reprinted here by permission of Henry Davis.

Edmond S. Meany's Chehalis Reservation field notes are housed at the University of Washington Libraries, Special Collections, Edmond S. Meany Papers, MS Collection No. 0106-001, and are reprinted here by permission of the University of Washington Libraries.

Chehalis materials are printed by permission of Don Secena and the Confederated Tribes of the Chehalis Reservation.

Boas Chehalis texts from the American Council of Learned Societies Committee on Native American Languages and the Franz Boas Papers are reprinted by permission of the American Philosophical Society.

Texts collected by Boas are reprinted from "Legends (Cathlamet, Chehalis, Chinook, Clatsop, and Salishan)," 1890, MS 1313, by permission of the National Anthropological Archives, Smithsonian Institution.

APPENDIX 1

Lower Chehalis Stories

Charles Cultee shared the following three stories — "Qonē'qonē," "The Women Who Married the Stars," and "The Sun" — with Franz Boas[1] at Bay Center on Shoalwater Bay[2] in the 1890s. The National Anthropological Archives holds these stories in typescript, and the American Philosophical Society holds two handwritten manuscripts, a short version and a long version, that are similar to the NAA "Qonē'qonē" typescript. A note with the APS manuscript indicates that Boas copied vocabulary from a manuscript Myron Eells[3] contributed to the Bureau of Ethnology. Eells's manuscript dates to 1882. The APS note indicates that Boas later corrected his own copy in the field.

In 1886 Boas made a self-funded research trip to British Columbia, one of the aims of which was "to learn enough of the languages to map the distribution of the Vancouver Island tribes and their linguistic relationships" (Cole 1999, 101). He returned to British Columbia on behalf of the British Association for the Advancement of Science in 1888 and then secured funding from that group as well as the Bureau of Ethnology for three summers of fieldwork in the Pacific Northwest (Cole 1999, 110). His 1889 fieldwork included Kwakiutl, Salish, and Nootka research. In 1890 his focus shifted to Chinookan languages. Douglas Cole notes, "Chinookan linguistics and ethnology were a diversion that had turned into a preoccupation. [Boas] had gone west in 1890 with the intention of spending three months studying the Salish of Oregon and Puget Sound for the Bureau of Ethnology. He needed, incidentally, to determine if the Chinookan languages of the lower Columbia River were Salishan, as Bureau linguistics believed, or a separate stock. There was so much to do on the Salish that Boas did not want to spend much time on the problematic Chinookan" (1999, 147). And so Boas traveled south: he visited Siletz, Grand Ronde, Astoria, and Seaside in search of Chinookan speakers. At Seaside Clatsop informants suggested Boas visit Bay Center, where Clatsop speakers still resided. There Boas noted that Clatsop and Chinook peoples had "adopted the Chehalis language," and he was assured "that the whole

country was occupied by the Chehalis" (1894, 6, 5). But Cultee still spoke ancestral Chinookan languages, remembered a number of stories from various
traditions, and could tell these stories in their language of origin. Boas worked
with Cultee during the summers of 1890 and 1891 and then returned to Bay
Center in December 1894 to clarify earlier work and collect more texts. This
work resulted in the Bureau of Ethnology's publication of Boas's *Chinook
Texts* (1894) and *Kathlamet Texts* (1901).

Boas kept a diary during his stay at Bay Center. When he first arrived at
the place (sometime between July 9 and 15, 1890), Boas thought he would
not need to stay longer than a week. Upon meeting Cultee, Boas wrote, "His
English is not very good, but he quickly caught on to what I wanted, and he
understands his own language. Thus I learned more about the Chinook language today than I had during all the time I worked so hard on it before,
and that is since June 30! This man is the only one left who really knows
the language. I hope to be finished with him by Sunday and then I will return to Astoria. That is, if no good Tsihelish (Chehalis) interpreter shows up"
(Rohner 1969, 121). But Cultee knew—and shared—much more than Boas
anticipated, prompting Boas to extend his stay at Bay Center. Boas notes that
he worked with Cultee on both Chinook and Chehalis. On July 20 Boas described the Chehalis work: "It is not easy, and that might be the reason why
I will leave here early on Tuesday—but that is not certain yet. Anyway, the
language is very difficult; its vowels and consonants are much more difficult
than the Chinook." In the same entry, after a series of complaints regarding
conditions in Bay Center, Boas conceded, "Well, it seems to me tonight I can't
do anything but fuss. That's because the language is so unexpectedly hard"
(Rohner 169, 124). Boas would return to this difficult language many times
over the next forty years, committing to its study and encouraging students
and colleagues to continue this work.

Boas provides a rough biographical sketch of Cultee in his introductions to
Chinook Texts and *Kathlamet Texts*. He notes that Cultee's "mother's mother
was a Katlamat,[4] and his mother's father a Quila'pax';[5] his father's mother
was a Clatsop, and his father's father a Tinneh of the interior"[6] living on the
"upper Willapa river." Still, Cultee spoke Chehalis "almost exclusively," as his
wife, Catherine, was Chehalis and Chehalis was "also the language of his children." Cultee's cultural background and proficiency in Chinookan languages

impressed Boas, who lauded Cultee as a "veritable storehouse of information" (1894, 6; 1901, 5).

In his introduction to *Chinook Texts*, Boas provides a glimpse into how the two men collaborated: "My work of translating and explaining the texts was greatly facilitated by Cultee's remarkable intelligence. After he had once grasped what I wanted, he explained to me the grammatical structure of sentences by means of examples, and elucidated the sense of difficult periods. This work was the more difficult as we conversed only by means of the Chinook jargon" (1894, 6). Although this explanation was first given in reference to the Chinook material, Boas gives a similar—nearly verbatim—explanation in reference to the Kathlamet material. In his introduction to *Kathlamet Texts*, Boas adds, "It will be noticed that the periods of the later dictations are much more complex than those of his earlier dictations" (1901, 6). It might be assumed, then, that the Chehalis stories were transcribed in Lower Chehalis—as the APS manuscript shows—but translated into English by way of Chinook Jargon, or Chinuk Wawa as it is presently known. It should also be noted that Boas published a German translation of "Qonē'qonē" in "Zur Mythologie der Indianer von Washington und Oregon," *Globus* (1893, 154). It is quite possible, then, that the story was translated into German before it was translated into English. The scars of translation are concealed in the National Anthropological Archives typescript—an English-only version with handwritten corrections made throughout—thus obscuring the transformation of the stories from oral tradition to published, and polished, texts.

Qonē'qonē

Charles Cultee

Qonē'qonē[7] and Crane lived at Toke Point[8] where they caught salmon, which they intended to dry. One fine day they encamped in an open country, made a fire, and sat down. Crane had a fine tail which Qonē'qonē envied him. While Qonē'qonē and Crane were eating he set fire to the dry grass, which singed Crane's tail. Qonē'qonē told Crane to put the tail into the dry grass, which would extinguish the fire. Crane did as told and set fire to the grass. Qonē'qonē said, "Put it into pitch wood. That will stop it." Crane did so and set fire to the pitch wood. He advised him to put it into everything that was dry and combustible and therefore Crane's tail was burned down. Only when it was quite short did he advise him to put it into water. Crane got angry and said, "Why didn't you advise me to put it into water before?"

They traveled up the river until they arrived at some rapids where there were salmon. Qonē'qonē made a trap above the falls so that the salmon when jumping up the river fell into his trap. Crane took his harpoon and speared the best fish that he saw passing by. Thus, it happened that Qonē'qonē obtained all the old, lean salmon while Crane got all the good ones. They caught a plentiful supply and began to dry them. Qonē'qonē envied Crane very much because he had very nice fish while his own were very dry. He thought, "I will kill Crane and take all his salmon." He began to sing and dance and continued to sing for a long time. Crane joined him and they danced. Qonē'qonē took a heavy stick and when his cousin in dancing bent his head he tried to strike him on the nape but Crane moved his head quickly aside and avoided the strike. He became very angry because he knew that Qonē'qonē tried to kill him. They traveled on across the mountains. Crane packed his fish in five bundles and carried one after another across the mountains. Qonē'qonē put his fish into a basket and told Crane, "I will make them go across the mountains by themselves. I will drive them over," and he told them to go. When they began to descend, Qonē'qonē's basket began to roll down faster and faster and when his dry fish came to the river they rolled into the water, came to life and swam away. Qonē'qonē tried to hold them but they pulled him into the water and he was almost drowned. He said, when he regained the shore, "I wish I could find Crane, who has played me this trick. Henceforth when people want to carry a load they shall work hard in doing so."

Qonē'qonē came to a place near the river where he built a salmon weir. He excreted twice near the weir and asked his excrements to call him if there should be any salmon in the weir and then went to sleep. After a while his excrements called him. He jumped up but when he looked in the weir he found only a little stick, so he went back. Soon his excrements called him again, and this time he found a larger stick. As this happened several times and he got angry and scattered his excrements about and excreted anew. He told the excrements, "Don't fail to call me if there are salmon in the weir but not otherwise." At the dawn of day they called him. He was very hungry and when he came down he found a salmon in the weir. He carried it ashore and roasted it. He took a milt and threw it under his bed, saying, "I wish you would become a man." The milt was very white and good. Every day he caught salmon. After five days he heard singing in his house but when he looked about in the morning he found nothing. Five times he heard singing when he returned at night. Then he took a torch and searched all over the house. He found two girls under his bed and he said, "Oh my children. Why did you hide yourselves? I am a poor man, and live all alone." Then the girls came forward from the bed. They dried the salmon and helped him in his work. They were very pretty and white. They combed their hair and washed themselves and were nice to look at. When they were grown up he thought, "I would like to marry them. They are not my children."

One day he wanted to go down the river in his canoe. He sat down in the bow of the canoe while the two girls were in the stern. Whenever they passed rapids the canoe would turn around and Qonē'qonē would say to his children, "Turn around the canoe," and they obeyed. After this had happened several times he said, "Turn around the canoe, my wives." One of the girls heard what he said and said, "Did you hear what he said? He called us his wives." The other one said, "No, he said, 'My children.'" They traveled on and when they came to the next rapids he said, "Turn around the canoe, my children." The girl said, "Now did you hear that? He called us his children." The next time, however, he said, "Turn the canoe around, my wives." One of the girls said,

"Do you hear that? He called us his wives." But the other did not believe her. When they came to the next rapid he called them again his children. They passed five rapids, then the second girl heard also that he called them his wives. They resolved to run away and the next time when the canoe turned around and the stern touched the bank of the river they put a large stick in the canoe and jumped ashore. They said to the stick, "When he says, 'Turn the canoe around, my wives,' you must turn it around," and the stick obeyed and therefore Qonē'qonē did not notice their escape. Finally, however, the wood did not turn the canoe when Qonē'qonē said, "Turn the canoe around, my children." He looked back and discovered that the girls had run away from him. He said, "Where are you my children?" The girls went up the country and finally reached a prairie. There they found a swing on which a cradle was placed. An old blind woman was swinging the cradle. The younger one of the two girls said, "Let us steal the child out of the cradle." They walked up to it and placed a piece of rotten wood in the cradle instead of the child. The old woman did not notice it as they had told the rotten wood to cry the same way as the child. But finally when she felt over the cradle she found that the child had been stolen. She cried, "Oh, my grandchild, you have become a piece of wood." Her daughter came home and said, "Why didn't you look out better for my child?"

The girls traveled on. The child's mother took her old blind mother on her back and pursued the girls. She went very quickly and almost overtook them. Then she threw down her mother, who urinated and made at once a large lake, but the girls who carried the baby succeeded in escaping before the water could overtake them. The woman again took her mother on her back and continued the pursuit. She threw down her mother, who urinated and made another lake. This time a smaller lake was made and the girls succeeded in making good their escape. Five times the woman threw down her mother but she was unable to overtake the girls, and she returned home with her mother. The woman took the cedar bark in which the baby had been bedded in the cradle, pressed it and molded it into the shape of a child. It was transformed into a boy.

The two girls continued to ascend the river and mountain and finally reached two rocks which were opening and closing continually. They passed in between them and reached a prairie on which they built a house in which they lived.

The baby's mother called all the good jumpers to go to the women's house and recover her child. Every year they tried but were unsuccessful as no one was able to pass through between the opening and closing rocks.

The boy who had been stolen grew up and became the husband of the two girls. They had many children, boys and girls. One day the young man's mother asked Blue Jay to try to recover her son. He went up to the rocks and after a while he jumped through when they opened and only his tail was caught when they closed. Then he reached the house in which the girls and their husband were living. He looked through the chinks in the wall and perceived the young man, who was making an arrowhead. He saw that he broke one and immediately after he broke a second and third one. Then the young man cried, "I think someone is looking at me. It makes me break my arrows." He threw them out of the door and hit Blue Jay's eyes. He said, "They stole him once and now he hits my face." When the young man heard the voice he went out and said when he saw Blue Jay, "Come in, young man." Then Blue Jay told him, "Your mother wishes to recover you and I have come to call you. Your wives are Qonē'qonē's children and they stole you when you were a baby." Then the young man got very sad. The women used to go out digging ginseng.[9] The young man waited for them, and when he saw them coming on their way home he cried, "O!" They looked up and when they saw him he arose and shook a stick. When they saw it they were transformed into elks and jumped away. He said, "You shall be elks and run away when you see a bow. Henceforth you will not steal children."

He had many children and when their mothers did not return they began to cry. One of them made his mouth very long and round in crying and he became the sucker. Another made his mouth very large and flat wide and he became the pike. The father gave these two children many little sticks which became their bones. Therefore the sucker and pike have many bones. Another of his sons became a bear and one of the daughters became a cedar. He said to her, "I send you away with your brother. Look out for him. In winter take him under your blanket." Therefore the bear sleeps in winter under the cedar.

He left his house accompanying Blue Jay and taking a large box filled with dentalia[10] along which was so heavy that no ordinary person could lift it. After a while they met a young man who was catching salmon. It was his brother who was made out of the cedar bark after he himself had been stolen. He lived on fish, lizards and snakes because he was very poor. When the young man saw this he said, "Oh, my poor brother." He seized him by the legs and shook him and all the bad things that were in him fell out of his mouth. He washed him and he became a Chief. The two brothers traveled on and they came to a village. They invited the daughters of all the Chiefs as they wanted to marry. When a girl came, Blue Jay, who had accompanied the two brothers, said, "Piss, piss, piss," and the girl turned back before entering the house as she felt compelled to urinate. Another one came and Blue Jay did the same thing. Finally only one homely girl remained whose skin was all covered with boils. She was lame. They painted her face and sent her to the house. Blue Jay cried when he saw her, "Don't let her in. She is not good enough for the Chief's wife." Then he said, "Piss, piss, piss," but it had no effect on her and she entered the house. When she entered Blue Jay was hardly able to breathe. She lifted the heavy box of dentalia which the young man had brought along and then the man married her. She gave the people blankets of deer, elk and salmon.

After a while he said, "I will go up to heaven and become the Sun and will always be able to see my people." He did so and when he went up it grew very hot so that the woods began to burn, and the waters to boil. When he came down again, the people said, "You are too hot. You will kill us." Then he sent his brother and when he traveled on the skies it was good weather and not too warm. Therefore the brother became the Sun and he himself became the Moon.

The Women Who Married the Stars

Charles Cultee

The daughters of a Chief used to go digging roots every day.[11] At night they returned home. One night they were rather late and the night overtook them before they could reach home. They lay down on the beach and looking up they saw stars. The youngest one said, "I wish that large star were my husband," and the older one said, "I wish that little one were my husband." After a while they fell asleep. When they woke, they found two men were lying with them. They took them to their houses. The girls found themselves in a large town. The man who had taken the younger girl was old and blear eyed. The husband of the older one was young and handsome. The younger one was ashamed and said, "My husband is homely. I will kill myself." She secretly made a long rope of spruce twigs by means of which she intended to let herself down to the earth. Then she made a hole in the ground and tied the rope around her belly and let herself down. When she had almost reached the ground the rope gave out and she was unable to descend any farther, neither was she able to ascend to heaven again.

The relatives of the girls missed them and searched everywhere for them all over the earth, but were unable to find them. Blue Jay, who was sleeping in the Chief's house, the roof of which was open, looked up and saw something just above his head. He said, "What is that up there? There is something black just above my head." The other people did not see it, but every time he looked up he saw something black just above the house. One day something fell down from the sky. Then he said, "Our Chief's daughter's head has fallen down." On the following day another part of her body fell down until all her bones had fallen into the house. Up to this time a strong gale had prevailed. It abated when all of her body had fallen down. Her father called all the people together. They danced and sung hoping to find a supernatural helper to bring the sky down to them so that they might go and take revenge. Some of the men were so strong that when they danced the sky began to come down but it went up again before it reached the ground. Finally Snowbird began to dance. Blue Jay said, "Oh, he is not strong. He cannot help us any." Snow-bird, however, told the people to blacken their faces, necks, and shoulders. They danced and the earth began to quake, then Blue Jay encouraged them to dance more. Then the sky began to tip over until it touched the earth on one side. They fastened it with strong ropes on the earth. They prepared to go up to the sky and tested their strength. Skate claimed to be a great warrior. Blue Jay said, "If you go and they shoot at you they will certainly kill you." Skate said, "Let us try and see if you can hit me." Blue Jay and Skate placed themselves opposite each other. Blue Jay shot first. As soon as he shot Skate turned so that his narrow side was towards Blue Jay and the arrow missed him. Then he shot and hit Blue Jay's foot and ever since that time Blue Jay's feet are weak. Blue Jay acknowledged that Skate was a good warrior.

The people began to ascend. They came to a very cold country. Then they saw a house and the salmon weir of the people who lived there, nearby. The Chief told Beaver to go and try to get some fire for they were afraid they would die of cold. Beaver jumped into the water and struck the surface with his tail. He allowed a man who was standing there with his dip net to catch him and to carry him into the house. He pretended to be dead and they singed him over the fire, but when his hair was burning he jumped up and ran away and they did not know what had become of him. He came to his people and they made a fire and warmed themselves. When they came to the village of their enemies, they sent Robin to see if their enemies were asleep. He sat down by the fire and warmed himself and forgot to return. After a while they sent Skunk. When he came to the house he laughed, "He, he, he," and ever since that time Skunk laughs this way. An old woman heard him and said, "I have never seen a skunk in this country." When the Chief's daughter, who lived with the younger star, heard it, she said, "There are many skunks in my country. Where may it have come from?" At midnight the Chief sent Mouse and Rat to see if their enemies were asleep. Mouse went up to the stolen girl and pulled at her blanket and told her to look out for them at night. "We have come to take you back." No one had noticed them. They gnawed through all the strings of the women's aprons and the bowstrings of the men and returned to their people without having been seen by anyone. Robin was still sitting by the fire but Skunk finally called him. Robin said then that he had forgotten all about the war. Two women heard this and said, "Didn't they speak about war?" Early in the morning when everyone was asleep the people from the earth attacked the village and killed everyone. When the people took up their bows to shoot, they found that the bowstrings were cut through. The women were unable to put on their clothes because Mouse had gnawed through the strings. Eagle attacked the West Wind, the oldest of five brothers. Red Eagle took hold of the South Wind, Owl took hold of the East Wind, [?] Eagle the North Wind, and Chicken Hawk attacked the youngest of the Wind brothers. They fought for a long time and tore off the heads of the four oldest brothers. Chicken Hawk, however, was unable to vanquish his adversary. He was unable to hold him and the latter made his escape. Then they returned with the women. When one-half of them had gone down, Blue Jay cut the ropes with which the sky was fastened to the earth and allowed it to jump back while one-half of the people were still in the sky. For this reason, forms of animals and birds may be seen in the constellations.

The Sun

Charles Cultee

Once upon a time[12] there lived a Chief who kept the Sun in a box.[13] When his daughter went to gather berries, she carried the box along and opened it a little so that she was able to see. When she had filled her basket she carried the box home to her father. The people in the other countries were very poor. They held a council in which they deliberated how they might obtain the Sun. Finally they decided to send K-ʼaliqōo[14] to the Chief to steal the Sun. When he reached the country he assumed the shape of an old slave. The people found him and took him home to their Chief.

Blue Jay lived in the house of the latter. He said, "Oh, that used to be my father's slave. He lost him one day. His grandfather has been my father's slave!" The people believed him and gave him to Blue Jay. When the Chief's daughter went picking berries they took him along to paddle the canoe. He was a very good oarsman, and Blue Jay said, "That is Tsīstīsāaʼtq, he was a very good oarsman too," and they believed him. When they were traveling along the slave began to say, "Tses, tses, tses." Blue Jay said to his brother Robin, "He always spoke so when he carried me about when I was a little boy," but Robin did not remember, and Blue Jay said, "Oh, you are good for nothing. You are older than I am and you do not remember him." Finally they arrived at the berry patch and the girl opened the box a little. As soon as the Sun appeared, the slave jumped up, seized the box and opened it and it became daylight. He ran away and they were unable to catch him. The people had almost killed Blue Jay because his lies had been the cause of their losing the Sun.

K-ʼaliqōo took the Sun home to his Chief, who gave it to the people, saying, "Henceforth we will all enjoy the Sun and not one man alone shall have it."

APPENDIX 2

Edmond S. Meany's Chehalis Reservation Field Notes

In 1905 Edmond S. Meany (1862–1935), a University of Washington history professor, made a tour of reservations throughout the state. He visited the Chehalis Reservation, collected history and stories, and took photographs of those who shared cultural knowledge with him. Meany's interest in Indian affairs spanned his career—his 1901 master's thesis focused on the life story of Chief Joseph and the plight of the Nez Perce people. He also worked with Edward S. Curtis, traveling with him to South Dakota in 1907 (Meany Papers, guide). The following is a transcription of Meany's field notes from the time he spent on the Chehalis Reservation. Most of these notes are based on stories told by Jacob Secena, sisína?xn, Jonas Secena's grandfather. According to Jonas, his grandfather "saw it before the whites came"; thus the fragments of Secena family stories preserved in these notes establish literary continuity from precontact to the present day (Adamson 1926–27, 379). sisína?xn died in 1907 at the reputed age of 117, two years after Meany recorded his stories. The stories here include a version of "The Flood," "Fire," "Bear and the Ant," and "Winter Story." Meany references the Choke and Heck families, whose stories are included in this volume, and he interviewed and photographed Peter Heck, teller of "The Flood." The Quinotle, Pete, and Smith families are also mentioned. Meany wrote a series of articles about Washington tribes for the *Seattle Post-Intelligencer*; these articles ran from June to November 1905. The article on the Chehalis tribe, sensationally titled "Washington Redmen Who Helped Palefaces In War: Chehalis Tribe of Twenty-Five Braves Who Fought for Whites," ran on October 15, 1905. Meany featured the legends of sisína?xn in this article, selections of which are reproduced here, reporting:

After some persuasion, See-see-nah told legends and stories of the old life, which I was very glad to write down with the aid of the two interpreters.

Long ago, before the whites came, his people owned all the prairies and land around the Chehalis river. Misp and his older brother, Kom-mol-owish, taught the Indians how to make fire by spinning one dry piece of wood on another. They also taught the people how to use fish and roots for food. Then they used flint and bluestone for arrowheads and axes.

Adamson includes "Mʊspʻ and Kəmoʻl," a Humptulip story shared by Lucy Heck, in *Folk-Tales of the Coast Salish*. In Heck's version, Mʊspʻ and Kəmoʻl are twins, the children of the son of Chief Woodpecker and a beautiful woman named Sɪlʼoʻcən. The twins are transformers and give xəné·xəne his name: "They went to Rock Creek. There they found a person, his face painted with charcoal, lying among the rocks. All around him in the sun were lying clam shells. The two brothers took the clams and stuck them on his front teeth but he did not wake up. They named him X̣wɑneʻx̣wɑne. (He was a great liar.)" (Adamson 1934, 338). These culture heroes are also featured in Quinault stories shared by Bob Pope with Livingston Farrand and by Billy Mason and Bob Pope and John Dixon and Jonah Cole with Ronald Olson.

Meany also includes sisínaʔx̣n's version of "The Deluge," which is similar to the one Peter Heck shared with Franz Boas and to those Peter Heck, Jonas Secena, Joe Pete, and Marion Davis shared with Thelma Adamson:

In the long ago the birds were like people.

Blue-jay told Field-wren to wash his face, but Field-wren pretended to do so and only made scratches on his dirty face with his claws. Blue-jay was wise and could not be fooled. Every day he kept telling Field-wren to go wash his face.

Field-wren at last grew tired and said he would now wash his face. He told his wife's mother to sit back from the stream for now he was going to bathe. When Field-wren had finished his bath he sounded a warning and then it began to rain in a terrible storm. For forty days the water poured down. There was a long tree on Miami prairie where the canoes were tied. The people rushed to this place when they saw the water rising over the land. Big fishes, porpoises, whales, seals and sealions came up from the sea.

Muskrat was the only fellow who went down into the water to the ground underneath. He brought up a handful of dirt and threw it off in one direction and where it fell a mountain grew up. Then he did so again and another mountain grew up. When the mountains grew up the waters began to pass away. Many of the animals and fishes could not find their way back to the ocean and their bodies can be seen to this day in the shape of mounds on the prairies. Near Boisfort, which the Indians call Tal-lo-lum, there is a big mound with a flowing spring on its crest. This was a whale and the spring was its spout.

After the flood went down the land and the rivers were left as they are now. Birds were no longer like people. After that people were only like men and women just as they are now.

This version provides an account not only of the flood but also of the transformation of the world to how it is today. sisína?xn places this story in Upper Chehalis territory: Mima Prairie is a little over ten miles northeast of the Chehalis Reservation, and Boistfort Prairie is located in the Willapa Hills, along the south fork of the Chehalis River. The mound described bears similarity to Grand Mound, ɬačʼís, which has been described as "a piece of star [that] broke off and plunged into the earth" (Miller 1999a, 16); the mound mentioned by sisína?xn could possibly be the site of the Old Boistfort Cemetery, a mound upon which up to seventy pioneers were buried between 1855 and 1887.

sisína?xn also shared a version of the story that received considerable attention from Boas and M. Dale Kinkade, "Bear, Yellow-Jacket, and Ant":

See-see-nah, the patriarch of the Chehalis tribe, in his cabin on the prairie, was just as interesting that day to the two interpreters as to his white visitor. He told a number of those rapidly fading legends. Here is another, the story of the bear and the ant:

"In that long ago when animals and birds talked like people the Bear said: 'Let all the people sleep one winter and then it will be daylight.'

"To this the Ant replied: 'That is too long a while to sleep. Let the daylight come just as it has been. The people would not get along well at all if they lay down to sleep all winter.'

"The Bear jumped up and down and stamped the ground, saying: 'Let us lay in the ground the whole year round.'

"But the Ant got the best of the Bear. He stamped on the ground and he drew his belt tighter and tighter until it almost cut his body in two. All this time he sang for the daylight and when the daylight came as usual and his victory was complete, he went to make his home in an old rotten log.

"The Bear was sullen and would not yield to the victory of the Ant. He went off by himself to den-up and sleep through the whole winter. Even to this day bears go to rotten logs to eat up the ants out of revenge for that old battle for the daylight."

This version is quite similar to the one shared by Jonas: Bear argues that people should sleep all winter; Ant argues that things should stay as they are. But while Yellow-Jacket is an important figure in Jonas's version—he is the one who disagrees with Bear and calls on Ant for support—sisína?x̣n does not mention Yellow-Jacket. Consistent with sisína?x̣n's version, Big John of Green River and Jonah Jack of Puyallup shared stories with Arthur Ballard in which the contest is between Bear and Ant only. In a Cowlitz version Mrs. Northover shared with and Adamson, Ant, Yellowjackets, Frog, and Grouse all go against Bear and argue that sleep should last only one night, not a full year (1934, 188). The figures who participate in the contest vary depending on who the storyteller is and the cultural tradition from which the story originates.

It is also worth noting that Meany served as editor of *Washington Magazine*, a short-lived periodical that focused on Pacific Northwest matters and preceded the *Washington Historical Quarterly*. The third issue of *Washington Magazine* features "The Story of Sun: A Legend of the Chehalis Indians," written by Robert J. Jackson, or Sard-Khom. The editor—presumably Meany—indicates that Jackson graduated from the Carlisle Indian School in 1896 and lived on the Chehalis Reservation at the time of publication. The connection between Meany and Jackson was likely established during Meany's visit to the Chehalis Reservation the previous year, though Meany does not mention Jackson in his field notes or the *Seattle Post-Intelligencer* article. Also, it is worth noting that, when speaking with Thelma Adamson, Marion Davis referred to Robert Jackson as his brother. Both Davis and Jackson attended Forest Grove Indian School in the 1880s. It appears that Davis returned to the Chehalis Reservation afterward, but Jackson continued his education at Carlisle before returning home.

"The Story of Sun" is an anglicized version of the story of x̣ʷə́n, whom Jackson calls "Mr. Whun." As in Secena's story, Mr. Whun, or Whun-nie, tricks twin girls, Misses White-skin, into making their way upriver with him. When they discover he intends to make them his wives, they run away. The twin girls then steal a child, replacing him in his cradle with a piece of rotten wood, with the intention of one day making him their husband. The child's mother, Mar-lhee, and his grandmother pursue the twin girls, but the Misses White-skin outrun them. As in Secena's version, the community gathers and attempts to rescue the kidnapped child, but a wall "that lifts up and leaves a small opening at the bottom and shuts again with great force" foils many of these attempts (Jackson 1906, 181). Mr. Blue-jay makes it through the opening and finds the kidnapped child, who is now a grown man. A major difference between Secena's version and Jackson's version is that in Secena's version, Moon is kidnapped, but in Jackson's version, Sun is kidnapped. Sun then returns, "traveling and changing everything in his way" (Jackson 1906, 184). He meets Miss Frog, whom he takes as a wife, and together Sun and Miss Frog come across Sun's younger brother. Sun is reunited with Mar-lhee, and then he and his younger brother plan to travel. Sun makes his way around the earth, but he scorches the people and vegetation as he goes. Since his younger brother is scared of the dark, Sun suggests that the younger brother travel during the day and that Sun travel at night. Jackson explains,

> So that arrangement was carried out and what was the moon is what we now call the Sun, the younger brother of the real Sun, who now travels in the night. You cannot make an old Indian believe otherwise. The medicine-man will prove to you that the moon is the Sun, because did not the Sun marry Miss Frog and took her with him in his travels. You can see her plainly hanging on to the moon every time he passes us in his travels. So the phrase "The man is the moon" is ridiculed by the oldest red-men as absurdly untrue. There is no man in the moon, they say, but it's Miss Frog and her descendents that are in the moon. The Sun goes home and stays with his mother quite often and rests from his travels and that is the reason we have no moon some nights. (1906, 186)

Jackson's editorial style is similar to the approach that Katherine Van Winkle Palmer would take in editing *Honne, the Spirit of the Chehalis: The Indian In-*

terpretation of the Origin of the People and Animals, in that Jackson explains the story as he tells it, clarifying passages that would be difficult for readers not familiar with Chehalis literary tradition.

Meany recorded, wrote, and edited much more Chehalis material than has previously been acknowledged, working nearly a generation before the salvage anthropologists of the 1920s focused their attention on this oral tradition. The field notes that follow are the foundation of Meany's work on Chehalis and provide a bridge between the scant work done by government agents, missionaries, and scholars in the nineteenth century and the corpus-building exercises of twentieth-century anthropologists. Annotations are mine and are largely drawn from ethnohistoric sources.

7r

Chehalis Reservation 23 Aug 1905
    See-Choke, William[1]
        wife[2] daughter of chief
        near Tenino
        —

    Ed. Smith[3] son of John
    Smith[4] <Shaker> thriftiest
    of farmers

    Secena[5]

    Peter Heck, policeman

    Hyas Pete[6]

7v

Che-neet-ya[7]—old
Chief of Chehalis.
Son still living—Shotty[8] on
Chehalis reservation.

Stevens'[9] chiefs
    Ah-yow-in-es[10] Head chief

    Treaty failed.

Old home of Chehalis on Ford
Prairie near ferry

Chehalis served 50 or 25
of them as soldiers for whites
in war.[11]

Old food.
    Dried salmon from Chehalis
    Deer, elk & bear
    Berries salal & blackberries
    June or service berrys dried

8r

Roots–lacamas,[12], fern
Tsat grey fern root[13]

    Cedar bark dresses
    Bear skin blankets

    Stone axes

Indians mail at Gate

Peter Heck ⟨Yon-num⟩[14]
Policeman
    Father and mother Chehalis

Mrs. Heck[15] [Se-a̱ls-t<u>um</u>][16]
father Humptulips
mother Chehalis.

Coyote's color; Hoop race[17]
in which coyote was beaten
by swift animals of forest. Dust
covered, he became gray

8v

George Quinotle[18] father
Humptulip. Got nickname
From Quinault

Very little fishing now.
Old forms gone

Boarding school closed 10
years ago.

    Produce of farm goes to Puyallup
    Day school at Chehalis

—

Promise that when school
closed lands of farm go back
to Indians.

Act of Congress 18 Jan 1881
20 yr plan of sale of land to
Indians

Mrs. Secena[19] blind and
old but expert basket weaver

9r

Lena Heck[20], weaver
Mrs. Lucy Quinotle, weaver

Secena

People used to be birds
Bluejay told field wren
to go and wash his face
just scratch his face with
nails
     Happened on Black River
near Miami Prairie[21]
[M-ne-qua-thol][22] — ~~lacamas~~
     Keep telling wren to wash
face every day he got
tired & said all right I'll
wash my face
     Wren went to wash his
face & told his mother-in
law to sit back because
he was going to bathe
     After wren got through

9v

giving warning, it started
to rain. Poured down
rain for 40 days
rivers came up and
covered country all over
water raised, fishes
whales, porpoises
pictures of them now
on ground in heaps of
earth.
    Muskrat only fellow
that dove into water &
reached ground he grabbed
dirt & came up & threw
it in different directions
making mountains &
water began to dry up.
People rushed for canoes
when water was raising
Long tree anchoring place
In Miami prairie
people tied canoes there
    Things were changed
to present conditions

10r

After water left, people
as now.
  Wren and blue jay passed
away

Fire

Misp, [name given by Mrs
Secena] young brother of
Kom–mol–owish [in
Chehalis]—Two of them
taught people to make
fire and to use lacamas
roots and fish for food
  Spinning dry piece of
wood to make friction ignite

10V

Bear and the Ant.

Bear says let all people
sleep one winter then it
will be daylight
Ant says: too long a
while to sleep. Let day
come just as it has
been. People would
get along at all if they
lay down and sleep
all winter.
Bear: jump up and
stamp ground. Let us
lay in ground year
around.

Ant got best of bear
stamp around. Drew his
belt tight that it nearly
cut him in two. He sang
for daylight.
Ant got best of it and
daylight came. He came
to old rotten log

11r

That is reason Bear
goes to logs and eats
ants for revenge. And he
alone dens up for winter.
—

Winter Story[23]
Falling of Snow
—

    Never used to allow children
to travel in snow because
snow comes for people to starve
them out covering up tracks
If no tracks weather change
Soon.
    Thinks it happened before flood
Swi-os-swi-ous[24] [snowbirds]
5 of them were warriors
then and started to fight
weather warriors. Whipped it
but one escaped and that is
why snow now comes once
in long while

11v

At time of flood
whale stranded near
Boisfort [Tal-lolum][25]
prairie. Large mound.
with spring on top. That
is spout of whale

Long ago Indians got
flint and blue stone for
arrow heads, spears
and axes
Reeds, seaweed, fix up
for houses all over this
country.
Found piece of metal
tied around wood near
Copalis on ocean beach
Very valuable
Cut off 4 inches to make
adze would cost one old
slave
For piece 6 inches one

12r

young able body slave
    Piece on end of stick
for sort of ax circle around
cedar like beam.
    Get tree down and form
boat with elk horn for
wedges.

Father's father Quinault
His father married a
Chehalis — owned lands
along river.
    His mother and father used to
live here. Summer near
Centralia.
    As far as this river goes
including Black Hills.

APPENDIX 3

Franz Boas's "A Chehalis Text"

A CHEHALIS TEXT.

By Franz Boas.

The following text is in the dialect of the Upper Chehalis *(Q'wăya·'ilq)* who live nowadays near their old home on a Reservation not far from Oakville, Wash. Their language is one of the Coast Salish dialects. It is closely related to the Cowlitz dialect from which it differs particularly by the regular change from *k* to *tc* which has been discussed by Haeberlin and myself.[1] A considerable number of Upper Chehalis pronounce *k* far forward, palatized, almost between *kᵘ* and *tᵘ*. Although Cowlitz belongs to the *k* dialects, Upper Chehalis to the *tc* dialects these two are very closely related. To the same group belong the Sä'tsep, Lower Chehalis, Humtolip, and Quinault, although the differences in vocabularies are greater than those between Upper Chehalis and Cowlitz. The dialects of Puget Sound belong to a distinct group.

BEAR AND BEE.

aⁱˡ ta² tu·'lapt³ aⁱˡ ta² swi·ns⁴
At past beginning at past their being

scama·'laxᵘ tit⁵ pǎ·'psayu', we⁴ na·'tc'ocin⁶
people these animals, was once

aⁱˡ ɔ·'ts's⁷ sq'e·'tatci⁸ itoˀ ta² tsɔ·'tnaxən⁹
on one day may be past said this

tit stcɔ'txvn, tit sq'e·'tatci we· siuᶜˡ⁰
this black bear, "This day is too

tɔ·'mlˡˡ. siul²⁷ tanin ankᵘs sxv'qwa·ncˡ²
short. Too much now always I am hungry

aⁱˡ t⁵ pantlᵛ'cˡ³. tˡ'aqᵘˡ⁴ tanin sa'astawtˡ⁵
in a wintertime. Well now we make

[1] See Sound Shifts in Salishan Dialects, International Journal of American Linguistics, 4 (1927): 120. A map showing the location of dialects will be found in the same paper p. 119.

it kwəslˡ⁶ na·tcpa·'nxᵘˡ⁷. tˡ'a·qᵘˡ⁴ tanin
a darkness one year. Well now

itwi iyuᵘ ɔ·'ts's⁷ pətxᵘ ɔ·ts's⁷ stˡ'icˡ⁸. we·
just one night one winter. It is

tˡ'aqᵘˡ⁴ na·tc'pa·'nxᵘˡ⁷ tˡ'aˡ⁹ sq'e·'tatcis²⁰,
well one year will (be) its day,

ɔ·'ts's məltc we· ɔ·'ts's sq'e·'tatci. we· tˡ'aˡ⁹
one summer is one day. It is will

s'e·'lənstawt²ˡ tit sxwas tca tˡ'a nukᵘ
we are eating these blackberries and again other

eta·'m'²² al tit panmə'ltc.ˡ³ we· al tˡ'a
things in this summer time. It is in future

stˡ'ica·'wms²³ we· tˡ'a sts'itclsᶜ²⁴ tit
they are winters, it is future disappear these

sq'vlna·'mts²⁵. panxᵘca·'nx²⁶ an ˡ²⁷
ripe fruits. At that time then future

kwɔ'swvnˡ⁶. we· al t xwa'qo' tit stˡ'icˡ⁸ we·
it is dark. It is in all this winter it is

xwa'qo' t scama·'laxᵘ we· ltˡ²⁷ mo·'səm ltˡ²⁷
all people it is future sleep future

ɔ·'ts's⁷ stˡ'ic. q'e·tsx²⁸ we· ai q'al sa's²⁹
one winter. Like this it is good must make

tit təmc tca t scama·'laxᵘ. — tsɔ·'tnaxən
this world and the people." — He said this

tit stsci·tcs³⁰, me·'tta·nin³ˡ laws³² ai
this bee, "Not now when past good

q'al we·ns²⁹ q'e·tx tit təmc. tˡ'a·qᵘ
must be like this this world. Well

tc'u sq'e·'tatcin³³ ăn ˡ²⁷ tˡ'a kwɔ'swvnˡ⁶.
always it is day then future again it is dark.

tɔ·'malteˡˡ,ˡ² t sq'e·'tatci tca t skwɔ'swvn.
Short are the days and it is dark.

tsɔ·'tnaxən⁹ tit stcɔ'txvn, si·'u' tanin tɔ·'ml t
He said this the bear, "Too much now short a

spatx̱ᵘˡ⁸ tca t sq'e·'tatci. t'e·x²⁶ wi
night and a day. This is

104 INTERNATIONAL JOURNAL OF AMERICAN LINGUISTICS VOL. VIII

*xwəni'notənl*³⁴ *me·'łta ixo*ˈ *smo*ˈˈ*səm änk*ᵘ*s*
tiresome, not enough(?) sleep always

ł'a q'e·'tatcin. *tso·'tnaxən tɨt stsci·tcs,*
again it is day." He said the bee

*xa'was*³⁵ *a·'ˈmq'la*ʾ³⁶. *s'e·'kwata·nc*³⁷ *ɨt*
"First wait! I am going for the

*sts'kä'eq*ʾ. *hɔi*³⁸ *än ta wa'ksən*³⁹ *tanin tɨt*
ant." Well, then past he went now the

*stsci·tcs cal*⁴⁰ *t xa·łts*⁴¹ *tɨt sts'kä'eq*ʾ.
bee towards the its house the ant.

*kwa'x*ᵘ*misən*⁴² *tɨt sts'kä'eq*ʾ. *o· na'we*⁴³ "Oh thou
He reached the ant.

*ən nä'stci*⁴⁴, *sa·'wlamina·nc*⁴⁵ *ä·'nəm*ʾ⁴⁶ how
my younger brother, I ask thee

*q'ał sa's*²⁹ *tɨt təmc. tso·'tnaxən tɨt stcə'txvn*
could do the world. He said the bear,

*tł'aq*ʾᵘ *tanin na·tc'pa·'nx*ᵘ¹⁷ *tł'a kwəs.*
'Good now one year future dark'."

*tso·'tnaxən tɨt sts'kä'eq*ʾ *q'ał tali'lna*⁴⁷
He said the ant, "Would it be kind for

*scama·'lax*ᵘ, *q'ał tali'lna scama·'lax*ᵘ,
the people, would it be kind for the people,

*q'ał si·'tɨt*⁴⁸ *tɨt təmc łt*⁴⁰ *q'e·tsx*²⁸.
it would change gradually the world by thus.

*tł'aq*ʾᵘ *me·'łta t sa's tɨt təmc łt q'e·tsx.*
Good not its making the world by thus.

q'ał wi·ns q'e·tsx t sa's tɨt təmc
It would its being thus its making the world

*wi q'ał ləpłtcl*⁴⁹ *ta·tc*⁴⁰ *sxwəq*ᵘ⁵⁰. *tso·'tnaxən*
be should we die with hunger." He said

*tɨt stsci·tcs cal tɨt sts'kä'eq*ʾ, *hɔi, o· na'we*
the bee to the ant, "Well, oh thou

ən nä'stci s'e·'kwatsitcən ¹²ˑ³⁷.
my younger brother I came to get thee.

*xə'ləmtcla*ʾ⁵¹, *o· swa'kstawt* ¹²ˑ³⁹. *tso·'t-*
Get yourselves ready! Oh we are going." He

*naxən tɨt sts'kä'eq*ʾ, *tɨt xte' nä·'c wi*
said the ant, "This here is

xatł'. tcən tɨt ləpłtcl. ä'ntsa wi
difficult. May be future we die. I am

*tɨt ä'xtkvlctcən*⁵². *wi aqa łt ta'laxəntcl*
the one I have power. It is shall we use

ən sä'xtkvlc. o· na'we ən xwał stsci·tcs.
my power. Oh thou my elder brother bee.

*tł'aq*ʾᵘ *sa·ˈmalstawt*⁵³ *ł'ə'qəyux*ᵘ. *hɔi, ał*
Good we are making a belt." Well at

*ta sna·msawmc*⁵⁴ *ł tɨt ł'ə'qəyux*ᵘ *tso·'tnaxən*
past their finishing the belt said

*tɨt stsci·tcs, xa'was to·ˈmalstawt*⁵⁵
the bee, "First we dance for power

*tula'płtsäne tł'a se·'kvntcł*³⁷ *stcə'txvn. hɔi,*
before future we go after bear.". Well,

än ta to·ˈmaliłte tula'płtsäne ta
then past they danced for power before past

swa'ksawmc cal tɨt stcə'txvn . . .
they went to the bear . . .

*kwa·'xvmisiłte*⁴² *tɨt stcə'txvn ał t*
They reached for a purpose the bear at the

*äts q'e·'tatci. sä'xtwalesyawmc*⁵⁶, *än ta*
complete day. He saw them, then past

*la'xlaxa·'wvn*⁵⁷. *o· ila·'pa äncnä'stcitən*⁴⁴
he laughed. "Oh ye younger brothers,

*a·'qa o·'k'wa st'o·'wap*⁵⁸ *cal to·ls*⁵⁹
now evidently you arrive to (?)

*naxe·'nwatəntcl*⁶⁰ *tɨt təmc.*
We arrange the world.

---

¹ Temporal subordination is expressed by
nominal forms; here with the preposition *ał* at,
on, in: *ał tɨt təmc* on this world; *ał t xa·'łtsawmc* in
their home; *ał ta sna·'msawmc* at their having
finished (see notes 20, 40).

² *ta* past tense; *l, tł'a* future (see notes 19, 27).

³ *tuˑl·* o start; *tu·'lap* to begin.

⁴ Stem *wi·, we·* to be; *s-* nominalizing prefix
(see note 18); irregular third person possessive *-ns*
(see note 20).

⁵ Like all other Coast Salish dialects attributive
demonstratives have separate forms for non-
feminine and feminine, the latter containing an
element *s*

non-feminine	feminine	
t	*ts*	general indefinite
ɨt	*ɨts*	general definite
tɨt	*tsɨts*	definite present
tat	*tsats*	definite absent

No distinction between feminine and non-feminine
is made in the plural. The non-feminine forms are

often used for feminine terms. At present at least, the usage is rather loose and feminine forms appear only when the distinction of gender is important. With names non-feminine forms are used: *t Malə'*, *tat k*wə'tcχwɛ* the *k*wə'tcχwɛ* (a female monster). We have *ts kă'is* his grandmother; but also *t k*o*'is* his mother.

⁶ The numerals one, two and three have two forms, one for counting, irrespective of objects counted, the other for counting objects that are compounded with the numerals. These are:

	Absolute	In compounds
one	*o·ts's*	*nătc'aw·*
two	*sa·'le*	*tsa·m·*
three	*tca·'la*	*tcanaw·*

Higher numerals are the same for both sets:

four	*mo·s*	eight	*tsa·'mos*
five	*tse·lătcs*	nine	*tă·ʷox*ᵘ*
six	*t'ăχăm*	ten	*pa·'natcs*
seven	*ts'ɔ·ps*	one hundred	*pa·ntcsto·mc*

Derivatives are formed from these stems by means of suffixes, for instance *nătc'a·'wets'a, tsa·'mets'a, tcana·'wets'a,mo·'sets'a* one,two, three, four blankets; *tsa·mstq, tcana·'wstq, mo·stq* two, three, four fires; *ts'opsta·'lx*ᵘ*,tsa·'mosta·'lx*ᵘ*, pa·ntcsta·lx*ᵘ* seven,eight, ten houses. There are many irregularities in the use of these suffixes (see note 34).

Numeral adverbs are formed with the ending *·(ta)cɪn* which shows also irregularities:

once	*na·'tc'ocɪn*	six times	*t'ăχă'mltacɪn*
twice	*tsa·'mcɪn*	seven times	*ts'ɔ·'pstacɪn*
three times	*tca·'nocɪn*	eight times	*tsa·'mostacɪn*
four times	*mo·'sacɪn*	nine times	*tăwi'x*ᵘ*stacɪn*
five times	*tsi'ltctacɪn*	ten times	*pa·'ntcstacɪn*

⁷ *o·ts's*, generally used in diminutive form *ɔ*ᵒ*ts's*.

⁸ Stem *q'e·'tatci* it is day; *s·* nominalizing prefix (see note 18).

⁹ Stem *tso·*, appears in two forms *tso·t* and *tso·n*. The form *tso·tn·* occurs always before direct discourse. The ending *χ* indicates definite, present statement (see note 28): *ti tso·tχ tl*a t wak*ᵘ*s* he said this his future going, i. e. he said he would go; *ɪt tso·'ntəmχ* he was told this; *ɪt tso·'nχtcən* I said it to him; *ɪt tso·t* he said; *ɪt tso·'ntwaleχ* he said to him (see note 12).

¹⁰ *siu*ᶜ too much.

¹¹ *to·m* short. For terminal *l* see note 12. Diminutives are formed by insertion of a glottal stop and vocalic changes: *o* to *ɔ*; *i, e* and *ă(ə)* to *ă'*. *a·ls*, dim. *a·'ls* chief; *man, ma'n* child; *sqɔ·'wun, sqɔ·*ᵒ*wun* to drink. — *io·'s, iɔ·*ᵒ*s* to work; *to·ml, tɔ·'ml* short. *wəll, wă'll* to fly; *wi·t, wă'lo* canoe; *pă'săn, pă*ᵒ*săn* younger sister; *sqwă'ləm, squă*ᵒ*ləm* heart; *sqe·wl, sqă'wl* to stink; *e·mts, ă'mts* grandchild. — Several are irregular: *sχwa'sănl, sχwa*ᵒ*se·nl*

blackberry vines; *qwa'il, sqwaya*ᵒ*il* child; *ăyă'lwun, ăyă'ă'lwun* pretty; *sχa'wq'meta·nc, sχă·*ᵒ*awq'meta·nc* I talk.

¹² All verbs have two forms, completive or momentary, and continuative. These are differentiated by two sets of pronouns. The subjective forms are regular:

	Completive	Continuative
I	*-tcən*	*-anc*
thou	*-c*	*-c*
he	—	*-ən*
we	*-tcl*	*-stawt*
ye	*-ap*	*-ap*
they	*-yawmc*	*-ilte*

English adverbs are verbs, and in combinations of two verbs the first verb (often our adverbs) takes the pronominal subjective endings while the second verb remains unmodified. If it is a transitive verb it retains the pronominal object. In other words, the association between the transitive verb and its object is firm, while the connection between verb and subject is loose.

*χə'k*ᵘ*tcən ăts kwanə·'n* I hold it firmly *(χək*ᵘ firm)
χe·'wntctcən a·'is   I am very sick *(χe·'wntc* very)

The objective forms of the pronouns are not the same in all verbs. I give here three classes:

Completive

	I	II	III
me	*-ts*	*-mc*	*-stomc*
thee	*-tse*	*-me*	*-stome*
him	*-ən*	*-l*	*-x*ᵘ
us, you	*-tol*	*-mol*	*-stomol*
them	*-ən-awmc*	*-l-yawmc*	

Continuative

	I	II	III
me	*-tsa·l*	*-ma·l*	*-tomal*
thee	*-tsin*	*-men*	*-tomen*
him	*-t*	*-l*	*-tw*
us, you	*-tul*	*-mol*	*-tomol*
them	*-t·yawmc*	*-l·yawmc*	*-tw·yawmc*

It will be seen that the common elements are

	Completive	Continuative
me	*(-s)-c*	*-al*
thee	*-e*	*-in(-en)*
us, you	*-ol*	*-ol*

The third persons of the various classes are quite distinct. Verbs ending in the third person in *l* are intransitive, and many have corresponding transitive forms. The four forms given in the following examples illustrate these forms.

	Intransitive		Transitive	
	Completive	Continuative	Completive	Continuative
to stretch	ɩt wʊlql	sʊʊ'lqwʊn	ɩt wʊ'lqən	sʊʊ'lqtən
to open	ɩt wa·q'l	swa·'q'wʊn	ɩt wa·'q'ən	swa·'q'atən
to be crosswise	ɩt wip'l	swi·'p'wʊn	ɩt wi·'p'ən	swi·'p'tən
to stick on	ɩt pət.l	spə'twʊn	ɩt pətə'n	spə'ttən
to spill	ɩt pɔqᵘl	spɔ'qᵘwʊn	ɩt pɔqʊ'n	spɔ'qᵘtən
to surround	ɩt yɩ'ləml	syɩ'ləmwʊn	ɩt yɩ'ləmən	syɩ'ləmtən
to drop	ɩt ä·pxᵘl	s'ä·'pxwʊn	ɩt ä'pxʊn	s'ä'pxᵘtən
to spin	ɩt ts'älpl	sts'ä'lpwʊn	ɩt ts'ä'lpən	sts'ä'lptən

Intransitive verbs in *l* form the continuative in -(*a*)*wʊn*. Some verbs with short stem vowel and single terminal consonant have the suffix -*a·wʊn*.

to run	ɩt äxᵘl	s'axwa·'wʊn
to fall over	ɩt yaq'l	s'yaq'a·'wʊn
to laugh	ɩt laxᵘl	s'laxwa·'wʊn

Stems with long vowel or bisyllabic stems with accent on the first syllable retain their accent in the intransitive continuative form:

to awake	ɩt p·a·ll	sp'a·'lawʊn
to enter	ɩt ma·'il	s'ma·'yawʊn
to emerge	ɩt sa·'latcl	sa·'latcawʊn

By far the greatest number of verbs of this class shorten the *a* and have the ending -*wʊn* with a strongly voiced *w*.

Intransitive verbs ending in -*m* have the continuative ending -*mitən*.

to sleep	ɩt mo·'səm	smo·'səmitən
to swim	ɩt sätc'ə'm	s'ä'tc'mitən
to boil	ɩt läpə'm	slä'pmitən
to make a humming noise	ɩt tə'mtaməm	sta'mtəm·i·tən

A small number of intransitive verbs ending in vowels or *n* form the continuative with the suffix -*nən* or -*ən*.

to sing	ɩt e·'lən	s'e·'lanən
to dive	ɩt i·'so'	s'i·'sonən
to bathe	ɩt ä''to	s'ä''tonən
to snow	ɩt a·cq	s'a·'caqən

Transitive verbs in -*ən* form the continuative in -*tən*. Stems with short vowel and ending in a single consonant shift the accent from the ultima to the penultima.

to pick out	ɩt yixə'n	s'yɩ'xtən
to see	ɩt äxə'n	s'ä'xtən
to close	ɩt täqə'n	stä'qtən
to cut	ɩt q'wäxʊ'n	sq'wə'xᵘtən
to pull	ɩt wʊcə'n	swʊ'ctən

Stems with long vowel or ending in consonantic clusters do not shift the accent.

| to cut | ɩt q'we·'tl'ən | sq'we·'tl'tən |
| to spread out | ɩt wʊ'lqən | swʊ'lqtən |

Others with long vowel of stem have the vowel *i* or *a* before the ending -*tən*.

to call a name	ɩt u·'matən	s'u·'matitən
to learn	ɩt po·'tən	spo·'titən
to stir	ɩt yu·'t'ən	s'yu·'t'itən
to gather	ɩt o·'laxən	s'o·'laxitən
to patch	ɩt q'ä'xən	sq'ä'xatən
to bother	ɩt tsa·ᵖyən	stsa·ᵖyatən
to throw away	ɩt 'a'xʊn	s'a'xwatən

Causative verbs in *xᵘ* have their continuatives in -*stʊʊn*.

to track	ɩt a·'yənqme·xᵘ	s'a·'yənqəmstʊʊn
to give to drink	ɩt qɔ·xᵘ	sqɔ·ᵖstʊʊn
to take home (to cause to go home)	ɩt ya·tl'xᵘ	s'ya'tl'stʊʊn

Some verbs in *xᵘ* have their continuative in -*yin*.

to kill, strike	ɩt yu·'tsaxᵘ	s'yu·'tsayɩn
to hide	ɩt i'pxvnexᵘ	s'i'pxvneyɩn
to teach	ɩt oxwa'naxᵘ	s'oxwa'nayɩn

Verbs with an indefinite object, derived from transitive verbs, have the endings -*äml* for the completive, and -*malən* for the continuative.

to beat time for a song	ɩt qä'säml	sqä'smalən'
to shoot with gun	ɩt tä'qᵘtcäml	stä'qᵘtcmalən
to take something home	ɩt ya·tl'twaml	s'ya·tl'twamalən

The use of the glottal stop at the end of the continuative form seems to depend upon the phonetic structure of the stem.

There are also distinct forms of the passive, a completive in -*əm*, a continuative in -*stc*, derived apparently from the transitive continuative.

to be drowned by someone	ɩt tc'ä'ltəm	stc'älstc
to be taken	ɩt kwana·'təm	skwana·'stc
to be hung up	ɩt xwi·'letəm	sxwi·'listc
to be taken away	ɩt asu·'ləm	s'asu·'lstc
to be taught	ɩt oxwa·'nayɩn	s'o·'xwanaɩstc

[13] *pan(xᵘ)* en element indicating time (see note 17); *tłᵖic* cold.

[14] *tłᵖa'qᵘ* a particle expressing the exhortative: well! let us!

[15] Continuative first person plural of *sa* to make (see note 12). This verb appears not only with nominal suffixes (see note 34) but is also compounded with independent nouns. Examples of the former type are *saa·'łtctən* he makes a bundle; *sao·'liłən* he is preparing food; of the latter: *sa'sɣalɣa·'stən* to make an arrow *(ɣalɣa's* arrow); *saᵒwina'wvn* he makes a wedge *(wina·'w·)* In the same way the verb *tłᵖa* to look for, to go to get, is used with suffixes and independent nouns: *tłᵖao·'liłən* to look for food; *tłᵖasxwa'stən* to look for blackberries *(sxwas)*; *tłᵖasqeno·'nłnəntən* to go after wolves *(sqeno·'nłən).* Although every now and then verbs appear with incorporated object the process is not frequently used: *syutswawa°ən* he kills a panther; *it ᾱɣtswawa°tcən* I saw a panther *(swawa°).*

[16] *kwəs-* dark, night; *-ł* see note 12.

[17] *na·tc'pa·'nxᵘ* one year; *natc'-* from *natc'aw-* (note 6); *pa·n(xᵘ)* expresses time, both as prefix and as suffix (see note 13); *al pan tca· tən stc'i·s* whenever I come (at time where my coming); *panxᵘ ca·'nɣ* at that time (at the time there (see note 26).

[18] *stłᵖıc* winter; *tłᵖıc* with nominalizing prefix *s-* (see note 4).

[19] *tłᵖa* future. There are two future particles *tłᵖa* and *ł.*

[20] *q'e·'tatci* it is day; with nominalizing prefix *s-* (see notes 4, 18). Here with possessive pronoun. These are:

my	*ən-*	our	*-tcl*
thy	*'a-*	your	*-ap*
his	*-s*	their	*-sawmc*

The first and second persons singular are prefixes, or better proclitics, the rest are suffixes. The plural forms agree with the completive subjects of the verb. Although the first and second persons singular are both proclitics they do not occupy the same position. This appears clearly when temporal particles are present (see notes 2,5)

ən ta tcᾱwł   my former wife
e·ta la tcᾱwł   thy former wife *(la* thy).

In all forms of this type in which the nominal element is accompanied by a qualifying element, the second person singular is *la-.* When combined with the articles ending in *t* and feminine *ts* (see note 5), these are glottalized:

it'a e·mts   thy grandson
its'a e·mts thy granddaughter

The first person is phonetically united with the article:

itən e·mts   my grandson.

Subordinate clauses are nominalized and have possessive pronouns for subject. Note 1 shows that a temporal clause is expressed by a nominal form. The use of the possessive pronouns with intransitive verbs is illustrated by the following examples:

ał ən ta swi· a·ls   when I was a chief
ał ta la swi a·ls   when you were a chief
ał ta swi·ns a·ls   when he was a chief

amo ən q'a ł wi· a·ls if I were a chief
amo q'a la ł wi· a·ls if you were a chief
amo q'a ł wi·ns a·ls if he were a chief

The negative *mełta* is treated in the same way:

mełta ən ta sᾱ'ɣtəm I was not seen (= it was not my being seen)
mełta ta la sᾱ'ɣtəm you were not seen

The pronominal object of transitive verbs remains attached to it while the subject takes the possessive form:

mełta ən sᾱɣə'n   I did not see him
mełta ən sᾱ'ɣtse   I did not see thee
mełta ən sᾱ'ɣtoł   I did not see you (pl.)
mełta t'a sᾱɣts   thou didst not see me
mełta t'a sᾱ'ɣtoł   thou didst not see us
mełta t sᾱɣts·   he did not see me
mełta t saᾱ'ɣtses   he did not see thee

Many nouns have irregular forms for the third person possessive; for instance from

tcᾱwl wife *tcᾱwa·'ləns* his wife
qa·'ɣa dog *qa·'ɣans* (but also *qa·'ɣas)*
qᾱncs his mouth *qᾱno's* its mouth (an animal's); his ugly mouth

Similar irregularities occur in verbs

ał ta swi·ns at his past being (from stem *wi·,* see note 4).

In the third person plural possessive the suffix *-wmc* follows the possessive suffix *-s.*
Irregularities occur also in the second person plural:

ɣa'cawap your house *(ɣac* house)
swi·'nap your being *(wi·* to be).

[21] *e·'łən* to eat.

[22] *ta·m* something; *e-* plural prefix.

[23] See note 12; *-wmc* third person plural.

[24] *ts'ıtc-* to disappear; *s-* nominalizing prefix; *-s* third person possessive: its disappearance.

[25] *q'ʋl-* to be cooked, done, ripe; *-na·mts* body (see note 34); the term for ripe fruits.

[26] *pa·nx* time (see note 17); *ca·n* is one of many demonstratives; here with the definite suffix *-ɣ* (see note 9).

Demonstrative adverbs refer to three positions; furthermore to rest, result of motion and motion

	Result of motion	Rest	Motion
near speaker	*cǎ'*	*nǎ'*	*cǎ'm*
near person addressed	*la·kʰᵘ*	*nic*	*la·'kʰvm*
near person spoken of	*ci·'n*	*ca·n*	?

The demonstrative pronouns corresponding to the three positions are

	Non-Feminine	Feminine
Near 1 person	*tɪt xte·'*	*tsɪts xtse·'*
Near 2 person	*tɪt xt'e·'s*	*tsɪts xts'e·'s*
Near 3 person	*tɪt xta'*	*tsɪts xtsa'*

There is a fourth form *t'e·x* probably related to the demonstrative of the second person.

²⁷ Future.

²⁸ *q'e·ts* like; *-x* definite (see note 9).

²⁹ See note 15; subordinate possessive form (see note 20).

³⁰ *stsci·tcs* all kinds of bees and wasps.

³¹ See note 20; *tanin* now.

³² *laws, taws* when, past; *lews, tews* present.

³³ Verbal form (see note 20).

³⁴ *xwən-* to be tired; suffix *-inot, -e·nwat* mind; *xwəni·'notənl* to get tired in mind; *q'ole·'nwat* he was happy. — Locative suffixes are widely used and, considering the divergence of vocabularies of the Salish dialects, remarkably stable in all the languages. Examples of Chehalis suffixes are:

-als, -lis head: *xǎ'lq'wals* curly headed; *sa·'qəlsəm* he scratches his head; *ts'axᵘli·'səm* he washes his head; *ta·'səlisitəm* he knocks him on the head

-a·lis eye: *pata·'lisitən* he closed his eyes; *k'vlq'a"lis* cross eyed

-a.is forehead: *tu·'ma.is* wrinkled forehead; *ca·'wa.is* bone of forehead

-o·s face: *ts'axo·'səm* he washes his face; *tsa·'qosəm* he paints his face

-qs nose, point: *stl'e·tcqs* skin of nose; *s'awqs* to sneeze; *snawa·'iqs* spear point, arrow point; *xǎtl'a·'yaqs* point breaks off

-lənl, -lnali, -lnatc mouth: *ta·'wlənl* big mouthed; *qwile·'mtənl* mouth bleeds; *qwatna·'lən* mouth wide open; *tə'qlnatctən* he shuts his mouth

-an' ear (not freely used): *taqa·'n'* deaf

-psəm neck: *tl'a'qpsəm* long necked

-na·mts body: *ts'axᵘna·'mts* to wash body; *q'vlna·'matstən* he scalds his body

-awq, -vq body: *tl'a·'qawq* tall; *xa·xwvq'* fast

-axᵘts chest: *ca·'wǎxᵘts* breastbone

-itcən back: *ts'axwi·'tcən* he washes the back; *ca·'witcən* backbone

-tl'tc belly: *ta·wtl'tc* big bellied

-atc'a hand: *sǎp'a·'tc'atəm* he knocks him on the hand (arm)

-axan upper part of arm, shoulder: *it xǎtl'a'xan* shoulder (of an animal) is broken

-e·q leg: *tsɪ'sǎwe·q* stiff legged

-ntc hip, hind part: *ta·wntc* big hipped

-ǎp thigh: *sp'ǎnǎ'p* back side of thigh

-yɪlps back side; tail: *ca·'wyɪlps* bone of tail; *tə·"mynlps* short tailed

-cən foot: *q'wa'lcən* he burnt his foot

-əlq penis: *ta·'wəlq* having large penis

-e·nawt, -e·'nwat mind (see before)

-a.itəmc land: *aya·'itəmc* good (level) land (see *təmc* land)

-mc people: *sma·'qwamo·mc* people of prairie

-lən woman: *stl'po·'miclən* Cowlitz woman

-il young: *sqa'nil* young gopher *q'a·'ma.il* girl

-stq fire: *ta·wstq* great fire; *tse·xᵘstaq* to throw into fire

-(e)ltci water: *xase·'ltci* bad water; *sqe·'wltci* ocean (= stink water)

-o·lxc, -xc, -a·lxᵘ, -a·lxc, -·xᵘ, -altxᵘ house: *xaso·'lxc* a bad house; *ayo·'lxc* a good house; — *tsa·mxc* two houses (cf. *xac* house, independent); — *pa·ntcsta·'lxᵘ* ten houses; — *mo·sa·'lxc* four houses; — *t'ǎxǎ'mxᵘ* six houses; — *suwala'ltcəlwaltxᵘ* mat house

-q'·, -aq voice: *tə·'laqən* to be ahead with voice (i. e. to start to sing); *tc'i'saqən* to come with voice (i. e. to assist in singing); *namq'* to finish talking

³⁵ *xa'was* first; used commonly to express: I shall first do so and so, then —.

³⁶ The imperative has the suffix *-a'* singular; *-la'* plural.

³⁷ *e·kᵘ-* to go to get someone. Completive *it e·'kvn*; Continuative *s'e·'kwatən* (see note 12).

³⁸ A frequent interjection: well!

³⁹ *waks* to go, Continuative *swa'ksən*.

⁴⁰ Chehalis has a number of prepositions: *al* at (see note 1); — *cal* towards, rarely *c* alone: *swa'ksa·nc c taa·"wvn* I am going towards *taa·"·wvn*; — *to* and *to al* from: *to lǎ'* from afar; *ə·'ts's to al snǎ'stcitən* to al one (from among) my younger brothers; — *l* by (with passives): *it yutsa'·ym l tɪt qa·'xa t sqeno·'nlən* it was killed by the dog the wolf; — *tac* and *tac al* across, through: *tac yɪ'lnaxᵘ* about around; *tac al sma·'na.ɪtci* all over the mountains; — *tǎtc* by means of; also: with (in company): *ɪt laqa'ntcən tǎtc t spǎta·'lən* I threw it with a stone; *ɪt ǎ'xtəm tǎtc na'we* he was seen with you; *ats tǎtc xaxa'* it is (with) taboo.

⁴¹ *xac* house; the form *xa·lts* is used for "his home"; *xacs* his house.

⁴² *kwaxᵘ-* to arrive; Continuative *skwa·'wvn*; *kwa'xᵘmisən* he arrived for a purpose

⁴³ Independent pronoun: *ǎ'ntsa* I; *na'we* thou; *tsǎ'ne* he, she; *ɪne·'m* we; *ɪla·'pa* ye; *tsǎnea·'wmc* they (f., non-f.).

⁴⁴ *nǎ'stci* younger brother; *xwal* elder brother. All terms of relationship form their collective plurals with the ending *-tən* and the prefix *ǎnc·*: *ən*

'ánɛná'stcitən my younger brothers. Exceptions are the terms for husband *scän*, pl. *scäni'sawmc*; man's sister-in-law *stcɑ·'wän* pl. *stcɑ·'wänqvlc*, or *sɑ·'pən* pl. *sɑ·'pənqvlc*.

⁴⁵ *sɑ·'wlaxᵘ* to ask (see note 12).

⁴⁶ *ɑ̇·'nəm'* how.

⁴⁷ *tali·'l* kind, tame; *-na* interrogative. There are two forms of the interrogative; one with the suffix *-na*: *tit ä'ɣtstcna* did you see me? *ta·wtna* is he big? — the other with a verbal (?) stem *'i·* followed by possessive forms (see note 20)

ats 'i·' tən ta skwana·'n am I the one who took it
ats 'i·' ta la skwana·'n are you the one who took it
ats 'i·' ta skwa·ts is he the one who took it
ats 'i·' smo·'smitap taws pətxᵘ, tľa·'qᵘna cal ila·'pa were you (pl.) asleep last night? Was it good for you?

⁴⁸ *si·t·* to be changed. Terminal reduplication expresses a slow, gradual movement

ɪt ɣɪpl	he walks	*ɪt yäppl*	he walks slowly back and forth
ɪt p'all	he awakes	*ɪt p'a·'lall*	he awakes slowly
ɪt ɣwənl	he gets tired	*ɪt ɣwana·'nl*	he is getting tired gradually

In stems ending with two consonants the first of these is duplicated:

ɣvtq-	hot	*sɣv'tətqwɛn*	it is getting hot slowly
mätsqᵘ-	to grind fine	*mätstsqᵘtən*	he keeps on grinding it slowly

⁴⁹ *a·təmən* to die, singular; *ləp-* plural.

⁵⁰ Nominalizing *s-*.

⁵¹ *ɣə'ləm* ready; *-tc* reflexive, *-la'* imperative plural: Reflexives are p. e. *t'oɣᵘtc* he bites himself; *sə'psptcta·nc* I strike myself repeatedly.

There are a number of verbal suffixes belonging to this morphological class:

-ci for: *yu·s* to work; *syu·'scimalən* he is working for him; *ɪt sa·'citctcan* I make it for myself (*-tc* reflexive)

-txᵘt for: *k'wə'ptxᵘtən* he straightened it for him *ɪt sa·txᵘts* he made it for me (> *sa·txᵘt·ts*) *ɪt ä'ɣtxᵘt t koma·'s* he saw the other one's father (he saw his father for him, used only to avoid ambiguity)

-tatci upon: *kwə'ctatcinɪlte* darkness came upon them *ɪt pä'ntatcɪtcən* it fell upon me *tľa äts qä'lxtatci t scama·'laxᵘ* light shall come upon the people *sɣasɪ''ltatcinanc* it is raining upon me

-toc each other: *ɪt ä'ɣtoctcl* we saw each other *-atci* quotative: *stc'i'smatci* it is said he came *tľa·'q'watci* good, it was said

-tľe· evidently: *ɪt a'təməntľe·* evidently he is dead *-xᵘ* to cause: *e·'lənxᵘ* to cause to eat (i. e. to give to eat)

-mis for a purpose: *kwa'xᵘmisən* he arrived for a purpose

There are also some nominalizing suffixes

-alatc'a nomen actoris (see *-atc'a* hand, note 34).
  yu·'salatc'a worker
  e·'lənalatc'a eater

-ano·m by means of
  e·la·'no·m by eating
  tac al tən sma'lqano·mc on account of my forgetting

-ən generally: place, but also; instrument
  tľaɔ·''ltnən fishing place
  q'a·''ləmən camp site
  yu·'sən tools

-tən abstract nouns
  səlä''tən distance
  s'ai'tən goodness

⁵² *ä'ɣtkvlc* to have supernatural power; the suffix *-kvlc* expresses something supernatural: *tso·'kvlc* to dream; *ɣa'skvlc* bad power.

⁵³ *sa·'malən* to make something. Here: Let us make something! A belt!

⁵⁴ *na·m* to finish

⁵⁵ *to·''malən*, stem probably *to·-*, form with indefinite object.

⁵⁶ Third person forms in *wale* are used when the object of an antecedent clause is the subject of a subsequent clause.

ɪt ta·'cis än yutsa·'walinən he chased it, then it killed him

ɪt ta·'cis än yutsa·'yin he chased it, then he killed it

When the object of the subsequent clause is not the same as the subject of the antecedent clause, the *wale* form is not used

ɪt q'eyo·'ts, hɔ'i än ta ä'ɣtwale he called her and she saw the one who called

ɪt q'eyo·'ts, hɔ'i än ta ä'ɣtən he called her and she saw it.

⁵⁷ *la·ɣᵘ* to laugh. Frequentatives are formed by reduplication of the first syllable of the stem including the first consonant following the first vowel. The vowel of the syllable following the reduplication is weakened in length and timber.

tä'ptən	to hammer	*tä'ptptən*
yu·'t'ən	to stir	*yu·'t'yut'ən*
s'e·lp	to shoot an arrow	*s'ä'lelp*
e·kᵘtq	to steal	*s'e·kwe'kᵘtq*
wa'kᵘtq	to go	*swa'kwvksən*

⁵⁸ *t'o·* to arrive coming.

⁵⁹ *to·l* means probably "the one who".

⁶⁰ *naɣ-* to promise; *-e·nwat* mind (see note 34).

110   INTERNATIONAL JOURNAL OF AMERICAN LINGUISTICS   VOL. VIII

THE PLURAL.

Plural formations are varied and speakers differ in their usage. The most frequent plural is formed by an *a* suffixed or inserted in the terminal consonantic complex:

eye	*mo·s*	plural	*mo·'sa'*
star	*la'tc'is*	,,	*latc'i·sa"*
alder	*lama'l*	,,	*lama'la'* (declined by some speakers)
ear	*q'wəla·'n'*	,,	*q'wəla·ᵇna'* (others *'qwəl'a·'n'*)

Stems ending with double consonant insert *a* between them:

knee	*ta·ns*	plural	*ta·'nas*
ghost	*ma·kᵘt*	,,	*ma·'k'wat*
oak	*skwisl*	,,	*skwi'sal*
lazy	*tso·'xvml*	,,	*tsə·'xvmal* (others *tsə·'-xwaáml*)

Stems ending in triconsonantic clusters insert *a* after the first of the three consonants, often with lenghtening of stem vowel

tongue	*texᵘtsl* plural *te·'xwatsl*
pack strap	*yănkᵘs* ,, *ye·'nakᵘs*
hole	*ləpxᵘl* ,, *le·'paxᵘl*

Stems containing syllabic *n (ən)* are treated in the same way:

tail	*su·'psəntc* plural *su·'pasəntc*
bear	*stcə'txvn* ,, *stcə'taxvn*
fish trap	*tsi·'tpən* ,, *tsi·'lapən* (others *tsi·'tpən)*

Collectives have the singular form with the ending *-qvlc*; partitives with the ending *-omc (-awmc)*.

In verbs a number of distinct types of plural formations are found.

1. A short vowel changes to *i·*, sometimes accompanied by a glottal stop:

tight	*k'wək'*	plural	*k'wi·'k'a*
to arise	*xwat'*	,,	*xwi·'t'a*
to heat	*xwətqᵘ*	,,	*xwi·'taqᵘ*
to spill	*k'wəl*	,,	*k'wi·'la*
tired	*xwən*	,,	*xwi·ᵇna*
down stream	*xwəl*	,,	*xwi·ᵇla*
to stick on	*pət.l*	,,	*pi·'tal*
to spill	*spə'qtən*	,,	*spe·'qwatən*
to sink	*nătcl*	,,	*ni·'tcal*
dry	*xăpl*	,,	*xe·'pal*

2. Others change their short vowel to *a*:

round	*yəmxᵘl*	plural	*ya'maxl*
to dig	*tc'ə'lqvn*	,,	*tc'a·'laqvn*
bright	*qəlxl*	,,	*qa·'laxl*
mad	*qəlxl*	,,	*qalaxl*

3. Long *e·* becomes *a·ya*. Possibly the primary form of these stems should be *ey*:

| oily | *kwe·xᵘl* plural *kwa·'yaxᵘl* |
| to cut | *q'we·tl'* ,, *q'wa·'yatl'* |

Here belongs also

to melt away *kwəyimə'n* plural *kwa·'yamən'*

4. The completive plural is often formed with *a* or a glottal stop added to the stem, while the continuative follows the types 1, 2 or 3 (see note 12):

to pierce	*ɩt păxə'n* pl. *păxaə'n spăxtən* pl. *spe·'xatən*
to spill	*păqv'n* ,, *păqwaə'n spă'qtən* ,,*spe·'qwatən*
to break	*xătl'ə'n* ,, *xătl'aə'n spă'tl'tən, sxe·'tl'atən*

A number of verbs insert glottal stops in very irregular ways:

to hang up	*xwi·'lən*	plural	*xwi·ᵇlaən*
to leave	*nəkwa"*	,,	*nək'wa"*
to teach	*oxwa·'naxᵘ*	,,	*ox'wa·'naxᵘ*
to open eyes	*waxa·'lisəm*	,,	*wax'a·'lisəm*

APPENDIX 4

"Bear and Bee": Narrative Verse Analysis of an Upper Chehalis Folktale

M. Dale Kinkade
University of British Columbia

Only one folktale has ever been published in Upper Chehalis, a Salishan language of southwestern Washington. This was the story of Bear and Bee, published in IJAL [*International Journal of American Linguistics*], Volume 8, in 1934 (Boas 1933:103–110).[1] The story was published solely to provide a basis for extensive grammatical notes on the language (and they are very good notes), and nothing whatever is said about the text itself. In fact, Boas only published about a third of the story. Had he continued, he would have had to print 20 highly repetitious songs, and little would have been contributed for his grammatical notes. The story is about the contest between Bear on the one hand and Bee and Ant on the other to decide whether a day should be a year long, half winter and half summer (Bear's position), or whether a day should be short.

I am presenting here the entire story of Bear and Bee, as transcribed in Boas' notebooks (now at the American Philosophical Society Library). The story was dictated to Boas on the Chehalis Indian Reservation near Oakville, Washington in the summer of 1927. The narrator was probably Jonas Secena, a highly respected tribal leader, and the source of most of the stories that Boas transcribed. Thelma Adamson apparently had some of the songs from this story recorded on cylinders, which are now located at the Archives of Traditional Music at Indiana University. I have retranscribed the story in my own phonemic system for the language, and rearranged it into the narrative

1. Volume 8 of IJAL began in 1933, and is so dated, but parts of it did not appear until the following year. My work on Upper Chehalis began in 1960, and has been supported over the years by the American Philosophical Society Library, Indiana University, the University of Kansas, the National Science Foundation, the University of British Columbia, and the Nederlandse Organisatie voor Zuiver Wetenschappelijk Onderzoek. Although I collected a few Upper Chehalis texts in 1960 and 1961, this was not among them.

verse format that I believe correctly portrays its structure (following the lead of Dell Hymes, and best explicated in Hymes 1981). Boas' printed version of the story differs little from that in his notebooks; he omitted a few words and a couple of lines, particularly at the end of what he published. The version presented here is based exclusively on the original notebooks. My procedure will be to explain why I have organized the story this way.

First of all, it is apparent that many units (acts, scenes, etc.) are grouped together in sets of three or five. This is entirely based on internal evidence, but upholds a principle that Hymes has explicated: "The regulating principle in verse relations appears always to go together with the pattern number (ceremonial number, sacred number) of a community. Where that pattern number is five, as in Chinookan, Sahaptin, and Kalapuyan, one finds relationships in narrative in terms of sequences of three and five units. Where that pattern number is four, as in Takelma and Tonkawa and Zuni, one finds sequences of two and four" (Hymes 1983).[2] Admittedly, accepting this principle helps in looking for structural units, but it cannot in itself justify them.

My first procedure is to divide the text into (verse) lines. This is relatively straightforward in Upper Chehalis if the main predication of each main or subordinate clause is assigned to a separate line with its complements and adjuncts. This sometimes makes for short lines and odd translations, but nevertheless accurately reflects the structure of the language, where virtually anything can be a main predication. I later adjust some of these line divisions, sometimes on what I consider purely aesthetic grounds. Arranging the text by lines puts many sentence particles at the left margin, and these prove to be useful in determining other groupings (note here the frequency of particles like *wi* and *húy* as line beginners).

Secondly, I look for the largest blocks, the acts. In Bear and Bee, these sort out naturally into three on the basis of plot structure. The five-day con-

2. In this same paper, Hymes gives a very convincing explanation of why different versions of the same story can be different and still be analyzed into narrative verse: ". . . details of motivation and outcome vary greatly in closely related texts. One response is to seek what is constant, as most important, because oldest in tradition, perhaps most basic, and the like, neglecting what varies as 'mere' detail. Another response is to welcome what is constant as a frame within which to recognize the play of imagination and personal interest. It is through reinterpretation of motivation and details of outcome that narrators find personal expression in traditional stories of which they are not considered authors, but knowers and performers." (Hymes 1983)

test forms a coherent unit, and what precedes it can be seen as presenting the argument and introducing the three protagonists. What follows the contest is denouement and telling how things are to be in the future. However, although action determines the number of acts (and scenes), it does not tell automatically where the divisions between the units occur. But in Upper Chehalis, major breaks of this sort in the stories I have analyzed are regularly marked by a particle (usually *húy*) or 'he said' (*cútnaxn*). Thus Act II might begin at line 133 or 136 just as well as at 134 in terms of plot, but 134 is strongly marked for a scene or act beginning, and no violence is done by making that the beginning of the act. Similarly, the song at the beginning of Act III might be seen as belonging in the preceding act, with all the other songs, but then what I have called a coda would not come at the end of the scene, as it seems regularly to do through the rest of Act II. In addition, *wi húy* is strongly marked for beginning an act. Act III thus ends up quite short, but that is not unusual in Upper Chehalis stories I have looked at; there is also some comparative evidence that more could have been done with this act. In a Cowlitz version, for example, there is a well-developed act at this point (in Cowlitz, Bear is opposed by a team consisting of Ant, big Yellowjacket, black Yellowjacket, Frog, and Grouse):

"'You've beaten me and now I'm going to eat you,' Bear said at last. He looked everywhere for Grouse but could not find him. He sat down again. 'One night, one night,' someone said. It was Ant and the Yellowjackets. He ate them. That's why bear always eats ants and yellowjackets. The others escaped him. He can never catch grouse and frog. The grouse always flies to a tree and the frog always goes under the water.

"'As for myself,' Bear said, 'I'll sleep a whole winter. You fellows can sleep one night.' He went to a cedar tree and made a door in it, just large enough to crawl through. He stayed there all winter, sleeping until springtime. After a while he opened the door and said, 'Is it warm yet?' It was perhaps January and still cold. He closed the door and slept and slept. A little later he got up. 'Perhaps it's light now, perhaps it's warmer,' he said and opened the door. 'Oh, it is warm! It must be about March now. Perhaps things are growing already.' He swam and swam. Then he found some skunk-cabbage. It was the first thing he ate after his long sleep. He ate and ate. He went close to a house and built a house of his own.

"'Before long the berries will be ripe; then I'll have a lot to eat,' he said. After a while he thought, 'Oh, I'm hungry.' He found a hollow log in which there were some ants and a yellowjackets' nest. The ants bit him and the yellowjackets stung him but he ate them anyway. 'I'm going to eat you fellows, you got the best of me,' he said." (Adamson 1934:189)

Division of acts into scenes follows similar principles. Act I can be seen to consist of three interactions, one between each possible pairing of protagonist. First Bear and Bee state their cases, then Bee solicits Ant's help, then Ant and Bear arrange the contest. The point of division between Scenes i and ii seems clear, but that between ii and iii is not. My first inclination was to divide these at the point where Bee and Ant have finished their dialogue (line 79), then, as I began to see the coherence of this part of the text, I tried it successively at lines 89 and 94. None of these seemed particularly satisfactory, although lines 79 and 94 at least begin in an acceptable manner. I eventually realized that stanza A presents a nice trio of actions: Ant and Bee declare that they will do something (this begins first at the end of Scene ii), they do it and declare they will do something else, they do this and declare they will do something else, and then they do this. Furthermore, each of these substanzas begins the same way (with the sequence *húy n ta-*), and there is in this stanza as a whole a series of five *húy*s, changing only at the sixth verse with the actual reappearance of Bear. But because most of the action of this stanza applies to Ant and Bee, it seems to be closely connected with Scene ii, and might be considered a coda to that scene or as some sort of entr'acte between Scenes ii and iii. I ended up putting it as I did largely because of the strong beginning of line 73—one that is much stronger for a scene beginning than line 94, the only other possible choice—and because it then begins in a way identical to the preceding and following scenes.

Act II automatically divides into five scenes, one for each day of the contest. Not all these scenes have strongly marked beginnings, but the counting of the days seems to dictate the divisions. What I have separated out as a coda to each scene could be placed at the beginning of the following scene, except

that then none of the scenes would begin in a usual way (whereas ii and iii
now do), and new problems would be raised for the division between Acts II
and III. These codas seem to summarize each scene and provide a bridge to
the following scene.

The division of Act III into scenes is more difficult because of the brevity
of the act. But three units can be seen: the first ends the contest and declares
the winner, the second declares how the world will be now, and the third explains bears' enmity toward ants and bees.

The divisions into stanzas seems to follow a general principle of Upper
Chehalis narratives. Each scene consists of two stanzas. This pairing principle
is not as consistently followed here as elsewhere, but is evident nevertheless.
Here, scenes sometimes have two parts each, and in three instances I have
divided scenes into three stanzas. The first of these is in Act I, Scene i, where
I simply do not know what else to do with the first four lines. Such beginning
lines sometimes constitute a separate title or introduction to the story, but
that does not seem to be the case here. The second set of three stanzas is in
Act I, Scene iii, the case just discussed in terms of scene divisions. The third
case is the final scene, where truncation seems to have affected the telling of
the story. Act I, Scene iii has another peculiarity: each of the stanzas seems to
consist of three parts, rather than a more expected two. Both stanzas of Act II,
Scene i also have three parts, although the reason for the multiplicity of songs
in this scene is not clear. It may have to do with the addition of a reference
to dancing in the middle of the scene, and this may have thrown the count
off or gotten the narrator mixed up when he added it. An alternative analysis
would be to recognize three stanzas in this scene, one for each sequence of
songs by Bear then Bee and Ant, although this puts the dancing reference in
the middle of a stanza.

Assignment of lines to stanzas is motivated on grounds of blocks of action,
and these blocks fairly consistently begin with one of the usual markers and
major divisions, especially throughout Act I. These markers are not always
used in Act II, where a song and its introductory line or two are enough to
mark the breaks, and they occur only twice in Act III.

Verse structure best portrays Hymes' principle of threes and fives. Sometimes particles suggest verses of three or five lines, sometimes semantic con-

tent suggests certain groupings. But the verse format is not so rigid in these stories that these are the only groupings found, although it is noteworthy that sets of three or five lines are so often used to present a particular theme. The songs of five lines each throughout Act II are the most obvious examples.

The verses of Act I are more interesting, and show many structural possibilities available to the narrator. In Scene I, Stanza B1, there are two sets of verses (or three; the relationship between my a1 and a2 is not so close as to preclude an analysis of this half-stanza intro three verses). The first of these verses is simply the three lines 6–8 expressing why Bear thinks the day is too short. The second verse is divided into three parts (versicles) by the exhortative phrase ƛǎqʷ *tanin*, the third instance of which is expanded with the particle *wi*, bringing the triplet to a close. (This closing device is used again in line 60, after a series of lines beginning with the modal particle *q'aɬ*.) Within this same verse, the units of time are expressed in a rather artful fashion: first we have dark:year, then one night:one winter; the third part changes these to day and summer, and reverses the order with the year and season — year:daylight, then one summer:one day. The actual structure of lines 17 and 18 is somewhat ambiguous; here *wi* could be either the particle frequently used to begin lines or the copula. I suspect that it is the latter here, but have left the lines as they are to show the parallel with lines 13 and 14. On the other hand, making 17 and 18 one line would result in a triplet of three-line versicles.

The following verse, b1-b2, has two parts each of three lines clearly marked by *wi*, followed by some transitional line or two. The unity of the two half-verses is that the first expresses what summers will be like, the second what winters will be like. The next two half-stanzas, B2 and C1, each contains three ideas, which I have expressed by designating three verses each.

In Scene ii, Bee's first address to Ant (lines 47–52) consists of five lines (the last of which I have divided into two half-lines, referring back to lines 9–18. The next half-stanza presents some problems. I see no semantic grounds for dividing it into two sets of three lines each, but it may be a five-line verse if the repetition in lines 54 and 55 is an error (either Boas' or his narrator's). Exact repetition of this sort is not usual; normally there would be some change, as between lines 56 and 57–58. On the other hand, the occurrence of five lines beginning with the modal *q'aɬ* is striking, if both 54 and 55 are kept.

Stanza B2 (lines 66–72) again consists of a trio of verses, each of two lines, each expressing a very different idea: this is difficult and may kill us, I am a shaman and we will use my power, and let's make us some belts.

Scene iii is divided (as discussed earlier) into three three-part stanzas, each division marked either with the particle *húy* or the predicate *cútnaxn*, and with the second verse of both A1 and A2 also marked with *húy*, giving special emphasis to these verses. The rationale for these divisions was given earlier: after the exhortation to make belts (line 72), they make the belts, then they will perform their ceremony (A1); they perform their ceremony, then they will go to Bear (A2); they get to Bear (A3). One might recognize further trios or quintets of lines in this section (for example, the five lines that make up the first verse of Stanza A3, 84–88), but I do not find the possibilities as convincing as those I have marked.

The next half-stanza, B1, consists of five versicles divided into three verses, the middle of which has three versicles beginning with *wi*. Meaning again supports this division: (a) we will sleep for a year, (b) people will be awake for the year of summer, and (c) that's how the earth will be. B2 also consists of five lines, and again a division into three verses would be possible: 106, 107–108, 109–110 (note that throughout I exclude the opening 'he said' lines from consideration in these counts of three and five within verses).

Stanza C1 again contains three verses, each divided into two closely related half-verses, all clearly marked by particles or predicates. In the first and third verses, the half-verses are each two lines long, in the second they are three lines long. In the second and third, the particle *wi* is again used in an emphatic way, somewhat like its use in lines 15 and 60, but at the beginning of a set rather than at the end. In verse b, this results in a series of five lines beginning with *wi*, in verse c, a series of three. All this produces a very deftly constructed stanza.

Act II has much less of this sort of verse structure, concentrating on the songs. But one might still note some sets of three and five, such as the three uses of the stem *túlap-* at the beginning of Scene i, or the three uses of *húy* in Stanza B1 (lines 165–167), or the five-line verse beginning Stanza A2 (lines 142–146). But the absence of introductory lines preceding the songs starting at lines 197, 239, 261, and 284 is also striking. The codas seem to use less structure, and express four ideas in Scenes ii, iii, and iv: they perform until it becomes daylight, they don't eat, they tighten their belts, and they perform until it becomes evening (Scene i omits reference to the belts).

The codas do display another feature of the language, however, which is used to striking effect. Vowels are systematically changed (usually involving lengthening) to indicate diminutive or to indicate emphasis and duration; it is the latter functions that are utilized here. In this process, *i* and *u* are lowered and lengthened to *e·* and *o·*, *a* is lengthened to *a·*, and *ə* becomes short *e* (and then can also be lengthened). In the five codas, there is a gradual increase in the use of this feature, suggesting that the performances are increasing in length and intensity each day, until they are finally effective on the fifth. The Scene i coda emphasizes 'become day' and 'become evening', Scene ii 'perform', 'become day', the negative, and 'become evening', Scene iii 'become day', the negative, 'perform', and 'become evening', Scene iv the same, and Scene v lengthens the vowels even more, indicating even greater effort, in 'perform', 'pretty soon', 'perform' again, and (surprisingly) a future particle and 'now'. First two words are emphasized, then four in the next three scenes, then five in the last scene, and here with much greater length.

Little can be said about verse structure in Act III because of its brevity. Scene i, Stanza B may consist of three one-line verses, since each expresses a different idea. Stanza A of Scene ii has a three-part verse (or three verses), the second and third beginning similarly (lines 294 and 296) with 'afterwards'. Lines 303–304 are curious, and seem out of place. These are normally the sort of lines that end a story (and note the similarity of the concluding line, 312). It is as though the narrator indeed started to end the story here, then realized he should have said something about the hostility that bears have toward ants and bees, and added it before concluding again. This sense of incompleteness may have been expressed again in the "addition" that Boas recorded after the story was ended. But this still does not add much; it recapitulates and emphasizes the tightening of belts, and then explains that this is why bees and ants have such narrow waists. As noted earlier, the Cowlitz version of this story gives a much more satisfying rendition of this part of the story.

Besides this Cowlitz version, Adamson records another Cowlitz version narrated by a different speaker, but the contest is only between Bear and Frog (rather than Ant, big Yellowjacket, black Yellowjacket, Grouse, and Frog in the first version), and the conclusion is not emphasized (Adamson 1934:

189–190). Other versions (all in English) can be found in the neighborhood. A Klickitat Sahaptin version (from territory southeast of the Upper Chehalis and east of the Cowlitz) has only the argument and the contest, and is between two factions of large animals (one led by Grizzly, and including Bear, Cougar, Wolf, Badger, Fisher, and Coyote, the other led by Rattlesnake, and including Bullsnake) opposing a group led by Bullfrog (whose younger brother Frog actually wins the contest) (Jacobs 1934:3–4). To the north of Upper Chehalis territory, three Lushootseed versions are available, all between Bear and Ant alone. Two are mere outlines of the story (Ballard 1929:54–55), but include the songs of the two sides. The third (Hilbert 1980:136–137) has nothing equivalent to the third act of the Upper Chehalis version.

REFERENCES

Adamson, Thelma. 1934. Folk-Tales of the Coast Salish. American Folk-Lore Society Memoir 27. New York: American Folk-Lore Society.

Ballard, Arthur C. 1929. Mythology of Southern Puget Sound. University of Washington Publications in Anthropology 3.2:31–150.

Boas, Franz. 1933. A Chehalis text. IJAL 8:103–110.

Hilbert, Vi. 1980. Huboo: Lushootseed Literature in English. Seattle.

Hymes, Dell. 1981. "In vain I tried to tell you": Essays in Native American Ethnopoetics. Philadelphia: University of Pennsylvania Press.

Hymes, Dell. 1983. Agnes Edgar's "Sun's child": verse analysis of a Bella Coola text. Paper presented at the 18th International Conference on Salishan Languages, Seattle.

Jacobs, Melville. 1934. Northwest Sahaptin Texts. Columbia University Contributions to Anthropology 19.1.

Bear and Bee

Act I. Scene i.

A	ʔał ta-túlapt	1	In the beginning
	ʔał ta-swins sšamʼálaxʷ tit péˑpsayuʔ,	2	when people were animals
	wi náčʼušn	3	and once
	ʔał [t] ʔóˑcʼs sqʼítači	4	on one day

B1	ʔitu ta-cútnaxn tit sčə́txʷnʼ,	5	then Black Bear said,
(a1)	"tit sqʼítači wi siw tóˑmł.	6	"The day is too short.
	síwł tanin	7	Too much now
	nkʷssx̣ʷə́qʷwanš ʔał t pənx̣ʼíš.	8	I am always hungry in the wintertime.

(a2)	x̣ʼáqʼʷ tanin	9	Well, now
	sáʔastawt ʔit kʷə́sł	10	we'll make darkness
	načʼšpánxʷ.	11	one year.
	x̣ʼáqʼʷ tanin	12	Well, now
	ʔit wi ʔíyu ʔóˑcʼs pə́tqʷx̣ʷ	13	it will be just one night
	ʔóˑcʼs sx̣ʼíš.	14	one winter.
	wi x̣ʼáqʼʷ taninʔ	15	All well, now
	načʼšpánxʷ x̣ʼa sqʼítačis.	16	one year will be daylight.
	ʔóˑcʼs mə́łč	17	One summer
	wi ʔóˑcʼs sqʼítači.	18	is one day.

(b1)	wi x̣ʼa sʔíłnstawt tit sxʷás	19	And we will eat the blackberries
	ča tʼa-núkʷ ʔitám ʔał tit pənmə́łč.	20	and other things in the summertime.
	wi ʔał x̣ʼa sx̣ʼišáwms	21	And when it becomes cold

	wi x̌ʼa scʼóčɬs tit sqʼʷlnámʼc.	22	and the berries will be all gone.
	panxʷšánʼx̣ n ɬ kʷóswn.	23	At that time it will become dark.
(b2)	wi ʔaɬ t x̣ʷáqʷuʔ tit sx̌ʼíš	24	And for the whole winter
	wi x̣ʷáqʷuʔ t sšamʼálaxʷ	25	all the people
	wi ɬ t mʼúsm ɬ t ʔó·cʼs sx̌ʼíš.	26	will sleep for one winter
	qʼícʼx̣ wi ʔóy	27	Thus it is good
	qʼaɬ sáʔs tit tómš ča t sšamʼálaxʷ."--	28	for the world and the people to be made."
B2 (a)	cútnax̣n tit cíčs,	29	The Bee said,
	"míɬtanin laws ʔóy	30	"No, it would not be very good
	qʼaɬ wins qʼícʼx̣ tit tómš.	31	for the world to be thus.
(b)	x̌ʼáqʼʷ čʼus sqʼítačin	32	Well, always it will become daylight
	n ɬ tʼa-kʷóswn.	33	and dark again.
(c)	tó·maɬti t sqʼítači ča t skʷóswn."	34	Daylight and darkness are short."
C1	cútnax̣n tit sčótxʷnʼ,	35	Bear said,
(a)	"síw tanin	36	"Now it is too
	tó·mɬ t spótqʷx̣ʷ ča t sqʼítači.	37	short a night and day.
(b)	tʼíx̣ wi xʷnínutnɬ;	38	This is tiresome;
(c)	míɬta ix̣ʷuʔ smʼúsm	39	one is not yet asleep
	nkʷstʼa-qʼítačin."	40	and it becomes daylight again."

C2	cútnaxn tit cícs,	41	Bee said,
	"xáwas ʔám'q'laʔ.	42	"First wait!
	sʔíkʷatanš ʔit c'skíyq."	43	I am going to fetch Ant."

Act I. Scene ii.

A1 (a)	húy n ta-wáksn tanin tit cícs	44	And so Bee went now
	šaɬ t xáɬts tit c'skíyq.	45	to the house of the Ant.
	kʷá xʷmisn tit c'skíyq.	46	He arrived at the Ant's.
(b)	"ʔu nə́wi nnə́sči,	47	"Oh you my younger brother,
	sá·wlaminanš	48	I ask you
	ʔé·nm q'aɬ sáʔs tit tə́mš.	49	how can it be done to the world?
	cútnaxn tit sčə́txʷn',	50	Bear said,
	'X̌'áq'ʷ tanin	51	'Well, now
	nač'špánxʷ X̌'a kʷə́s.'"	52	one year will be darkness.'"
A2	cútnaxn tit c'skíyq,	53	Ant said,
	"q'aɬ talíl-na sšam'álaxʷ,	54	"It would be dangerous for the people,
	q'aɬ talíl-na sšam'álaxʷ,	55	it would be dangerous for the people,
	q'aɬ sítit tit tə́mš ɬ t q'íc'x̣.	56	for the world to change gradually thus.
	X̌'á q'ʷ míɬta	57	Well not
	t sáʔs tit tə́mš ɬ t q'íc'x̣.	58	will the world be made thus.
	q'aɬ wins q'íc'x̣ t sáʔs tit tə́mš	59	If the world be thus made
	wi q'aɬ ɬə́pɬčɬ táčsx̣ʷqʷ."	60	then we could die of starvation."

B1	cútnax̣n tit cíčs šałt tit c'skíyq,	61	The Bee said to the Ant,
	"húy, ʔo· nə́wi nnə́sči,	62	"And so, oh, you my younger brother,
	sʔík^waci čn.	63	I came to fetch you.
	x̣ə́lmcšlaʔ.	64	Get ready!
	ʔo· swáksstawt."	65	Oh let us go."
B2	cútnax̣n tit c'skíyq,	66	Ant said,
(a)	"titx̣tí né?š wi x̣áƛ̕.	67	"This here is difficult.
	čn łit łə́płš čł.	68	Maybe we will die.
(b)	ʔə́nca wi tit ʔə́x̣tk^wlš čn.	69	As for me, I have received spirit power.
	wi ʔaqa ł t tálax̣n čł nsʔə́x̣tk^wlš	70	And now we shall use my spirit power.
(c)	ʔu nə́wi nx̣^wał cíčs.	71	Oh you my elder brother Bee.
	ƛ̕áq'^w sá·malstawt t'ə́qix^w."	72	Well, let us make belts."

Act I. Scene iii.

A1 (a)	húy n ta-sáʔatiłt tit t'ə́qix^w.	73	And so they made the belts.
(b)	húy, ʔał ta-sná·msyamš ł tit t'ə́qix^w,	74	And so when they had finished with the belts,
	cútnax̣n tit cíčs,	75	Bee said,
	"x̣áwas tóm'alstawt	76	"First we will perform our spirit power ceremony
	tulápłcəni	77	before
	ƛ̕á sʔík^wnčł sčə́tx^wn'."	78	we go fetch Bear."
A2 (a)	húy, n ta-tóm'aliłt	79	And so they performed their ceremony
	tulápłcəni	80	before
	ta-swáksyamš šał tit sčə́tx^wn' . . .	81	they went to bear . . .

(b)	"húy x̌'á q'ʷ tanin	82	"And so well, now
	swáksstawt šał tit sčə́txʷn'."	83	we will go to Bear."
A3 (a)	húy n ta-námawiłt	84	And so they finished,
	n ta-túl'alimitn,	85	and they started out,
	wá··ksiłt.	86	they wa··lked.
	n kʷáxʷmisiłt tit sčə́txʷn' šał tit xáłts.	87	And they arrived at Bear's house.
	kʷáxʷmisiłt tit sccə́txʷn' ʔał t ʔó·c's sq'ítači.	88	And they reached Bear one day.
(b)	sʔə́xtwalisyamš tit sčə́txʷn',	89	Bear saw them,
	n ta-láx̌ʷlax̌ʷawn.	90	and he laughed.
	"ʔu ʔilápa nšnə́sčitn,	91	"Oh you my younger brothers,
	ʔáqa ʔuk'ʷa st'úwap	92	now you are arriving
	šał túłs naxínuwačł tit tə́mš."	93	so we can arrange the world."
B1	cútnaxn tit sčə́txʷn',	94	Bear said,
(a)	"x̌'áq'ʷ tanin	95	"Well, now
	načšpánxʷ x̌'á sm'úsmčł.	96	we will sleep one year.
(b)	wi ʔał t pən x̌'aq'á·m'	97	And in the springtime
	n ł q'ítačin.	98	daylight will come.
	wi panxʷšán'x	99	And at that time
	n ł p'álawn x̌ʷáq'ʷ t sšam'álaxʷ.	100	all the people will awaken.
	wi ʔó·c's smə́łč	101	And one summer
	x̌'á sq'ítačis.	102	it will be daylight.
(c)	ʔacwé·x tanin	103	It is thus now
	x̌'á sáʔs tit tə́mš."	104	the world shall be made."

B2   cútnax̣n tit c'skíyq,

"mé·łta q'ał sáʔs q'íc'x̣ tit tə́mš,

q'ał talíl-na t sšam'álaxʷ

q'ał wínsx̣ tit tə́mš.

ƛ̓áq'ʷ ʔiyu sq'ítačin

n t'a·kʷə́swn ł tó·małti."

105	Ant said,
106	"The world should not be made thus,
107	for it would be dangerous for the people
108	for the world to be thus.
109	Well, it is just daylight
110	and darkness will be short."

B3   cútnax̣n tit sčə́txʷn',

"míłta."

111 Bear said,
112 "No."

C1   húy cútnax̣n tit c'skíyq,

(a1)   "ƛ̓áq'ʷ tanin

ʔiyu ʔit x̣íx̣q' čł.

113 And so Ant said,
114 "Well, now
115   we will just gamble (race).

(a2)   ƛ̓áq'ʷ tanin

sʔílan'stawt.

116 Well, now
117   we will sing.

(b1)   wá· tuł m'úsmitn tuláp,

wi táx̣

wi ł c'ə́čitm;

118 Whoever will go to sleep first,
119 that one
120 will be defeated;

(b2)   wi wá· míłta ƛ̓á m'úsms,

wi cniáwmš

wi ł t c'ə́čm'ł.

121 and whoever doesn't go to sleep,
122 they are the ones
123 who will win.

(c1)   ʔamu ł c'ə́čn čł tit nə́wi,

124 If we defeat you,

	wi t čús ƛ̓á tó·maɬti t spə́tqʷx̣ʷ ča t sq̓ítači.	125	then always night and days will be short.
(c2)	wi ʔamu ʔala ɬ c̓ə́čituɬ,	126	And if you defeat us,
	wi načšpánxʷ ƛ̓á sm̓úsmčɬ."	127	we will sleep for one year."
C2	cútnax̣n tit sčə́txʷn̓,	128	Bear said,
	"t̓íx̣ wi ʔéy."	129	"This is good."
C3	cútnax̣n tit sčə́txʷn̓,	130	Bear said,
	"ƛ̓áq̓ʷ tanin	131	"Well, now
	ʔú· stúm̓alstawt."	132	we will perform a spirit power ceremony."
	ʔaqa n kʷə́swn.	133	And now it became dark.

Act II. Scene i.

A1	húy n ta-wə́ɬqtiɬt tit qə́syačasawmš tulápap u,	134	And so they spread out their drumsticks to begin with,
	n túlapn sčə́txʷn̓.	135	and Bear began.
	túlapn tit sčə́txʷn̓,	136	The Bear began,
	"ʔó·c̓s syawə́q ƛ̓á sq̓ítačis,	137	"One year it will be daylight,
	ʔó·c̓s syawə́q ƛ̓á sq̓ítačis,	138	one year it will be daylight,
	ʔó·c̓s syawə́q ƛ̓á sq̓ítačis,	139	one year it will be daylight,
	ʔó·c̓s syawə́q ƛ̓á sq̓ítačis,	140	one year it will be daylight,
	ʔó·c̓s syawə́q ƛ̓á sq̓ítačis."	141	one year it will be daylight."
A2 (a)	túlapn tanin tit cíčs ča tit c̓skíyq.	142	Now Bee and Ant began.
	x̣áwas ɬə́mtiɬt tit t̓ə́qixʷs.	143	First they tied their belts.
	húy tó·laqn cíčs;	144	And so Bee started singing;

	tulápap u čísaqn c'skíyq,	145	to begin with Ant helped sing,
	huy ʔéꞏlann tit cíčs,	146	and so Bee was singing,
	"sq'ítači,	147	"Daylight,
	sq'ítači	148	daylight,
	sq'ítači	149	daylight,
	sq'ítači	150	daylight
	sq'ítači."	151	daylight."

(b)	húy čísaqn c'skíyq,	152	And so Ant helped sing,
	"sq'ítači,	153	"Daylight,
	sq'ítači	154	daylight,
	sq'ítači	155	daylight,
	sq'ítači	156	daylight,
	sq'ítači."	157	daylight."
	(high voice; then Bee starts and all sing with him) *(after this response they all sing)*		

A3	húy, túlapn tanin,	158	And so he began now, (first)
	cútnaxn tit sčə́txʷn',	159	Bear said,
	"ʔóꞏc's x̣'íš x̣'á skʷə́s,	160	"One winter it will be darkness,
	ʔóꞏc's x̣'íš x̣'á skʷə́s,	161	one winter it will be darkness,
	ʔóꞏc's x̣'íš x̣'á skʷə́s,	162	one winter it will be darkness,
	ʔóꞏc's x̣'íš x̣'á skʷə́s,	163	one winter it will be darkness,
	ʔóꞏc's x̣'íš x̣'á skʷə́s."	164	one winter it will be darkness."

B1	húy wətšə́nmitn sčə́txʷn'.	165	And so Bear danced.
	húy wətšə́nmitn cíčs ča t c'skíyq.	166	And so Bee and Ant danced.
	húy ʔaqa łə́mtiłt tit t'ə́qixʷsyamš ł t x̣ə́k'ʷł.	167	And so now they tied their belts tight.
	"sq'ítači,	168	"Daylight,
	sq'ítači	169	daylight,
	sq'ítači	170	daylight,
	sq'ítači	171	daylight,
	sq'ítači."	172	daylight."
B2	tit sčə́txʷn' yá·nslaws,	173	Bear's tune,
	"ʔó·c's ƛ'íš ƛ'á skʷə́s,	174	"One winter it will be darkness,
	ʔó·c's ƛ'íš ƛ'á skʷə́s,	175	one winter it will be darkness,
	ʔó·c's ƛ'íš ƛ'á skʷə́s,	176	one winter it will be darkness,
	ʔó·c's ƛ'íš ƛ'á skʷə́s,	177	one winter it will be darkness,
	ʔó·c's ƛ'íš ƛ'á skʷə́s."	178	one winter it will be darkness."
B3	cútnax̣n cíčs,	179	Bee said,
	"sq'ítači, *(Bee low, Ant high and quick)*	180	"Daylight,
	sq'ítači	181	daylight,
	sq'ítači	182	daylight,
	sq'ítači	183	daylight,
	sq'ítači."	184	daylight."

CODA

túmʼaliłt n qʼéˑʔtačin.	185	They performed until daylight.
túmʼaliłt ʔał tat sqʼítači.	186	They performed during the day.
míłta t qʼał sʔíłnsyamš.	187	They didn't eat.
túmʼaliłt n kʷéswn.	188	They performed and it became evening.

Act II. Scene ii.

A	cútnaχn sčə́txʷnʼ	189	Bear said
	ʔał tʼa-stóˑlʼalms	190	when they started out
	ʔał t sáˑlis t spə́tqʷχʷ,	191	on the second night,
	"načʼšpánxʷ ƛʼá skʷə́s,	192	"One year it will be darkness,
	načʼšpánxʷ ƛʼá skʷə́s,	193	one year it will be darkness,
	načʼšpánxʷ ƛʼá skʷə́s,	194	one year it will be darkness,
	načʼšpánxʷ ƛʼá skʷə́s,	195	one year it will be darkness,
	načʼšpánxʷ ƛʼá skʷə́s."	196	one year it will be darkness."
B	"sqʼítači, *(Bee and Ant)*	197	"Daylight,
	sqʼítači	198	daylight,
	sqʼítači	199	daylight,
	sqʼítači	200	daylight,
	sqʼítači."	201	daylight."

CODA

tóˑmʼaliłt n tʼa-qʼítačin,	202	They performed until it became daylight again,
qʼéˑʔtačin.	203	it became daylight.

mé·ɬta t sʔíɬnsyamš.	204	They didn't eat.
húy n x̌áwas	205	And so first
x̌ə́k'ʷtn t t'ə́qixʷs cíčs ča tit c'skíyq.	206	Bee and Ant tightened their belts.
túm'aliɬt n kʷéswn.	207	They performed and it became evening.

Act II. Scene iii.

A (a)   húy ʔaɬ čá·ɬas pə́tqʷx̌ʷ   208 And so on the third night

       x̌áwas ʔayá·laq'n sčə́txʷn',   209 first Bear changed his tune,

"ʔó·c's smə́ɬč x̌'á sq'ítačis,	210	"One summer it will be daylight,
ʔó·c's smə́ɬč x̌'á sq'ítačis,	211	one summer it will be daylight,
ʔó·c's smə́ɬč x̌'á sq'ítačis,	212	one summer it will be daylight,
ʔó·c's smə́ɬč x̌'á sq'ítačis,	213	one summer it will be daylight,
ʔó·c's smə́ɬč x̌'á sq'ítačis."	214	one summer it will be daylight."

(b)   húy t'a-sʔayá·laq'n   215 And so again he changed his tune,

"ʔa ʔa načšpánxʷ x̌'á skʷə́s,	216	"Ah, ah, one year it will be darkness,
ʔa ʔa načšpánxʷ x̌'á skʷə́s,	217	ah, ah, one year it will be darkness,
ʔa ʔa načšpánxʷ x̌'á skʷə́s,	218	ah, ah, one year it will be darkness,
ʔa ʔa načšpánxʷ x̌'á skʷə́s,	219	ah, ah, one year it will be darkness,
ʔa ʔa načšpánxʷ x̌'á skʷə́s.	220	ah, ah, one year it will be darkness."

B   húy túlapn c'skíyq ča t cíčs   221 And so Ant and Bee began

     ʔaɬ čá·ɬas t spə́tqʷx̌ʷ,   222 on the third night,

"tó·maɫti x̌'á sq'ítačis,	223	"Short will be the daylight,
tó·maɫti x̌'á sq'ítačis,	224	short will be the daylight,
tó·maɫti x̌'á sq'ítačis,	225	short will be the daylight,
tó·maɫti x̌'á sq'ítačis,	226	short will be the daylight,
tó·maɫti x̌'á sq'ítačis." *(and Ant high)*	227	short will be the daylight."

CODA

t'a-q'é·tačin.	228	It became daylight again.
mé·ɫta t sʔíɫnsyamš.	229	They didn't eat.
cútnaxn tit c'skíyq,	230	Ant said,
"x̌áwas x̌ók'ʷwstawt tit t'ɔ́qixʷčɫ."	231	"First let us tighten our belts."
tómʔaliɫt n kʷéswn.	232	They performed and it became evening.

Act II. Scene iv.

A (a)	túlapnɫ sčɔ́txʷn' ʔaɫ t mús t spɔ́tqʷx̌ʷ,	233	Bear began on the fourth night,
	"ʔó·c's x̌'íš x̌'á skʷɔ́s,	234	"One winter it will be darkness,
	ʔó·c's x̌'íš x̌'á skʷɔ́s,	235	one winter it will be darkness,
	ʔó·c's x̌'íš x̌'á skʷɔ́s,	236	one winter it will be darkness,
	ʔó·c's x̌'íš x̌'á skʷɔ́s,	237	one winter it will be darkness,
	ʔó·c's x̌'íš x̌'á skʷɔ́s."	238	one winter it will be darkness.
(b)	"ʔó·c's smɔ́ɫč x̌'á sq'ítačis,	239	One summer it will be daylight,
	ʔó·c's smɔ́ɫč x̌'á sq'ítačis,	240	one summer it will be daylight,

	ʔó·c's sməłč x̌'á sq'ítačis,	241	one summer it will be daylight,
	ʔó·c's sməłč x̌'á sq'ítačis,	242	one summer it will be daylight,
	ʔó·c's sməłč x̌'á sq'ítačis."	243	one summer it will be daylight."
B	tó·l'aqn t cíčs ʔał t smúss t spə́tqʷx̌ʷ,	244	Bee started singing on the fourth night,
	"sq'ítači, *(Ant as tenor, rapid)*	245	"Daylight,
	sq'ítači	246	daylight,
	sq'ítači	247	daylight,
	sq'ítači	248	daylight,
	sq'ítači."	249	daylight."

CODA

túm'aliłt n q'é·tačin.	250	They performed until it became daylight.
mé·łta t sʔíłnsyamš.	251	They didn't eat.
cútnax̌n t c'skíyq šał tit cíčs,	252	Ant said to Bee,
"x̌áwas x̌ə́k'ʷwstawt tit t'ə́qixʷčł."	253	"First let us tighten our belts."
húy n tó·m'aliłt n kʷé·swn.	254	And so they performed and it became evening.

Act II. Scene v.

A (a)	ʔał t'a-stó·lps ʔał t cílačs spə́tqʷx̌ʷ,	255	In the beginning on the fifth night,
	"ʔó·c's x̌'íš x̌'á skʷə́s,	256	"One winter it will be darkness,
	ʔó·c's x̌'íš x̌'á skʷə́s,	257	one winter it will be darkness,
	ʔó·c's x̌'íš x̌'á skʷə́s,	258	one winter it will be darkness,

	ʔóc's x̌'íš x̌'á sk^wə́s,	259	one winter it will be darkness,
	ʔóc's x̌'íš x̌'á sk^wə́s.	260	one winter it will be darkness.
(b)	ʔóc's smə́łč x̌'á sq'ítačis,	261	One summer it will be daylight.
	ʔóc's smə́łč x̌'á sq'ítačis,	262	one summer it will be daylight.
	ʔóc's smə́łč x̌'á sq'ítačis,	263	one summer it will be daylight.
	ʔóc's smə́łč x̌'á sq'ítačis,	264	one summer it will be daylight.
	ʔóc's smə́łč x̌'á sq'ítačis."	265	one summer it will be daylight."
B	húy tó·laqn t c'skíyq,	266	And so Ant started singing,
	"tó·m'ałti x̌'á sq'ítačis, *(Ant, high voice)*	267	"Short will be the days,
	tó·m'ałti x̌'á sq'ítačis,	268	short will be the days,
	tó·m'ałti x̌'á sq'ítačis,	269	short will be the days,
	tó·m'ałti x̌'á sq'ítačis,	270	short will be the days,
	tó·m'ałti x̌'á sq'ítačis."	271	short will be the days."

CODA

	tó···m'aliłt q^wó···cannł q'ítači	272	They performed almost (until) day
	ʔał t cílačs spə́tq^wx̣^w;	273	on the fifth night;
	tulápłcəni t sq'ítači	274	before daylight
	ʔaqa n yúlwn sčə́tx^wn'.	275	now Bear became heedless.
	tó···m'aliłt x̌'á·· sq'ítačinn.	276	They performed just until it became morning.
	ʔáqa m'úsmitn t sčə́tx^wn'.	277	Now Bear is sleeping.

Act III. Scene i.

A (a)	wi húy Ɂé·lan'n tit cíčs,	278	And so Bee was singing,
	"tó·m'ałti x̣'á spə́tqʷx̣ʷ, (also Ant as tenor)	279	"Short will be the nights,
	tó·m'ałti x̣'á spə́tqʷx̣ʷ,	280	short will be the nights,
	tó·m'ałti x̣'á spə́tqʷx̣ʷ,	281	short will be the nights,
	tó·m'ałti x̣'á spə́tqʷx̣ʷ,	282	short will be the nights,
	tó·m'ałti x̣'á spə́tqʷx̣ʷ.	283	short will be the nights.
(b)	tó·m'ałti x̣'á sq'ítači,	284	Short will be the days,
	tó·m'ałti x̣'á sq'ítači,	285	short will be the days,
	tó·m'ałti x̣'á sq'ítači,	286	short will be the days,
	tó·m'ałti x̣'á sq'ítači,	287	short will be the days,
	tó·m'ałti x̣'á sq'ítači."	288	short will be the days."
B	Ɂacm'úsm t sčə́txʷn'.	289	Bear was asleep.
	námawiłt Ɂał t cílačs t spə́tqʷx̣ʷ ča t sq'ítači.	290	They finished after five nights and days.
	c'ə́čm'ł tanin t cíčs ča t c'skíyq.	291	Now Bee and Ant won.

Act III. Scene ii.

A	cútnax̣n t cíčs ča t c'skíyq,	292	Bee and Ant said,
	"Ɂiyu x̣'á sá·Ɂs tuł sšam'álaxʷ.	293	"Just so it will be for the people.
	Ɂał t Ɂáw t'm	294	Afterwards
	x̣'á tó·m'ałti t spə́tqʷx̣ʷ ča t sq'ítači.	295	nights and days will be short.
	Ɂał tuł Ɂáw t'm	296	Afterwards
	Ɂúxʷł tanin	297	different now
	x̣'á sšam'álaxʷ.	298	will be people.

B   wi talá·xʷ tanin sčə́txʷn'   299   And now only Bear

      ƛ̓á sm'úsmitn ł t ʔó·c's ƛ̓íš.   300   will sleep for one winter.

      m'úsmitn   301   He will go to sleep

      ƛ̓išáwmłtn sčə́txʷn'."   302   (when) Bear starts getting cold."

      t'íx̣ tanin   303   That now

      t'a-snámus tu šán'x̣ tanin.   304   is the end of that now.

Act III. Scene iii.

A   wi t č'ús   305   And always

      ʔactaxʷásmn t cíčs ča t c'skíyq.   306   he is an enemy of Bee and Ant.

B   táx̣ cu t č'ús   307   Why, therefore always

      ʔamu ł t'úqʷł ł t sčə́txʷn' t x̣á łts c'skíyq ča t cíčs   308   if a bear finds a house of ants or bees

      wi ł c'ə́łqn t x̣áłts.   309   he will destroy their house.

C   nám c'ə́łqó·txʷn,   310   He will just destroy the house,

      húy n ł ʔupáln c'skíyq ča t cíčs.   311   and so he will eat the ants and bees.

      t'íx̣ snáms.   312   That is the end.

ADDITION

      tulápłcəni ta sx̣ix̣q'sáwmš   Before they gambled

      wi ta k'ʷə́pł náwc'isawmš.   their bodies were straight.

      wi cílačs t spə́tqʷx̣ʷ ča t sq'ítači   And five nights and five days

      ta stóm'asawmš.   they performed.

      wi t č'ó·sač'a sx̣ə́k'ʷtiłti tit t'ə́q'ayuxʷ sawmš.   And always they tightened their belts.

      ʔał ta snámsawmš   When they finished

      wi q'ʷó·canin ł ta ʔacq'ʷiƛ̓ə́lwas.   they were almost cut in two.

      wi ʔał ta námsawmš   And when they finished wi t č'ús tanin k'é·mɬ t ƛ'áčsawmš.

now their bellies are always slender.

ʔə́y tan u tas sáʔsawmš

That was just all they could do

ʔaɬ ta sɬə́mt'sawmš ɬ t x̣ə́k'ʷɬ tit t'ə́q'ayuxʷsawmš.

when they tied their belts tight.

wi ta ʔam táyliɬn

And so without eating,

taláxʷ tanin wá·ʔ ta stálax̣itiɬti

except now they used water,

táʔx̣ cicu q'ʷó·canin ɬ ʔacq'ʷiƛ'álus

therefore almost cut in two

t cíčs ča t c'skíyq.

are the bee and ant.

APPENDIX 5

"Daughters of Fire": Narrative Verse Analysis
of an Upper Chehalis Folktale

M. Dale Kinkade
University of British Columbia

Upper Chehalis is a Salishan language formerly spoken in southwestern
Washington along the middle and upper course of the Chehalis River and its
tributaries. It is now reduced to only one reasonably fluent speaker, and the
last speaker who could tell traditional stories died several years ago. Fortunately, a fair number of stories of the Upper Chehalis have been collected. In
1926 and 1927, Thelma A[damson] collected stories in English (at least only
English versions survive; Adamson 1934), and Franz Boas collected 578 notebook pages of texts in Upper Chehalis. In late 1952, Leon Metcalf recorded
two or three stories in Upper Chehalis, but without translations, and, in 1960
and 1961, I collected a dozen or so. Both Metcalf and I recorded on tape, and
Boas and Adamson only recorded a few songs from stories on wax cylinders.
The bulk of these stories in the original language, then, is in Boas's manuscripts, which are now in the Library of the American Philosophical Society
in Philadelphia (Boas 1927).[1]

I have recently begun working with the texts that I collected, as well as
those collected by Boas and Metcalf, to investigate the narrative structure to
be found in them. Some time ago, I became convinced that Dell Hymes was
on the right track in his analysis of Chinook myths into dramatic verse, and
his claims that this format was more widely applicable. His recent book on
the subject, *In Vain I Tried to Tell You* (1981), makes his technique quite clear.
I have so far worked out this structure on only four Upper Chehalis stories,

1. My work on Upper Chehalis has been supported over the years by the American Philosophical Society Library, Indiana University, the National Science Foundation, the University
of Kansas, the University of British Columbia, and the Nederlandse Organisatie voor Zuiver
Wetenschappelijk Onderzoek. In particular, I wish to thank Dell Hymes for his extremely useful
comments on the early version of this paper, and for his continued enthusiastic support of my
attempts at this sort of analysis of narrative structure.

but have begun doing so on several others, and believe that not only is it a possible way of presenting these stories, but it is the best way. This sort of structure is certainly there, as a look at "Daughters of Fire" should make clear. Furthermore, I find that presenting the texts in this way turns them into far more beautiful and often exciting drama than is apparent from a reading of them in prose form.

This particular story, "Daughters of Fire," is one of those collected by Boas, in 1927, in or near Oakville, Washington. It is one of the very first he wrote down, and it is given as a self-contained story. Actually, however, it is only one episode of an extensive cycle, all of which Boas also collected. Well into this cycle, there is a note by Boas that his informant said that that was where the "Daughters of Fire" story belonged. The informant was Jonas Secena, a distinguished member of one of the most prominent families on the Chehalis Reservation. It is clear from Boas's transcriptions that Mr. Secena was an accomplished story-teller, and the more I work with his stories, the more I am impressed with his narrative ability.

The story begins in a way usual for Upper Chehalis stories, with one or two lines that constitute a combined title-introduction. The title I have put at the beginning of the story was probably provided by Boas; my informant never gave titles to his stories, and these introductory lines make them unnecessary. The drama breaks up naturally into three acts. The second act, in particular, seems to set itself off—at least there is clearly a second act. The actual division between acts, scenes, and stanzas is not always obvious. But the flight to various objects, Moon's request for help, and the refusals constitute a clear unit. The three acts present three distinct episodes: the first focuses on singing and tells of Moon's encounter with the Fire girls and his persuading them to sing for him; the second tells of his flight and attempts to escape from the resulting conflagration; and the third tells of how he is saved and then reorders the world (many of the episodes in the long cycle to which this story belongs conclude with some such reordering).

The division of each act into five scenes of two stanzas apiece does not seem to be accidental either (this same structure is present in other Upper Chehalis stories I have analyzed). In Act I: the first scene gives the background of the Fire girls; the second scene focuses on the singing of the youngest and Moon's hearing her; the third is his first request of her to sing again and her refusal; the fourth is his second request and her consent; and the fifth is the consequence of the singing. Note the parallels in the structure of the two stanzas of the first scene: both begin with ʔacwé· x̣ 'live, stay', and both end with two lines that convey the same information—they are daughters of Fire and they are pretty women. The fire song first appears in the second scene at the end of the first stanza. Note that it has two verses, virtually identical, echoing the dualistic structure of scenes. The song reappears at the end of the fourth scene (Boas did not write it out again, so we can only assume that it was sung identically). At first these positions may not look parallel, but they are if it is kept in mind that the song is only part of a stanza and not the stanza in itself. The first singing comes at the end of the initial stanza of the second scene of Act I; the second singing comes at the end of the stanza just preceding the last scene of Act I:

Act I.	Scene 1.	a
		b
	Scene 2.	a + SONG
		b
	Scene 3.	a
		b
	Scene 4.	a
		b + SONG
	Scene 5.	a
		b

The dualistic structure that exists within each scene, and within the fire song, also occurs in Moon's request to the youngest daughter; he twice asks her to sing. Her initial refusal is based on her knowledge of the danger in the girls' singing for strangers—an injunction we were told about in Scene 1. But Moon insists, and she relents, with dire consequences.

Act II tells of Moon's efforts to escape. The fact that Moon goes to five objects is not accidental; five is the pattern number in Upper Chehalis, and stories are full of specific references to five—five brothers, five prairies, five wedges, five baskets, or, in this case, five daughters of Fire in Act I and five days of bathing in Act III. So it is natural here that there should be five escape efforts, and it is the last that saves him. It could be argued that this fifth effort belongs in Act II, but I believe that it is more appropriately placed within a separate concluding act, wherein everything is set right. The first four scenes of Act II are exactly parallel (I will return to this in a moment). The fifth scene is a delaying action on the part of the narrator to build up tension (a technique called "extraposition" by Hymes, and noted by him in Chinookan and Zuni). After all, the whole world is in peril, and this is the climax of the story. The final object to which Moon runs, and the one which saves him, is treated a little differently from the others. Each of these was dealt with in one fairly short scene, but two longer scenes are devoted to Trail, and each of these is parallel to a single stanza of the comparable events of Act II. In the first stanza of each of the first four scenes of Act II, Moon runs to an object of nature and asks for help. In the second stanza he is refused because the object realizes that it can offer him no real help. Note that the second stanza of Scene 2 is missing; the exactly parallel structures of Scenes 1, 3, and 4 show that there should be a second stanza here (such an omission becomes particularly obvious when the story is set out in this sort of verse form). The first four objects asked for help (Rock, Lake, Wind, and Creek) are probably somewhat arbitrary, although if one attempts to think of other objects from which it would be reasonable to request help, there are not very many. My reason for assuming the selection here to be arbitrary is that Adamson gives a similar story from the Cowlitz (southern neighbors to the Upper Chehalis; Adamson 1934) where these objects are Tree, Big Rock, Little Creek, Prairie, and Rotten Log (and then Trail; five is also the pattern number in Cowlitz, but there the narrator chose to have five objects before Moon comes to Trail).

In Act III, Moon is saved. In Scene 1 he reaches Trail and asks for help. Trail notes the problem and the destruction caused by Fire. In Scene 2, Trail tells Moon that he cannot burn, and that if Moon lies down on him the fire will pass over him. In Scene 3, Moon does so and is saved (this is the most difficult scene in the drama to divide into stanzas, and the division might be more appropriate a line earlier or later than where I have put it). Scenes 4 and 5 return the story to the longer cycle. In Scene 4, there is a ritual cleansing after the escape from death (note again the use of five), and before Moon starts out again on his journey through the world, reordering things from the myth age to their present state. Scene 5 gives the details of this reordering; there will not be general conflagrations just because the daughters of Fire sing.

I have demonstrated that the story can be divided into acts and scenes on the basis of its dramatic structure. But this is not enough. I have not yet justified the overall poetic structure. In terms of language structure, my divisions into stanzas and lines are not arbitrary. There are twenty-nine stanzas in the story (there should be thirty, but one was obviously omitted from Act II). Of these, twelve begin with cútnaʔχn 'he said', and eleven begin with húy 'and so'. Since the use of these words so often correlates with natural dramatic divisions, their placement at these points and as structural markers cannot be accidental. In fact, they occur similarly in other Upper Chehalis stories, whether told by Secena or by other narrators. They do appear elsewhere in this story than at stanza divisions, it is true, but not often, and sometimes these other occurrences are structurally motivated (as at lines 68 and 69, where húy appears in two successive lines, emphasizing an event). This is, in part, the reason for some reservation concerning my division of Act III, Scene 3: táxʷl is not the sort of word that normally begins stanzas, and there is a huy in the preceding line. Two stanzas begin with wi, which may be a reduced form of húy. Usually wi begins lines, however. Throughout Act I, from Boas's transcription it is unclear whether I should have written wi or húy; because huy is not stressed and because húy seems out of place there, I chose the former. Thus my stanza divisions seem appropriate in terms of both linguistic and dramatic structure.

Line divisions are fairly straightforward. Essentially I assume only one main predication per line; dependent predications, and sometimes prepositional phrases, also make up lines. Complements (that is, subjects and objects) remain with their main predications. Since virtually any word (the rather restricted class of particles constitutes the exception) may constitute a main predication, this makes line divisions rather easy, but may make the English translation difficult, as for lines 46 and 47, where both 'very' and 'tired' are independent predications. Sentences in the language, in general, tend to be rather brief, and this also accords with the line divisions. Ideally, one would hope that these divisions would correlate with pauses and specific intonation patterns. But since this particular text exists only in Boas's manuscripts, this cannot be checked. In another text that I have worked into verse structure, and for which I do have a taped version, pauses and intonation patterns do, in fact, correlate with such divisions (I worked out the divisions before listening again to the tape to check pause and intonation correlations).

There are many other features to which attention could be directed, both as features of language structure indicating verse structure and as features of drama, but I will not go into them here. However, the main point should be clear: "Daughters of Fire" is a highly dramatic and beautifully told story.

POSTSCRIPT

Since the above was written, Hymes has suggested to me that my stanzas might be divisible into verses as an intermediate level between stanzas and lines, and these tend to occur in groups of three. He expects these verse triplets to reflect a three-part logic in the action. Although it is difficult to discern this structure in every stanza, it does indeed seem inherent in many, and the interested reader can undoubtedly perceive it. I will here indicate only a few of these, and note one very important instance.

Each of these stanzas in Act I, Scene 1 can be seen to consist of three verses (I thank Hymes for this suggested breakdown), each consisting of two sentences (which I sometimes divide further into lines). Verse 1 includes lines 3 to 4 and 5, verse 2 is lines 6 and seven to 9, and verse 3 is lines 10 and 11. Line 6 could conceivably be placed in the preceding verse on the grounds that this verse constitutes a general description of the girls. But the meaning of x̣ax̣á·ʔ suggests a closer connection of line 6 with what follows; it means not just 'forbidden', but also 'powerful, sacred, tabu', all important attributes for upper-class people. The second stanza has a similar structure: verse 1 is lines 12 to 13 and 14 (the youngest daughter), verse 2 is lines 15 and 16 to 17 (all the daughters), and verse 3 (which exactly parallels verse 3 of the first stanza) is lines 18 to 19 and 20.

The two stanzas of Act III, Scene 1 also lend themselves to this kind of analysis. The first verse contains lines 145 and 146 (pertaining to Moon), the second, lines 147 and 148 to 150 (a group which is itself a triplet of descriptions of Fire: 'near', 'everywhere', 'around'), the third lines 151 to 152 and 153 to 154 (introducing Trail). In the second stanza, the first verse includes lines 155 and 156 to 157 (Moon's plight), the second, 158 and 159 (his plea for help), and the third is a series of five actions: 'look', 'blaze', 'crackle', 'fall over', 'boil'.

Act III, Scene 3, which earlier appeared somewhat problematical as to its proper division, now seems to me to have the clearest internal structure in the story, and is one of the most superbly crafted and dramatic scenes. This scene is the climax of the whole story; here Fire catches up to Moon and is defeated. Each stanza falls naturally into three verses.

stanza 1:	184	/	185
	186	/	187–188
	189		
stanza 2:	190	/	191–192
	193		
	194		

Each of the three verses of the first stanza begins with húy; although this particle usually marks stanzas, it is used here to mark verses, emphasizing the importance of this scene, and, together with the terseness of the three one-line verses, adds to the dramatic force of the scene. Note too the alternation of the protagonists verse by verse. In the first stanza we find Fire, then Moon, then Fire. In the second stanza we find Moon (although Fire is the one mentioned, he is in a subordinate clause, and the verse is about Moon), then Fire, then Moon. The dominance thus switches from Fire to Moon between the first stanza and the next, expressing Moon's overcoming the danger of Fire, which leads him subsequently to transform it into something less dangerous.

Continued examination of this story will undoubtedly lead to further insights into its structure.

REFERENCES CITED

Adamson, Thelma
   1934   Folk-Tales of the Coast Salish. American Folk-Lore Society, Memoir 27. New York: The American Folk-Lore Society.
Boas, Franz
   1927   Chehalis field notes. Manuscript in the American Philosophical Society Library, Philadelphia.
Hymes, Dell
   1981   In Vain I Tried to Tell You. Essays in Native American Ethnopoetics. Philadelphia: University of Pennsylvania Press.

ʔinamałsqʼʷə́tʼwn (Daughters of Fire)

Introduction

ʔacwé·x tit sqʼʷə́tʼwn.	1	There was the Fire,
wi ʔacqʼámayałqʷlš̓ tit sqʼʷə́tʼwn ł t cílačs.	2	and the Fire had five daughters.

Act I. Scene 1.

ʔacwéx̣yawmš ʔał t x̣áłtsawmš	3	They stayed at their house
yáʔ čm̓š ʔał t smániči.	4	near a mountain.
wi čʼús skáwmitn ʔał t x̣áššawmš.	5	And it always burned at their house.
wi cəniáwmš wi ʔálisumš.	6	And they always were chiefs/royalty.
wi ʔə́yu x̣ax̣á·ʔ	7	And it was just forbidden
qʼał sʔíln̓sawmš šał t mə́yšawł	8	for them to sing to a young man
ča tʼa nukʷ t sšam̓álaxʷ.	9	or for any other people.
wi ʔinamał t sqʼʷə́tʼwn	10	And they are children of Fire
wi ʔəyálʼiwn t čawałúmš.	11	and they are pretty women.
húy ʔacwé·x c ʔúcʼs	12	And so there was one
t·sxʷqʷáyʼis tu ʔáłcəniawmš	13	the youngest of them.
wi t čʼús nkʷsʔé·lʼann.	14	And she was always singing a little.
wi náčʼawšn	15	And once in a while
wi x̣ʷáqʷyamš	16	and all of them
nkʷsʔílanʼn.	17	they sang.
míłtanin t wá·	18	Nobody
qʼícʼ x̣ ł tit ʔinamałsqʼʷə́tʼwn.	19	is like the daughters of Fire.
cəniáwmš wi ʔəyálʼiwn t čawałúmš.	20	They are pretty women.

Act 1. Scene 2.

wi náčʼušn ʔał pétqʷiʔ x̣ʷuʔ.	21	And once it was early in the morning.
wi sʔé·lʼilʼanʼn cic ʔó·cʼs	22	And there was singing away the one

tu ʔał ʔinamałsqʷ'ə́t'wn	23	of the daughters of Fire,
sxʷqʷáy'is.	24	the youngest.
ʔé·l'il'an'n:	25	singing away:
sq'ʷə́t'wn, sq'ʷə́t'wn	26	Burning, burning / Fire, fire
lámqsmitn	27	putting out tongues
lámstaqn	28	blazing
skáwmitn, skáwmitn.	29	flaming, flaming.
sq'ʷə́t'wn, sq'ʷə́t'wn	30	Burning, burning
lámqsmitn	31	putting out tongues
lámstaqn, lámstaqn	32	blazing, blazing
skáwmitn.	33	flaming.
hee hee hee.	34	haa, haa, haa.
ʔítu sč'ísn ta šał t šə́wł	35	Then there came along the road
ʔeyál'iwn nułtámš.	36	a nice-looking person.
ʔə́xtm ʔał cic q'ámaył.	37	He was seen by the girl.
námawn ł t sʔíln'.	38	She stopped singing.
t'úwn tit mə́yšawł šʔáłcəni.	39	The young man got to her.

Act I. Scene 3.

cútnaʔxn tit mə́yšawł,	40	The young man said,
"ʔu ʔə́y	41	"Oh, it was good,
nstó·lixʷ ʔit ʔasʔíln'.	42	what I heard you sing.
ʔə́nca wi ʔáls čn.	43	I am a chief.
čen ʔack'ʷálanmn č t łukʷáł,	44	Maybe you have heard of Moon,
ta syə́pwanš ł t lé·ʔ.	45	I have been walking from far away
wi k'ʷə́pł čn	46	And I am very
ʔacxʷə́nł.	47	tired.
háy t'aʔíln'laʔ	48	Hey! Sing again
ł t q'íc'x łit ʔasʔé·ln'."	49	your same song."
cútnaʔxn ł titxtí cic q'ámaył,	50	The girl said this,
"mélta nq'ał sʔíln'šici,	51	"I cannot sing for you;

t'íx̣ wi x̣ax̣á·ʔ	52	that is forbidden
nq'ał sʔíln̓šn t ʔiwát.	53	for me to sing to anyone.
ʔə́nca wi namałsq'ʷə́t'wn čn.	54	I am a daughter of Fire.
q'ał talíl na tit tə́mš	55	The world would be in danger
nq'ał ʔíln̓šici."	56	if I should sing for you."

Act I. Scene 4.

cútnaʔx̣n tit łukʷáł,	57	The Moon said,
"ʔó· táx̣ʷl ʔó· q'íc'x̣.	58	"Even though it is thus,
wi ʔə́y	59	And it was good
nstó·lixʷ tu lé·ʔ	60	what I heard from far away—
ʔit ʔayán̓sulš.	61	your tune.
wi k̓áq'ʷ č	62	You'd better
t'it ʔasʔíln̓."	63	sing again."

cútnaʔx̣n cic q'ámaył,	64	The girl said,
"ʔiním wi ʔinamałsq'ʷə́t'wn	65	"We are the daughters of Fire,
wi ʔaqa ł t ʔíln̓šn čł tit nə́wi	66	and now we will sing for you.
ʔó· [same song]."	67	Oh! . . ."

Act I. Scene 5.

hú-i ʔé·l̓il̓an̓n.	68	And so she was singing away.
hú-i č'ísn tanin	69	And so there came now
x̣ʷáqʷu tit q'ámayałqʷlal̓s t sq'ʷə́t'wn.	70	all the daughters of Fire.
č'ísaqn tit nukʷ tit ʔinamałsq'ʷə́t'wn.	71	The other daughters of Fire help sing.
ʔé·l̓an̓iłti.	72	They sang.
k'ʷéčcštn tit ʔáls.	73	The chief listened.
ʔítu lámstaqn t sq'ʷə́t'wn	74	Then fire blazed up
p'étlm̓.	75	everywhere.

húy káwmitn tanin	76	And so it is burning now,
x̣ʷáqʷu ʔał ʔ itám.	77	everything,
cútnaʔx̣n tit łukʷáł,	78	The Moon said,

"ʔóʔ k'ʷə́pɬ uk'ʷa	79	"Oh, I suppose truly
ɬ t q'ʷə́t'	80	it will burn,
x̣ʷáqʷuʔ tit tə́mš."	81	the whole world."

Act II. Scene 1.

húy n ta wə́q'wn tanin t ɬukʷáɬ.	82	And so now Moon was running.
yáʔčm̓š tanin t sq'ʷə́t'wn šʔáɬcəni.	83	Now Fire got near to him.
kʷáxʷmisn t spatáln.	84	He came to Rock.
cútnaʔx̣n tit ʔáls šʔaɬ spatáln,	85	The chief said to Rock,
"ʔóʔ nx̣ʷáɬ,	86	"Oh, my elder brother,
ʔi q̓alaɬ tal̓íčc?	87	could you help me?
sč'ísn tit sq'ʷə́t'wn."	88	Fire is coming."
cútnaʔx̣n t spatáln,	89	Rock said,
"ʔóʔ nnə́sči.	90	"Oh, my younger brother,
méɬta t ʔínanum	91	there is no way
nq̓aɬ sxʷtalíčstumi.	92	I can help you.
ʔamu nkʷst̓úmc t sq'ʷə́t'wn	93	When Fire comes to me,
wi nkʷstxʷƛ̓alə́qʷ čɬ,	94	we will crackle,
x̣ʷə́ɬq'ɬ čɬ."	95	we will burst."

Act II. Scene 2.

húy šán̓x̣ tanin	96	And so there now
n wə́q'wn	97	he ran
ɬ t x̣íwicš tit ɬukʷáɬ.	98	hard, the Moon.
kʷáxʷmisn t cál̓ɬ.	99	He came to Lake.
sáwlayn,	100	He asked him,
"ʔí t q̓alaɬ stál̓ičc?	101	"Could you help me?
sč'ísn tit sq'ʷə́t'wn.	102	Fire is coming.
čən ɬ t q'ʷə́t' čn."	103	Maybe I will burn."

Act II. Scene 3.

húy t'aʔáys wóq'wn t łukʷáł.	104	And so Moon ran again.
wó··q'wn.	105	He ran and ran.
kʷáxʷmisn słóčiyq.	106	He came to wind.
"ʔí t q'alał stál'ičc?	107	"Could you help me?
sq'ʷót'wn tit tómš."	108	The world is burning."
cútnaʔxn słóčiya,	109	Wind said,
"méłta nq'ał stal'íčici.	110	"I cannot help you.
ʔamuʔ nkʷspúxʷm'ł čł	111	When we blow
wi čát tan uʔ	112	then instead
nkʷsq'ʷót' ł t xiwícš.	113	it will burn harder.
wóq'łlaʔ šał ʔicá·pš.	114	Run to the creeks!
čən cəniámš q'ał tal'íčici."	115	Maybe they can help you."

Act II. Scene 4.

huy t'aʔáys wóq'wn t łukʷáł	116	And so Moon ran again.
kʷáxʷmisn t cá·pš.	117	He came to Creek.
cútnaxn ł tit ʔicá·pš,	118	He said to the creeks,
"ʔu sʔátminanš."	119	"Oh, I am dying."
cútnaxn cá·pš,	120	Creek said,
"ʔu k'ʷópł č	121	"Oh, truly
ʔit kʷáxʷmn ʔinamałsq'ʷót'wn.	122	you got to the daughters of Fire.
náxʷł uʔ sʔátminš.	123	Indeed you are dying.
míłta ʔínanum	124	There is no way
nq'ał stal'íčici.	125	I can help you.
ł t'ó·s taláʔla t sq'ʷót'wn	126	When Fire comes after a while
wi ł t xʷalaʔáwm tit tómš.	127	then the world will get hot.
wi ʔónca wi ł t lópm čn.	128	And then I will boil.
wi q'ał t'it q'ʷółł č uʔ	129	And you can get roasted all the same.
náxʷł uʔ sʔátminš.	130	Indeed you are dying.
wákʷsaʔ.	131	Go on!"

wə́q'ɬaʔ q'íc'x̣ u	132	Run just the same
ɬ tala sx̣áx̌ʷtn."	133	with all your speed!"

Act II. Scene 5.

húy n wə́q'wn tanin.	134	And so he ran now.
cútnaʔx̣n t ɬukʷáɬ.	135	Moon said,
"ʔə́nca wi ʔáls čn.	136	"I am a chief.
wi x̣ʷáqʷu ʔitám	137	And everything,
wi nkʷsɬíwxʷ čn ʔaɬ tit tə́mš.	138	and I always take it off the world.
x̣ʷáru ʔitám	139	Everything
wi ʔacx̣ʷálaxʷ čn.	140	I have overpowered.
húy ʔaɬ titx̣í tanin tit sq'ítači	141	And so on this day
wi sʔatminanš uk'ʷa.	142	I guess I will die—
sq'ʷə́t'anum uk'ʷa,	143	by burning, I guess,
t n x̌'a sʔátmn."	144	I will die."

Act III. Scene 1.

húy x̣íwicštn tanin	145	And so now hard
wə́q'wn.	146	he ran.
húy wá kʷsn	147	And so he went
yáʔ čmʔš tanin tit sq'ʷə́t'wn.	148	near now, the Fire.
p'éʔtlanm' tanin,	149	Everywhere now,
yə́lmɬcni tit sq'ʷə́t'wn.	150	Fire was around him.
x̣ʷél tanin téʔmš	151	Now a small piece of land
t míɬta t sq'ʷə́t's.	152	was not burning.
iwə́q'wn šín'x̣.	153	He ran there.
kʷáx̣ʷmisn t šéw'ɬ.	154	He came to a little trail.
cútnaʔx̣n t ɬukʷáɬ,	155	The Moon said,
"ʔó ʔaqa sʔátminanš.	156	"Oh, now I will die.
čən ɬ t q'ʷə́t' čn.	157	Maybe I will burn.
nə́wi nčúp'a	158	You, my grandfather,

ɁacɁí t q'alał stal'íčcɁ"	159	could you help me?"
Ɂéxnn' tit šéw'ł šał tit skáwmitn.	160	The Trail looked at the fire.
lámstaqn sq'ʷə́t'wn.	161	Fire was blazing.
sʎ'ə́lqʷmitn xʷáqʷu Ɂitám.	162	Everything was crackling.
syaq'áwn t ʎ'ə́š ʎ'š.	163	Trees were falling over.
lə́pmitn t cápaš	164	Creeks were boiling,
ča t cáɁlał.	165	and so were lakes.

Act III. Scene 2.

cútnaɁxn tit šéw'ł,	166	The Trail said,
"Ɂu náxʷł uɁ	167	"Oh, indeed
k'ʷa q'ʷó·Ɂcanin	168	it is almost so
yáčapici t sq'ʷə́t'wn.	169	that fire has caught up with you.
taláxʷ Ɂə́nca	170	Although I—
wi míłta nq'isq'ʷə́t'.	171	I cannot burn.
ɁiyuɁ nkʷsq'ʷə́t' t sq'ʷə́t'wn taš yalə́mšc	172	Fire just burns around me,
nkʷstánmaln taš ʎ'úk'ʷ.	173	passing above me.
č'ísaɁ nɁímc,	174	Come, my grandson!
cákʷlaɁ Ɂał t nsłáwličn!"	175	Lie down on my back!"
cútnaɁxn tit šéw'ł,	176	The Trail said,
"tá xʷl č	177	"Although you
xʷalaɁáwm,	178	will get hot,
wi míłta Ɂast'áq'awicš.	179	don't move.
čáwcixʷ č t Ɂamús	180	Lay down your eyes
ča t Ɂaqə́ns	181	and your mouth
xíwicš Ɂáłtm'š."	182	firmly to the ground."
məy cə́kʷwn šał tit šéw'ł.	183	He just lay down on the Trail.

Act III. Scene 3.

húy n yáčaptwalinn tit sq'ʷə́t'wn.	184	And so the Fire caught up with him.
lámstaqn p'étlm'.	185	It blazed everywhere.

húy ʔaqa x̣ʷ ślwn' t łukʷáł.	186	And so now Moon sweated.
míłta láws x̣ʹáqłnł	187	Not very long
ta čáwanis	188	he was lying down
húy n tánwalinn t sqʹʷə́t'wn.	189	and Fire went past him.
táxʷl ʔit tánwali tit sqʹʷə́t'wn,	190	Although the Fire went past him,
wi qʹʷó·ʔcanin	191	he almost
ł ʔátmn.	192	died.
wákʷsn t sqʹʷə́t'wn.	193	Fire went on.
ʔúcx̣ʷmitn t łukʷáł.	194	Moon stood up.

Act III. Scene 4.

cútnaʔx̣n,	195	He said,
"míłta ukʹʷa nx̣ʹa sʔátmn,	196	"I guess I'm not going to die.
wi cílačs sqʹítači	197	And five days
nx̣ʹa swé·x̣ néʔx̣.	198	I will stay here.
x̣áwas ł t ʔé·t'u čn	199	At first I will bathe,
n ł t'a túl'alimitanš."	200	then I will start out again."
wé·nnax̣n ł cílačs sqʹítači.	201	He stayed five days.
ʔé·t'unn t łukʷáł.	202	Moon bathed.
ʔał t snáms sʔé·t'us	203	When he finished bathing,
x̣áwas ʔə́yqcštn.	204	first he dressed up.

Act III. Scene 5.

cútnaʔx̣n,	205	He said,
"ʔał titx̣í qʹʷó·ʔcanin	206	"At this time, almost
qʹʹał ta ʔátmn čn	207	I could have died
ʔał ʔə́yu ʔit ʔíln'šitm čn	208	just because it was sung for me
ł t qʹámaył t sqʹʷə́t'wn.	209	by the daughters of Fire.
wi ʔúxʷł tanin	210	And different now
x̣ʹa sšam'álaxʷ	211	shall people be
ʔał tuł wákʷs.	212	in the future.
wi ʔə́yu x̣ʹa sʔílan'n t qʹám'ayałqʷlš̌	213	And the daughters will just sing,

mílta ƛ̓a sq'ʷə́t's t təmš	214	the world will not burn.
wi ʔə́yu ɬ t ʔíln̓šitm	215	And he will just be sung for
ɬ t q̓ámay ɬ t ʔáls	216	by the daughters, the chief—
mílta ƛ̓a sq'ʷə́t'wnamc."	217	they will not burn his body up."

SYNOPSIS

Title/ Introduction.			Fire had five daughters (lines 1–2).
Act I.	Scene 1.	A.	Fire daughters are forbidden to sing to strangers (3–11).
		B.	Youngest daughter always sings (12–20).
	Scene 2.	A.	Youngest daughter sings her song (21–34).
		B.	Moon comes along and she stops singing (35–39).
	Scene 3.	A.	Moon asks her to sing again (40–49).
		B.	She refuses, saying it would be dangerous (50–56).
	Scene 4.	A.	Moon asks again (57–63).
		B.	She consents and sings (64–67).
	Scene 5.	A.	Other daughters join in (68–75).
		B.	General conflagration ensues (76–81).
Act II.	Scene 1.	A.	Moon runs to Rock for help (82–88).
		B.	Rock can't help (89–95).
	Scene 2.	A.	Moon runs to Lake for help (96–103).
		B.	[missing]
	Scene 3.	A.	Moon runs to Wind for help (104–8).
		B.	Wind can't help (109–15).
	Scene 4.	A.	Moon runs to Creek for help (116–19).
		B.	Creek can't help (120–33).
	Scene 5.	A.	Moon tells of his power (134–40).
		B.	Moon thinks he will die (141–44).
Act III.	Scene 1.	A.	Moon runs to Trail (145–54).
		B.	He asks Trail for help (155–65).
	Scene 2.	A.	Trail says he doesn't burn (166–75).

B. He tells Moon to lie down on him (176–83).

Scene 3. A. Fire comes and passes over Moon (184–89).

B. Fire passes and Moon is saved (190–94).

Scene 4. A. Moon says he will bathe (195–200).

B. Moon bathes and fixes himself up (201–4).

Scene 5. A. Moon comments on his near death (205–9).

B. Moon transforms the daughters of Fire (210–17).

NOTES

Introduction

1. Special thanks to Fred Shortman for talking to me about the importance of Seven Generations and explaining the belief that gathering is the privilege of the sixth generation and sharing is the privilege of the seventh.

2. This work is now known as salvage ethnography. Many early twentieth-century anthropologists and linguists believed that the cultures and languages they were documenting would be lost in another generation, and as such, they aimed to document these rapidly disappearing cultures. Leading figures in the discipline articulated as much. In his forward to *Argonauts of the Western Pacific*, Polish anthropologist Bronisław Malinowski captures the urgency motivating much of this work: "Ethnology is in the sadly ludicrous, not to say tragic, position, that at the very moment when it begins to put its workshop in order, to forge its proper tools, to start ready for work on its appointed task, the material of its study melts away with hopeless rapidity. Just now, when the methods and aims of scientific field ethnology have taken shape, when men fully trained for the work have begun to travel into savage countries and study their inhabitants—these die away under our very eyes" (1961, xv). I choose to highlight Malinowski's words here—callous in retrospect—to call attention to the attitudes of European scholars vested in the study of indigenous peoples worldwide.

   Franz Boas, at times guilty of similar insensitivity, describes these efforts in gentler language. Biographer Douglas Cole notes that Boas's "emphasis was on the urgency of the work, on the duty of the present generation to collect information before it passed way. 'It is only a question of a few years, when every thing reminding us of America as it was at the time of its discovery will have perished,' he wrote. 'Our generation is the last that will be able to collect the data which will form the basis of the early history of America'" (1999, 205). And thus Boas and his students engaged in the impressive task of documenting and preserving endangered cultures and languages, salvaging what remained of them in the wake of global expansion and enterprise.

3. Palmer was the daughter of the local doctor, Jacob Van Winkle. Palmer studied geology at the University of Washington and taught paleontology at Cornell University. She was a founding member and served as director of the Paleontological Research Institution at Cornell. See Miller 2012a for more thorough biographical sketches of both Palmer and Sanders and discussion of their collaboration.

4. Vine Deloria Jr. explains the difference between linear and cyclical time. Time "must begin and end at some real points, or it must be conceived as cyclical in nature, endlessly allowing the repetition of patterns and possibilities" (2003, 70). The prominence of Moon and Sun in Chehalis stories, and Moon's role as a transformer, is indicative of time as "patterns and possibilities." Chehalis understanding of the length of seasons and days is brought to light in "Bear, Yellow Jacket, and Ant."

5. Lucy Heck's husband was Silas Heck; her brother-in-law was Peter Heck.

6. Much of Adamson's introductory material prepared for *Folk-Tales of the Coast Salish* applies to the stories Boas collected as well. Adamson explains that most of the tales she collected "refer to the time 'when all the animals were people'. The Upper Chehalis term for this type of tale is sielɔ''pt." Adamson continues, "According to the Upper Chehalis, after the appearance of the transformer Moon, the birds and animals could no longer speak the human language. Moon was 'master' of the animals and told them how the people in time to come should use them. Most of the characters in these tales are animals or birds, but in a few cases, the characters seem entirely human" (1934, xii). One person whom Adamson interviewed (likely Peter Heck) clarified Moon's role in this transformation, explaining that Moon changed everything to how it is today and that Indians, animals, and people could talk to each other before the transformation but that "after Moon changed animals and bird's can't talk the language of the people" (1926–27, 81). In his introduction to *Twana Narratives: Native Historical Accounts of a Coast Salish Culture,* William Elmendorf provides commentary that relates to Adamson's notes. He explains that there were "four kinds of Twana stories: mythic, semimythic, semihistoric, and, in the present collection, historical." Mythic stories occur "before the change of the world known as the sp'əlɑ'č' (the turning over or capsizing)" (1993, liii).

7. Moon builds fish traps in the river, x̌ʷə́n gathers berries in the mountains, k'ʷə́cx̌ʷe digs camas and fern roots, Bluejay travels over burning prairies, malé and her daughter pick juniper berries at Claquato, and s'yawyu'wun shows the people how to catch lamprey eels at Chehalis River rapids (likely Rainbow Falls).

8. In 1960 Silas Heck told Kinkade about the battle that divided the Lower Chehalis and Upper Chehalis, a battle that occurred well before contact.

9. Kinkade explains, "The Satsop were politically affiliated with the Lower Chehalis, but the language is predominately Upper Chehalis" (1991, v). Cloquallam Creek near Elma has been referred to as the boundary between Lower Chehalis and Upper Chehalis.

10. The Swaal, also known as Kwalhioqua or Willapa Athabaskan, lived in these hills.

11. Or Fort Nisqually to Cowlitz Farms.

12. A sample of these stories—collected in the early twentieth century (or a little before)—gives a sense of geographic distribution of shared narrative traits as well as the scope of salvage ethnography projects contemporaneous with the work of Adamson and Boas. See, for instance, Livingston Farrand's *Traditions of the Quinault Indians*, specifically Bob Pope's Transformer tales (1902). Eells summarized two Twana legends "in regard to the origin of the sun" (1985, 259), and Mary Adams shared a Skokomish version of "Moon and Sun" with Adamson (1934, 374). Further north, Erna Gunther collected *Klallam Folk Tales*. This volume features a version of "Star Husband" told by Jennie Talicus and interpreted by Vera Ulmer, as well as six versions of "Mucus Boy" and one version of "Gum Husband." In "Gum Husband," told by Mrs. Robbie Davis, two brothers become the sun and the moon (1925, 135–36, 125–31, 131–34). "Star Child" is prominent in many Lushootseed traditions: Snuqualmi Charlie, a Snoqualmie man, shared "Moon, the Transformer," with Arthur Ballard (1929, 69); Little Sam shared another Snoqualmie version, which Herman Haeberlin titles "Symplegades" after the "two big rocks" that "were always opening and closing" (Haeberlin and Boas 1924, 372), and there are similarities between two Snoqualmie versions of "Star Husband," told by Skookum George and Henry Sicade, and both Secena's "x̌ʷəné·x̌ʷəne: A Story" and Cultee's "The Women Who Married the Stars" (appendix 1). Jerry Meeker shared a Puyallup version of "Moon and Sun" with Adamson (1934, 356). Joe Hunt shared Klikitat tales "Moon transformer teaches domestic crafts and kills dangerous beings" and "Wild Cat plays tricks on Coyote" with Melville Jacobs (1934, 40, 76). Coyote takes the place of x̌ʷə́n in these stories. Jacobs also worked with Sam Eyley Sr., who shared the Cowlitz tales "Coyote loses his milt daughters. They steal Moon baby; Moon becomes transformer" and "Coyote pretends to die, returns to cohabit with his daughters" (1934, 139, 146), and Jim Yoke, who shared the Upper Cowlitz tale "Coyote kills the Soft Basket Woman-with-vagina-dentata" (1934, 188).

13. Many of the family members of the people who shared these stories were not aware that Boas's field notes, manuscripts, and typescripts exist. It is imperative that archives, libraries, museums, and other repositories share the materials they hold with the families and communities of those who shared them. The caretakers at these institutions should not assume that these families and communities are aware that these materials exist and should take the initiative to share what they hold.

14. It seems that members of families who have continuously carried stories hold that the stories belong to a particular family tradition, while members of families who have not (or do not appear to have) carried stories are more ambivalent.

15. To my knowledge, there is no record—oral or written—of Jonas Secena having children.

16. In February and March 2015 I conducted a series of interviews with younger Chehalis tribal members regarding these stories specifically, and Chehalis story-telling more generally. I asked each person who was willing to spend time talk-ing with me how he or she would like to be identified. Some people asked to be identified by their initials only, some by first name, and some by full names. Some wanted to make their family affiliation known. Others preferred to be rec-ognized according to their position within the Chehalis Tribe. These positions are very fluid, and some of the people I interviewed have held multiple posi-tions in the seven years since I started working on this project. Though names and titles appear to be presented inconsistently throughout the introduction, respect for how individuals asked to be identified is consistent.

17. Questions asked elicited the use of the word *ownership* in many of these re-sponses; questions rephrased in terms of carrying a story, rather than owning a story, might have yielded different answers.

18. Unless otherwise indicated, subsequent quotations are from interviews and per-sonal communications.

19. Ford was an early settler in the area, coming to the Chehalis River valley in 1846. He served as Indian agent and was present at the failed treaty negotia-tions at Cosmopolis in 1855.

20. MDC confirms this generational difference. She says, "I would say, it's typical that families do know which stories belong to them and which can be shared. There might be some general knowledge stories of the Tribe, but I think even those could probably have been claimed by some family or other, and you know, sometimes the youth . . . might not know if it's a family story or not, but I would say there's always an elder that can say, 'No, that's a Secena family story. We don't get to tell that,' or, 'No, that's a Hazel Pete family story. You can't tell it'" (interview).

21. Chehalis storyteller Curtis Du Puis, son of Hazel Pete, talks about how he learned stories from his grandparents, Frank and Harriet Pete. Recordings of some of these stories are available on *American Indian Stories of the Pete Family* (Du Puis 2012). For more on Hazel Pete's contributions to living cultural traditions at Chehalis, see Collins 2000/2001.

22. MDC says:

    It's unfortunate, but I feel like if we're going to really preserve a lot of these things, they probably do have to be written down, and that makes me sad because that's not really the way of our people. And I think that stories lose a significance or a sense of reality, like you could picture them really happening, when they're being told to you, but when you're reading them, it's a dry account, it's a stale account, it doesn't have the emphasis you would get verbally when you're reciting them. It doesn't have those little bits that make it feel real, or make it feel alive. (interview)

23. MDC gives an example of this loss of control, providing a glimpse as to how published volumes have been perceived within the Chehalis community. She explains:

   [The x̣ʷə́n stories] are an example of something that was taken from the Tribe, and then somebody else made a profit, and the Tribe never benefited from it. Those stories, although they were requested and asked, they were basically stolen because I don't think it was said that they were going to be published, that a book would be made, that money would come in, but not for the Tribal people; it's going to come in for the people who collected these stories. And I think the mistrust was already there before that, but I think that that was one of the most blatant experiences that the Tribe had, and I've heard that those stories are incorrect, that people didn't want to pass on the real stories, in case something like that happened, so people would use these different versions of stories that were non-traditional, and then they were relieved when they found out, you know, exactly what had happened, and I think that that brought some relief, that those weren't correct stories. (interview)

   This serves as a reminder that scholars should be completely transparent regarding their intentions for use of material collected. If profit is made from the publication of this material, funds should find their way back to the community where the stories originated.

24. Filler words have been removed.

25. Helen Sanders, daughter of George Sanders and lead plaintiff in the historic Supreme Court cases, including *United States v. Helen Mitchell et al.* (1983).

26. This hybridity is apparent in Pike Ben's sharing of "Origin of the Fish," "Origin of Beaver and Deer," and "The Traveller" with Adamson — stories in which Jesus travels and transforms, doing the things that x̣ʷə́n does in traditional Chehalis stories (1934, 138–40). New religious beliefs are woven into old narrative structures — or, perhaps, old narrative structures are preserved because the storyteller appears to have converted.

27. The Chehalis Culture and Heritage Department and Education Department do an excellent job sharing cultural material with Chehalis students. John Shortman Jr. has already suggested that these stories be shared with students through the reservation-based afterschool and summer programs.

28. The 1940s and early 1950s.

29. MDC, Gleason, and Thoms each remember Curtis Du Puis sharing stories with the youth and with the community (interview). I have not written about Du Puis's contributions out of respect for the tradition that he carries, which is distinct from, yet intertwined with, the traditions featured here.

30. The subtitle of this section is an adaptation of a phrase used by Richard Bauman and Charles Briggs (1999, 486).

31. Boas is often referred to as "the father of American Anthropology." This is due

to his pioneering work in the study of culture, language, and race as well as his role as advisor and mentor to many of the discipline's founding members. His students had another paternal nickname for him: "Papa Franz."

32. The ethics of Boas's collection practices of both texts and objects have been scrutinized by many. These practices included the collection and purchase of ceremonial items, grave goods, and human remains. Cole provides details of Boas's collection work for the British Association for the Advancement of Science (1999, 110–12). For discussions of Boas's ethics, see Bauman and Briggs 1999; and Pöhl 2008.

In his introduction to the *Handbook of American Indian Languages*, Boas notes that "the essential object in comparing different types of man must be the reconstruction of the history of the development of their types, their languages, and their cultures." Boas and his students worked painstakingly to gather linguistic data along the Northwest Coast, and Boas explains the importance of such a project, that the "linguistic investigation may disclose the history of languages, the contact of the people speaking them with other people, and the causes that led to linguistic differentiation and integration" (1911, 14).

33. Willapa Athabaskan, or Swaal.

34. A Lower Chehalis variation of x̣ʷə́n.

35. Adamson and Jacobs both worked with Mary Iley (Eyley in Jacobs's spelling), an Upper Cowlitz woman who described myth as a canoe that, at the end of a night of storytelling, "had to be moored to a log or a tree along the river until the next night's myth journey." The next night the storyteller would say, "Now I will untie the myth," and begin the story from where he or she left off. Listeners discouraged digressions such as "a side channel of gossip or other irrelevance" by calling out, "Your myth might float away" (Jacobs 1934, x).

36. These transcriptions are included as an appendix to *Folk-Tales of the Coast Salish* (Adamson 1934), and the recordings are available through the Indiana University Archives of Traditional Music.

37. Boas and Hunt's collaboration resulted in major works such as *Kwakiutl Texts* (1902–05, 1906) and *Ethnology of the Kwakiutl* (1921). For more thorough discussion and analysis of their collaboration, see Helen Codere's introduction to Boas 1966; Berman 1994; and Bauman and Briggs 1999.

38. Some sources, such as Upton 2003, suggest other biographical details; these have been strongly contested. The biographical details presented here come from Adamson's notes from Davis directly.

39. According to Miller and MDC, Barr remembers her father working with Adamson and Boas. She was six or seven at the time. Davis was ill, but he told stories from a cot brought out into the yard and set up under a tree. Barr was some-

times present for this but was sometimes asked to go along and play (Miller 2010, 360; interview).

40. Bertha later married Fred Bobb.

41. Chinook Jargon is also known as Chinuk Wawa.

42. Curtis Du Puis describes this as someone's personal spirit or power.

43. Adamson's dissertation, "Trickster and Transformer Myths of the Coast Salish," is also missing. There is some speculation that a draft may have been given to Marian Smith.

44. Miller gleaned the following information from Kinkade's *Upper Chehalis Dictionary* and Adamson's ethnographic notes: "Mary Heck's husband, the father of Peter and Silas, was named *xekwim/* and then *kʷuqʷła* after his father's father" (1999a, 30; Kinkade 1991, 336). In addition, "At his wedding, Peter Heck was named *yanm* after his father's father, with the announcement that 'the dead man has now returned'" (Miller 1999a, 30, from Adamson 1926–27, 82).

45. See Kinkade 2008.

46. An interlinear transcription is one in which the translation of an original native-language text is presented between the lines of the original. This can be done word by word or morpheme by morpheme and often retains the grammatical structure of the original.

47. Chehalis-language students might be interested in working through this unfinished translation.

48. Special thanks to Roberta Secena, daughter-in-law of Murphy Secena, for sharing this knowledge.

49. Kinkade's note indicates that the Kitsap relation was through Jacob Secena, sisína?xn, but Jacobs's interview with Mrs. Dan (Alice) Secena indicates that the Kitsap relation came through Alice's marriage to Dan. It is possible that the relation is through both sides of the family, and it should be noted that there were at least three Chief Kitsaps. A family historian might be able to clarify these connections.

50. Boas paid Dawson for the work she continued after he left the Chehalis Reservation, as discussed in the letters exchanged between the two of them.

51. Probably Alice.

52. For examples of the use of X-rays in the study of sound, see Russell 1928; or Russell 1929. Roman Jakobson (1978, 7–12) details the history of the use of X-rays in the study of linguistics.

53. Ethel and her husband, Bernard (Burt) Aginsky, both studied under Boas. The couple worked with the Pomo Indians in California and published *Deep Valley: The Pomo Indians of California* in 1967. Ethel specialized in Puyallup Lushootseed.

54. See Seaburg and Sercombe 2009; Miller 2012a.
55. See Swadesh 1950.
56. It is possible that Kinkade also gave copies of this material to Secena family members in the early 2000s.
57. In developing this form, Hymes sought to retain "the surprising facts of device, design, and performance inherent in the words of the texts, the Indians who made the texts, and those who preserved what they made," to let the text not only speak, but sing (1981b, 5, 6). See Hymes 1974; Hymes 1981; and Hymes 2003.
58. Gladys A. Reichard expresses similar frustration in "A Comparison of Five Salish Languages: I." She explains:

    A major criticism of Boas' Chehalis is his failure to define the phonetic system he uses. Apparently he hewed pretty closely to the line of the Phonetic Transcription of Indian Languages with modifications introduced between 1916 and 1934, changes with which I am familiar. But his representation of the vowels is not clear, and I can find no note to indicate whether he used his old system for palatals or revised it. I assume that X is what we now write x, and that former x is X. I deduce this from a comparison of the text, notebooks, and a few remarks, none of which is explicit. (1958, 293)

59. A digital edition of this material would be preferable to an interlinear print edition. Both English and Upper Chehalis material could be transcribed, with various layers of the text (field notebook, typescript, digital transcription) available to readers simultaneously. This would connect readers to the source material, and not another copy of a copy.
60. Adamson was institutionalized soon thereafter. For more on Adamson's life and work, see Seaburg 1999.
61. According to Miller, when Kinkade first presented "Bear and Bee" as a conference paper, he "humorously prefaced it by hoping the academic audience's fifty years of anticipation would be met at last" (pers. comm.).
62. The broader context for this research is outlined in Elaine L. Mills's guide to Harrington's field notes. Harrington was especially interested in studying "the now extinct neighbors and predecessors of Athapascan tongue" (1981, 37). Emma Luscier, who was fluent in Lower Chehalis and familiar with other Salish languages, "was the original source for most of the linguistic data and she reheard and commented on published and manuscript vocabularies or on the information given by other informants" (31, 37).

A Story

1. "Beasts" in the typescript (1). However, *pé·ps* is often translated as "animal" (Kinkade 1991, 95).
2. Thelma Adamson and Franz Boas worked with many of the same storytellers,

and *Folk-Tales of the Coast Salish* contains episodes that correspond to stories Boas collected. See the abstract for "Moon" in *Folk-Tales of the Coast Salish* for associated stories (Adamson 1934, 379). There are many similarities between this story and George Sanders's *Honne, the Spirit of the Chehalis: The Indian Interpretation of the Origin of the People and Animals.* Secena's version is evenly divided between the travels of xʷen and the travels of Moon, whereas Sanders's narration is almost entirely devoted to xʷen, with only a brief mention of Moon and Sun. Ki-kai-si-mi-loot, an Upper Chehalis woman better known by her nickname "Queen," shared a version of "The Story of Sloqualm (The Moon)" with George Gibbs in the 1850s. Robert Jackson's "The Story of Sun: A Legend of the Chehalis Indians" is much shorter than Secena's version but features many of the same episodes. In 1952 Murphy Secena, Jonas's brother, shared his version of this story with Leon Metcalf. Murphy shared the story in Upper Chehalis and made explanations in English. Metcalf's audio recordings of Chehalis people are housed at the University of Washington. In 1960 M. Dale Kinkade recorded Silas Heck's "The Kidnapping of Moon." This story is published in *Salish Myths and Legends: One People's Stories*, with Kinkade providing commentary on how various Coast Salish versions of Moon's kidnapping are interconnected and the story itself presented in narrative verse format (2008, 349–68).

3. In her introduction to *Folk-Tales of the Coast Salish,* Thelma Adamson notes that the tales therein refer to a time "'when all the animals were people'. The Upper Chehalis term for this type of tale is sielɔ''pt, the Cowlitz sɔ''pt. According to the Upper Chehalis, after the appearance of the transformer Moon, the birds and animals could no longer speak the human language. Moon was 'master' of the animals and told them how the people in time to come should use them. Most of the characters in the tales are animals or birds, but in a few cases, the characters seem entirely human" (1934, xii).

The storyteller of "Snowbird," this volume, puts it another way: "In the beginning there were the new people in the world. All the animals were people. In the beginning of the world the people were transformed. All the people were animals." Curtis Du Puis, Chehalis storyteller, shared that his grandparents, Frank and Harriet Pete, said, "When birds, people, and animals lived together." This phrasing is common among Northwest Coast traditions.

4. "Chief Y" in the typescript (1). The *Y* is actually the particle *čaʔu,* meaning "why" (Kinkade 1991, 34). The particle begins the next sentence.

5. Boas frequently uses an *X* to indicate xʷəné·xʷəne, Jonas Secena's form of xʷə́n. The field notebooks and typescript contain variations of this spelling, with xwna' xun most commonly repeated in the typescript. Spellings correspond to storytellers and represent different dialects. Adamson identifies Secena's xʷə́n as X̣wanä'x̣wane. Kinkade represents Boas's rendering of Secena's trickster figure

as x̣ʷəné·x̣ʷəne, and that is the form that will be used consistently herein when it is clear that Secena is the storyteller. Otherwise, the standard x̣ʷə́n will be used. Other variations include Palmer's anglicization of George Saunders's central figure as Honné; Curtis Du Puis indicates that Harriet and Frank Pete said T'whannah; and Boas presents Cultee's Lower Chehalis version as Qoné'qonē.

6. Boas's handwriting is difficult to decipher, but the word used here may be *I-lo-kwát*, the Upper Chehalis word for cattail grass (Kinkade 1991, 16). In that case, *rushes* would be a better word choice here than *brushes*.

7. The name qʷcx̣ʷé appears in many different forms. Boas uses the spelling "Kwɑtsx̣wɛ̈" in his field notebooks, and Aginsky simplifies this to "kw' tsxw" in the typescript. Kinkade represents Boas's rendering of this female monster as "k'ʷə́cx̣ʷe," used herein.

8. Camas, a purple-flowering bulb, is an Upper Chehalis food staple and, as this story illustrates, an integral part of Upper Chehalis trade networks. Gunther (1945) identifies Chehalis, Cowlitz, Klallam, Lummi, Makah, Nisqually, Puyallup, Quileute, Quinault, Skokomish, and Squaxin names for camas. She notes that camas "was universally used in the area, and traded from others if it is not available in the home territory. Except for choice varieties of dried salmon there was no article of food that was more widely traded than camas." She continues, "Camas grows best in prairies (open spaces in the heavily wooded landscape of this area), and is dug in the late spring. Camas bulbs are usually cooked in a pit in the ground." Specific to Upper Chehalis, Gunther explains, "The Chehalis smash the bulbs and press them together like a cheese to preserve them. These are boiled in a stew with salmon." She also points out that "the Skokomish get camas from the vicinity of Chehalis through trade, since the plant does not grow in their own lands" (1945, 24). Upper Chehalis gathering and processing of camas is evidenced by archaeological data (an earth oven in the Chehalis River Basin dates to nearly three thousand years BP) as well as oral tradition (language and literary traditions included) (Foutch, Punke, and Fagan 2012, 2). In *The Chehalis People* it is noted that "when going to dig roots, [women] left early in the morning for the open prairies and did not return until the end of the day. They used a digging stick of ironwood (spirea) about two and half feet long fitted with a handle of elk horn. Women from several villages might congregate at camas-picking grounds when the bulbs were ready to dig. In the Upper Chehalis area there are many prairies where the blue flowers of camas still appear abundantly in late spring." Preparation methods are also explained: "Camas was cooked using the ancient pit-baking method. The bulbs were placed in a pit four to five feet deep and lined with ferns, then covered with more ferns and earth, and a fire built on top. The fire burned all night long and by morning the roots would be all cooked. Sometimes the cooked bulbs were smashed and made into a loaf

like bread, dried so that it could be eaten during the winter. Camas was also smoked whole and then used in soup with fish and salmon eggs" (Marr, Hicks, and Francis 2001, 6). Today Chehalis people gather and process camas and promote camas prairie restoration.

9. Both Peter Heck and Jonas Secena shared stories regarding the use of dentalium (Adamson 1934, 82, 83). Heck shares:

They gave the men a canoe but refused to give them dentalia (xaL'e'' ı k·). The Qwesta'imuχ had great heaps of little shells piled up. They had sucked the insides out and had thrown the shells away. (These shells were the dentalia.) The two men, however, wanted very much to have some of the dentalia, so they put pitch on the bottoms of their canoes to pick the shells up. There were various kinds—the short variety and the long variety; they stuck to the bottom of the canoe. That's how dentalia first got here. (Adamson 1934, 83)

Miller summarizes Adamson's ethnographic notes—likely shared by Peter Heck—regarding these highly valued, tusk-like shells. Dentalium, "dangling in strings, were used for earrings and other objects of wealth. . . . As elsewhere along the Pacific coast, natives did not know that their source was Nootkan traders from the west coast of Vancouver Island, where the shells were ingeniously dredged up from the ocean floor several hundred feet deep" (1999a, 13). George Gibbs observed dentalium used as currency, noting that it "was procured on the northern coast by letting down long poles, to which was attached a piece of wood filled with spikes, or teeth, between which the shells became fixed." Gibbs explains that the value "depended entirely on its length," noting that "single shells were shown to me on the Tsihalis [Chehalis] for which the owner refused a dollar apiece. This money is, however, becoming scarce, and is far less used than formerly" (1877, 213). In *A Guide to the Indian Tribes of the Pacific Northwest*, Robert Ruby, John Brown, and Cary Collins note that "well-established trade routes lay between the Lower Chehalis and the Kwaiailk [Upper Chehalis] lands. Over those routes the Kwaiailks obtained goods such as dentalia and seal oil, which were traded along the Pacific Coast from Neah Bay southward to the Columbia River" (2013, 157).

10. Field notebook II, 90: "whenever"; typescript, "A Story," 1: "hereafter."

11. Field notebook II, 90: "he"; typescript, "A Story," 2: "they."

12. Field notebook II, 102: "Could you help me? Could you make . . ."; typescript, "A Story," 5: "Can you help me? How can you make . . ."

13. Typescript, "A Story," 6: "says."

14. Ironically, tamanous—spelled a number of different ways—is not an Upper Chehalis word but a word borrowed from Chinook Jargon. Thus the language used to discuss precontact traditions is a postcontact construct. According to Adamson, the word is "the Chinook jargon [Chinuk Wawa] term for guardian

spirit, now in common usage. The one term is used to express either the singu-lar or the plural" (1934, 2). Gibbs includes "Ta-máh-no-us" in *A Dictionary of the Chinook Jargon; or, Trade Language of Oregon*, defining it as *"a sort of guardian or familiar spirit; magic; luck; fortune; any thing supernatural.* One's particu-lar forte is said to be his *tamahnous"* (1863, 25). Tamanous refers to the guard-ian spirit as well as the power it bestows. This power takes many forms, as Peter Heck explained to Adamson in 1927. These include (1) doctoring the sick, (2) dancing, (3) going to the Land of the Dead, (4) hunting, (5) fishing, (6) being well off, (7) inheriting tamanous from ancestors or relatives, and (8) borrowing ta-manous from the same (Adamson 1926–27, 42–43, 245; Miller 1999a, 45–46). In Upper Chehalis, these powers are linguistically differentiated. For instance, stá-ličamš is the "fisherman's guardian spirit" and sqép is the "guardian spirit giving good luck, lucky spirit power, having good songs, general good luck" (Kinkade 1991, 293). Each of these powers could be used to help people, but they could also be quite dangerous: a doctor had the power to cure, but he also had the power to kill. In this specific case, Secena refers to a gambling power, which he told Adamson was a good luck tamanous for anything—"gambling, sing-ing, earning things"—given by Bluejay, Flying Squirrel, Wolf, Coyote, Chicken Hawk, or Hoot Owl (1926–27, 343).

15. According to Miller, "Hoop Disks was played at night with lots of betting be-fore the two sides sat on mats. These disks were eight black and red, one black, and one white. Each side had five and hid them inside shredded cedar bark. They played to a count of 40, using split sticks for tallies, guessing for the solid color" (1999a, 39). These notes pertain to Chehalis specifically, but the game was played throughout the region. Myron Eells illustrates this traditional gambling game, relating how the game is played, its purpose, and the traditions behind it. Eells describes the round disks:

> The disks are about two inches in diameter and a third of an inch thick. They are made of hard wood, quite smooth, and by long continued use become highly pol-ished. One edge of most of them is partly painted, either red or black, while one is left unpainted; or else the edge is entirely painted. There are ten blocks or disks in a set. (1985, 205)

16. Field notebook II, 113: "Chief of the Geese"; typescript, "A Story," 8: "Chief of the Bees."

17. Typescript, "A Story," 9: "tales."

18. Field notebook III, 147: "stick"; typescript, "A Story," 10: "spot."

19. Peter Heck shared the following cultural knowledge with Adamson:

> When the salmon comes up, that's the time to put up fish trap. Always have a trap for spring salmon—just some people. Same way when the salmon come up in Octo-

ber months when river is dry. . . . Spear or any way. Cook. Boiled, or roasted. . . . Spear, cause always dug on the riffle, spear dry back bone. Dried, soaked over night on the river side. . . .

Two or three or five different parties would make a fish trap so could help one another cut lots of sticks to make it with. Cut from maple. . . . Maybe five feet long about an inch or more in diameter. Poles sharp on bottom and. Tied together with willow bark about a yard apart clear across the river. That is, make each section a yard wide. . . . Then tie them together and put the sharp stick on the ground where the riffle is slanting, so gets on the hollow on bottom and one on top. The bottom one is perhaps a foot from the water. Three . . . or four . . . across river. Make a hoop round about . . . about three quarters of a yard round, and make it from p'an nkɬ, and always split it and tie it to hoop with willow bark. Maybe eight feet long, and when all round, they'll put a little pole around it so will bend until it ets [?] to the tail, to keep hoop over, just tie one on the end. Now, just tie it round. They'll make another about yard wide, make it same way but half size one-half circle. Tie . . . string at bottom, like bow and arrow to hold it in round shape. Will tie the ends, tied here, bowed put round bark. Salmon [go] in here then turn around and go back into cylinder and stay there where are caught. (1926–27, 27–28)

20. Field notebook III, 162: "hewing" or "chipping"; typescript, "A Story," 11: "tipping."
21. A clearer translation of "x̌ʷəné·x̌ʷəne Makes a Self-Acting Maul" is provided in the second version (see p. 85).
22. Field notebook III, 164: "Spring Salmon"; typescript, "A Story," 12: "salmon."
23. Field notebook III, 174: "roots of ferns"; typescript, "A Story," 14: "fern woods."
24. Field notebook III, 174: "all things"; typescript, "A Story," 15: "everything."
25. Field notebook IV, 186: "so"; typescript, "A Story," 15: "that."
26. Field notebook IV, 190–91: "she put it on" or "she put it aboard"; typescript, "A Story," 16: "she put it on."
27. Field notebook IV, 191: "The canoe is getting heavy"; typescript, "A Story," 16: "The canoe was getting heavy."
28. Field notebook IV, 193: "First, I walk"; typescript, "A Story," 17: "First, I take a walk."
29. "Country of the Spring Salmon" and "Land of the Salmon" are used interchangeably. When the elder sister refers to the Country of the Spring Salmon, Boas provides *ts a w ɬ*, his form of *c'áwɬ*, which is the Upper Chehalis word for spring, or Chinook, salmon. However, in reference to the Country or Land of the Salmon the more generic term, *sčanánxʷ*, is used (field notebook IV, 204–5).
30. This was a time of perpetual twilight, before Moon and Sun separated day and night.
31. Claquato; typescript, "A Story," 18: "Kilakwito"; according to Boas, "a prairie south of Chehalis" (Kinkade 1991, 332).

32. Field notebook IV, 206: "malɛ'"; typescript, "A Story," 18: "Male'"; Kinkade notes that "malé" is the "name of the mother of Moon" and, according to Boas, "Moon's grandmother" (1991, 79) In this version malé is the name of Moon's grandmother, but the name occasionally refers to Moon's mother as well. Peter Heck shared his understanding of these differences with Adamson, which Adamson preserves in a footnote to a story titled "Malɛ'": "Some people call Moon's mother Male'' (or Mali'); others call Moon's grandmother this instead. These people maintain that Male'' is a native term. On the other hand, Mr. Heck maintains that they had never called Moon's mother or grandmother this until after they had heard about the Virgin Mary from the Catholics. He said, however, that there was a native term similar to Male'', but that it was the name of a male character in a story" (1934, 74–75). In regard to a landform (exact location unknown) said to be malé, Heck notes, "doesn't know whether man or rock near Lequito—woman—large rock which looks like a person. Has no arms—two smaller ones are her dogs. Was not moon's mother, but some people are using it for that" (Adamson 1926–27, 275).

33. Moon is consistently referred to as "he" and as malé's grandson; however, in both this version and the second translation he is referred to as a daughter. The passage might also be translated as "Her daughter was picking berries. Her daughter had a child by immaculate conception from the bursting of red hot stones in front of her body. From these her child was born," leaving the gender of the child ambiguous (field notebook IV, 206).

34. Field notebook IV, 207: "her grandmother"; typescript, "A Story," 18: "her granddaughter."

35. Field notebook IV, 211: "with"; typescript, "A Story," 19: "by."

36. Field notebook IV, 212: "child"; typescript, "A Story," 20: "grandchild."

37. Field notebook IV, 212: "stole"; typescript, "A Story," 20: "had stolen."

38. Field notebook IV, 213: no "all" indicated; typescript, "A Story," 20: "the girls are all different kind."

39. According to Kinkade, the word $t'aq'^w\text{-}i\text{=}q^w\chi^w\text{\l{}}\acute{a}\text{-}w\text{-}n$ can be translated "she talked about her power" (1991, 148).

40. No translation provided.

41. Hermann Haeberlin titled a Snoqualmie story featuring a similar opening and closing of the earth "Symplegades," referencing the Cyanean Rocks of Greek mythology (Haeberlin and Boas 1924, 372). In his introduction to "The Kidnapping of Moon," Kinkade discusses the two mythic sites specified in this story. Kinkade explains, "One is the land of the salmon, where the kidnappers take the baby; this is considered their home, since they were made from milt. The other site is the border between that world and our own. Here the sky repeatedly and rapidly crashes against the earth, making it impossible to cross. This sort of bor-

der is widespread in mythology, and in Greek mythology is called the Symplegades" (2008, 352).

42. Field notebook IV, 221: "Children of Spring Salmon"; typescript, "A Story," 22: "children of salmon."

43. In the second version, malé says, "Now I give it up, my daughter," which is much more faithful to Boas's transcription (see p. 93; field notebook IV, 222).

44. Boas indicates this is a swear word.

45. Field notebook IV, 227: "tamanous"; typescript, "A Story," 24: "supernatural."

46. No translation provided.

47. Again, a clearer translation is provided in the second version (see p. 94; field notebook IV, 229).

48. "Oh, our elder brothers, let Mountain Lion go first" comes from the second version of this story, as the first version is ambiguous (see p. 94).

49. Kinkade glosses this as "what Bluejay says" (1991, 47).

50. Field notebook V, 258: "What are you doing to me, my master?"; typescript, "A Story," 29: "What are you doing to my mask?"

51. Traditionally made of woven cedar bark.

52. Field notebook V, 285: "penis"; typescript, "A Story," 35–38: "tool or tools."

53. Boas's field notebook scrawl under "meat"—"woman/meat, i.e. cohabit"—does not make it into the typescript. The bawdiness of this passage is toned down (field notebook V, 286).

54. Field notebook V, 291: "headband"; typescript, "A Story," 36: "cap"; *headband* and *cap* are interchangeable, but Boas uses *headband* more frequently.

55. Number is inconsistent in this passage, and pronouns do not always agree with antecedents.

56. Field notebook VI, 300: "hats"; typescript, "A Story," 37: "heads."

57. This translation leaves a space where these utterances should be; the second translation presents the shouting as "eh" (see p. 102).

58. Breechcloth.

59. Boas notes that this is Lower Chehalis dialect (typescript, "A Story," 39).

60. Field notebook VI, 320: "wooden bucket"; typescript, "A Story," 45: "wooden basket."

61. Boas's notes confirm that xʷəné·xʷəne says, "You shall go make a fire at the foot of the tree. After you have made a fire, sit down at the foot of the red fir tree," and then completes the action himself (field notebook VI, 339).

62. Boas (field notebook VI, 355) translates this as "fry" or "trout," but Kinkade (1991, 80) translates *mánc* as "salmon fry."

63. A source of Adamson's, likely Peter Heck, spoke about xʷə́n, often regarded as a trickster, and what ultimately became of him:

Xw&n was a person. Xw&n kind of a Cowlitz man, the way he talks, he talked
Cowlitz language when he traveled. "Maybe he was the Cowlitz tribe, but he traveled everywhere." (Never knew him to change himself. Mrs. Heck, all he does is try
to steal and cheat others.) I think he is over on Cowlitz side. (When I asked what
become of him.) Mrs. Heck seems to disagree.) Turned into a rock, he thinks, don't
know who did it, maybe somebody changed him, Moon, or the Devil. Was going
toward Cowlitz—something whistled behind him—turned to rock—little pack on
his back—there yet.)" (1926–27, 81)

Many of the important figures featured in these stories are present in the landscape of the river valley. Cultural memory is embedded in the hills, prairies,
rivers, and stones that make up Chehalis geography.

64. Boas glosses this as "you displease yourselves" and "you hurt your own feelings"
(field notebook VII, 377).

65. The second translation of Moon's speech is much different, emphasizing that it
is disgraceful for people to come just to eat. Speech giving and tamanous performance are integral to these gatherings.

66. Field notebook VII, 415: "his mother-in-law" or "her father-in-law"; typescript, "A Story," 37: "her mother-in-law." Using context as a guide, this has been
changed to "her mother-in-law," as Frog is consistently referred to as female, and
she is cooking with Moon's mother, her mother-in-law.

x̣ʷəné·x̣ʷəne: A Story

Field notebook I–VII, 57–62, 72–78, 87–116, 144–48, 161–95, 204–34, 245–311, 311–45,
353–60, 373–88, 404, 407–13, 404–5, 416–28; typescript, "Xuná Xune, a Story," 20–85,
5–8.This is the second translation of Secena's story, utilizing the same field notebook
passages as the first. This version is more polished, and passages left in Upper Chehalis
in the first version are translated here. Most of the first version's footnotes apply to the
second version as well; therefore this text has not been explicated with the same level
of detail.

1. Field notebook II, 87: "brushes"; typescript, "Xuná Xune, a Story," 20: "bushes."
However, "rushes" might be more appropriate.

2. Field notebook II, 93: "like this"; typescript, "Xuná Xune, a Story," 21: "with this."

3. From here on in the typescript, "Owl" is used instead of "Hooting Owl." However, Boas consistently writes the same word, *skʷinútčič*, in his field notes. Thus
"Owl" has been changed to "Hooting Owl" (Kinkade 1991, 267).

4. Boas translates *qat̓ q̓ʷáxnł* as "screecher" in the alternate version, and Kinkade
indicates that this word can be translated as both "gracious!" and "scratcher"
(1991, 118).

5. Field notebook IV, 189: "push"; typescript, "Xuná Xune, a Story," 35: "pull." Kinkade translates *xáx̓api-mal-ilaʔ* as "push out to the water!" (1991, 159).

6. As noted in the first version, this is likely a mistranslation. Moon is consistently referred to with male pronouns as malé's grandson.

7. In the first version, Boas and Aginsky use variations of "supernatural" and "tamanous" to refer to tamanous; in the second version, "shamanistic," "supernatural," and "witchcraft" are substituted for tamanous. These substitutions are not faithful to the original, and thus "tamanous" has been reinserted into the text when appropriate.

8. Field notebook IV, 216: "charming"; typescript, "Xuná Xune, a Story," 39: "witchcraft." According to Kinkade, *čə́c'stani* can be translated as "use power to influence a person" or "charm, send one, 'to talk long distance'" (1991, 41).

9. The first version is less fragmented: "The sky went up and rejoined the earth. There was a little opening so that a person could almost go through where it rejoined the earth" (see p. 50).

10. Again, the first translation is more complete: "Then she was going to get in but she failed to get hold of it" (see p. 50).

11. Field notebook IV, 221: "Children of Spring Salmon"; typescript, "Xuná Xune, a Story," 41: "children of the salmon."

12. Field notebook IV, 228: "I am a hero"; typescript, "Xuná Xune, a Story," 44: "I am terrible." The word used, *pə́saʔ*, can be translated as "monster, mean person, mean thing," "evil spirit," "dangerous being" (Kinkade 1991, 97).

13. Field notebook VI, 306: "breech clout"; typescript, "Xuná Xune, a Story," 61: "bread cloth."

14. Dialogue is more clearly attributed to speaker in the first translation (see p. 62).

15. Field notebook VI, 315: "she"; typescript, "Xuná Xune, a Story," 64: "he."

16. Boas translates the alternate version as, "It is a real monster. It is not a person." The field notebooks indicate that this first translation is correct (see p. 67).

17. Field notebook VI, 337: "big tree with thick needles"; typescript, "Xuná Xune, a Story," 68: "a large trail with thick leaves."

18. The first translation is less muddled: "Among them was x̌ʷəné·x̌ʷəne, among the monster people. There were as many as there were animals" (see p. 72).

19. Boas notes, "Listeners say this. It is said if they do not do so, they will become hunchback" (typescript, "Xuná Xune, a Story," 85).

Bear, Yellow Jacket, and Ant

Field notebook I, 30–44; typescript, "Bear, Yellow-Jackets and Ant," 1–7. This is the first story Boas transcribed in his field notes, and it immediately follows introductory vocabulary and grammar work.

Boas published an excerpt of this story as "A Chehalis Text" in the *International Journal of American Linguistics* in 1935, reproduced in this volume as

Appendix 3. Kinkade revisited Boas's translation in "Bear and Bee: Narrative Verse Analysis of an Upper Chehalis Folktale," available here for comparison as Appendix 4.

Adamson's *Folk-Tales of the Coast Salish* contains three alternate, much shorter, Upper Chehalis versions of this story. Adamson attributes versions of "Bear and Ant or the Contest for Day and Night" to Maggie Pete, Dan Secena, the father of Jonas Secena, and Joe Pete, respectively (1934, 132–33). Two Cowlitz versions are also featured in the volume: Lucy Youckton's "Bear, Ant, Grouse, Frog and the Yellowjackets" and Mary Iley's "Frog and Bear" (1934, 188–89). The episode is also present in *Honne, the Spirit of the Chehalis* as "Why We Have Days and Nights" (Palmer 1925, 51–53).

Boas does not indicate who told him this story, but Kinkade notes that "the narrator was probably Jonas Secena" (1984, 246).

1. Typescript, 3: "Then Bear said, 'This is good,' said the Bear, 'let us dance.'"
2. Field notebook I, 78–79; typescript, "Daughters of the Fire," 8.

A Visit to the Skokomish

Field notebook I, 18¹–19¹; typescript, "A Visit to the Skokomish," 9.

Gossip

Field notebook I, 20¹–23¹; typescript, "Gossip," 10.

Snowbird

Field notebook I, 28¹–38¹, 48¹–62¹ and field notebook II, 63¹–68¹; typescript, "Snowbird," 11–19. Another Upper Chehalis version of this story, "Northeast Wind and Southwest Wind," was published in Adamson's *Folk-Tales of the Coast Salish* (1934, 75). Adamson attributes this story to Jonas Secena. Cultee shared "Myth of the Southwest Wind," a Kathlamet tale, with Boas (1901, 67–71).

1. Snowbird is identified as the Oregon junco, xʷayóʔsxʷayʔs in Upper Chehalis (field notebook I, 28¹; Kinkade 1991, 291).
2. Field notebook II, 65¹. According to Kinkade, *xʷalínwat-* can be translated as "give up hope" (1991, 228).
3. Typescript, "Snowbird," 19: "left of."
4. Probably "up north."

Rabbit and Mountain Lion

Field notebook VIII, 447–72; typescript, "Rabbit and Mountain Lion," 86–94. Two Upper Chehalis versions of this story, "Mountain Lion and Rabbit Gamble," were published in Adamson's *Folk-Tales of the Coast Salish* (1934, 52). Adamson attributes the first version to Jonas Secena and the second version to Marion Davis.

1. Slahal, an ancient gambling game, is also known as the bone game. For Chehalis ethnography, see Miller 1999a, 39. Eells provides a description of the bone game, explaining game pieces and rules (1985, 208–10). Slahal tournaments were, and are, often accompanied by drumming and singing. Tournaments are still popular at Northwest Coast gatherings, including potlatches, pow wows, and tribal days.

Bluejay

Field notebook VIII, 473–88; typescript, "Bluejay," 1–5. Four Upper Chehalis versions of this story, "Bluejay Goes to the Land of the Dead," were published in Adamson's *Folk-Tales of the Coast Salish*. Adamson attributes the first version to Peter Heck, the second version to Marion Davis, the third version to Maggie Pete, and the fourth version to Jonas Secena (1934, 21). A Satsop version by the same name was told by Mrs. Simon Charlie (Adamson 1934, 349). "Bluejay and His Sister Yo'I," a Humptulip tale, was shared by Lucy Heck (Adamson 1934, 293). "Jay Goes to the Other-World," an episode in *Honne, the Spirit of the Chehalis*, also corresponds to this story (Palmer 1925, 202–3). In "Bluejay and His Sister," Kinkade (1987, 255–96) presents Silas Heck's version of this story in ethnopoetic form, in both Upper Chehalis and English. He then makes a comparative analysis of multiple versions of this story, including the version presented here. Ki-kai-si-mi-loot shared a similar story, "The Mo-Kwo-Tah-Oom," with Gibbs, though Bluejay is absent from the narrative.

Mink

Field notebook IX, 493–513; typescript, "Mink," 1–7. Pike Ben provides three Mink stories in Adamson's *Folk-Tales of the Coast Salish*: two versions of "Mink Kills Whale" and one version of "Mink and the Girl" (1934, 133). However, Adamson notes that these are not Upper Chehalis tales. Mary Adams tells a similar tale, "Mink," which Adamson categorizes as a Skokomish tale (1934, 364). In *Honne, the Spirit of the Chehalis*, "Story of Jay and Girl Who Died and Came Back to Life" and "Mink Takes the Girl Away" correspond to Davis's story (Palmer 1925, 54–62, 62–64).

1. Typescript, "Mink," 3: Nisqualli.
2. Field notebook IX, 508: "folks;" typescript, "Mink," 5: "relatives."
3. Kinkade indicates that *yaləm-* can also be translated as "helpers," which is a euphemism for "slaves" (1991, 235).
4. Boas's translation of this material is unclear. Boas provides, "She took her child and Mink the boy swam. When Mink came up he said, 'My child shall stay with your grandchildren'" as a translation. Field notebook IX indicates that "She took her child and Mink the boy swam" should be divided into two sentences. In the first clause, Boas provides "and" as a translation for *ča*, and Kinkade indi-

cates that *ča* can also be translated as "with." "The boy swam" is an independent clause. Thus the last two sentences could be translated as "She took her child with Mink. The boy swam," or some variation thereof. The first part of the second sentence, "When Mink came up he said," is not problematic, but the second part, "'my child shall stay with your grandchildren,'" is more difficult. In Field notebook IX Boas writes the last words of the story as "nax · kop!aten." The *nax* prefix gives a sense of future children, or children yet to be born (see Kinkade 1991, 91, entry 1188, náxʷ-). It might be possible to translate Mink's statement as "My child will be with the children you are yet to have."

In the second version of "Mink Kills Whale," Pike Ben tells Adamson, "Then they paddled away from Mink and his son. 'You shall be a mink and stay there forever. They'll sell your hide for a lot of money,' the woman called back. Before this Mink had been a man" (1934, 136). In "Mink and the Girl," Pike Ben says, "The woman picked up her little son and threw him overboard. He went in as a real little boy but came out as a mink" (Adamson 1934, 137). Mary Adam's version might provide the most insight. It goes, "The woman paid no attention, only directed her slaves to keep on paddling. She threw her son overboard. As the boy floundered about, Mink cried, 'Try to reach those snags! Try to swim ashore to your grandfather's root.'" The story ends with the Creator, Dukwe'bał, becoming pregnant after drinking Mink's urine. Because of this, the trickster Mink "was in everything!" (Adamson 1934, 366, 367).

The Flood

Field notebook IX, 514–18; typescript, "Untitled," 1–2. Adamson provides three alternate Upper Chehalis versions of "The Flood" in *Folk-Tales of the Coast Salish*, as told by Peter Heck, Jonas Secena, and Joe Pete, respectively (1934, 1). She also provides one Cowlitz version, told by Mary Iley (178).

1. Boas notes, "a small brown-striped bird," that is, thrush (typescript, "Untitled," 1).
2. Kinkade identifies this as Muskrat Mountain, possibly Rock Candy Mountain or Capitol Peak (1991, 329).

Skunk

Field notebook IX, 519–29; typescript, "Skunk," 1–4. Boas does not indicate a storyteller for "Skunk," although it directly follows "The Flood" and a short section on "Hunting" in field notebook IX. Peter Heck told "The Flood." Adamson attributes another version of "Skunk" to Marion Davis and "X̣wanä'x̣wane and Skunk" to Jonas Secena, both Upper Chehalis (1934, 46, 142). A Davis version of "Skunk," recorded in Adamson's ethnographic notes, features a pretty hoop "like good red fire" and ends with the explanation, "These Skunks we have now, are just little Skunks, but don't kill the people with their gas, just smells strongly" (1926–27, 175, 177). Adamson revises this, "We shall not have skunk again like this—killing people. He used to be large and killed people, but now he is small and wouldn't kill anyone" (1926–27, 177).

1. As Boas does not indicate the storyteller, it is difficult to determine the most appropriate spelling of x̣ʷə́n to use in "Skunk." A variation of x̣ʷəné·x̣ʷəne is used in the typescript, but a variation of x̣ʷə́n is used in Field notebook IX. For the sake of consistency, the spelling "x̣ʷə́n" will be used throughout.
2. Field notebook IX, 525; typescript, "Skunk," 3: A shift from plural "them" to singular "it" is indicated.

x̣ʷə́n and Raccoon

Field notebook IX, 529–35; typescript, "Untitled," 1–2. As with "Skunk," Boas does not indicate a storyteller for "x̣ʷə́n and Raccoon." This story directly follows "Skunk," "The Flood," and a short section on "Hunting" in field notebook IX. Adamson attributes another Upper Chehalis version of "X̣wan and Coon" to Peter Heck (1934, 140). She attributes a Cowlitz version of "X̣waʼni and Coon" to Mary Iley (250).

1. As in "Skunk," the spelling "x̣ʷə́n" will be used throughout.

x̣ʷə́n Kills k'ʷə́cx̣ʷe

Field notebook IX, 549–68; typescript, "Untitled," 1–5. The first part of Jonas Secena's "Moon" in Adamson's *Folk-Tales of the Coast Salish* is very similar to this story (1934, 158). Jack Williams's "X̣wəneʼ," a Wynoochee tale, and Mrs. Simon Charlie's "X̣wəneʼ and the Woman," a Satsop tale, are also similar (343, 347). The Cougar stories—"Cougar and Wildcat," "Cougar and his Younger Brothers," "Cougar and Mink," and "The Cougar and their Brothers"—are also related.

x̣ʷə́n and Bluejay

Field notebook X, 570–89; typescript, "Untitled," 1–3. This is an abridged telling of the kidnapping of Moon.

1. Boas notes that this is poisaɬ, a lake below Chehalis known as "bent lake."
2. Field notebook X, 576: "son"; typescript, "Untitled," 2: "story."
3. Kinkade translates núkʷimaɬ as "strange person travelling" (1991, 92).
4. Italicized words are my suggested translation. The rest of this story was not translated, with the typist noting, "Story not finished, too muddled" (field notebook X, 570–80; typescript, "Untitled," 3). Translated fragments reveal that this story is similar to episodes in Peter Heck's version of "Moon" (Adamson 1934, 158). Moon is looking for a wedge and comes across a woman on a swing. In Heck's version, this woman is k'ʷə́cx̣ʷe.

S'yawyu'wun

Field notebook X, 600–606 (607–10 not translated); typescript, "Untitled," 1–2. No storyteller indicated. Adamson provides an alternate Upper Chehalis version of "Syuyu'wən," told by Peter Heck (1934, 41).

1. Adamson spells this name "Syuyu'wən." Boas spells it "S'yawyu'wun" in field notebook X and "Syau yuwun" in the typescript. The name, Adamson notes, means "great hunter" (1926–27, 336). Phonetically similar to *syowen*.
2. Boas notes that this is Puget Sound.
3. Lamprey eels, a Chehalis dietary staple, are harvested from riffles and falls along the Chehalis River and its tributaries. For a thorough ethnography on Chehalis past and present use of lamprey eels, see Miller 2012b, 65.
4. The typist notes that the rest of this story is not translated (typescript, "Untitled," 2). However, the corresponding pages in the field notebook are not a continuation of the story but an explanation of the powers of the chief and a discussion of what is and is not taboo. While this information might directly relate to S'yawyu'wun, the passage seems more closely connected to the "The Chief and his House," "A Farewell Speech," and especially, "The Way of the q'ʷay'iɬq'."

xʷə́n

Field notebook XI, 639–41; typescript, "Untitled," 1. Field notebook XI, 642–48, is left in Upper Chehalis and may be a continuation of this story. After xʷə́n takes the Daughter of the Rock as a mistress, he is found by Crane. This Upper Chehalis text should be compared to "xʷə́n and Crane."

1. Field notebook XI, 640, "woman"; typescript, "Untitled," 1: person.
2. Field notebook XI, 640, "woman"; typescript, "Untitled," 1: person.
3. The typist notes that the rest of this story is not translated.

One-Legged Monster

Field notebook XI, 656–84; typescript, "Untitled," 1–7. Again, Boas does not indicate who told him this story. Corresponding tales in Adamson's collection include Peter Heck's Upper Chehalis "The One-Legged Man," James Cheholts's Cowlitz "Wolf, Coyote, and Dog," Mary Adams's Skokomish "The Sharptailed Man," and Lucy Heck's Humptulip "The Wolves and Their Brother Dog" (1934, 121, 191, 371, 307).

1. The One-Legged Monster, referred to as the Sharptailed Man in other versions, is possibly Beaver.
2. Field notebook XI, 666: "it was hooped on it of hazel bush"; typescript, "Untitled," 2: "He made it dry [blank] of hazel bush."
3. Field notebook XI, 669: "Wildcat"; typescript, "Untitled," 3: "Muskrat."

4. Bob Pope, a Quinault storyteller, situates his version of this story, "The Magic Flight," on "the north side of Greys Harbor, just below James Rock" (Farrand 1902, 114).

5. Field notebook XI, 678: "shall fight"; typescript, "Untitled," 5: "fight."

Chipmunk

Field notebook XIII, 721–23, 732; typescript, "Chipmunk," 1–2. According to Amelia Susman Schultz, Boas included this story in his curriculum at Columbia University (Miller, personal correspondence). This tale is similar to Mary Iley's Cowlitz "Chipmunk and the Dangerous Woman" (Adamson 1934, 218).

Why the Dog Has Marks on His Paws

Field notebook XII, 732–34; typescript, "Why the Dog Has Marks on His Paws," 1. Boas does not provide the name of this storyteller, but it was probably shared by Dawson, as the handwriting matches that of "Chipmunk" and "The Flood."

The Flood (The Deluge)

Field notebook XII, 739–40; typescript, "The Deluge," 1.

1. Typescript, "The Deluge," 1: "But never the world will be flooded now."

The Crows

Field notebook XII, 741–42; typescript, "The Crows," 1. Storyteller not identified. Peter Heck's "Crow and the Women," an Upper Chehalis tale recorded by Adamson, is very similar (1934, 40).

1. Typescript, "The Crows," 1: "berries" is crossed out.

Untitled Story

Field notebook XII, 752–63; typescript, "The Crows," 1–6. This story immediately follows "The Crows" in the typescript, but the division within the field notebook justifies dividing these texts into two stories. Peter Heck's Upper Chehalis "The Young Man Who Was Stolen by Lion" is similar (Adamson 1934, 83).

1. Field notebook XII, 753: "They always played and they always ate. They did everything as is done by other people. They were good-natured children"; typescript, "The Crows," 2: "They always came and they ate everything as is done by other people. They did so they were good-natured children."

2. As Boas does not indicate the storyteller, it is difficult to determine the most appropriate spelling of xʷə́n to use in this story. For the sake of consistency, the spelling "x̣ʷə́n" will be used throughout.

Beaver and the Woman

Field notebook XII, 765–80, field notebook XIII, 832–33; typescript, "Beaver and . . . ,"
1–7. Boas provides "Beaver and . . ." as an unfinished title for this story. Considering the
story's content, "Beaver and the Woman" seems appropriate. No storyteller indicated.
"Wildcat," a Cowlitz story Mary Iley shared with Adamson, is similar (1934, 193).

1. Both the typescript and the field notebook provide muddled translations of this
passage. The editor has intervened, but some difficulty remains.
2. "Leavened" is cumbersome. "Were level" or "were equal" is more appropriate
considering the context. Kinkade translates a similar clause as "In the beginning
when people were animals" (1991, 4).
3. Boas notes, "father."
4. Field notebook XII, 777: "She gagged" or "She felt like vomiting"; typescript,
"Beaver and . . . ," 5: "She felt qualmish."

x̣ʷə́n and Crane

Field notebook XIII, 785–828; typescript, "Untitled," 1–16. No storyteller is indicated.
Adamson collected two similar Upper Chehalis tales: Jonas Secena's "X̣wanä'Xwane
and Crane" and Mary Heck's "X̣wan and Crane" (1934, 143, 145).

1. As no storyteller is indicated, the spelling "x̣ʷə́n" will be used throughout.
2. Field notebook XIII, 787: "He dressed and put on his clothes. He ran that far";
typescript, "Untitled," 2: "He put on his clothes and he ran that far."
3. Field notebook XIII, 793: While this sentence is ambiguous, it seems to indicate
that the thin bark Crane uses to make his net is found near the bank of the river
and that he then dips this net to catch the fry; typescript, "Untitled," 4: "[un-
translated] the branch of the river. It was taken by Crane with a thin bark net.
He dipped up the fry and threw it out on shore on the sand bar."
4. Field notebook XIII, 801; Kinkade glosses sx̣'úk'ʷaʔx̣ʷ as a "temporary roof"
(1991, 280).
5. This dialogue was left in Upper Chehalis in both the typescript and the field
notebook. I suggest "I have found a deep water for bathing" or "where we can
bathe" as a translation here (field notebook XIII, 802; typescript, "Untitled," 7).
6. Boas provides "qwɛ'qʷsnate" as the coastal variation of k'ʷə́cx̣ʷe.
7. Field notebook XIII, 820: "fine drums"; typescript, "Untitled," 13: "fine dress."

Raccoon and His Grandmother

Field notebooks XIII, XIV, 850–62; typescript, "Raccoon and His Grandmother," 1–5.
Boas does not indicate the storyteller of "Raccoon and His Grandmother." Adamson indicates Pike Ben told a short Upper Chehalis version of "Coon and his Grandmother"
and Mary Iley told a Cowlitz version of the same (1934, 43, 220).

1. This passage was left in Upper Chehalis; however, it is very similar to a sequence of events in "x̣ʷə́n and Crane." I suggest "he dressed and put on his clothes," though it could be simplified to "he put on his clothes" (field notebook XIII, 852; typescript, "Raccoon and His Grandmother," 1).

The Five Brothers

Field notebook XIV, 892–94; typescript, "The Five Brothers," 1.

1. Field notebook XIV, 892: "In the long ago . . ."; typescript, "The Five Brothers," 1: "In the time long ago . . ."
2. Field notebook XIV, 892: "was seen"; typescript, "The Five Brothers," 1: "never the same again."

The Chief and His House

Field notebook XIV, 865–72; typescript, "The Chief and his House," 7-1–7-3. No speaker indicated, but very likely Jonas Secena.

1. Chehalis people.
2. Boas notes, "Rochester."
3. Chehalis River.
4. Satsop River.
5. Nisqually people.
6. The "people of Oyster Bay, Mud Bay, Squaxin Island, and Tumwater" (Kinkade 1991, 3).
7. Satsop people, in this instance.
8. Puyallup people.
9. Puyallup people, "water coming out" (Kinkade 1991, 143).
10. Boas notes, "a little prairie near Lincoln Creek."
11. Black River.

The Way of the q'ʷay'iɬq'

Field notebook XIV, 872–73; typescript, "The Way of the q'ʷay'iɬq'," 7-4. No speaker indicated, but very likely Jonas Secena.

1. In Field notebook XIV, Boas uses the word x̣ax̣áʔ here, which he translates as "holy." In the typescript, however, the word is translated as "taboo." Kinkade defines x̣ax̣áʔ as "sacred, taboo, forbidden, holy" (1991, 160). The word is also used to mean "deity."

A Farewell Speech

Field notebook XIV, 881–85; typescript, "A Farewell Speech," 7-5.

1. Field notebook XIV, 882: "then"; typescript, "A Farewell Speech," 7-5: "that."

2. Typescript, "A Farewell Speech," 7–5: Rochester. The rest of the speech is not translated; however, Boas's rough field translation serves as a starting point: "*We were writing the teachings of the* q'ʷay'áyiłq', *and we were writing the stories of the* q'ʷay'áyiłq'. *We were counting the lakes and the rivers, and we were finding out how the ways were before.*" Jonas then talks about how Moon is the Chief of the q'ʷay'áyiłq' and came to the people in the beginning. The Chief gave the people good ways and good thoughts to follow. He says that the Chief's heart is light—it is the light of the stars in the morning. He encourages everyone to follow the shining road of good plans that come from the Chief's heart. Jonas concludes as many Chehalis speakers do, by generously thanking everyone: "*I give you my thanks from my heart . . . I thank you, my people.*"

Appendix 1

1. Boxberger and Taylor 1986 provides more detail on Cultee and Boas's work together.

2. Shoalwater Bay is a historic name for Willapa Bay, a Pacific estuary at the mouth of the Willapa River. Bay Center is located on the south side of this bay, near the confluence of the Niawiakum and Palix Rivers. Toke Point, a fishing site featured in Cultee's "Qoné'qoné," is located on the north side of the bay. This is also the location of the Shoalwater Bay Reservation, established in 1866.

3. Myron Eells (1843–1907) served as a missionary on the Skokomish Reservation, where his brother Edwin Eells (1841–1917) worked as the Indian agent on the Puyallup Consolidated Indian Reservation. Myron Eells recorded languages and legends of Northwest Coast people, making contributions to the study of Chinookan and Salishan languages (Powell 1894, 43). Eells's *The Indians of Puget Sound: The Notebooks of Myron Eells* contains a collection of myths, including an origin story of Chehalis and Chinook people, as well as stories similar to "Bear, Yellow-Jacket, and Ant," and "The Flood" (1985, 254, 265). Boas enlisted Myron Eells's help in "gathering a collection of Puget Sound Salish" material for the World's Columbia Exposition, which was held in Chicago in 1893. Boas also corresponded with Edwin Eells regarding fieldwork logistics. The Eells brothers provided considerable support to Boas during his 1890s visits to the Northwest Coast.

4. Kathlamet.

5. A Chinook form indicating Willapa, phonemicized as xʷiˑlápaχ (Krauss 1990, 532).

6. Kwalhioqua, which "consisted of two groups": Willapa and Suwal (or Swaal) (Krauss 1990, 530).

7. "Qoné'qoné" is a Lower Chehalis form of xʷə́n. This story is taken from "Legends (Cathlamet, Chehalis, Chinook, Clatsop, and Salishan)," 1890, MS 1313, National

Anthropological Archives, Smithsonian Institution. This Lower Chehalis version of the story of xʷə́n features cultural activities and settings important to Lower Chehalis people.

8. A point on the north side of Willapa Bay.

9. In other versions of this story, the women are digging camas. However, this wild ginseng may be pəsʔáynɬ, or devil's club, a plant traditionally used as a medicine for childbirth (Kinkade 1991, 97). In *Ethnobotany of Western Washington: The Knowledge and Use of Indigenous Plants by Native Americans*, Erna Gunther cites Leslie Haskin regarding the use of devil's club: "Haskins speaks of the widespread use of this plant on the coast as a medicine, as a charm for fishing, and an emetic" (1945, 41). According to Haskin, "Next to the hellebore this was undoubtedly the Coast Indians' most valued medicine" (1934, 231).

10. See "A Story," note 9.

11. This story is present—even foundational—in many Northwest Coast traditions. Star Child is an important figure in Lushootseed stories. See Hilbert 1985; Langen 1984; and Miller 1999b, 54–57. Adamson recorded two Upper Chehalis stories titled "Star Husband," one told by Peter Heck and another told by Jonas Secena, and a Puyallup version titled "Star Husband" told by Jerry Meeker. Secena's version is similar to a Quinault story, "The Ascent to the Sky," which Bob Pope shared with Livingston Farrand. In the abstract for "Moon," Adamson explains the connection between the "Star Husband" and "Moon" traditions: "Two girls are taken to the sky as wives of two stars. . . . They descend to earth by means of a rope, and the elder brings her baby. Their blind grandmother minds the child in a swing. Two girls steal it" (1934, 381). Snuqualmi Charlie shared "Moon, the Transformer" with Arthur Ballard; his telling also connects the two narratives, with the two sisters' journey to the sky resulting in the birth of Moon, who is subsequently stolen by Dog Salmon.

12. This story appeared in the *Chehalis Tribal Newsletter* in October 2009. It is a version of the widely dispersed "Raven Steals the Sun" legend. Many versions of this story were collected by Boas and his contemporaries in the early twentieth century. In "The Development of the Mythologies of the North Pacific Coast Indians," Boas identifies seven variations of "Raven Steals the Sun" in the texts he collected, from Tlingit, Tsimshian, Bilqula, Hɛ́'ltsuk, Newettee, Nutka, and Coast Salish traditions (2002, 639). John R. Swanton, who studied under Boas at Columbia University, recorded a Tlingit "Raven" tale in which Raven liberates Sun, who had been kept in a box by a rich man (1909, 2–21), and Livingston Farrand collected a Bella Bella tale, "Raven Obtains the Sun" (Boas 1916, 884–85). See Carlson 1977 for Halkomelem, Lushootseed, Kwak'wala, and Nitinaht tellings of this story. Boas cites a related Raven story in *Tsimshian Mythology* (1916, 60–62, 631). In his "Comparative Study of Tsimshian Mythology," a subsection

of this major work, Boas compares twenty-nine Northern and nine Southern and Inland forms of the "Origin of Daylight." In these versions, Gull or Seagull "is described as the owner of daylight, and only the incident of the sun being kept in a box is retained" (646). Boas briefly explicates the Lower Chehalis story, which "in details resembles the Bluejay tales of the Quinault, Chehalis, and Chinook" (647). Boas summarizes:

The chief keeps the sun in a box. His daughter takes it out when she goes berrying, and opens it a little in order to see. The people hold a council in order to get the sun, and send Chief Kalixo, who takes the form of an old slave. Bluejay claims that he is his own slave, but his brother Robin does not recognize him. They take him paddling, and Bluejay claims that he used to paddle for him, which Robin denies. When the girl opens the box, he takes it away and runs home and opens it, then it gets daylight, Chehalis. (647)

Boas refers specifically to this Chehalis version in "The Development of the Mythologies of the North Pacific Coast Indians," noting,

Coast Selisch retains the more important element that Raven, by a ruse, forces the owner of daylight to release it from the box where he keeps it locked up. The same element, transferred to Jay, is still found with the Chehalis of Grey's Harbor (*Globus*, Vol. [63], No. 12). Here, and in Newettee, Seagull is the owner of daylight. (2002, 639).

13. "Basket" appears in the typescript but is crossed out and amended to "box."
14. K-'aliqōo is a form of *kʷálaxʷ*, meaning seagull.

Appendix 2

University of Washington Libraries, Special Collections, Edmond S. Meany Papers 1883–1935, MS Collection No. 0106-001, box 86, folders 2–3.

1. Grandfather of Robert Choke.
2. Sally Choke.
3. Ed Smith was Blanche Pete Dawson's uncle, her mother Maggie Pete's brother.
4. John Smith and Peter Heck (named three lines below) were charter members of the Indian Shaker Church.
5. Jacob Secena.
6. Related to Blanche Pete Dawson.
7. cinítiya was "a chief of the Upper Chehalis, under Yawnis" (Kinkade 1991, 336). Peter Heck told Adamson that "tsinitis" was "the most important chief" who had "many wives" and "was well-off" (1926–27, 268).
8. Old Shotty is mentioned on Indian Census Rolls from the late nineteenth and early twentieth centuries. The 1885 Indian Census Roll for Nisqually and Skokomish Agencies identify him as Shutta Squatta, and Old Squatta was an early landholder on the Chehalis Reservation, receiving his patent in 1888. Meany

mentions these patents in his *Seattle Post-Intelligencer* article, noting that Peter Heck and George Quinotle "dread the time when the patents on the Chehalis reservation begin to mature in another year or two. . . . They would like to hold their lands indefinitely just as at present, without the right to sell and without the risk or necessity of paying taxes" (1905, 6).

9. Governor of Washington Territory Isaac Stevens.

10. Yowannus served as the head chief of the Upper Chehalis at the Chehalis River Treaty Council in 1855. Kinkade transcribes the name as yáwniš; Yawnish is another common form.

11. Meany highlighted this fact in his article, supplementing accounts provided by Chehalis people with accounts provided by pioneers.

12. Camas.

13. Gunther identifies s'a′q as brake fern roots (1945, 14), and Kinkade identifies sʔə́q as bracken root, which was used to make bread (1991, 220).

14. Kinkade transcribes Peter Heck's name as "yánm".

15. Mary Heck, Peter's mother.

16. Kinkade transcribes Mary Heck's name as si·lst m or Silstem.

17. *Folk-Tales of the Coast Salish* contains multiple versions of this story: the Upper Chehalis "Fox and Stehe′n," the Wynoochee "The Hoop," and the Skokomish "The Hoop."

18. In his caption to a photograph of George Quinotle, Meany notes that Quinotle served as an interpreter in recording Jacob Secena's stories.

19. Likely Ann Secena, wife of Jacob.

20. Wife of Peter Heck.

21. Mima Prairie.

22. Possibly manə́č′uw'ɬ, which Kinkade identifies as the "name of a prairie just east of the Gray's Harbor-Thurston County line, and north of U.S. Highway 12" (1991, 329).

23. Similar to "Snowbird," collected by Boas, and "Northeast Wind and Southwest Wind," which Jonas Secena shared with Adamson.

24. Lillian Young identifies xʷayóʔsxʷayʔs as the Oregon junco (Kinkade 1991, 291).

25. Kinkade identifies Boistfort as t'á·lɑlɑn.

Appendix 4

First published in the *1983 Mid-America Linguistics Conference Papers*, edited by David S. Rood, 246–61.

Appendix 5

First published in University of Oklahoma Papers in Anthropology 24(2) (1983): 267–78.

REFERENCES

Unpublished and Archival Sources

Adamson, Thelma. 1926–27. "Unarranged Sources of Chehalis Ethnography." Melville Jacobs Papers. Special Collections, University of Washington.

Aginsky, Ethel G. 1935. "Comparison of Puyallup and Chehalis." American Council of Learned Societies Committee on Native American Languages. American Philosophical Society Library.

American Council of Learned Societies Committee on Native American Languages. American Philosophical Society Library.

"Annotated Maps and Notes to Maps of the Pacific Northwest." MS 47.3.B63c. American Council of Learned Societies Committee on Native American Languages. American Philosophical Society Library.

Boas, Franz. Ca. 1890. "Lower Chehalis Vocabulary and Text." American Council of Learned Societies Committee on Native American Languages. American Philosophical Society Library.

———. 1890. "Legends (Cathlamet, Chehalis, Clatsop, and Salishan)." Numbered Manuscripts, ms. 1313. National Anthropological Archives, Smithsonian Institution.

———. 1897, 1927–35. "Chehalis Lexical File." American Council of Learned Societies Committee on Native American Languages. American Philosophical Society Library.

———. 1927a. "Chehalis Field Notes." American Council of Learned Societies Committee on Native American Languages. American Philosophical Society Library.

———. 1927b. "Chehalis Folklore." American Council of Learned Societies Committee on Native American Languages. American Philosophical Society Library.

———. 1927, 1934–36. "Chehalis Materials." American Council of Learned Societies Committee on Native American Languages. American Philosophical Society Library.

———. 1927–35. "Chehalis Myths." American Council of Learned Societies Committee on Native American Languages. American Philosophical Society Library.

———. 1934. "Chehalis Vocabulary." American Council of Learned Societies Committee on Native American Languages. American Philosophical Society Library.

———. Ca. 1935. "Chehalis Lexicon." American Council of Learned Societies Committee on Native American Languages. American Philosophical Society Library.

Boas, Franz, Professional Papers. American Philosophical Society Library.

Boas, Franz, and Myron Eells. 1882. "Chehalis Field Notes." American Council of

Learned Societies Committee on Native American Languages. American Philosophical Society Library.

———. Ca. 1890. "Chehalis Texts." American Council of Learned Societies Committee on Native American Languages. American Philosophical Society Library.

Harrington, John P. 1942–43. "Quinault/Chehalis/Cowlitz/Yakima/Chinook/Chinook Jargon, 1942–1943." John Peabody Harrington Papers. National Anthropological Archives, Smithsonian Institution.

Heck, Silas, and M. Dale Kinkade. 1960. "Upper and Lower Chehalis Battle." Upper Chehalis (Salish) Language Material, audio recording. American Philosophical Society Library.

Indiana University Archives of Traditional Music.

Jacobs, Melville, Papers. Special Collections, University of Washington.

Meany, Edmond S., Papers. MS Collection No. 0106-001. Special Collections, University of Washington.

Published Sources

Adamson, Thelma. 1934. *Folk-Tales of the Coast Salish*. American Folk-Lore Society Memoir 27. New York: American Folklore Society.

Aginsky, Burt W., and Ethel G. Aginsky. 1967. *Deep Valley: The Pomo Indians of California*. New York: Stein and Day.

Ballard, Arthur. 1929. *Mythology of Southern Puget Sound*. Seattle: University of Washington Press.

Bauman, Richard, and Charles Briggs. 1999. "'The Foundation of All Future Researches': Franz Boas, George Hunt, Native American Texts, and the Construction of Modernity." *American Quarterly* 51(3): 479–528.

Berman, Judith. 1994. "George Hunt and the Kwak'wala Texts." *Anthropological Linguistics* 34(4): 482–514.

Boas, Franz. 1893. "Zur Mythologie der Indianer von Washington und Oregon." *Globus* 63(10): 154–157.

———. 1894. *Chinook Texts*. Bureau of American Ethnology, Bulletin 20. Washington DC: Government Printing Office.

———. 1901. *Kathlamet Texts*. Bureau of American Ethnology, Bulletin 26. Washington DC: Government Printing Office.

———. 1911. *Handbook of American Indian Languages*. Bureau of American Ethnology, Bulletin 40. Washington DC: Government Printing Office.

———. 1916. *Tsimshian Mythology*. Thirty-First Annual Report to the Bureau of American Ethnology to the Secretary of the Smithsonian Institution, 1909–1910. Washington DC: Government Printing Office.

———. 1923. "James A. Teit." *American Folklore* 36(139): 102–3.

———. 1927c. *Primitive Art*. Oslo: H. Aschehough.

———. 1935. "A Chehalis Text." *International Journal of American Linguistics* 8(2): 103–10.

———. 1966. *Kwakiutl Ethnography.* Edited by Helen Codere. Chicago: University of Chicago Press.

———. 2002. *Indian Myths and Legends from the North Pacific Coast of America.* Edited and Annotated by Randy Bouchard and Dorothy Kennedy. Translated by Dietrich Bertz. Vancouver BC: Talonbooks.

Boas, Franz, and Herman Haeberlin. 1927. "Sound Shifts in Salishan Dialects." *International Journal of American Linguistics* 4(2): 117–36.

Boas, Franz, and George Hunt. 1902–05. *Kwakiutl Texts.* Publications of the Jesup North Pacific Expedition 3(1–3); Memoirs of the American Museum of Natural History 5(1–3). New York.

———. 1906. *Kwakiutl Texts (Second Series).* Publications of the Jesup North Pacific Expedition 10(1); Memoirs of the American Museum of Natural History 14(1). Leyden: E. J. Brill; New York: G. E. Stechert.

———. 1921. *Ethnology of the Kwakiutl.* Washington DC: Government Printing Office.

Boxberger, Daniel L., and Herbert C. Taylor. 1986. "Charles Cultee and the Father of American Anthropology." *Sou'wester* 21(1): 3–7.

Carlson, Barry F., ed. 1977. "Northwest Coast Texts: Stealing Light." Native American Text Series. *International Journal of American Linguistics* 2(3).

Chalcraft, Edwin L. 2004. *Assimilation's Agent: My Life as a Superintendent in the Indian Boarding School System.* Edited with an introduction by Cary C. Collins. Lincoln: University of Nebraska Press.

Clark, William, and Meriwether Lewis. 1983–2004. *The Journals of the Lewis and Clark Expedition.* 13 vols. Edited by Gary E. Moulton. Lincoln: University of Nebraska Press.

Cole, Douglas. 1999. *Franz Boas: The Early Years 1858–1906.* Seattle: University of Washington Press.

Collins, Cary C. 2000/2001. "A Future with a Past: Hazel Pete, Cultural Identity, and the Federal Indian Education System." *Pacific Northwest Quarterly* 92(1): 15–28.

Deloria, Vine, Jr. 2003. *God Is Red: A Native View of Religion.* Thirtieth anniversary edition. Golden CO: Fulcrum.

Du Puis, Curtis. 2012. *American Indian Stories of the Pete Family.* Compact disc. Lake Forest Park: Northwest Heritage Resources.

Eells, Myron. 1985. *The Indians of Puget Sound: The Notebooks of Myron Eells.* Edited with an introduction by George Pierre Castile. Seattle: University of Washington Press.

Elliot, T. C. 1912. "Journals of John Work, November and December, 1824." *Washington Historical Quarterly* 3(3): 198–228.

Elmendorf, William. 1993. *Twana Narratives: Native Historical Accounts of a Coast Salish Culture.* Seattle: University of Washington Press.

Farrand, Livingston. 1902. *Traditions of the Quinault Indians.* Assisted by W. S. Kahnweiler. Memoirs of the American Museum of Natural History, vol. 4; Publications of the Jesup North Pacific Expedition 3. New York: American Museum of Natural History.

Foutch, Amy E., Michelle L. Punke, and John L. Fagan. 2012. *Archaeological Synthesis Report for Site 45LE611, Centralia, Washington.* Portland OR: Archaeological Investigations Northwest.

Garfield, Viola, and Pamela Amoss. 1984. "Erna Gunther (1896–1982)." *American Anthropologist* 86(2): 394–99.

Gibbs, George. 1863. *A Dictionary of the Chinook Jargon; or, Trade Language of Oregon.* New York: Cramoisy Press.

———. 1877. *Tribes of Western Washington and Northwestern Oregon.* Department of the Interior, U. S. Geographical and Geological Survey of the Rocky Mountain Region, Contributions to North American Ethnology, vol. 1. Edited by J. W. Powell. Washington DC: Government Printing Office.

Gunther, Erna. 1925. *Klallam Folk Tales.* Seattle: University of Washington Press.

———. 1926. Review of *Honne: The Spirit of the Chehalis*, edited by Katherine Van Winkle Palmer, and *Ancient Warriors of the North Pacific*, by Charles Harrison. *Washington Historical Quarterly* 17(1): 66–67.

———. 1945. *Ethnobotany of Western Washington: The Knowledge and Use of Indigenous Plants by Native Americans.* Seattle: University of Washington Press.

Haeberlin, Herman, and Franz Boas. 1924. "Mythology of Puget Sound." *Journal of American Folklore* 37(145/146): 371–438.

Haeberlin, Herman, and Erna Gunther. 1930. *The Indians of Puget Sound.* Seattle: University of Washington Press.

Hajda, Yvonne. 1990. "Southwestern Coast Salish." In *Northwest Coast*, vol. 7 of *Handbook of North American Indians*, edited by Wayne Suttles, 503–17. Washington DC: Smithsonian Institution Press.

Haskin, Leslie L. 1934. *Wild Flowers of the Pacific Coast.* Portland OR: Metropolitan Press.

Hilbert, Vi. 1985. *Huboo: Native American Stories from Puget Sound.* Forward and introduction by Thom Hess. Drawings by Ron Hilbert. Seattle: University of Washington Press.

Hodge, Tové. 1995. "The Family of Sidney S. Ford, Senior." In *Centralia, the First Fifty Years: 1845–1900*, edited by Herndon Smith, 76–103. Rochester WA: Gorham Printing.

Hymes, Dell. 1974. *Foundations in Sociolinguistics: An Ethnographic Approach.* Philadelphia: University of Pennsylvania Press.

———. 1981. *"In Vain I Tried to Tell You": Essays in Native American Ethnopoetics.* Philadelphia: University of Pennsylvania Press.

———. 1983. "Agnes Edgar's 'Sun's Child': Verse Analysis of a Bella Coola Text." Paper presented at the Eighteenth International Conference on Salishan Languages, Seattle.

———. 2003. *Now I Only Know So Far: Essays in Ethnopoetics.* Lincoln: University of Nebraska Press.

Interview of Chehalis Tribal Elders. 2005. Volume 3, Barr, K. M. & Dupuis, C. Video recording. Evergreen State College, Olympia, Washington.

Jackson, Robert. 1906. "The Story of Sun: A Legend of the Chehalis Indians." *Washington Magazine,* May, 178–86.

Jacobs, Melville. 1929. *Northwest Sahaptin Texts.* Seattle: University of Washington Press.

———. 1934. *Northwest Sahaptin Texts.* New York: Columbia University Press.

Jakobson, Roman. 1978. *Six Lectures on Sound and Meaning.* Cambridge MA: MIT Press.

Kinkade, M. Dale. 1963a. "Phonology and Morphology of Upper Chehalis: I." *International Journal of American Linguistics* 29(3): 181–95.

———. 1963b. "Phonology and Morphology of Upper Chehalis: II." *International Journal of American Linguistics* 29(4): 345–56.

———. 1964a. "Phonology and Morphology of Upper Chehalis: III." *International Journal of American Linguistics* 30(1): 32–61.

———. 1964b. "Phonology and Morphology of Upper Chehalis: IV." *International Journal of American Linguistics* 30(3): 251–60.

———. 1983. "'Daughters of Fire': Narrative Verse Analysis of an Upper Chehalis Folktale." In *North American Indians: Humanistic Perspectives,* edited by James Thayer. University of Oklahoma Papers in Anthropology 24(2): 267–78.

———. 1984. "'Bear and Bee': Narrative Verse Analysis of an Upper Chehalis Folktale." In *1983 Mid-America Linguistic Conference Papers,* edited by David S. Rood, 246–61. Boulder: University of Colorado Department of Linguistics.

———. 1987. "Bluejay and His Sister." In *Recovering the Word: Essays on Native American Literature,* edited by Brian Swann and Arnold Krupat, 255–96. Berkeley: University of California Press.

———. 1991. *Upper Chehalis Dictionary.* University of Montana Occasional Papers in Linguistics 7. Missoula: University of Montana.

———. 2004. *Cowlitz Dictionary and Grammatical Sketch.* University of Montana Occasional Papers in Linguistics 18. Missoula: University of Montana.

———. 2008. "The Kidnapping of Moon: An Upper Chehalis Myth Told by Silas Heck." In *Salish Myths and Legends: One People's Stories,* edited by M. Terry Thompson and Steven Egesdal, 349–68. Lincoln: University of Nebraska Press.

Krauss, Michael E. 1990. "Kwalhioqua and Clatskanie." In *Northwest Coast,* vol. 7 of *Handbook of North American Indians,* edited by Wayne Suttles, 530–32. Washington DC: Smithsonian Institution Press.

Langen, Toby C. S. 1984. "Four Upper Skagit Versions of 'Starchild.'" *Working Papers of the Linguistics Circle of the University of Victoria* 4(2): 241–54.

Malinowski, Bronisław. 1961. *Argonauts of the Western Pacific.* New York: E. P. Dutton.

Marr, Carolyn J., Donna Hicks, and Kay Francis. 2001. *The Chehalis People.* Oakville WA: Confederated Tribes of the Chehalis Indian Reservation.

Meany, Edmond S. 1905. "Washington Redmen Who Helped Palefaces in War: Chehalis Tribe of Twenty-Five Braves Fought for Whites." *Seattle Post-Intelligencer,* October 15.

Miller, Jay. 1999a. "Chehalis Area Traditions: A Summary of Thelma Adamson's 1927 Ethnographic Notes." *Northwest Anthropological Research Notes* 33(1): 1–72.

———. 1999b. *Lushootseed Culture and the Shamanic Odyssey: An Anchored Radiance.* Lincoln: University of Nebraska Press.

———. 2010. Review of *Folk-Tales of the Coast Salish,* edited by Thelma Adamson, new introduction by William Seaburg and Laurel Sercombe. *Folklore* 121(2): 359–61.

———. 2011. *Traditional Cultural Place (Property) and Ethnographic Study for Twin-Cities (Centralia-Chehalis) Flood Damage Reduction Project Study Area.* Seattle: U. S. Army Corps of Engineers.

———. 2012a. Introduction to *Honne, the Spirit of the Chehalis: An Indian Interpretation of the Origin of the People and Animals,* edited by Katherine Van Winkle Palmer and narrated by George Sanders, v–xxxi. Lincoln: University of Nebraska Press.

———. 2012b. "Lamprey 'Eels' in the Greater Northwest: A Survey of Tribal Sources, Experiences, and Sciences." *Journal of Northwest Anthropology* 46(1): 65–84.

———. 2012c. "Skookumchuck Shuffle: Shifting Athapaskan Swaals into Oregon Klatskanis Before Taitnapam Sahaptins Cross the Cascades." *Journal of Northwest Anthropology* 46(2): 167–75.

Mills, Elaine L., ed. *The Papers of John Peabody Harrington in the Smithsonian Institution, 1907–1957.* Vol. 1. Millwood NY: Krause International.

Palmer, Katherine V. W., ed. 1925. *Honne, the Spirit of the Chehalis: The Indian Interpretation of the Origin of the People and Animals.* Narrated by George Saunders. Geneva NY: Press of W. F. Humphrey.

Pöhl, Friedrich. 2008. "Assessing Franz Boas' Ethics in his Arctic and Later Anthropological Fieldwork." *Études/Inuit/Studies* 32(2): 35–52.

Powell, J. W. "Report of the Director of the Bureau of Ethnology for the Year Ending June 30, 1893." In *Annual Report of the Board of Regents of the Smithsonian Institution.* Washington DC: Government Printing Office.

Reichard, Gladys A. 1958. "A Comparison of Five Salish Languages: I." *International Journal of American Linguistics* 24(4): 293–300.

"Reservation News Notes." 1927–32. *Oakville (WA) Cruiser.*

"Robert Choke." 1965. *Daily Chronicle* (Centralia, Washington), April 30.

Rohner, Ronald P., ed. 1969. *The Ethnography of Franz Boas: Letters and Diaries of Franz Boas Written on the Northwest Coast from 1886 to 1931.* Introduction by Ronald P. Rohner and Evelyn C. Rohner. Translated by Hedy Parker. Chicago: University of Chicago Press.

Rosaldo, Renato. 1989. "Imperialist Nostalgia." In *Culture and Truth: The Remaking of Social Analysis,* 68–87. Boston: Beacon Press.

Ruby, Robert H., and John A. Brown, and Cary Collins. 2013. *A Guide to the Indian Tribes of the Pacific Northwest.* Norman: University of Oklahoma Press.

Russell, G. Oscar. 1928. *The Vowel.* Columbus: Ohio State University Press.

———. 1929. "The Mechanism of Speech." *Journal of the Acoustical Society of America* 1(1): 83–109.

Seaburg, William R. 1999. "Whatever Happened to Thelma Adamson?: A Footnote in the History of Northwest Anthropological Research." *Northwest Anthropological Research Notes* 33(1): 73–83.

Seaburg, William R., and Laurel Sercombe. 2009. Introduction to *Folk-Tales of the Coast Salish,* by Thelma Adamson, v–xxiii. Lincoln: University of Nebraska Press.

Shortman, Fred, ed. 2009a. "Chehalis Legend: Unnamed Story on How the Sun Was Stolen." *Chehalis Tribal Newsletter* (Oakville WA). October.

———. 2009b. "Honoring Our Elders: Katherine Davis-Barr." *Chehalis Tribal Newsletter* (Oakville WA). March.

———. 2010. "Honoring Our Elders: Cindy Davis-Andy." *Chehalis Tribal Newsletter* (Oakville WA). February.

Smith, Joshua, Regna Darnell, Robert L. A. Hancock, and Sarah Moritz. 2014. "The Franz Boas Papers: Documentary Edition." *Journal of Northwest Anthropology* 48(1): 93–106.

Swadesh, Morris. 1950. "Salish Internal Relationships." *International Journal of American Linguistics* 16(4): 157–67.

Swan, James G. 1857. *The Northwest Coast; or, Three Years' Residence in Washington Territory.* New York: Harper & Brothers.

Swanton, John R. 1909. *Tlingit Myths and Texts.* Bureau of American Ethnology, Bulletin 39. Washington DC: Government Printing Office.

U.S. vs. Hilary Halbert Jr., et. al. 1929. U.S. Circuit Court of Appeals for the Ninth Circuit.

Upton, Judith. 2003. *Glimpses of Gate: A Pictorial Journal of Gate, WA: 1880–1920*. Rochester WA: Gorham Printing.

Voegelin, Charles F., and Zellig S. Harris. 1945. "Index to the Franz Boas Collection of Materials for American Linguistics." *Language* 21(3): 5–7, 9–43.

Wickwire, Wendy. 2003. "Teit, James Alexander." *Dictionary of Canadian Biography*, vol. 15. University of Toronto/Université Laval. http://www.biographi.ca /en/bio/teit_james_alexander_1884_15E.html.

Wilkes, Charles. 1844–49. *Narrative of the United States Exploring Expedition during the Years 1838, 1839, 1840, 1841, 1842*. 5 vols. Philadelphia: C. Sherman.

INDEX

References to unnumbered notes are represented by the page number followed by an *n* and no following note number. If multiple unnumbered notes appear on one page, a key term from the chapter title follows the *n*. Similarly, if multiple instances of any note number can be found on a page of notes, a term from the chapter title follows the note number.

Adams, Mary, 279n12, 295nMink, 295n4, 298nOne-Legged

Adamson, Thelma: on animals as people, 285n3; "Bear and Bee" translation of, 212, 234, 293n; and Bluejay story, 20, 295nBluejay; and Crows story, 299nCrows; and Daughters of Fire story, 263; on dentalium, 287n9; dissertation of, 283n43; and fish traps, 288n19; and Flood story, 210, 296nFlood; on Heck family, 283n44; illness of, 31; on "malé," 290n32; and Marion Davis, 212, 282–83nn38–39; and Mink story, 295nMink; and Moon story, 297nkʷə́cxʷe; and "Muspˀ and Kəmoˀl," 210; and Northeast Wind story, 294nSnowbird, 305n23; and One-Legged Monster story, 298nOne-Legged; and Rabbit and Mountain Lion story, 294nRabbit; and Raccoon story, 297nRaccoon, 300nRaccoon; research by, 15–18, 22–26, 32, 282n35; and Skunk story, 296nSkunk; as source, x, 2; and star stories, 303n11; stories told to, 3, 19–21, 30–31, 70, 260, 278n6, 281n26, 284n2; on story ownership, 6; and Sʼyawyuˀwun, 298nSʼyawyuˀwun, 298n1Sʼyawyuˀwunn; on tamanous, 287n14; and xʷə́n, 291n63, 300nxʷə́n; and "Wildcat," 300nBeaver

Aginsky, Bernard, 283n53

Aginsky, Ethel, ix–x, 26, 27, 28, 283n53, 286n7, 293n7

American Council of Learned Societies Committee on Native American Languages, 29

American Folklore Society, 31

American Indian Stories of the Pete Family, 280n21

American Philosophical Society (APS), 22, 26, 27, 29, 197, 199, 234, 260

animals: and Beaver's wife, 173–74, 176; in Flood story, 210–11; as people, 35, 77, 79, 112, 117, 126, 127, 170, 171, 173, 190, 211, 219–21, 278n6, 285n3, 300n2Beaver; pursuit of Moon by, 51–55, 93–98; race of, 217; as stars, 205. *See also specific animals*

Ant, 119–23, 211–12, 222–23, 234, 236–38, 241, 242

Argonauts of the Western Pacific (Malinowski), 277n2

arrowheads, 62–63, 103, 203, 210, 224

arrows, 161, 170, 171

"The Ascent to the Sky" (story), 303n11

assimilation, 1, 12, 32, 281n26

Astoria OR, 197, 198

Seattle Post-Intelligencer, 30, 209, 212, 304n8
Secena, Alice, 22, 24, 221, 283n49
Secena, Ann, 218, 305n19
Secena, Dan, 22–23, 293n
Secena, Jacob, 2, 21, 23, 30, 209–12, 215, 304n5, 305n18
Secena, Jonas: biography of, 22–26, 283n49; on dentalium, 287n9; family of, 2, 6, 8–10, 209, 279nn15; and q'ʷay'iɬq', 301nChief, 301nWay; as source, 17, 18, 209; spelling of x̣ʷə́n, 285n5; stories of, 2, 11, 16, 27, 28, 35, 79, 119, 194, 210, 212, 213, 234, 261, 264, 279n12, 284n2, 292n, 294nRabbit, 294nSnowbird, 295nBluejay, 296nFlood, 296nSkunk, 297nk'ʷə́cx̣ʷe, 300nx̣ʷə́n, 303n11, 305n23; on storytelling, 6–7; on tamanous, 287n14
Secena, Murphy, 9, 23, 284n2
Secena, Roberta, 24
Secena family, 22–24, 209
Sercombe, Laurel, 20
service berries, 216. *See also* berries
shaman(s): Alice Secena as, 24; in Beaver story, 175, 176; Mink's girl to, 143; Snowbird as, 127; in "A Story," 53, 95, 96, 112–13; on Sun and Moon, 213. *See also* illness; medicine
Sharptailed Man, 298nOne-Legged, 298n1One-Legged
shells, 210. *See also* dentalium
Shoalwater Bay, 4, 14, 197, 302n2Appendix
Shortman, John, Jr., 8, 9
Shutta Squatta. *See* Old Shotty
Sicade, Henry, 279n12
sielɔ"pt, 278n6, 285n3
Siletz OR, 197

Sɪl'o'cən, 210
si·lst m. *See* Heck, Mary
Silstem. *See* Heck, Mary
Simon Charlie, Mrs., 295nBluejay, 297nk'ʷə́cx̣ʷe
sisínaʔx̣n, 23. *See also* Secena, Jacob
Skate, 206
Skokomish (Twana) Indians: and camas, 286n8; census of, 304n8; research on, 15, 31; reservation of, 19, 302n3; stories of, 279n12, 295nMink, 305n17; territory of, 5. *See also* Twana Indians
Skookum George, 279n12
Skunk, 147–49, 160, 206–7, 296nSkunk
"Skunk" (story), 18, 20, 147–49, 297nRaccoon
sky, 77–78, 117–18, 126, 127, 130–32, 205–7. *See also* horizon; world
Skylark, 67–68, 108
slahal, 132, 133–37, 295n1Rabbit
slaves, 208, 224–25, 295n3
sleeping, 120–23, 183–86, 203, 211–12, 222–23
Slug, 38–39, 82–83
Smith, Ed, 215, 304n3
Smith, John, 21, 215, 304n4
Smith, Marian, 283n43
Smith family, 209, 215
Snake, 53, 95, 127–30, 176, 185–86. *See also* Rattlesnake
snakes, catching of, 204
Snoqualmie Indians, 279n12, 290n41
snow, 130, 131, 223
Snowbird, 126–31, 205–6, 223
"Snowbird" (story), 126–31, 285n3, 305n23
Snuqualmi Charlie, 279n12, 303n11
songs: of Bear, Yellow Jacket, and Ant, 120–23, 211–12, 222, 234, 236, 242; of Bees, 83; of Bluejay, 138–40; in bone

water (*continued*)
Jacket and Ant's use of, 123. *See also* "The Flood" (story); lakes; ocean
Waterman, T. T., 15
wa′xə́mlut. *See* Secena, Jonas
"The Way of the q′ʷay′iɬq′," 298n4
wealth, 13, 30–31, 287n14. *See also* poverty
weaving, 1. *See also* baskets
Westport, 4
West Wind, 207
whales, 139, 142, 210, 211, 220, 224
wheel game, 39–40, 83, 288n15
White Horsefish, 70, 110. *See also* fish
White River Indians, 15, 20, 31
whites: Chehalis soldiers with, 216; culture of, 12; earliest contact with, 2–3, 23, 209; effect of, on Chehalis history, 3, 13–14; graves of, 211; and origin of tamanous, 287n14; ownership by, 7; salvage ethnography of, 214, 277n2; sharing knowledge with, 9–10; trade with, 4–5
Whun-nie. *See* Sun
"Why the Dog Has Marks on His Paws" (story), 167
Wild Cat, 163, 164, 171, 189
"Wildcat" (story), 300nBeaver
"Wild Cat plays tricks on Coyote" (story), 279n12
Willapa Athabaskan Indians, 302n6. *See also* Kwalhioqua Indians
Willapa Bay. *See* Shoalwater Bay
Willapa Hills, 211
Willapa River, 198, 302n2Appendix
Williams, Jack, 297nkʷʷə́cxʷe
Williams family, 2
Wind, 64, 105, 126–31, 207, 263
winter, 25, 119–23, 163, 191, 192, 203, 211–12. *See also* seasons

"Winter Story," 209, 223, 305n23
Wishkah, 4
wives: of man with headband, 60; of Moon, 55, 70, 73–74, 97, 110–11, 113–15; purchase of, 173–74; of Qonē′qonē, 201–2; of Sun, 213; of xʷə́n, 43–46, 86–89, 156, 213. *See also* families; girls; mistresses; women
Wolf, 52, 94–95, 128, 129, 176, 190, 242, 287n14
"Wolf, Coyote, and Dog" (story), 298nOne-Legged
"The Wolves and Their Brother Dog" (story), 298nOne-Legged
women: apron strings of, 206–7; and camas, 286n8; as Chief of Southwest Wind, 126–27; children stolen from, 156–57, 202–3, 213; and Crane, 182; creation of husbands by, 188–89; double children of, 170–72; gossip about, 125; loving men, 106, 155; making fun of, 40, 84; as monsters, 186; with xʷə́n, 156. *See also* "Daughters of Fire" (story); families; girls; k′ʷə́cxʷe; malés; mistresses; people; wives
"The Women Who Married the Stars" (story), 14, 197, 205–7, 279n12, 303n11
wood: ants in rotten, 211–12, 222–23; for basketmaking, 180; of Bluejay, 139; children as rotten, 48, 90, 156, 202, 213; and Daughters of Fire story, 263; for fires, 74, 110, 114, 178, 179, 185–86, 221; tools for cutting, 56, 60–62, 98, 101–2; whittling of, 57–58, 99, 157. *See also* cedar; ironwood; sticks; trees
Woodpecker, 38–39, 81–82, 210
woods, 161–62, 204. *See also* land
Work and Wilkes, 3
world: day and night in, 119–23, 236;

CPSIA information can be obtained
at www.ICGtesting.com
Printed in the USA
LVHW022104110119
603646LV00002B/2